Dedicated to Perry DeAngelis,
A friend and skeptic of some note

NINE AGAINST THE UNKNOWN

A Record of Geographical Exploration

by

J. LESLIE MITCHELL

AND

LEWIS GRASSIC GIBBON

The lights begin to twinkle from the rocks,
The long day wanes ; the slow moon climbs ; the deep
Moans round with many voices. Come, my friends,
'Tis not too late to seek a newer world.
Push off, and sitting well in order smite
The sounding furrows ; for my purpose holds
To sail beyond the sunset and the baths
Of all the western stars, until I die.
It may be that the gulfs will wash us down :
It may be we shall touch the happy isles.

—*Ulysses*

Polygon

First published by Jarrolds (London) in 1934

This edition published in 2000 by Polygon
An imprint of Edinburgh University Press Ltd
22 George Square, Edinburgh

Printed and bound in Great Britain by
Redwood Books, Trowbridge

A CIP Record for this book is available from the British Library

ISBN 0 7486 6270 7 (paperback)

For

IVOR BROWN

CONTENTS

LIST OF ILLUSTRATIONS

MAPS

INTRODUCTION

Nine Against the Unknown – subtitled *A Record of Geographical Exploration* – appeared on 2 November 1934, not long before James Leslie Mitchell's unexpected and terribly early death from peritonitis. It was a handsome book, costing eighteen shillings, handsomely illustrated by specially commissioned plates of the subjects (the originals of which remain in Mitchell's family) reproduced in a striking grey shade. The dedication was to Ivor Brown, who was to do much to popularise *A Scots Quair* after Mitchell's death in 1935; the title page, not inappropriately, quoted Tennyson's *Ulysses* to the effect that "'Tis not too late to seek a newer world", a world sought "beyond the sunset and the baths/of all the western stars".

And that, in brief, was the purpose of *Nine Against the Unknown* – to chart the careers of the earth wanderers who captured the imagination of an author fascinated – almost obsessed – by the spread of humankind through the unpopulated areas of the world, by the spread of "civilisation", by the overlay of one civilisation by another by assimilation or by force. His short stories of Egypt and Persia are about the clash of ideologies and religions, the attempt of one civilisation to rule over and run the affairs of another; his distaste for Mungo Park and Hanno (both of whom he wrote about) was in part their wish to impose an ideology on the countries they opened up to the West. In his science fiction, he is openly appalled by a future world (in *Gay Hunter*) where one dominant ideology tries to enslave the world, as he is fascinated and drawn to the past world (in *Three Go Back*) where there is no dominant ideology, indeed none at all – a world where people feel free to live and love according to their own wishes, unashamed and unburdened by guilt, the hunters of an earlier age, "tall and naked, the sunshine glistening on golden bodies, their hair flying like the horses' manes. Golden and wonderful against the hill-crest they ran . . ." (Polygon ed., Edinburgh, 1995, p. 69). This is the state

Mitchell evokes in his introduction to *Nine Against the Unknown*, the "happy-go-lucky tribes of Early Man, hunters and fishers", who led "dangerous and happy lives, generation on generation, in a great artistic flowering of the human spirit in a world slowly recovering from the Ice Age rigours" (p. 12).

The author of *A Scots Quair* – to say nothing of the essay on "The Antique Scene" of *Scottish Scene* (1934) – marks a firm division between those happy freedoms and "the coming of civilization, . . . the swift rise of gods and the study of death and decomposure" (p. 13) which follows with startling abruptness from this natural life, once people found the Nile basin and its ready fertility, and gave up the natural life for settling down – farming – the beginnings of civilisation. Chris Guthrie in *Sunset Song* sees momentary visions of that far-off time before civilisation in Scotland: *Nine Against the Unknown* is the work of an author to whom that distant "natural" state, and the present degenerate "civilisation" of 1934, is a major concern.

What characterises these nine studies is a terrible hunger for knowledge, for adventure, for the land beyond the horizon's edge. Leif Ericsson endures terrible privation to try to find the "western wonderlands" (p. 31), while Marco Polo follows tales of "colourful myths and terrible beasts and dreadful tribes" in his journeying (p. 49). Don Cristóbal Colon has his fortunate islands, "somewhere out in the dark Atlantic" (p. 89) while Cabeza de Vaca opens the path for generations behind him "the Americas resounding, north and south, to the tread of the feet of following adventurers on those trails he had beaten through wild leagues of bush and swamp while he sought the golden cities of mirage, the unknown lands where he would win wealth and many souls to God" (p. 166). Vasco da Gama embarks (p. 172) for the West, while "his mind strayed off unceasingly on that question? – Columbus's Cuba – how did it lie in relation to the Moluccas?", while Bering has his strait to find, building on report, on supposition – and on dangerous supposition, for as Mitchell notes "Myth flowered from legend and sometimes from lies" (p. 200) and Bering had to disentangle them at his own peril. For Mungo Park, the challenge was "interior Africa", long a mystery as the Americas were explored and looted, and "the rumour of the Niger, a great river . . . rivalling the Nile, a river on the banks of which stood fabulous Timbuctoo" (p. 227). For Francis Burton, the challenge was simply the Fortunate Isles of the unknown, wherever found:

> None of that multitude of hardy and strong and gifted men who opened up the continent of Africa from the darkness of black barbarism to the new and spreading darkness of White exploitation and industrialism possessed that driving unease of curiosity on the geographically unknown to such force and urge as Burton, questing the ancient Fortunate Isles with a wry sneer of disdain, pursuing them out of Africa and abroad four continents, and escaping the sound of them at last in denial of their existence. (p. 265)

And the fortunate isles of quest, for Mitchell's ninth explorer, are at the earth's extremes, where Nansen finds his destiny in the "only the great white stretches of *terra incognita* about the Poles where the last of the great earth conquerors touched with the wings of that ancient quest" (p. 288). The fortunate isles – the dream of an undiscovered, unexplored, "undeveloped" source of riches or beauty – often, it has to be admitted, riches rather than beauty – are the linking theme of Mitchell's choice of explorers. He traces them from "the burial of the dead on Nile Bank five thousand years before the birth of Christ" – and the growth of organised religion – through Amazonia and Africa and "thin little tracts of Arabia and Indo-China" to the poles, where Nansen completes the ninth chapter of exploration.

Like everything Mitchell did, *Nine Against the Unknown* was written professionally, tidily, neatly compiled. Its subjects are admittedly diverse, the logic of the book not immediately apparent in 900 years' spread and several continents, but easily apparent if the reader accepts Mitchell's premise of the Nile valley as cradle of civilisation as we know it, and the drive of the Earth Conquerors to settle, to explore, to push back the limits of knowledge – to convert, to "civilise". While the lives might be heroic, the circumstances in the chronicles are often quite the opposite. Mungo Park dies in the attempt to open up Africa, but Timbuctoo, the fabled city, turns out "no city of magic and mystery, but a decaying, dusty mart, mud-built, odoriferous, squalid" (p. 263). Siberia was opened up for "fur-looting" once the Russians discovered it (p. 202); Vasco da Gama sailed in a ship with "a supply of oil, capable of being boiled and used for the questioning of recalcitrant natives" (p. 172). To Mitchell the transition from "the darkness of black barbarism to the new and spreading darkness of White exploitation and industrialism" has little of the heroic, whatever the human courage of the nine who faced the unknown. The book is a constant counterpoint between the raw courage of the individual explorer, and the more squalid motives of the society who sent them, grudgingly paid them (if at all), and gleefully set about exploiting the territories they opened up. The fabulous city, the golden countries of imagination turn out, in this book, often to be assets to be exploited, gold, slaves, furs, money.

Nine Against the Unknown is a valuable book to read to settle firmly in the mind the implications of Mitchell's diffusionist beliefs. Clearly, he saw in the civilisation of his own mature years, war-scarred and slowed by Depression, a dreadful debasement of the kind of natural life he had written about in *Three Go Back*, and recalled the lingering death of in *Scottish Scene*. The flashes of time-travel which enliven *Sunset Song* are something of the same technique we see in *Nine Against the Unknown*, the juxtaposition starkly of present decadence and past simplicity, neither romanticised nor presented in black-and-white. The primitive Scot who sees the ships of Pythias approaching and wrings his hands in despair, the Roman soldier preparing for the battle of Mons Graupius and (doubtless) his own death in the Roman quest to "civilise" the Scots are moments of clarity granted to Chris and to Chae, characters sensitive to the complexity of past and present in a Scotland violently changing during the First World War years. *Nine Against the Unknown* is a less fantastical, more straightforward set of juxtapositions: nine hundred years of history throwing up adventurer after adventurer, different countries, different backgrounds, different motives – but united by the quest for those fortunate isles which either remain tantalisingly out of reach, or turn out (like fabulous Timbuctoo) to be rather more prosaic once they are found, and once civilisation sets to work on them.

One interesting quirk lies in Jarrolds' advertisements at the end of their 1934 London edition, of THE CONQUEST OF THE EARTH By LEWIS GRASSIC GIBBON, author of "*Sunset Song*", "*Cloud Howe*", "*Grey Granite*", "*Niger: A Life of Mungo Park*", *and (in collaboration with Hugh MacDiarmid)* "*Scottish Scene*". Illustrated, 18s. net.

This betrays some haste on the part of Jarrolds, quite apart from the wrong title for one of the books (*Niger: The Life of Mungo Park* was published by the Porpoise Press). For NINE AGAINST THE UNKNOWN is plainly the same book as EARTH CONQUERORS, bearing on the title page and dust jacket the joint names of James Leslie Mitchell and Lewis Grassic Gibbon, whom he disingenuously had referred to in *Scottish Scene* as his "distant cousin". *Earth Conquerors* became the title of the

American edition, with the change of authorship on the title page to LEWIS GRASSIC GIBBON alone, a different title page and price.

Written in ill health, alongside projects as substantial as *Scottish Scene* (for which Mitchell did the greater part of the work, MacDiarmid being in the Shetlands) and *Grey Granite* which proved very difficult to round off and complete, *Nine Against the Unknown* shows an author of complete professionalism, with a strong message to get across, never losing sight of the focus of a substantial book, nor of the need to give the audience rounded biographies of each individual explorer while clinging to the theme of the Fortunate Isles of legend, and the quest to shed light on the great Unknown. It has long deserved to be better known as part of Mitchell's great burst of productivity in his last year of life.

Ian Campbell
Edinburgh

Ian S. Munro discusses the publication and reception of *Nine Against the Unknown* in *Leslie Mitchell: Lewis Grassic Gibbon* (Edinburgh, 1966, pp. 191–4), with details of publication and reception in America, and also of the strong similarities in detail to Mitchell's earlier *Hanno*. In his important *A Blasphemer and Reformer* (Aberdeen, 1984), William K. Malcolm discusses *Nine Against the Unknown* valuably in relation to the tradition of the Absurd (pp. 32–6) which is at the heart of his book's excellent analysis of *A Scots Quair*. Douglas F. Young remains the best writer on Gibbon's diffusionist ideals: in *Beyond the Sunset* (Aberdeen, 1973 pp. 13–22) Young relates some of these ideas to *Nine Against the Unknown*.

The essays (particularly "The Antique Scene") in *Scottish Scene*, jointly produced with Hugh MacDiarmid in 1934, are now available in *The Speak of the Mearns*, Polygon's 1994 re-issue of the unfinished Mearns novel with the essays and short stories and a valuable brief essay by Jeremy Idle on Mitchell's exploration writing. On *Scottish Scene* and its genesis see "Gibbon and MacDiarmid at Play: The Evolution of *Scottish Scene*", *The Bibliotheck* 13/2 (1986), pp. 44–52, and on *Gay Hunter* and early civilisations "The Science Fiction of John [sic] Leslie Mitchell",

Extrapolation 16,1 (December, 1974), pp. 53–63. More republication of material from *Scottish Scene* is expected shortly. Meantime *Persian Dawns, Egyptian Nights* (which concerns itself very much with exploration in Egypt and the Middle East) is available from Polygon (Edinburgh, 1998), as is *Three Go Back* (Edinburgh, 1995, 2000).

Nine Against the Unknown

I

THE GLAMOUR OF GOLD AND THE GIVERS OF LIFE

§ 1

IF Man the Artist and Man the Agriculturist have lengthy histories and pre-histories, it is certain that Man the Explorer has an even greater antiquity. His antiquity extends far back beyond his humanity to the distant wanderings of the common ape-stock which fathered such divergent near-humans as the Peking Man of China, Pithecanthropus of Java, the great-jawed Heidelberg man of Germany. Exploration is among the most ancient of urges, nor need we assume that even in the pre-human days of humanity it was always exploration in search of more pleasant foods and pleasing shelters. Curiosity was a continual urge, even though only that spasmodic and uncontinued curiosity that a modern man may study in the antics of the monkey-cage. Beyond the next forest, the next line of hills, went a dim reasoning, *there might be something new.*

Twenty or thirty thousand years ago the great ice barriers of the Fourth Glacial Age began to break down all over the northern half of the Old World. The Ice retreated from Europe and Asia, leaving the great Russian plains seeping swamps, breaking down the Central Asian mountain-and-snow-ring in which it is possible that Man himself had attained (sheltered in that nook from the glacial rigours) his humanity. It was the Spring-time of the world, and different groups of men set out on slow wanderings, millennium on millennium, to the ultimate homes of racial differentiation. They were probably medium-sized, browny, indeterminate beings, those early forerunners who turned their backs on each other and set out to found the various races of mankind.

Neither the bleached pallor of the White, the curled hair and flattened face of the Black, the yellowness and eye-folding of the Mongol were yet in evidence. Climate and mutation were to play their parts in effecting those changes that are now so obtrusive to our eyes: Man the Early Explorer in his explorations was to father all the racial prides and fond prejudices of Modern Man.

That Early Man appears to have approximated very closely indeed to the Natural Man of Rousseau and the Encyclopædists; indeed, the Natural Man of Rousseau was no chance imagining of a dreaming sage (as is so often supposed), but a personification of the qualities of the last surviving groups of early men discovered by civilized Europe—the primitives of America. He was cultureless, houseless, godless; he had no devils, no classes, no agriculture, no clothes, no domestic animals. He was merely an animal, and not unrare on this planet in that he was also a tool-using animal. And, to judge by the evidences from the scarce Primitive groupings which until lately survived in this and that corner of the world, he was on the whole a happy and kindly animal, easily amused, a singer and hunter, unoppressed by strange fears, unstirred by strange hopes. The Golden Age was for long a reality on our planet: the first explorers who wandered west into Europe, east into China, south into Africa, were of the very stuff of the wistful dreamings of poets in the cities of civilization a long twenty thousand years later.

In Europe Cro-Magnard and Magdalenian man hunted the horse and the bison through long ages, painted great pictures, led dangerous and happy lives, generation on generation, in a great artistic flowering of the human spirit in a world slowly recovering from the Ice Age rigours. South and around the Mediterranean were folk of like blood and quality: their rock-paintings astound the modern traveller in the nullahs of the Sahara. But gradually a period of desiccation set in. Slowly the forested, swampy Sahara grew arid and brittle. Ungulates and carnivores drifted eastwards along the Mediterranean coasts with that shrinkage of the verdure of North Africa. With them went the happy-go-lucky tribes of Early Man, hunters and fishers. So doing, they came at last to the banks of the lower Nile.

The Nile resisted the desiccation. Year after year, most

uniquely flowing of rivers, it brought down the warm equatorial waters to generate the seeds of the plants along its shores. Wild barley grew along those shores in great natural fields, sprang to greenness, ripened, fell to the ground to be revived again, surely and certainly, on a fixed, unwavering day, by the next year's floods. It was a process profoundly and plainly impressed on the mind of the Primitive who had come hunting into that region: in no other region could the process have been so plainly impressed. He found the barley easy and succulent food. And at last one of his number, long afterwards deified as Osiris, the First King-Irrigator, was moved to assist the processes of the river, to dig a channel to further stretches of land for the river to fertilize, to inaugurate the first attempt at basin-agriculture.

So, suddenly, man became an agriculturist, storing the surplus of the seeds for next year's flood-sowing, creating architecture in building sheds for that storage, creating villages and so towns and so civilization in the necessity to carry out those operations communally. So classes came into the world with the differentiation of men into Kings (Chief Irrigators), Priests (Followers and Tenders and Interpreters of the Kings)—and Plebs (the Labourers at the Sowing and Reaping). In a few hundred years there came into being on our planet—and at the time on no other portion of it than the Nile basin—civilization: not slowly evolved from barbarism as barbarism was once supposed in its turn to have sprung from savagery, but a direct transition from the life of wandering, carefree Natural Man.

Now, godless and devil-less though he had been, Natural Man like all other animals had always sought to avoid death, and had reasoned that the cause of death was the loss of blood, that blood itself, in fact, was Life. Consequently, long before the coming of civilization, he had in various parts of the world greatly prized objects and materials the colour of blood—red carnelian and the like. He had prized the cowrie-shell as an amulet because of its life-giving shape—its obvious similarities in shape to the portal of mammalian birth. He had traded in such objects over wide areas, and valued them greatly.

With the coming of civilization, with the swift rise of gods and the study of death and decomposure, that search for life-givers became intensified if also diversified. Green was now looked upon as a Giver of Life—any object of green—

because of its likeness to the life-giving corn. Jade and malachite were searched for and valued accordingly. So was gold—the colour of the sun which warmed and ripened the crops—a great Life-Giver. With the surplus of energy and population that agriculture created the ancient Nilotic kings sent out their captains and mariners far and near in quest of those seemingly necessary things.

Exploration of the world was launched again—exploration not originally for trade or conquest or the seizing of rich lands; but for amulets against death and misfortune, precious metals which would ensure the wearer long health and earthly immortality, residence in a happy eternity of terrestrial bliss.

§ 2

The urge of this irrational quest for irrational Givers of Life spread civilization abroad the Old World. The exploring miners and traders and exploiters of Egypt carried agriculture, its banes and blessings, to Sumer, to Syria, to Crete. There the autochthonous primitives, learning practice and theory, in their turn erected altars to strange gods, upbuilt their characteristic civilizations, quested like their mentors the Egyptians out and abroad the unknown lands for gold and pearls, jade and amber. Sumer carried the seeds of civilization into India, rearing Mohenjo-Daro and its attendant glories, into Central Asia and from there engrafting the tree of Chinese civilization. So with Crete, civilizing the Mediterranean basin and the Greek lands, penetrating remotely to Spain, and from there to Britain. Civilization fathered the first deliberate exploration, exploration in its turn fathered the great divergent and diverging cultures of the ancient world.

But gradually the irrational element in the quest died out. Gold came to be prized not as a magic metal, a mystic Giver of Life, but (owing to its scarcity) assuming direct and ascendant values over other commodities as a means of exchange and therefore of definite social wealth. In a measure this was mere transmutation of the original idea of gold—a transmutation which still holds the world in thrall. But it was of definite consequence. The fantastic element in the quest lapsed, or, as the poets of the succeeding Greek and

Roman civilizations saw it, the Silver Age which had succeeded the Golden Age in its turn departed, to be followed by the Iron Age of brute exploitation and conquest, the ages which produced the warring armies of Assyria and the throat-cutting raids abroad Europe of the early Greeks and Celts. And, just as the value of gold was transmuted in men's minds, its direct and urgently personal-appealing importance to some measure lapsed. Sargon sought territory rather than the metals within it: he sought subject peoples and subject cornlands. So with Alexander the Great, so with most of the great military conquerors.

Encouraging their merchants to trade afar, the Mesopotamian and Mediterranean civilizations had already, by the close of the last millennium before Christ, fairly definite knowledge of many countries outside the range of their own political sway. Pytheas, a Greek trader from Marsala, had sailed up the coasts of Spain, circumnavigated Britain, and voyaged to a remote Thule which was perhaps Iceland, more probably Norway. The Greek Alexander (the trader, not the king), had coasted Southern Asia remotely to Hanoi. The east coast of Africa had been definitely explored as far south as Dar-es-Salaam: perhaps even further, for Herodotus has a story of an expedition despatched by the Egyptian Pharaoh Necho which circumnavigated Africa, taking several years to do so, keeping close to the coasts, landing and planting crops, awaiting their ripening, and pushing on till finally it came to the Pillars of Hercules, and so at last the Mediterranean. Two at least of these three great journeys were journeys in the interests of trade, colonization, land-seizing.

Necho's expedition is perhaps the exception. It brings us to other exceptions which still dwindlingly survived. In 500 B.C. Himilco the Carthaginian visited the West Coast of Europe, perhaps touched on Ireland, and then penetrated far out into the Atlantic—attaining the Sargasso Sea, as some think. He could hardly have done so in quest of definite spoil. Here and there in the drabness of the records other attempts erupt into notice—inexplicable attempts upon this and that point of the compass from the view of the new commercialist orientation of exploration.

For the explanation of such attempts it is necessary to glance again at those first beginnings of all civilizations in the Valley of the Nile. As we have seen, the First God was the deified King-Irrigator. Dying, he yet lived in his successor; and also, in the hazy theological metaphysics of those days, individually and personally, in remote lands of the sun. For he was a Child of the Sun and his flesh might not put on corruption.

So arose the idea of immortality, a play and a counter-play of thought and surmise upon a very prosaic happening. Assembling for the first time in villages, men no longer, as did their primitive progenitors, left their dead to decompose where they fell. They carried the bodies remotely from the villages to the sandy Western bank of the Nile and thrust them into holes, kings, commons, priests, heaping the sand well upon them.

But it was a peculiar burial-place. The hot Egyptian sands did not, as sands in burial elsewhere, decompose the body. Instead, they preserved it uniquely. Astounded Egyptians carrying their dead there would find that hungry jackals had been at work and had torn out corpses and partially devoured them. This was understandable enough, but not (for hunters accustomed to seeing the decay of death) the state of the cadavers. The dead Egyptians looked almost as in life, dead hardly at all, surely in a sleep, surely awaiting the coming of some fresh life. . . .

To ensure that life yet more fully—that mystic life in some unnameable land—mummification, tomb-building, was introduced, and spread everywhere in the tracks of the Archaic Civilization. With that diffusion—to Europe, to Asia, remotely into Africa—spread the myths and legends that went with the practice, legend of a mythic land in the West (originally the Nile *West* Bank) where the happy dead lived a new life, free and immortal,

> the island-valley of Avilion,
> Where falls not hail, or rain, or any snow,
> Nor ever wind blows loudly.

The idea and belief took root in theology, in folklore, as the Garden of the Hesperides, the Fortunate Isles, Valhalla, Wineland, the Land of Gold. And it was regarded not as a distant land in the skies, not in exact essence the Heaven or Hades of the various mythologies, but as a definite terrestrial paradise. Generally its direction was adscripted to the West.

As geographical knowledge enlarged it receded more quickly and quickly into the Atlantic. Sometimes, though seldom, the East found it its home, what with the tales that came to Europe of the magic Spice Islands—inextricably confused with the Fortunate Isles though indeed they were but the East Indies.

So again the irrational element had come into exploration, the quest for a land of geographical fantasy, a land of Youth and Fortune and Gold.

§ 3

Men being of the lowly clay they are, concerned with food and mating and the begetting of children, drowsing by chimney corners, yawning in peace in long summer days, worshipping with benignant incomprehension the incomprehensible Gods, that Quest of the Fortunate Isles was never in itself in any age a deep and passionate racial urge. At the most it was the main motif in a number of exploring lives, it gave hope and fear and a dim uncertainty to the far land and sea-wanderings of many men in the days before Christ. A man set out on a new trade route in the hope, as a remote ambition, of finding the Golden Land of Youth. If he failed en route he might at least fill his pouch with good terrestrial treasure by the way.

The origin of the belief and quest, as we have seen, was a fantastic misapprehension of the action of Nature in a matter of human burial. But, spreading through the Mediterranean, throughout all Europe, interweaving with fresh by-products of religious and theological fancy, it acquired a surer belief to foundation it. That belief was built on vague race memories of the world that once had been—that world of Early Man which those first civilizations (even while they enjoyed the fruits of civilization) looked back on regretfully as the vanished Golden Age when good King Cronos reigned in heaven and Zeus the warlike usurper was still inapparent. Some fragment of that ancient world, went the poet's misty dream, might still survive—far off under the setting of the sun. . . .

The fourth and fifth Christian centuries saw the overthrow of the Roman Empire. Europe was plunged into political and cultural anarchy; trade languished as did imagination; exploration as motif or desire vanished from the European scene. Slowly a version of Christianity, garnished with many an odd notion from the older religions, spread abroad Europe; slowly the kingdoms and principalities of the Middle Ages took more or less permanent shape; slowly the great trading, exploring, debating class came into prominence—the middle class. Men read the ancients in a new-found leisure, speculated in monasteries and the great guild towns, carried the seeds of those speculations from the Mediterranean to the Baltic. Populations grew at considerable pace: in the less kindly agricultural regions the press of population was the root cause of the unending moving and raiding and colonizing of the first Christian millennium. That spread of population was to father the Crusades, with which this record is unconcerned. But also it was an urge to find new ways of trade: it begat anew the desire for geographical exploration: it begat the long line of earth-conquerors who were to subjugate the earth.

And in the medley of reasons that have urged European explorers abroad the planet since that year A.D. 1000—desire for loot, for fame, for fun—the quest of the Fortunate Isles, sometimes deliberate, sometimes unapprehended, has moulded innumerable lives and journeys and voyages. Until the beginning of the present century one may trace it as a thin vein of unauthentic gold in all the grey fabric of geographical adventure. And in the lives of at least Nine of the great representative Earth-Conquerors its influence was predominant; and with them is this chronicle.

It was a quest curiously mixed and—by the time of the last of the Nine—transmuted. Yet Leif Ericsson and Fridtjof Nansen, separated by a space of nine hundred years, both quested the unattainable same. They did it under different names and guises: the essence remained. Marco Polo alone belongs to this record not so much because of the influence of the quest upon his life as the influence of his life upon the quest. Columbus and Cabeza de Vaca were seekers of the Fortunate Isles naked and unashamed in intention; Magellan's search was darker and colder, his Fortunate Isles the isles of clove and nutmegs, but the urge to their attainment drawn from Columbus's; Vitus Bering slowly and unwilling sought the same fleeting land in the fogs of the North Pacific; Mungo Park pursued it inland, with a cold fire, to its abiding place by the bank of an unknown river, Richard Burton (who would have laughed the imputation of the quest to scorn) sought the same Debatable Land in Harar, in Arabia, in the Lakes that give birth to the Nile; Nansen quested it, disguised as "knowledge of a mathematical point" towards the utmost Pole.

How that quest interwove in their lives and thoughts and actions, was acknowledged, repudiated, foregone, but yet was the principal thing in the lives of those Nine; how the sought-for Land of Youth sometimes betook itself to strange shapes, to the likeness of the City of God, to the likeness of a mental refuge from a half-integrated self, to the likeness of the realm of icy knowledge: is the theme of this book.

In all its changings—from a definite Island in a definite sea to a definite standpoint in human thought—it remained and remains *terra incognita*, the Unknown Land; and it may be said truly that the lives of those Nine, all of whom were great and successful explorers, are all in a fashion tragic epics. So in a fashion is all human life. But tragedy itself has no part in that belief in the happy Fortunate Isles which dominated the lives of those Nine who were representative of so many men: it was glamour gloriously unescapable. Leif at Brattalid, Burton at Aden, Mungo Park in Peebles, Bering toil-worn on the Yenisei, Magellan glowering eastwards from Goa:

> Whether at feast or fight was he
> He heard the noise of a nameless sea
> On an undiscovered isle.

II

LEIF ERICSSON'S LANDFALL IN WINELAND THE GOOD

§ 1

BY the tenth Christian century the Northmen of Scandinavia had definitely established themselves as the great seafaring folk of Europe. Their longships, inherited from the shipyards of Egypt and Crete not by way of the Atlantic but by way of the trans-European rivers, were stout and strong, capable of long sailings and travaillings, made of hard woods and well constructed; their crews were men from a bitter and infertile land whence it was scarcely possible in the agricultural techniques of the time to wring meagre sustenance, far less the luxuries of existence. For the latter they turned to adventure beyond the creaming surfs pelting the long Norse coasts.

These Northmen in their narrow fjords, winter-surrounded through great portions of the year, rearing scant crops of oats and barley, pasturing lean herds in the uplands in summer, fishing in turbulent seas, were in essence no remarkable folk. From the Archaic culture they had passed, as all Europe had passed, to a civilization compounded of a congeries of small kings and small gods, the local chief the head of a Thing or Parliament of free-men, the lowlier tasks relegated to slaves or bondmen, the Gods the War and Hate and Wonder Gods of a people bitterly reared on the sharpest edge of the Iron Age. Their development of seafaring was inevitable, granted supplies of wood and iron and those initial impulses to boat-building which had filtered up from the Mediterranean; loutish, hungry, and poverty-stricken, they quested adventure for the sake of loot, not love.

South-east across the North Sea they raided the coasts of Scotland, the Western Islands, England, France, Spain, North Africa, Italy: they penetrated even remotely to Egypt the mother-home of all sea-farers; they returned with loot and scalps and chained gangs of thralls, wonder-stories of half-mythic lands, the virginal insignia of murdered maids, the skulls of men they had slain—skulls they kept as drinking cups. They have been much romanticized, those sea-raiders, as strong and hardy and gallant men, great drinkers and lovers and fighters, but the picture fades and dims to unlovelier colours in the light of research. We may now, unimpassioned, envisage them for what they were—a race that for long deserved the epithet savage far more than any race ever known to the earth before or after. Their home lives were built on the thin dregs of European civilization seeping north. They had no native literature, no native culture, no religion, though much brutish superstition ; no single thought or impulse to stir our later sympathies. Their sagas tell of a mean and bloody and cowardly life, comrades throat-cutting on minor matters like the stealing of fish or firewood, mean squabbes on little roods of land, clownish cruelties and clownish curiosities in that cruelty. To the harassed and divided peoples of the lands they raided they appeared as no superior type—they appeared for what they were, brutish and implacable bands of pirates.

To clear the picture to a truer vision of their quality is not to denigrate them or their achievements. Rather the reverse. They were amongst the most bitterly tortured of our species in its maladjustments both to climatic conditions and to the unnatural phenomenon of civilization. In the throes of those maladjustments they put to sea on quests for food and rape and loot and blood, and in those quests, suddenly, unexpectedly, looked again and again on the face of wonder, pushed back the frontier of the world's geographical knowledge, saw strange islands and peaks in running tides at twilight, and returned to Norway with the tale of them—tales that drifted south and became one with those Fortunate Islands that first rose as a dream from the priestly imaginings on the banks of the primal Nile.

They were amongst the first of the Europeans deliberately to "put to sea"—to leave the hugging of coasts and steer by stars, by wind-direction, by the finding of birds, across great open spaces of water. That is the preliminary and prelude to their voyagings ; that is the essential thing to be apprehended. Not until the eleventh century at earliest, when Leif of this record was sleeping his last sleep in Brattalid, did the primitive lode-stone that foreshadowed the true compass reach to navigational knowledge in the fjords of the north. The Pole-star was their lode-stone by night, the sun and the positioning of clouds and tides and rains their guides by day. Yet before the opening of the eleventh century they had voyaged with only those aids to Iceland, to Greenland, to Spitzbergen, to Novaya Zemlya—and, as that century broke, to a land even yet more distant.

About the year A.D. 870 they had reached Iceland—led there by the accidents of storm and tide, or deliberately seeking a refuge—the tale is sadly confused. There they found an older population in uncertain residence—it seems to have been settled by Christianized Celtic harmosts long centuries before. Of these Celts we hardly hear again, folk hardly emerging even in name from one of those many Celtic twilights that have haunted the West European fringe. No doubt the Northmen slew them, enslaved them, or gradually absorbed them into the Norse family-groups, the Norse language. Name-places of the aliens long haunted the Iceland scene. By A.D. 900 extensive settlements had been carried out in Iceland by the newcomers, for Harold Haarfager had arisen in Norway subduing the little kings to a central power. Many of them refused that subjection, and instead put to sea for Iceland, preferring an even harder life on the inhospitable island to the unlikely comforts of Norway ruled by an autocrat.

They found their preference tested in bitter rigours. Land was scarce; and so remote was Iceland out in the Atlantic wastes that it was impossible to supplement life-resources as easily as in the old country—by thief-raids on North Europe. As a consequence there speedily developed throughout the island, with no definite centralized authority, such unending anarchic orgy of private claim and counter-claim, private murder and retaliation, as clouds the early sagas with a wearisome steam of blood. A desperate and intolerable land-hunger drove those men. It gave birth to an even more mean and desperate courage and ruthlessness. Among the most warlike and homicidal of the Iceland farmers in A.D. 980 was that Eirik Raude who was presently to father on the Icelandic scene the son who was to be dubbed of all voyageurs The Lucky.

§ 2

Eric (Eirik in his Norse) and his father Jaederen had both been exiled from Norway for murder about the Christian year 970. Emigrating to Iceland, they bore with them untarnished the family penchants. The father died some little time after the move—possibly and righteously of a slit throat. Thereon Eric decamped to the south of the island. Here he speedily quarrelled with the neighbours around Eirikstad; finally, he killed several of them, probably very cold-bloodedly for the local indeterminate Thing, no squeamish body, condemned him to banishment from the district.

He and his wife and household of carles—gangster-assistants—and thralls—slaves captured on sea-raids—then moved to a farm on a small island off the Iceland coast. But neither Eric's nature nor his circumstances seem to have changed greatly. Soon he was blood-letting again. At the Thing of 980 he and his gangsters were declared outlaws and were hunted to and fro the Iceland strands.

In this strait Eric, banished from Norway, banished from Iceland, recalled a remarkable tale. This had been passed to and fro in the winter gossip of the Iceland kitchens from the lips of a certain Gunnbjörn who had sailed by accident and the force of contrary winds far out into the Western sea and had there glimpsed the snow-peaks of unnamed lands. Eric resolved to load his boats and seek those lands himself.

In the brevity of the saga compiled long afterwards we hear little more than of the resolution and the departure. But it seems that he and his followers were in considerable strength, we can vision them strong and sea-skilful men, living possibly in a kind of communal kindness among themselves, mentally savages, culturally pre-palæolithic, ignorant very greatly of even the fears that the world of their time entertained regarding the limits of that Western Ocean and the great Gulf of Dread into which all story told the waters of the earth in some place poured—beyond the Fortunate Isles.

Their ignorance held them in good stead. The eastern coast of Greenland, tall and uninhabited, ice-sheathed, was sighted amidst considerable excitement. But it was rocky and bare, and Eric saw that it would be useless to land there. Accordingly, he sailed south for uncertain days, rounded the point that in modern geographies is called Cape Farewell, and there made a ragged fringe of country on which the eternal snows did not intrude, though they reared up their glacier-points far northwards, pale blue and unmoving on the skyline. In a wildered jumble of fjords and nullahs Eric drew in his long-ships, his men standing and staring at the land and water, the cattle on board—for there were cattle—lowing at the whiff of the autumn grasslands, wonder and speculation stirring in the dull Norse peasant brains. Presently they found good anchorage and landed.

They were the first Europeans in Greenland. But they were not the first inhabitants. Sailing up the Western coasts, black and barren and desolate, they landed and found there stone traps and bones, metal implements even, tell the sagas; and at these they stared in a considerable amaze, and from them no doubt round about them, gripping their axes, waiting the sight or sound of trolls who could only be enemies to the Norse kind. But the place was silent and forsaken, but for the crying of seabirds and the rustling of the long Autumn grasses. . . . Eric resumed his explorings.

For three years he explored and quested those coasts with a surprising diligence that we find hard enough to account for unless on the supposition that farming bored him intensely, he preferred the chances of the sea and—who knew? —coming at last perhaps far up those fjords on some rich city of the trolls which he could comfortably loot. No city was found, though much of frostbite and hardship. At Eiriksfjord down in East Settlement a collection of dwellings of un-mortared stone had meantime been reared to shelter men and cattle; there were no trees growing anywhere, but up the Western coast the Northmen (thenceafterwards to be called the Greenlanders) found a point where drifted wood shored in great piles.

They made expeditions to this spot, wood-gathering for fuel and carpentry, whale-hunting, fishing. They endured the winters and cried at the first sight of the summer sun; they pastured their cattle and sowed scant seeds, and through three long years as they turned in sleep at night heard the thunder of the southward-going bergs. . . . And amidst this scene the four children of Eric—sons Leif, Thorwald,

LEIF ERICSSON

Thorstein, and Freydis, his illegitimate daughter—grew up in a hasting adolescence.

Eric seems to have been glad of the passing of those three years. He was an outlaw; and though that must have troubled little a heart and a mind without ethic notions of citizenship or communal kinship, it probably irked him that he had so few companions to dominate and browbeat and fight with. He sailed again for Iceland.

His outlawry was up. But he found Iceland little to his taste. His worst enemy, one Thorgest, promptly challenged him to combat; and, as the saga briefly relates: "Thorgest won." One approves of Thorgest. Eric seems to shrink a little after that. The indomitable bully, suddenly pricked, his bellowings at home and against his wife and children had perhaps thereafter an uneasy note in them. Pricked and prudent, he resolved to forswear Iceland, but not to sail back to Greenland without inducing as large a population as possible to accompany him.

Accordingly, he spread the tale of the land he had found, dubbing that land by the name it has borne since the day of Eric's infamous mis-christening—"because, said he, men would be more willing to go thither if it had a good name!" By the year 990 the inhabitants of Greenland were a large number, as the Northmen reckoned numbers. Over a thousand European souls had made the great venture from the Eastern to the Western hemisphere, to rear their stone huts and byres in Eastern and Western Settlement, to pasture their cattle and dream of Iceland and set forth for it or even distant Norway on trading ventures of wild hazard and wilder legend.

Very early it became clear to those Greenlanders how anomalous was their position, how poverty-stricken this life to which they had exiled themselves. The ruins of their habitations are to be seen to this day: the byres are small and suggest goats and sheep rather than cattle; the houses themselves have a terrifying smallness and closeness. In the howl of the Greenland nights they must have been draughty and odoriferous and uncomfortable enough, when the wolves gathered round the Greenland garbage-heaps and bayed the stars, and the vikings nodded in slumber before inadequate heaps of driftwood fire, and the dull and squat and harassed Northwomen went about their household tasks with so many restrictions upon their housekeeping. They limned in a strange and almost unparalleled episode in history, those folk of that remote venture of European civilization on the fringes of the American Arctic.

§ 3

In the year 999, a fine concatenation of numbers, the eldest son of Eirik Raude, Leif, took out his longship and sailed for Norway.

There has been little of Leif hitherto in the Saga of Eric the Red. It is uncertain when or where he was born, though almost certainly in Iceland. But men grew rapidly to maturity in that milieu; we may guess he was a little over twenty years of age, in outward appearance a typical Norseman, tall and burly, in blue cloak and sober grey leggings, a personable youth--"Leif was a large and powerful man, and of a most imposing bearing, a man of sagacity and a very just man in all things"—says the Saga.

His mental content was a strange admixture of hunting and whaling lore, the life-formulae of a land-pressed peasant, lore of the wielding of arms in the conflicts and squabbles of the colony, lore of the gods of war and sea; and a dim geographical horizon in which Iceland bulked immensely, Norway more dimly, and south of that tenebrous Norway a vision of Europe dim peak on peak fading into lands of legend as the towering Jokulls back of Eirikstad faced into the Northern Mists. He called himself a Greenlander without prejudice to being a Norseman; and sailed in a young man's hope of adventure, loot, lust, and odd pickings by the way.

Probably the direct passage from Greenland to Norway, without touching Iceland, had been made before ever Leif put to sea; but his is the first recorded transatlantic crossing on record, though his plan to reach Norway direct did not mature. Gales came on, heavy Spring storms, and the longship was driven out of its course into some island of the Hebrides. Here they were welcomed and given hospitality by the islanders, Norse like themselves, and here they sat down to await a favourable wind to carry them to Norway.

But it was a still and drowsing summer that followed that Spring. No winds came. The Atlantic slept through the long hours of daylight, unruffled except by the passing wing of a seagull; night-time it flung up a great radiance of stars back to the starry skies and the lodestar of the Northmen. To tack or row into favouring currents in that sea with his single-sailed ship was apparently beyond Leif's seamanship. He awaited a favourable gale, and meanwhile fell in love with an island woman, Thorgunna, so bringing one of the first authentic love-stories into saga literature, a whisper of clear and lovely and tragic happenings in those long records of land-squabblings and mixed and impatient voyaging.

To fall in love in that time between such two as Leif and Thorgunna meant to share more than kisses or looks. So Leif perhaps had his first awakening to wonder and the strange beauties behind the barren greyness of life in the bed of the kind and passionate Thorgunna as the summer waned to autumn and their idyll waxed to fruit. Then at last the winds came.

When Leif went to part with Thorgunna, she begged that he take her with him. He seems to have hesitated for a while, and then perhaps thought of the smoke and glower of the Norse court where he intended to sojourn. He answered that he could not take one of her lineage on such seas, in a boat protected by so few men. Here they must end their summer months.

Then Thorgunna told him that she was pregnant, and Leif the father of her child; but even that did not move him. Perhaps he had tired of her, perhaps his refusals were for her sake only. One peers down those caverns of the years to seek into motives and hopes and repulsions long not even a flicker in human thought, with Leif and his Thorgunna bidding farewell. But she swore she would follow him to Greenland, somehow, in some fashion, though it took all her life, and bring their son if she should bear one. That he does not seem to have denied her. Perhaps he thought it merely the passionate protest of a woman in her state. So he gave her a "gold ring, a Greenland mantle of frieze, and a belt of walrus ivory" and parted with her, dourly, and without tears, as was their kind, putting to sea with a following wind and reaching Norway without further mishap or goodhap.

Olaf Tryggvason, that strange barbarian who had become such a queerly fanatic Christian, ruled Norway at the time. Leif made his way to the court and seems to have been well received there, albeit he was a heathen savage from the uttermost bounds of the Northman king's domains. Perhaps he had come on some semi-official mission; perhaps it was a likeness in mental bent and content and dream that drew Olaf and Leif together. For it seems that he became a favourite, that for the king's sake he listened to the priests. Before that year 999 was out he had become a Christian.

There were probably priests from the South, from the Baltic and Germany, with whom he talked in Norway, traders and missionaries and curious men come to the court of the savage Christian king. And Leif told much of distant Greenland and in return was patient with queries and questions. Were there other lands out there? Warm lands, fruitful lands? Had he or the Greenlanders yet seen the fair Isle of St. Brendan rising in the seas beyond Ireland? Had he seen the unipeds and the clustering grapes of Wineland, the Fortunate Isle?

Out of such strands of gossip and rumour and speculation we may imagine the mind of young Leif Ericsson, the White Christ's new man, fashioning a web of geographical curiosities far beyond the vision of his father Eirik who had hunted Western Greenland for things understandable and solid enough —food and loot and wood. Wineland the Good, the Fortunate Land. . . .

He wintered with the court at Nidaros, but in the spring prepared to sail again for Greenland. Then at Olaf's urging —or perhaps his own request—he took with him a priest to convert the Greenland heathen, and parted with Olaf, and set sail on as straight a route across the Atlantic as had ever been followed, between the Faröes and the Shetlands, his design to strike Cape Farewell and no other land before that.

The design was completely successful. Cape Farewell was reached and rounded and before the eyes of Leif and his crew uprose again the ragged, barren lands of Eiriksfjord, with behind it the great Jokull, the Glacier, rearing up its blue peaks unchanged. Of the homecoming there is no record; the sagas treat with a decent severity such matters. But however indifferent or surly the greeting of the ageing Eric himself, Leif's two brothers, Thorstein and Thorvald, must have received him with questions enough on what strange strand he had ever made captive the beings with whom he was companioned—the shaven priest of the White Christ and two thralls presented him by Olaf in Norway—Scots thralls, the man named Haki and the woman Hekja. What these three newcomers themselves thought of Brattalid, Eric's house, goes also unrecorded. The two thralls stared at the Jokull and set to their toil, unaware their sterner life destinies in the Fortunate Land of legend.

§ 4

This was the year 1000 of the Christian era. Before it was spent there had come changes at Brattalid and up and down both Eastern and Western Settlements. The missionary's efforts met with a singular success—backed probably by the strong hand or the strong recommendation of Leif. Everywhere the White Christ was accepted and the ancient feasts and sacrifices to the Norse gods suppressed. Tjodhild, Leif's mother, was one of the first converts and was instrumental in building the first church in Eastern Settlement. The ancient gods and the ancient rites were abandoned with a singular unanimity which suggests very strongly what a feeble hold the creeds of blood and war had truly upon the Northmen: they were as willing as most of the rest of humankind when unbedevilled, to acquire a gentler faith and a saner superstition.

With one exception. The exception was the aged and scoundrelly Eric the Red himself. He would have none of the new doctrines, or the shaven hypocrite—the 'skaemannin' —who propounded them. He saw in them, no doubt, a weakening of his own authority, the uprising of a shadowy moral wall of disapproval against those acts of blood and rapine that had enlivened the tediums of his bare existence. And this was more than fulfilled.

His persistent refusal even to listen to the new creed brought about an unexpected reaction on the part of his wife Tjodhild. They might indeed be wedded in the sight of the heathen gods, between them have brought three sons into the world: but she was a Christian now and would share neither bed nor board with a heathen. At this news and the acts that accompanied it the sagas relate, dryly, that Eric was "greatly displeased'

In that land beyond Cape Farewell the year passed slowly

and eventfully enough, we may suppose, though the changes and alterations of feeling and belief are a dim tale now. When the winter came down it brought to Eiriksford a new sound in those sub-arctic wastes—the chanting of the mass, hymn-singing in lonely wastes where few and alien gods had come. It needs indeed a sudden urge of vision to realize the strange and unexpected turns of fortune and fashion that diffused abroad the ancient world creed and custom from one remote part to another. In Greenland they worshipped a thousand years after his death a Jewish prophet who had lived and died in the heat and sunglare of the unknown Levant. Neither planning nor faith could have won that result, merely the play and counter-play of the tides of chance and change.

And presently, as the Spring came to Brattalid and all the snow-entrenched byres and house-roofs slowly thawed and the grass put forth its blades in the narrow scaurs, there came news of how those tides of chance had brought to the eyes of men sight of a land of wonder and legend in the seas of the unknown south.

§ 5

One of the settlers in Greenland was a Heriulf from Iceland. Coming originally to the new country in the west, he appears to have left some part of his household gear and family behind. . . . The story is a faint one, in the faintest outline. But early in the spring of 1002 a son of this Heriulf, one Biarni Heriulfsson, set sail from Iceland in his longship, with intent to visit his father in Eastern Settlement. He appears to have been a young man of no great distinction or character, as subsequent events were to prove to his disgusted crew.

For presently storms arose, driving the ship violently from its course. With them came raining fogs till presently the Northmen had completely lost bearings and for "many days drifted about in the sea". Then at last the storm subsided, the fog lifted, and there, close on the western skyline, they sighted land—where no land should have been.

The sea flung up long breakers along a flat and wooded shore; over all raced the clouds of Spring. The Northmen stared their excitement and wonder and steered the longship nearer. But now Biarni proved his lack of quality. He refused to make a landing. Of this land they had no knowledge, and he himself no need. It was Greenland he had set out for, and Greenland he intended to make.

Muttering their resentment, his crew obeyed, and sailed the longship north. Presently it vanished from sight, the mysterious land, and the fogs came down again, though there was a good following wind that drove the ship north-east. Once again, days later, that fog lifted, and they saw land again on the port—flat, inhospitable land. And once again Biarni refused a landing.

At last Cape Farewell was sighted, the great sail of the longship lowered, and the much and strangely travelled Northmen rowed into Eiriksfjord. They were the first of their kind to sight the American Continent.

§ 6

The story fired Leif Ericsson. Perhaps he had never forgotten those tales of western wonderlands he had heard in Nidaros when he heard also for the first time of the new faith. And they were more than tales—Biarni could have proved them more than tales, had he had the courage and energy. Biarni, indeed, must have led an ungay life in Greenland, scoffed at and jeered at for his failure to land on the new shores. All through that summer and the following autumn and winter talk and controvery on that glimpsed land went on in Eiriksfjord. At last, his plans complete, Leif took them beyond talk. His own longship no longer seaworthy, he went to Biarni and offered to purchase his.

Biarni seems to have acceded without any regrets. As long as he himself owned a longship, so long would it be expected that he would some day man it and sail south-west in quest of that infernal shore that ill-luck had allowed him to glimpse. Instead, as he now gathered, here was Leif Ericsson bent on that mission without any pressing at all.

It was summer when Leif mustered his crew to the longship, thirty-five men in all and one woman. That woman was the Scotswoman slave Hekja. Among the men was her lover or husband Haki. Leif himself apart, all the others are nameless except Leif's foster-father, a German named Tyrker, which is possibly a corruption of the Norse word for a German

—Tysker. Tyrker was small and swart and given to jolly living and shrewd planning, and was greatly devoted to Leif. His devotion to yet other things was to prove the name for the unknown land. Neither Thorstein nor Thorvald, Leif's brothers, appear to have been invited on the expedition.

Eric himself, however, was so invited, and at first refused. But he was accounted lucky in his findings, and still remembered as a great explorer. Under pressure from his son—he appears to have had considerable affection for Leif in spite of the fact that the latter had inflicted Christianity upon the Settlements—he at last agreed to accompany the ship. Farewells were said at Brattalid on a summer morning and the shipmen set out for the strand where the longship lay. Eric rode on a pony, and had gone but a little way when an accident occurred—he fell from the horse and broke his ribs and hurt his shoulder. His only comment on the accident, tells his Saga, was "Ah, Yes!"

The expedition does not seem to have delayed. It embarked and hoisted the great square sail and slowly took the wind and held out from Eiriksfjord. Here a good south-westerning wind was found and the Greenland coasts vanished in the summer haze from the Jokull.

For two or perhaps three days they ran before that wind, caught in the great coasting current that sweeps down towards Labrador. Then at last there appeared hull down a long stretch of coastland, towering in the sky great icy mountains. The Northmen, resolved to have done with such cravenness as Biarni's, shortened sail and put into shore.

It was no Fortunate Island. The shore was covered with great rounded stones, the land stretched bleak and barren back to the edge of the unfrequented, snow-tipped hills. Leif and his companions appear to have regarded it without enthusiasm but also undespondently. This was not the land they sought.

They christened it Helluland, glumly, the Land of the Flat Stones, that portion of modern Labrador, and re-embarked and put to sea again. Soon Helluland sank behind; next day brought a new country—undoubtedly the country that Biarni had sighted.

For it was wooded down to the shore, the Nova Scotia of that day, with a foreshore of white sand such as the Norsemen had never seen before and stared at in amaze. Leif and his men put ashore in a boat, and found water and wood and explored a little, and were still unsatisfied. This Markland appeared a good and hearty land enough to their Northern mind; had they been in search of merely another land for settlement this would have appeared paradise in comparison with the stiff and unyielding Greenland. But there was something else that urged on at least their commander—the knowledge that somewhere in these seas the happy Fortunate Islands each morning lifted up their fruit-laden trees to sunrise. He ordered a re-embarkation.

So they re-embarked and put to sea once again, with a north-east wind behind them. And that wind indeed drove them through the space of two days' sail towards a land that was to seem to Leif the fulfilment of the tales he had heard afar in Nidaros.

§ 7

It took them two days' sail. Then this new land, south-west of Markland, hove in sight, with beside it an island where the grass was spring-green in the summer sunlight. Again they put in and landed.

> And they looked round them in the fair weather and found that there was dew on the grass, and it happened that they touched the grass with their hands, and put them in their mouths, and they thought they had never tasted anything so sweet as it was.

It was probably the modern Nauset Island, the honey-dew on the grass a minute insectine excrement. Near at hand rose the great bulk of that alien land, the black point thrusting far out into the sea and long, low coasts shimmering away southwards into the rising sun. Undoubtedly the better of lands lay south. Delaying but a little while on the island, they sailed south and were presently coasting down the long shores of Nova Scotia, with its wheeling openings of bays and broken land, its forests gleaming hot in the dry air, Leif's companions, as we may imagine, urging him to put ashore. Here was rich and good land.

But Leif was possessed of an urge beyond theirs. It was not yet the great fruitland of the Fortunate Isles. Refusing a landing, he held south all that day, glimpsed what he imagined yet another island, and coasted in near the shore of modern Maine.

Two days thereafter they "sighted land and sailed towards it. There was a promontory where they first came. They cruised along the shore, which they kept to starboard. It was without harbour and there were long strands and stretches of sand. They went ashore in boats, and found thereon the promontory of a ship's keel, and called it 'Kjalarnes' (Keel-ness) ; they also gave the strands a name and called them Wonderstrands, because it took a long time to sail past them."

They had attained and rounded Cape Cod. The mystery of the keel, so casually mentioned in the Saga, remains unexplained to this day. Had ever a ship been there before ? It is not improbable ; indeed, it is not improbable that many ships, in the long first Christian millennium, may have passed across the Atlantic, by accident or design, and never again returned. Wrecked ships on the Iceland-Greenland route may often have strewn their keels by the chance of wind and wave on some cove about Cape Cod. But there is another possibility. Cape Cod itself has a keel-like look, and Leif and his men may have noted the fact. There is less likelihood in the second supposition. We of later days look on Cape Cod with a map in our minds. To Leif and the like of his sailings it must have appeared merely low sand-land stretching grey-blue into unguessable distances.

Rounding Wonderstrands and passing the site of modern Chatham, Leif's ship came in a "land of Bays, and they steered the ship into a bay". Perhaps it was Buzzard's Bay. Here the Scots thralls were put to use, the man Haki and the woman Hekja. They were both lightly built and sinewy folk, still clad in some primitive foreshadowing of kilt plus plaid that the Norsemen called a 'kiafal.' Leif had them rowed ashore and gave them directions. They were to explore southwards at top speed, examining the country and returning to report before three sailing-days had elapsed. They quickly disappeared inland.

Possibly they were despatched to scout both for the fact of their speedy feet and because, as slaves, liable to mischief in this unchancy new country, their loss would be no great strain upon the expedition. Leif cast anchor and waited and stared at the new country.

The adventures and chances that attended the two antique

Scots have not come down to us. They were the first true explorers of the Americas, and their feet trod land busy and familiar enough now, their eyes looked on hills and rivers familiar and named to our eyes. What they encountered and saw and hid from in the way of beast and bird we can only surmise : it is probable that they set eyes on no human being. Indeed, in all its Expedition, Leif's party was to set no eyes on those alien Skraelingr who were so to vex subsequent expeditions of the Northmen—finally to vex them from America.

At the end of the three sailing days the Northmen in the longship lifted their eyes and saw Haki and Hekja come running down to the shore, safe and unharmed, much travelled, bringing wild vines and "self-sown wheat" in their hands. Leif and Tyrker stared at the former : Vines! What could this be but the edge of Wineland the Good itself ?

He raised anchor again and "sailed into a certain sound, between island and cape", the island surely Martha's Vineyard itself ; and thenceafter, in the confusion of the Greenland and Icelandic Sagas from which this account is drawn, proceeded to actions mistily indeterminate. The Northmen landed at some place and beached the ship in considerable haste, for Leif had awakened to the fact that they were short of provisions, that summer (as he reckoned it) was past, and that they must put up shelters for the coming of the winter. It was perhaps in the western tip of Martha's Vineyard that they landed, with the Rhode Island shore still in their vision ; more probably the mainland itself was their early habitation, and a later flitting made to either Martha's Vineyard or the island that is now called No Man's Land.

Here there were so many birds that one "could hardly put one's foot between the eggs" ; and here they found a river that ran from a central lake, and proceeded to build there booths of wood and stone against the threatened coming of the winter.

But they found, building the booths in some haste and carrying ashore there their hammocks and arms, that they had been over-hasty. The fine weather went on. The river swarmed with salmon, and between it and the eggs there was little chance of starvation. Leif resolved that in this situation booth-building was not enough ; they must erect a permanent stone house.

In between whiles of directing these activities he set about plans for exploring the mainland. Every now and then parties of the Northmen rowed across to that mainland, sometimes in Leif's command, sometimes apparently leaving him behind to attend to affairs in Leifsfjord. He appears to have commanded his men with great skill and to have had no grumblers, recognized, says the Saga, as a kind and just man—strange enough epithets for the hero of a Saga!

But though it seems they penetrated into the Rhode Island country, no doubt tramped their way by forest edges and up the banks of streams for long days, they made little progress in knowledge of the fact that the great mainland was truly a mainland. They were a folk accustomed to islands and the seas, oppressed by the thought of the coming winter, Leif himself infrequently in their command, in spite of his haunting vision of Wineland the Good.

Tyrker the German, as later events were to prove, was the chance discoverer who was to prove Wineland and its name. In one of the exploring parties ashore he must have strayed from his fellows, and come on a sight such as they had hitherto missed or disregarded. At that his German tongue, long unsolaced, grew dry in his throat. He took many rowings to the mainland, after that; always eager to go hunting at Leif's command. And in between whiles he would slip away, watched by the bland Rhode Island sky, about his secret business.

§ 8

Their preparations for winter had been thrown away. Little or no winter came. Instead, in this Hollow Land of the poets and myth and now a strange reality—no frost or snow came, and the grass did not wither. The sunlight filtered down through unwithering leaves and warmth was long on the land. Here was fishing of larger salmon than they had ever encountered, here the shortening of the days brought none of the iron winds of winter. . . . So the Greenland saga tells, in words that were once taken as poetic licence, as myth imported into the adventures of Leif Ericsson. Now we know it true of the continental fold around Martha's Vineyard, so that Leif's Landfall is now as certain as though he had verily carved with his own hand that rock on No Man's Land which has aroused so much controversy and dispute and has now gone from the arena of controversy, shamefacedly—the rock on which is carved in Runic letters the inscription .

Leif Eriksson
MI

and below it, mutilated,

Vinland.

It is doubtful if Leif or any other in his party could write. Some of the Runic letters used are such as were scarcely known to the Norway of his time; and had there indeed been a litterateur in the longship of the Northmen, he would have written the name Leifr Eiriksson, he would not have used the Roman dating 'MI'. So modern research discards the enigmatic rock as a forgery, ingenuous and puzzling.

Puzzling indeed it is how anyone on even a lonely island these modern days could have carved out that inscription, undetected, in the splash of sea-water, for nothing but the remote chance that it might some day be discovered to astound America. There is surely another explanation—and that explanation Leif's foster-father, Tyrker.

Tyrker was a German, a foreigner among the Northmen, perhaps one who had learned writing in his own land and Runic later in life, using the latter with a barbarous freedom that mutilated Norse construction. And, for it was no habit of the Norse of that time to erect such inscriptions, who would have carved it in that long summer-winter but Tyrker himself in pride of the achievement of his foster-son—and some puzzlement as to the correctness of dating and spelling ?

A possible picture, and a fascinating one, we summon from nine hundred years of limbo: the flat-faced, fugitive-eyed, freckled little German, swart and puny, seated on the Rhode Island rock on a sultry afternoon those centuries ago, carving out that enigmatic misspelling while he awaited the fruition of the vines of Vinland.

But a new worry had come on Leif himself. Food unexpectedly began to grow scarce in Martha's Vineyard as the Spring came in. The Northmen, seeing and enduring but little winter, had taken no precaution to smoke and dry the salmon they caught so readily, and now the salmon were gone. It seems also that the hunting must have declined on the mainland ; perhaps there came illness as well. In the midst of this situation, Tyrker disappeared.

Leif was troubled the first day of his disappearance, and even more the next. On the third day he organized a search party and rowed across to the mainland. They searched far from the beach haunts of their exploration, and finally, deep in the woods, came on the German sitting on the ground in a strange condition.

> First he spoke for a long time in German, and rolled his eyes in many ways and twisted his mouth ; but they could not make out what he said. After a while he said in Norse : I did not go much further, and yet I have a new discovery to tell of : I have found vines and grapes.

His condition, in fact, was that of intoxication, and it makes an amusing tableau to the mind, in that silent North American forest the armed Norsemen surrounding and staring at the drunken little German babbling of his grapes and the secret brewing of them which (there can be little doubt) he must have carried on through many weeks. He kept the secret no longer, but apparently led Leif and his companions to the wild vineyard.

Leif seems to have seen the event as the end of his troubles. Perhaps other food became more plentiful then, but he resolved to fill the ship with a cargo of pressed grapes both as a commercial proposition and an earnest to Greenland of the quality of the land he had found. The ship was sailed or poled over to the mainland, and the work of loading her (the grapes no doubt in casks) commenced.

The spring days went by, and at last the ship was full, as the wild geese honked one night south over the deserted booths on Martha's Vineyard. Leif set his plans for sailing home.

And from there the saga tells nothing more of Wineland the Good, of how they must have carried gear and arms down to the strange 'new fjord' and hoisted the long-resting sail, and looked back as they clambered aboard at the great stone-foundationed hut Leif had reared beside his first booths. Leif himself may have turned a look on that shore he had hardly touched, in spite of his diligent explorings—the shore undoubtedly of the Fortunate Isle, Wineland the Good—

for did he not carry its vines with him back to Greenland to tell them if he lied ?

So they sailed up Nantucket Sound, on their left the Wonder-strands gleaming white, and out into the rolling Spring waters of the Atlantic, till presently the points of Keelness were left far behind, and the first expedition of Europeans to America of which we have any record was homeward bound laden with the first Argosy of the West.

§ 9

The longship sailed north for three days. On the third Leif looked out on the sea and saw a point of land—perhaps an island, and something that seemed to move thereon. He called Tyrker to look, and asked what he saw. The German could see nothing.

But Leif had not been mistaken. It was the shipwrecked crew of a longship belonging to one Thori, on a voyage from Iceland to Greenland companioned by his carles and his wife Gudrid, and driven out of his route. Perhaps this encounter was off the North Labrador coast, and if so proves yet again how frequent such discoveries and re-discoveries of the Americas must have been—only the chance of surviving manuscripts preserving Leif's venture for us. His luck was with him, even in this rescue. Thori and Gudrid and fifteen men were taken into the longship, and Greenland made in a short run.

So "Leif came to land in Eiriksfjord, and went home to Brattalid ; there they received him well. . . . He was then called Leif the Lucky."

Thus, briefly, the Saga ; but adds with a laconic humour that Eric himself commented that he saw little luck in this son of his who had brought the hypocrite monk to Brattalid and dispossessed a good man from his bed. . . .

Of what became of the cargo from Wineland there is no tale ; of the story told and retold, we may be sure, around the fireplaces of Brattalid that winter there survive to us only the most meagre of details.

But it would seem that with the coming of the next year Brattalid was deeply engaged in preparations for a further voyage, and we cannot but suppose but that Leif himself intended to captain it and question the further mysteries beyond the Rhode Island swamps.

An insurmountable obstacle arose. Eric died that Spring, full of years and sin, and Leif was left in command of Eastern Settlement; himself to settle down and rule and deal with disputes, and measure crops and plan the shearing of sheep, the collecting of driftwood, the rearing of churches—all the life of a ruler in a bleak little Norse community, instead of sailing the sounding seas free and unhampered in quest of the wonderlands whose Wonderstrands he had barely touched. . . .

Such we may imagine to have been his feelings that next year as Thorfinn Karlsevne, a trader from Iceland, arrived at Ericsford and declared his intention of raising a great expedition of many boats, loaded with cattle, and setting out to colonize the land that The Lucky One had discovered.

§ 10

Karlsevne presumed Leif's exploring days over, and asked the Greenlander to give him the house he had built in Wineland. Leif answered shortly that "he could only lend it". Karlsevne, unsnubbed, accepted the offer, and went on with his preparations—including marriage. Thori had died and his widow Gudrid was a comely and healthy-looking woman, fit mother for a race of colonists. She would accompany Karlsevne.

Karlsevne sailed with a hundred and sixty (some tell a hundred and forty) men on his ships, Gudrid, Leif's brother Thorvald his second in command, and Eric's illegitimate daughter Freydis one of the party. Three days sail brought them to Bear Island, perhaps in Baffin Land, and thence two days' further sail, with a following wind, to Helluland. Down those dim coasts they cruised without much incident, touching at Keelness, as Leif had done, and rounded the point, "and reached Leif's booths, and unloaded the ships and established themselves there. They had with them all kinds of cattle, and sought to make use of the land. . . . They did nothing else but search out the land."

They repeated throughout the winter, in fact, Leif's mistake, and Spring found them short of food, perhaps killing the cattle they had brought. It seems that they had not

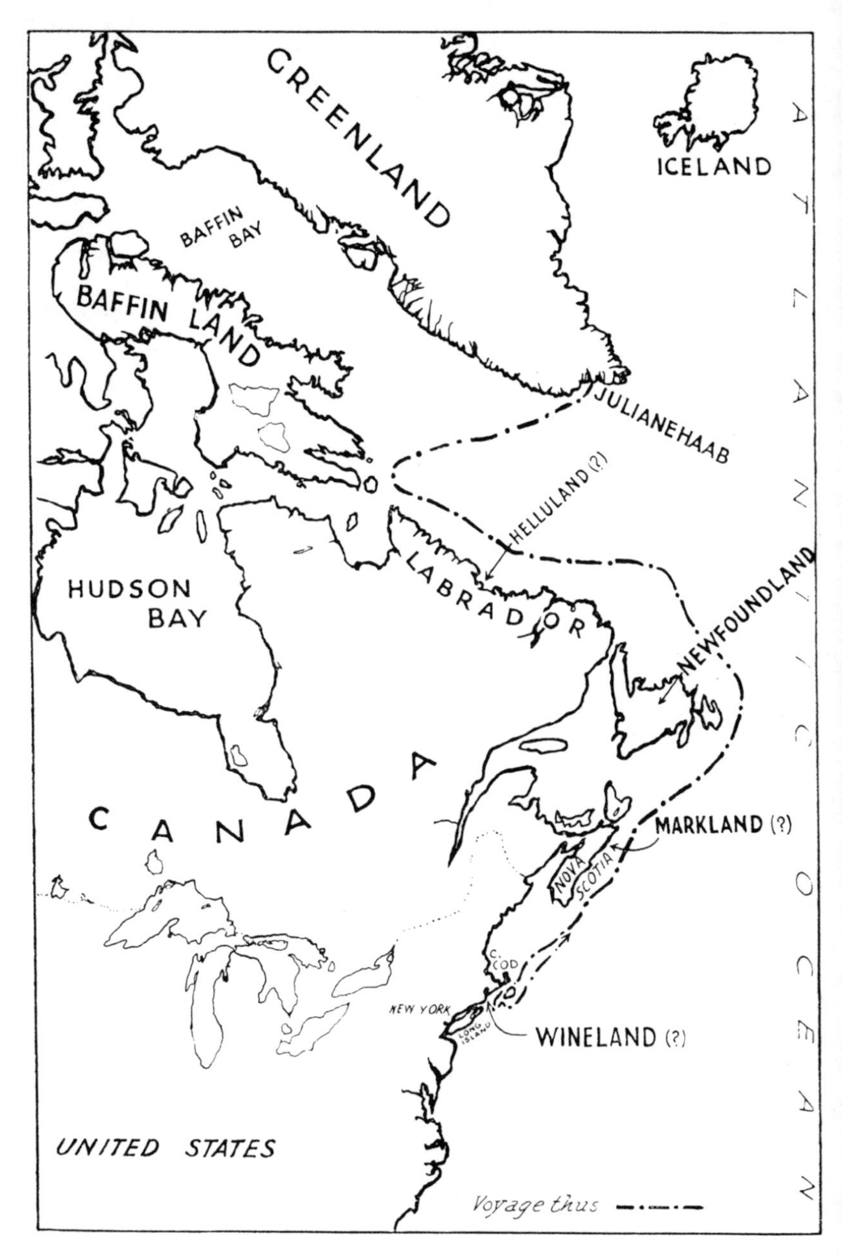

LEIF ERICSSON IN AMERICA

settled on Martha's Vineyard, or No Man's Land, but on the mainland, "for they prayed for food . . . and rowed out to the island, expecting that there they might find some fishing". But there was nothing to be found until one of them, a heathen, went apart and prayed to the Old Gods. Next day a whale was washed ashore, and all were violently ill in consequence of eating of this heathen provender.

Soon afterwards conditions improved, however, with hunting on the mainland and good fishing grounds discovered. The first European to be born in America, Snorri Thorfinnsson, the child of Gudrid and Karlsevne, added his voice to the other sounds about Leif's booths. The settlement of Rhode Island was well under weigh.

But dissensions broke out among the colonists. Karlsevne, a restless man, determined to seek better land yet further south. Nine of the colonists refused this new expedition, and sailed for home. Undaunted, Karlsevne re-embarked his remaining followers and coasted south.

After sailing "for a long time" they came to the mouth of a great river. Perhaps it was the Hudson. Here every beck was full of fish, and there was good hunting in the surrounding forests. The Northmen disembarked and took their cattle ashore to graze. They erected fresh booths and appear to have determined on a permanent settlement.

All went well for the first fortnight. But one morning they looked out on the sea and saw nine hide boats approaching, laden with small squat men, "very ugly". These gestured towards them in an indeterminate way, and then turned about their flotilla and disappeared behind a headland.

This was the first encounter with the American natives. It appears that these Skraelingr were Eskimos, not Red Indians, as has sometimes been supposed. The Amerindian was as yet inapparent upon the coasts of North America; a great tribal movement had drawn the Eskimo from Greenland—where they had left their implements and ancient camp sites to the inquiring gaze of Eric a score of years before—down to the fresh lands and good hunting of North America. Mysteriously they were later to retrace the steps of that migration and at last wipe out and destroy the Norse settlements in Greenland itself. Possibly, here on the Hudson, they stared an astonishment at the Norse even greater than the latter, troll-believers, albeit Christians, stared on them.

However, Karlsevne decided to go on with his house-building. The Northmen stayed the winter there, and found it pass easily, though not with the lack of frosts that had characterized the shoreland by Martha's Vineyard. The cattle grazed and grew fat, and were doubtless milked and the milk turned to butter and cheese in the Norse fashion. They may even have prepared the land for crops, though that on the whole is unlikely. With the coming of Spring, unexpectedly, the Skraelingr returned as well—in a flotilla of hide boats that seemed to cover the bay.

For a time relations were amicable enough: the Norse set up a market, trading cloth with the Eskimo who swarmed ashore. These newcomers gave signs that they also wanted to purchase swords and shields, but Karlsevne prudently forbade the trade. This thriving mart was going on apace until a ludicrous accident occurred:

An ox, which Karlsevne had, ran out of the wood and began to bellow. The Skraelingr were scared and ran to their boats and rowed south along the shore. After that they did not see them for three weeks. But when that time was past, they saw a great multitude of Skraelingr boats coming from the south, as though driven on by a stream. Then all the wooden poles were waved against the sun (wither-shins), and all the Skraelings howled loudly. Then Karlsevne and his men took red shields and bore them towards them. The Skraelings leapt from their boats and then they made towards each other and fought; there was a hot exchange of missiles. The Skraelings also had catapults. Karlsevne and his men saw that the Skraelings hoisted up on a pole a great ball about as large as a sheep's paunch, and seeming blue in colour, and slung it from the pole up on to the land over Karlsevne's people, and it made an ugly noise when it came down. At this great terror smote Karlsevne and his people, so that they had no thought but of getting away and up the river, for it seemed to them that the Skraelings were assailing them on all sides; and they did not halt until they had reached certain crags. There they made a stout resistance. Freydis came out and saw that they were giving way. She cried out: "Wherefore do ye run away from such wretches, ye gallant men? I thought it likely that ye could slaughter them like cattle, and had I but arms I believe I should fight better than any of you." None heeded what she said. Freydis tried to go with them, but she fell behind, for she was with child. She nevertheless followed them into the wood, but the Skraelings came after her. She found before her a dead man, Thorbrand Snorrasson, and a flat stone was fixed in the head of him. His sword lay unsheathed by him, and she took it up to defend herself with it. Then the Skraelings came at her. She takes her breasts out of her sark and whets the sword on them. At that the Skraelings are afraid and run away back to their boats, and go off. Karlsevne and his men meet her and praise her happy device. Two men of Karlsevne's fell, and four of the Skraelings; but nevertheless Karlsevne had suffered defeat. They now go to their houses, bind up their wounds, and consider what swarm of people it was that came against them from the land. It seemed to them now that there could have been no more than those who came from the boats, and that the other people must have been glamour. The Skraelings also found a dead man, and an axe lay beside him; one of them took up the axe and struck at a tree, and so one after another, and it seemed to delight them that it bit so well. Then one took and smote a stone with it; but when the axe broke, he thought it was of no use, if it did not stand against stone, and he cast it from him.

Karlsevne and his men now thought they could see that although the land was fertile, they would always have trouble and disquiet with the people who dwelt there before. Then they prepared to set out, and intended to go to their own country. They sailed northward and found five Skraelings sleeping in fur jerkins. . . . They thought they could understand they were outlaws, and killed them.

They reached Martha's Vineyard again in safety, and stayed there another year, but apparently uneasily, exploring the country far and near. On one of these expeditions Thorvald, Leif's brother, was killed at a place called Crossness by a creature who, the Saga solemnly informs us, was a Uniped, a one-footed man. Him they did not catch.

On the fourth summer they cruised north—apparently the entire colony—to Markland, and captured two young Skraelingr there. These new thralls, learning Norse, entertained them with a variety of tales of Eskimo life, some of which ring true enough, others fantastically improbable. They told that a land of white men was indeed near, "where white-clad priests marched down to the shore with a great shouting." This the Christian Norse knew must be Great Ireland, Huitramanna-Land. Was it perhaps some rumour or reminiscence of the Toltec civilization then nearing its end in distant Mexico, some knowledge or legend of the Mound Builders of the Mississippi?

Of that we shall never know for certain. Karlsevne had sickened of the adventure. It was a fat land, but ill to settle in with the pressing attentions of the Skraelingr. He resolved to sail for Greenland. The expedition was one with him in the resolution.

So presumably such cattle as survived were reloaded on the longship, Gudrid and Snorri, Freydis and her husband Thorvard and all the rest of the men re-embarked and the second and unfortunate European attempt to explore and colonize North America abandoned. Karlsevne reached Greenland in safety, and was welcomed there by the lucky voyager, Leif, eager for news of his Wineland, again deserted.

There was to be yet another attempt upon it.

§ 11

It is now to be added, that Freydis, Eric's daughter, set out from her home at Gardar, and waited upon the brothers Helgi and Finnbogi [adventurers who had meantime arrived from Norway] and invited them to sail with their vessel to Vinland, and to share with her equally all the good things which they might succeed in obtaining there. To this they agreed, and she departed thence to visit her brother, Leif, and ask him to give her the house which he had caused to be erected in Vinland, but he made her the same answer (as that which he had given Karlsevne), saying, that he would lend the house, but not give it. It was stipulated between Karlsevne and Freydis, that each should have on ship-board thirty able-bodied men, besides the women; but Freydis immediately violated this compact, by concealing five men more and this the brothers did not discover before they arrived in Vinland. They now put out to sea, having agreed beforehand, that they would sail in company, if possible, and although they were not far apart from each other, the brothers arrived somewhat in advance, and carried their belongings up to Leif's house.

Now when Freydis arrived, her ship was discharged, and the baggage carried up to the house, whereupon Freydis exclaimed: "Why did you carry your baggage in here?" "Since we believed," said they, "that all promises made to us would be kept." "It was to me that Leif loaned the house," says she, "and not to you." Whereupon Helgi exclaimed: "We brothers cannot hope to rival thee in wrong-dealing." They thereupon carried their baggage forth, and built a hut, above the sea, on the bank of the lake, and put all in order about it; while Freydis caused wood to be felled, with which to load her ship. The winter now set in, and the brothers suggested that they should amuse themselves by playing games. This they did for a time, until the folk began to disagree, when dissensions arose between them, and the games came to an end, and the visits between the houses ceased; and thus it continued far into the winter.

One morning early, Freydis arose from her bed, and dressed herself, but did not put on her shoes and stockings. A heavy dew had fallen, and she took her husband's cloak, and wrapped it about her, and then walked to the brothers' house, and up to the door, which had been only partly closed by one of the men, who had gone out a short time before. She pushed the door open, and stood, silently, in the doorway for a time. Finnbogi, who was lying on the innermost side of the room, was awake, and said: "What dost thou wish here, Freydis?" She answers, "I wish thee to rise, and go out with me, for I would speak to thee." He did so, and they walked to a tree, which lay close by the wall of the house, and seated themselves upon it. "How are thou pleased here?" says she. He answers: "I am well pleased with the fruitfulness of the land, but I am ill-content with the breach which has come between us, for, methinks, there has been no cause for it." "It is even as thou sayest," says she, "and so it seems to me: but my errand to thee is, that I wish to exchange ships with you brothers, for that ye have a larger ship than I, and I wish to depart from here." "To this I must accede," says he, "if it is thy pleasure."

Therewith they parted, and she returned home, and Finnbogi to his bed. She climbed up into bed, and awakened Thorvard with her cold feet, and he asked her why she was so cold and wet. She answered, with great passion: "I have been to the brothers," says she, "to try to buy their ship, for I wished to have a larger vessel, but they received my overtures so ill, that they struck me, and handled me very roughly; what time thou, poor wretch, wilt neither avenge my shame nor thy own, and I find, perforce, that I am no longer in Greenland; moreover I shall part from thee unless thou wreakest vengeance for this."

And now he could stand her taunts no longer, and ordered the men to rise at once, and take their weapons, and this they did, and then proceeded directly to the house of the brothers, and entered it, while the folk were asleep, and seized and bound them, and led each one out, when he was bound; and as they came out, Freydis caused each one to be slain. In this wise all the men were put to death, and only the women were left, and these no one would kill. At this Freydis exclaimed: "Hand me an axe!" This was done, and she fell upon the five women, and left them dead. They returned home, after this dreadful deed, and it was very evident that Freydis was well content with her work. She addressed her companions, saying: "If it be ordained for us, to come again to Greenland, I shall contrive the death of any man who shall speak of these events. We must give it out, that we left them living here, when we came away." Early in the spring, they equipped the ship, which had belonged to the brothers, and freighted it with all of the products of the land, which they could obtain, and which the ship would carry. Then they put out to sea, and, after a prosperous voyage, arrived with their ship in Ericsfirth early in the summer. . . .

Freydis now went to her home, since it had remained unharmed during her absence. She bestowed liberal gifts upon all of her companions, for she was anxious to screen her guilt. She now established herself at her home; but her companions were not all so close-mouthed, concerning their misdeeds and wickedness, that rumours did not get abroad at last. These finally reached her brother, Leif, and he thought it a most shameful story. He thereupon took three of the men, who had been of Freydis' party, and their stories entirely agreed. "I have no heart," says Leif, "to punish my sister, Freydis, as she deserves, but this I predict of them, that there is little prosperity in store for their offspring." Hence it came to pass, that no one from that time forward thought them worthy of aught but evil.

§ 12

It is the last note in the explorer's life of Leif. Speedily, with the tale of Freydis's bloody venture, there spread throughout the hamlets of Greenland and Iceland the conviction that Wineland was a haunted and evil place, too distant for hope of succour, terrestrial or celestial, did misfortune come, over-swarmed year on year ever more thickly by the hostile Skraelingr—a fat country, but not to be enjoyed.

It is unlikely that such considerations would have stayed a further venture on the part of America's first European discoverer—that just and large and visioning man who followed Biarni's accidental glimpse and attained (as he believed) the fabled country of Wineland; who gave up much for the care and comfort of others but refused to surrender that Wineland house he had built for his habitation against the day when he would come to it again and watch the strange forests climbing saffron into the dawns of Straumoy. . . . But that further adventure remained a wistful dream, time, labour and the press of the days forbade the search.

He died at Brattalid in the year 1025, and, though there is no record of him marrying, a son succeeded him—no other son than Thorgils, child of that Thorgunna of the Hebrides with whom he had lived a summer long before while he waited a wind for Norway. Thorgils crossed the seas to Greenland and sought out his father; it is even told that Thorgunna herself, by then as age went in those days an old woman, set out in her son's sea-tracks to reach her lost lover in Brattalid. But she died at Iceland on the way there (and was buried "wearing a gold ring and clad in a mantle of Greenland frieze") and Leif never saw her again.

They are one with dust and snow now, seeker and sought, legendary shades perhaps in some eternal Hebridean summer untroubled by the cry of mysterious seas running west to the shores of the Fortunate Isles.

§ 13

The tale of the Wineland discoveries was carried abroad to Iceland by Karlsevne and his wife, the much married Gudrid, and that son Snorri, the first European born in America. From there it spread to Norway, and so, we may believe, to the Europe of the time. When Karlsevne died Gudrid girded up her widow's gown and journeyed "south on pilgrimage"—to Rome, it is told, and on the journey no doubt told much of wild lands in the mythic west. Legend and fable intermingled itself with the true story of the explorings and colonizings, but sufficient reached the Mediterranean to confirm the tales of antiquity, to reinforce the dreamings of the imaginative cosmographers, to sway very profoundly indeed the thought of such later earth-conquerors as Columbus and that Marco Polo whom this record awaits to set on their travels again.

But the colonizing urge had died out in Greenland itself. The Northmen there were presently too bitterly engaged in fresh encounters with the Skraelingr at their own doors to seek them afar in Wineland. For the Eskimos, the Red Indian migrations of the Archaic Culture pressing behind them, trekked up into Greenland again and presently came in contact with the Norse Western Settlement. Years of trade and seasonal bickering went on till finally, long after Leif's bones were set in their mound, the Skraelingr descended on the Norse settlements in a great raid and despoiled and destroyed them, carrying captives away into the mists of Northern Greenland.

Before that, indeed, a Greenland Bishop, Bishop Eric Uppsi, had sailed in search of Wineland in 1121 and never returned. A long three and a half centuries after Leif a Greenland ship went down to Markland, and loaded a cargo of timber, and came back in safety. . . . And the *Landnamabòk* has a tale of one Are Marsson who set out on yet another expedition and penetrated far to Great Ireland—a templed place where white priests with banners "went to sacrifice with a great noise". Some have thought this stray Norseman may have reached Mexico of the time, or perhaps the Maya New Empire in Yucatan. But these were ventures and adventures beyond even the half-lights of pseudo-history that follow the ships of Leif.

III

SER MARCO POLO JOURNEYS TO THE ISLANDS BEYOND CATHAY

§ 1

BEYOND the frontiers of Europe of the early thirteenth century the continent of Asia loomed as a strange confusion of lands—the harbourage of colourful myths and terrible beasts and dreadful tribes. Prester John had his Christian kingdom there; there lived the roc and the unicorn and worshippers of idols; there was gold in great quantities and spices of great pungency in the rumoured Spice Lands, the Fortunate Isles; there was wonder and heathenism, inextricably blended.

That Asia had always had this seeming in European eyes was by no means the case. The Mediterranean world of classical times had adventured in Asia and traded with Asia, consciously and deliberately, through long centuries. India and Ceylon knew the Roman ships and the galleys of Tyre; beyond India itself, as Ptolemy knew, was the dim but certain geographical land of Seres (which was China) where silk and the silkworm flourished. At one time and one point the outposts of the Roman and Chinese Empires had touched in south-central Asia. Men stared a mistily hostile greeting one upon the other, the immemorial East and the immemorial West as the romantic mind would visualize this meeting, eternally coexistent, eternally different. Alexander's great raid into Asia had led to an ebb and flow of cultural custom and sculptural motif between the southern halves of the two continents: myth and ritual and philosophical system had changed and interchanged by land and sea-routes for several hundred years, Asia and Europe discovering each to the other for the first time in history, it has been said.

But this second popular belief is as little warranted as the belief set in the jingle on the eternal differentiation of East and West. The civilization of the two continents—indeed, of all continents, of a West much more westernly than Europe, of an East much more in the sunrise than even Cipangu—had a common origin. From neither of the two continents had that civilization originated, but from Africa, the shallow valley of the Nile. From there, east and west and north, though but slowly south, that first and earliest civilization sent far afield those groups of surveyors and colonists who reared the megalithic circles and devil stones and chambered barrows around and encircling the world from Spain to the Yenisei, from the Shetlands to Alaska. These colonists reared the great civilizations of Crete and the Mesopotamian valleys, the wonders of Sumer and palaced Knossos. From Sumer it was that pre-Semite colonists had crossed the roof of the world into India, in one direction, into the land that was not yet China, in another, bearing with them the seeds of agricultural practice and king-worship, religion and class organization, slavery and culture. From those seeds rose the great Dravidian states, the kingdoms of the Chinese rivers.

Through long millennia after that first bursting of civilization upon the pristine world of the primitive, Asiatic, European, African, an ebb and flow of cultural custom and trade and treasure flowed to and fro between the sister-continents. But to a great measure it seems to have passed anonymously and unnamed. Porcelain and silk and jade came to the Mediterranean: but out of dim lands that sheltered behind the name of Asia. And to Asia, as there is now ample evidence to prove, Europe transmitted not only new motifs in sculpture and art and weapon-making, but important intellectual elements of culture which resulted in two of the world's great religions.

By 540 B.C., when Thales of Miletus died, a new thing had come into the world—the envisagement of the world and all the terrors of life and death and time through individual eyes and independent reasoning, that development that its world called philosophy. It was the beginning of the first breakdown in the bonds of the ancient fertility religions which had enslaved the minds of men since the rise of the first civilization in Egypt. Thales was at first little more than a single blasphemer, a lonely antagonist of the irrational gods, the Givers of Life who had dominated humankind for a long three thousand years. Yet, within the space of a century, remote from Ionia, and remote one from the other at the thither side of Asia, two codes or creeds of non-religious ethic, very similar to Thales', were abroad in the minds of men. These were Confucianism and Buddhism, separated by the great mountain-chain of the Himalayas and the stretching deserts of China. The seeds of Thales's rationalism had been diffused by nameless traders and travellers far from the Mediterranean into new lands of strange speech and custom, and earthed and grew and bloomed the strange flowers and fruits of the philosophies of K'ung-fu-tze and Sakya Muni.

With the downfall of the Roman Empire, Europe's knowledge of Asia had been to a great extent lost or cretinized under the influence of Christian myth and Christian barbarism. Religious intolerance raised a febrific barrier of intellectualist superstition against Asia if it left the trade routes still open. Yet presently these also were severed with the coming of Islam, thrusting a new wall of arrogance and mislike across Asia Minor and Syria, shutting in Europe from her ancient (and still unquenched) curiosities on the lands beyond the Tigris. Merchants no longer journeyed freely within the verges of those debatable tracts. The ancient sea-route to India was lost and forgotten.

But, early in the thirteenth century, there rose out of that dim Asia, long lost to European knowledge, the rumble and cry of a great and inexplicable storm. This was the rise of the Tartar tribes: speedily the coming of the Tartar invaders.

The great nomadic tribes roaming the fringes of civilization in Central and Northern Asia had awakened under one of the world's great military leaders, Jenghis Khan, and set out on the conquest of the earth for themselves. Almost they succeeded. The flimsy Mohammedan states of near Asia were swept away: the Tartar armies poured across Russia into Europe. For a little it seemed, in that breathless year A.D. 1242, as though Europe and Asia would be welded together for all time, fused by the Tartar-Mongol blood and iron into some magic, impossible world-state. But the centre of the new Mongol power was remote in Karakorum, on the borders of China; it was a military dominance, entirely lacking a civil service; road and route-connections, as we shall have occasion to note, were fantastically bad over that great stretch of Central Asia; and presently Jenghis Khan died. The

Tartars were recalled from Asia, and Europe sighed its relief, still staring eastward at that world glimpsed for a tantalizing moment when the blanket of the dark which divided the two continents had been thrust aside under the impetus of the Mongol spear.

§ 2

The veil closed down on the rumbling retreat of the Tartar baggage-waggons. Relieved Europe thought of another possibility : the horrendous invaders had been merely pagans. It was a well-known fact that they were indifferent to their own gods, they were horse-riding rationalists and sceptics, cheerfully throat-cutting in mosque and church alike. Might it not be possible to win them to the Christian faith, to win them as political allies against the Mohammedanism of Egypt and Saracen Spain ?

So it came that, forerunners of the great Traveller with whom this record is concerned, two men were despatched beyond the fringes of that veil into remote Asia in the track of the Tartars. Commissioned by the Pope to interview the Great Khan on his sentiments in the matter, the Franciscan John de Plano Carpini set out on April the 16th, 1245. He reached Kiev in February of the following year and then crossed into Siberia. He was in a new land, the Steppe :

> In certain places thereof are small store of trees growing but otherwise it is altogether destitute of woods. Therefore all warm themselves and dress their meat with fires made of dung. The air also in that country is very intemperate. For in the midst of summer there be great thunders and lightnings, and at the same time there falleth great abundance of snow . . . there is oftentimes great store of haile also. Likewise in the summer season there is on the sudden extreme heat and suddenly again intolerable cold.

He noted of the Mongols :

> Their inhabitations be round and cunningly made with wickers and staves in the manner of a tent. But in the midst of the top thereof they have a window open to convey the light in and the smoke out. For their fire is always in the midst. Their walls be covered with felt. Their doors are made of felt also. Some of these tabernacles may quickly be taken asunder, and set together again, and are carried upon

MARCO POLO

beasts' backs. Others some cannot be taken in sunder, but are stowed upon carts. And whithersoever they go, be it either to war or to any other place, they transport their tabernacles with them. . . . And they think they have more horses and mares than all the world beside.

He crossed the Aral-Caspian depression to the basin of the Syr Darya, thence by the western prolongation of the Tian Shan mountains through a land

full of mountaines, and in some other places plains and smoothe ground, but everywhere sandie and barren, neither is the hundredth part thereof fruiteful. . . . Whereupon they have neither villages nor cities among them except one which is called Cracurim and is said to be a proper towne.

But he himself never penetrated to the "proper towne" of Karakorum. He was halted at Syra Orda for three months, given the Khan's reply to the Pope's letter—a singularly neat and astounding reply, asking penetratingly discourteous questions on the warlike behaviour of Christians, the supposed followers of the prince of peace—and set out again for Europe. He reached it by almost the same route as he had taken in his outward passage, and arrived in Kiev on June the 9th, 1247, a little over two years after first setting forth on his mission.

He is a cold and cool and dispassionate traveller, albeit his chronicle is filled with personal details of halt and trek completely missing from those of his great follower. He penetrated beyond the veil and returned with the report, and the news of it vanished into obscurity for two hundred years after his death. He lacked supremely that gift that the explorer must have in good measure: ardent curiosity. He brought out of the mysterious lands of Asia a dispassionate report that the world refused for its very dispassion.

The next of these forerunners was an envoy, despatched to the same Great Khan in 1252, of Louis IX of France, engaged at the moment on the Sixth Crusade. This was William of Rubrick, another ecclesiastic, of a more genial and ardent disposition than his predecessor of Carpini. Reaching Sudak in the Crimea from Acre, he engaged carts for the journey to Karakorum at the thither side of Asia. It was a doubly rugged journey in consequence. His trail was almost that of Archbishop John's, and the sights and sounds of that great desolate stretch of Asia were borne to his eyes and ears in much the same images as to his predecessors. Penetrating across the country on this northernmost route, these two travellers indeed missed all that means for us Asia—Persia and India and China and the rich lands between. But William especially was a keen and acute traveller: if in Asia he saw little that added to the information gathered by Johannes, on the borders of the continent he finally determined that the Caspian was indeed an inland sea, no branch of the Euxine, as the geographers of the time held. Also, reaching Karakorum and interviewing the Great Khan in December of 1253, he heard rumours of a country still further to the east—"Great Cathaya, the inhabitants whereof (as I suppose) were of old time called Seres. For from them are brought most excellent stuffs of silke."

So William of Rubrick rediscovered that vanished people known to the Greeks and the voyageurs of the Roman Empire. As he turned to ride lurchingly and perspiringly the years-long journey back to Europe, young Marco Polo, far away in Venice, was greeting his first glimpse of this world of wonder and terror with the birth-cry common to all human-kind.

§ 3

Two great sea-republics dominated the coasts of Italy by the middle of the thirteenth century. These two republics were Venice and Genoa, republican only in that they were kingless, oligarchies or corporative states as we might call them in the jargon of our own era. By 1250 Venice was outstripping her rival in enterprise and wealth alike: she was fast becoming the strongest and most ruthless power in all the eastern Mediterranean. She was the great Moloch of Trade, wealth her aim, her being and her justification. She hired great fleets and armies to protect her gains or to attack her rivals and unfriends. Amidst her labyrinthine, walled sea-streets and towering walls she crouched in the warm, malarial hazes of summer and the thin, bright air of her frostless winter, looking west with cruel, cool eyes at the prizes of the Levant. . . .

Some such picture earlier writers, and of as great an honesty, found representational enough of the great city where Marco Polo came into this world of travel and travail from the first of all travails. Nor, though we may doubt much of the personification and personation, is it perhaps a picture completely false. Venetians were of the common stock of men, no doubt, kindly and cruel and wayward and homely, no two alike, patriots and traitors, revolutionists and reactionaries. Only the shoddy symbolism of nationalism would foist a definite personification upon those life-warring, life-wandering multitudes. Yet it seems to have been an especially greedy, cruel, cowardly, and yet queerly courageous class which ruled in that mid-century Venice, and, indeed, for long centuries thereafter. Art was for it gaudy architecture and floriferous sculpture ; religion was a Name, a fast, a gesture, a supplication, a horrifying Fear or a comforting Hope : never a fine distillation of exultant altruism or passionate pity ; science was bright and young, with the wind of the Mediterranean in its hair : young, but a moron youth, unchanging and unprogressing beyond the days of the Ptolemies. Philosophy was the Medieval synthesis. Men of this class (and no doubt the subordinate classes of the republic in lesser measure) turned all their energies to the pursuit of wealth, to lust after and long for, suffering dreadfully in the pursuit thereof and causing suffering with complete callousness to others—because there was nothing else for them to do.

On the mainland of Europe and Asia of that day the bored among the governing classes turned to war. The Venetian, with a stable and unmalcontent plebs, turned to trade. In Venice the patrician was a trader in excelsis in consequence of being a patrician—not a patrician-plutocrat in consequence of being a trader. And among those lordly seekers after the most ancient Giver of Life was one, Andrea Polo, Nobilis Vir, of the Parish of S. Felice.

This Andrea is a shadowy figure ; indeed, the Polos, as if foreseeing the undue and unwarrantable curiosities of later generations, all cultivated the shade. In that state of obscurity, however, Andrea had fathered three sons, Marco Nicolo, and Maffeo. Marco and Maffeo were old family names : they had occurred before, and, somewhat confusingly, they were to occur again.

Growing up, the three sons appear to have entered with considerable zest on the common pursuit of their race. They traded. They traded up and down the Levant, and beyond, into the Black Sea, the Ancient Euxine with its turbulent tides and its half-known tribes of coast-folk. Marco established himself as depot-chief in Constantinople—a Constantinople not yet Turkish but seat of the decadent Byzantines—and made of himself in the tripartite partnership the static if not the sleeping partner. His kind go richly robed and bearded in the Italian pictures of only a little later day: one may visualize him flat-capped, with a jewelled hand and grave mien and a notary's mind as he checked his ledgers and his bonds and warehouses, and stroked that indubitable beard, gazing out at night across the Hellespont, his thoughts, uneasy, far in Asia with those two brothers of his who had vanished into the unknown wastes of the north-east.

Commercial travellers of their era, Nicolo and Maffeo had apparently plied their pursuits within fairly normal ranges until the year 1255. Two years or so before that, Nicolo Polo was certainly in Venice, lending that minor male assistance in gestation that was minor even for a Venetian merchant prince. As a result, and somewhere, it seems, in the year 1254, his eldest son Marco, destined for so much of wandering and adventuring, so much of obloquy and so much of praise, was born. It is said that Marco's mother died at his birth in the Ca' Polo, the dark family house in the Subbiataco above the Venetian canals. Obstetrics of the time were crude and pitiless: perhaps when Nicolo looked on his dead wife the emptiness within him cried for wider wanderings than those ventures in Near Asia. Perhaps, like many another helpless male in such circumstances, he looked on the unlucky newcomer with no great gratitude, consigned him to the care of relatives, and returned to Constantinople and a ready enthusiasm for the extended market-plans of his elder brother Marco.

Their latest venture carried them far up the Euxine to the Crimean Peninsula. Here, in trade in furs and amber and the like products, they seem to have prospered greatly. They penetrated a considerable distance inland to the east. This was Tartar country, under the dominion of governors left after the withdrawal of the great hordes which had followed Jenghis Khan.

Suddenly a minor war of considerable intensity broke out between their base and the country leading back to the Black Sea. They were cut off from Constantinople. With feelings that are left unrecorded, they decided that it was hopeless to make the attempt, and came to an astonishing conclusion:

to push forward into Asia itself, and carry on trading operations there.

Their inwards route in that year 1255 must have paralleled closely the outwards route of William of Rubrick, pantingly joggled in his cart from distant Karakorum. Perhaps they actually encountered and exchanged confidences and notes on routes—a meeting that would account for the later readiness of the Polo brothers to seek the court of the Great Khan. Meantime, and with unrecorded travails and difficulties, they reached the ancient city of Bokhara and took up residence there. Perhaps they were already trading in jewels. If so, they found the trade profitable: Bokhara housed them for a full, if incredible, three years.

The war which disturbed the Black Sea country was long over, as we know from other histories. But they were either unaware of the fact, or indifferent to it. The East had them in thrall—presumably its wealth-getting, not its glamour. Yet there is good reason to believe they would have speedily returned to Constantinople but for the arrival of a remarkable embassy in the city of Bokhara.

This embassy had been despatched by Hulagu, the Tartar conqueror of Persia and Baghdad, on a mission to his brother Kublai in far Karakorum. The great Jenghis Khan, the first overlord of those Mongol hordes which had overrun all northern Asia, had left five sons, Mangu, Batu, Hulagu, Kublai, and the indefinite Artigbuga. Mangu had succeeded to the title of Grand Khan and had despatched Hulagu to the conquest of Persia and the Moslem kingdoms, Kublai to the conquest of China. Mangu himself led a part of the Mongol host against China. In 1258 he died at the siege of Ho-cheu, in Sechuen, while Kublai was south warring against the emperor of Song. Now a remarkable event took place. Hulagu, the brutish conqueror of Baghdad, appears to have been next in succession—he was an older son than Kublai. But (so the Chinese historians tell) he despatched an embassy across Asia to his brother in China, urging Kublai to accept the overlordship of the Mongols. In this unwonted charity and forbearance Hulagu rendered his only service to civilization: he allowed the ascent to the throne of an incomparably greater ruler than himself; and he allowed the passage of the first European traders to the court of Karakorum.

For Hulagu's ambassador, encountering the Polo brothers,

"was gratified in a high degree at meeting and conversing with these brothers, who had now become proficient in the Tartar language; and, after associating with them for several days, he proposed to them that they should accompany him to the presence of the Grand Khan, who would be pleased by their appearance at his court, which had not hitherto been visited by any person from their country; adding assurances that they would be honourably received and recompensed with many gifts. Convinced as they were that their endeavours to return homeward would expose them to the most imminent risks, they agreed to this proposal, and, recommending themselves to the protection of the Almighty, they set out on their journey in the suite of the Ambassador, attended by several Christian servants whom they had brought with them from Venice. The course they took at first was between the north-east and north, and an entire year was consumed before they were enabled to reach the imperial residence in consequence of the extraordinary delays occasioned by the snows and the swelling of the rivers, which obliged them to halt until the former had melted and the latter had subsided. Many things worthy of admiration were observed by them in the progress of their journey, but which are here omitted, as they will be described by Marco Polo in the sequel of the book."

§ 4

In April of the year 1269 the Papal Legate in Acre, on the coast of Palestine, one M. Tebaldo de' Vesconti di Piacenza, received word that two merchants desired an audience with him. He seems to have been a gracious and worldly and courteous man, and possibly stared only a mild surprise at the appearance of the merchants. They were clad in half-Tartar robes, their faces were browned with alien suns, their Italian was a slow and halting speech. They gave their names as Nicolo and Maffeo Polo, and told him how it was fourteen years since they had set foot in a Christian town.

Of those fourteen years there have come down to our time only the tiniest scraps of record. They had reached the court of the Grand Khan in the company of Hulagu's ambassador, and Kublai (as we know from other sources) had then had himself crowned emperor, and in some stretch of the subsequent ten years had granted several audiences to the Venetians. With his character the son of Nicolo will deal: but the Chinese annals describe him as inquisitive and restless, mentally as physically. He had never before seen those strange fauna, the Europeans, but he had a considerable interest in them. He questioned the Polos closely on their kings and countries, their methods of war and their habits in peace, and finally came to a decision: he would send an embassy to the Pope in Rome, asking for a hundred Christian missionaries to come and expound to his people the Christian faith.

This conduct was to be emulated by a later emperor of China, who welcomed impartially Nestorians and Buddhists and Moslems. It is probable that Kublai had only a mild and passing interest in the subject. But while the whim was upon him, he pursued it with energy. He appointed a Tartar envoy, Khogatal, to accompany the Polo brothers to Rome and despatched them across the wilds of Asia, protected by his Grand Seal.

So protected, bearded like the pard, with perhaps little gain in wealth from their eleven or twelve years' absence in Asia, the Polo brothers had taken the long road back to Europe. On that road Khogatal had fallen ill and had been left behind, and thereafter, indeed, vanished from the tale. The two brothers had pushed on through long months of the usual difficulties: swollen rivers and impassable swamps and deserts where the tracks were lost and their feet failed them. So journeying through an incredibly tedious three years, they had at length reached a seaport in Lesser Armenia, and from thence had made their way here, to the audience of the Papal Legate.

The Pope?

But the Pope in Rome, Clement IV, had died six months before their arrival in Acre. The Acre Legate considered the matter, and gave them his advice. The best thing they could do was to see to their own affairs, awaiting meanwhile the election of a new pope by the council of cardinals.

Nicolo and Maffeo took ship to Negropont and thence to Venice. Of their reception there there is no record, nor of the fortunes of the elder Marco, abandoned all these years in Constantinople. But they found Nicolo's son, young Marco, a "young gallant"—which may mean much or little.

Boys matured rapidly in that age and city. No doubt there was much feasting and rejoicing, and, within the family-circle at least, much story-telling. They had ample time in which to indulge in these refreshments. The election of a new Pope delayed scandalously: there were plots, intrigues, and cabals innumerable in the Sacred College—a state of affairs which might have greatly interested Kublai remote in China awaiting his hundred Christian missionaries. Nicolo and Maffeo grew impatient and apprehensive: The Grand Khan might suspect they had no intention of returning, and all their hopes of ultimately winning out of Asia a great treasure would be lost for ever. Minus the hundred missionaries, but with a gift of oil from the lamp which burned eternally in the Holy Sepulchre in Jerusalem, they determined to depart for China without further delay—they had already delayed two years—taking young Marco with them.

In such fashion was Marco Polo launched on the quest that was to be his life—the quest of the Golden Ruler, Kublai Khan: a quest successful, fulfilled, and yet never ended.

It was 1271. They set out from Venice for Acre, journeyed up to Jerusalem, obtained a gift of the Holy Oil, and set sail for the port of Laiassus in the Black Sea—a port in the kingdom of Armenia. There, while they waited to equip a caravan, a message reached them from their friend Tebaldo of Piacenza in Acre. He himself had been elected Pope: they were to return at once to Acre and receive from his hands despatches for the Grand Khan of the Tartars in distant Cathay.

§ 5

Towards the end of the year 1271 or the beginning of 1272 the three Polos, much-harried from pillar to post, recommenced their journey from Acre. They carried with them the Papal letters and "several handsome crystalline vases" as presents to the Grand Khan; companioning them went, instead of the hundred Christian missionaries requested, two friars of the Order of Preachers to whom had been given authority to ordain priests and consecrate bishops. Probably they had various servants and retainers with them as well, but note of them is omitted from the tale of the younger Marco.

For it is now his tale. Before his journeying we have done no more than peer through a vague mist at those distant lands that haunted the fringe of the consciousness of Europe. Now, eschewing personal memoir except where it was essential, Marco seems to have set about recording on the tablets of his mind everything of importance or startling appearance or rumour in the lands through which they passed.

They came again to the port of Laiassus in Armenia—in Armenia Minor. It was ruled by a Christian prince, given to the "administering of strict justice", but unfortunately greatly harried by the heathen. The heathen in question were the Moslem under Bibars, the Mameluke Sultan of Egypt. As the three Polos and the two friars reached Laiassus rumours of the raiding depredations of the "Babylonians" filled the air, and the friars who had set out to consecrate bishops and ordain priests in far Cathay took fright at this very portal to their journey. They handed over the Papal letters to the Polos, wished them God-speed, and placed themselves under the protection of a band of Knight Templars in Layas. The Polos were probably staggered enough at this conduct. But, having come so far themselves in other years through situations far worse than the present, they determined to hold on their journey un-friar'ed.

They held through the Armenia which we call Anatolia, a land of "degenerate gentry" and busy ports, till they emerged into the northwards region of Turcomania. This had been conquered and partly settled by a southwards overflow of the Tartars, "a rude people, and dull of intellect" who had become Mohammedans. Pushing onwards, past Casaria and Sivas, they reached the city of Arzingan in Greater Armenia. No Armenians ruled here. The country was under the domination of the Tartars. Here it was that the Polos discerned Ararat's cloudy summits, on which the Ark had rested. They were suitably impressed at sight of this mythic mountain made visible. On the summit of it, according to Marco, the snows never melted, but went on "increasing by each successive fall". At what rate of progress the summit would finally vanish entirely into the heavens he did not stop to calculate. Instead, he noted "near Zorzania" a great oil fountain which discharged unceasingly an oil good as both an unguent and for purposes of burning. This is geography's first mention of the oil-wells of Baku.

But it is improbable that they penetrated up into Georgia, though they heard many tales of that land. They turned, unaccountably, to the south-east, following the course of the Tigris to Bandas, through the province of Mosul, which they found in that age inhabited by a medley of races and faiths, noting particularly the Christian Nestorian sect. The Nestorians, says Marco, even sent missionaries as far afield as India. En route, they heard also of the Kurds, then, as now, an "unprincipled race, whose occupation is to rob the merchants". This variation upon the custom of taking in one another's washing lingered in Marco's mind.

They came to Baghdad, and perhaps halted there for a while, savouring the best of possible routes to take in their journey to the Grand Khan's court. Here Marco heard the tale of the miserable end of the last of the Abbasite khalifs at the hands of Hulagu twelve years or so before. The khalif had been an oppressor of the Christians, and Marco solemnly ascribed his horrible death to the instigation of "Our Lord Jesus Christ".

The Polos seemed to have decided here to journey down to Ormuz in the Persian Gulf and from there take ship to distant China. They held south-east through Persian Irak, halting at Tabriz, which manufactured cloth of gold and traded in precious stones and pearls. Marco gathered no good opinions of the Mohammedan section of the population, but an excellent opinion of their Tartar overlords, who restrained the common Mohammedan desire to hamstring the straying Christian. Passing onwards, down through Persia proper, they heard of the city of Saba, from which the Three Wise Men journeyed to Bethlehem at the birth of Christ. The tale had become inextricably mixed with lingering doctrines of Zoroastrianism: there were cities where the Parsees still pursued their ancient faith. Persia bred excellent horses, as Marco noted and afterwards specified in detail, as well as asses which sold at even higher prices than horses. The roads were unsafe, the "savage inhabitants making a common practice of wounding and murdering each other". This genial custom Marco notes (gratefully) had been strongly restrained by the Tartars. We may suppose that large parts of the country were overrun by bands of hopeless and desperate men whom the Tartar invasion had ruined. Marco had no sympathy for them, they impeded his road to Cathay.

Mohammedans, he found, evaded the prohibition against wine in an ingenious manner. They boiled the wine, and then regarded it as forbidden no longer. For it had a different taste, a different appearance, and therefore could not be wine! Southwards, through a land of date-palms and wild asses, the travellers came to Kerman, where turquoises were found, and much fine needlework made. In the mountains they bred the "best falcons that anywhere take wing".

They went southwards through the mountains, making the Persian Gulf, and suffering greatly from the cold, against which young Marco found it difficult to defend himself even with the aid of "many pelisses". No doubt the thinner blood of his father and uncle suffered even worse.

But beyond the mountains, in the plain, they found themselves in the granary of Persia, a rich land of wheat and rice and fruits, the air a-whirr with pheasants and francolins. Here Marco saw his first humped cattle and heavy-tailed sheep. It was a land vexed by robbers and with tales of the greatest of them all, a Mongol Nikodar Khan who had raised a great army of desperate men and descended on India, conquering Delhi. Settled there, Nikodar and his companions had intermarried with the dark-skinned Indians with great speed and fecundity, producing in a generation (if the real historical facts, unknown to Marco, had been to hand, it would have shown as in about a third of a generation!) a race of browny half-breeds, the Karaunas. These Karaunas, robbers like their fathers, spread back into Persia in wandering bands, and, by means of diabolic arts acquired in India, "could produce darkness and obscure the light of day". This is the first mention of gas-warfare: no doubt the hooves of the raiders' horses at sunrise or sunset were the *dei ex machina*.

They were nearing Ormuz. But the Karaunas were active, slave-raiding and cattle-stealing on the plains beyond the city where the Ormuz merchants grazed their mounts. The three Polos found themselves in the midst of a raid—they would seem to have been travelling in company with other pilgrims. Various of their companions were killed and others dragged off as slaves. Marco and his father and uncle escaped to a near-by fortress. Perhaps some of the Venetian servants perished here: perhaps this was Marco's introduction to terror and war. But, youth though he was, he seems to have been little disturbed.

Through a dangerous road where robbers still swarmed, they descended for two days' journey till they came to the ancient port of Ormuz itself. They were in the East of fable and fact, in that hot, dusty town on the shores of the Persian Gulf—a port "frequented by traders from all parts of India, who bring spices and drugs, precious stones, pearls, gold tissues, elephants' teeth, and various other articles of merchandise. These they dispose of to different sets of traders by whom they are dispersed throughout the world." Here Marco heard of the sirocco which blew with such dread effects on respiration and trade in the summer months—the inhabitants, he tells us, would make for the water when the sirocco came, immersing themselves to the chin, and "continuing in that situation until it ceases to blow". It was an altogether dreadful wind: it blew while the Polos themselves were in Ormuz. The richer inhabitants retreated to the mainland, seeking coolness there. Meantime, the ruler of Ormuz had neglected to pay his annual tribute to his overlord in Kerman. Kerman despatched an expeditionary force. It slept a night on the verge of a grove of trees verging these hellish lowlands, and recommenced its march in the morning in ignorance that this was the sirocco's hour. The entire army was suffocated by the sand-wind. Marco himself, it seems, went out and inspected the dried-up, desiccated bodies, a tale of wonder and horror, a second Sennacherib's army that had perished in the breath of God.

§ 6

Inspecting the ships at Ormuz, the Polos found them of deplorable quality, "exposing the merchants and others who make use of them to great risks". They were built without nails and had no anchors. Despite the rigours of their previous overland journeyings, Nicolo and Maffeo agreed that the land-route would be better than to entrust themselves and their "young gallant" to these unchancy craft.

They turned north again, reaching Kerman by a different route and holding towards the borders of the land that we now call Afghanistan. It was a land of plenty again, on this new route to Kerman. But beyond Kerman was a great desert, where the springs met with in the first three days'

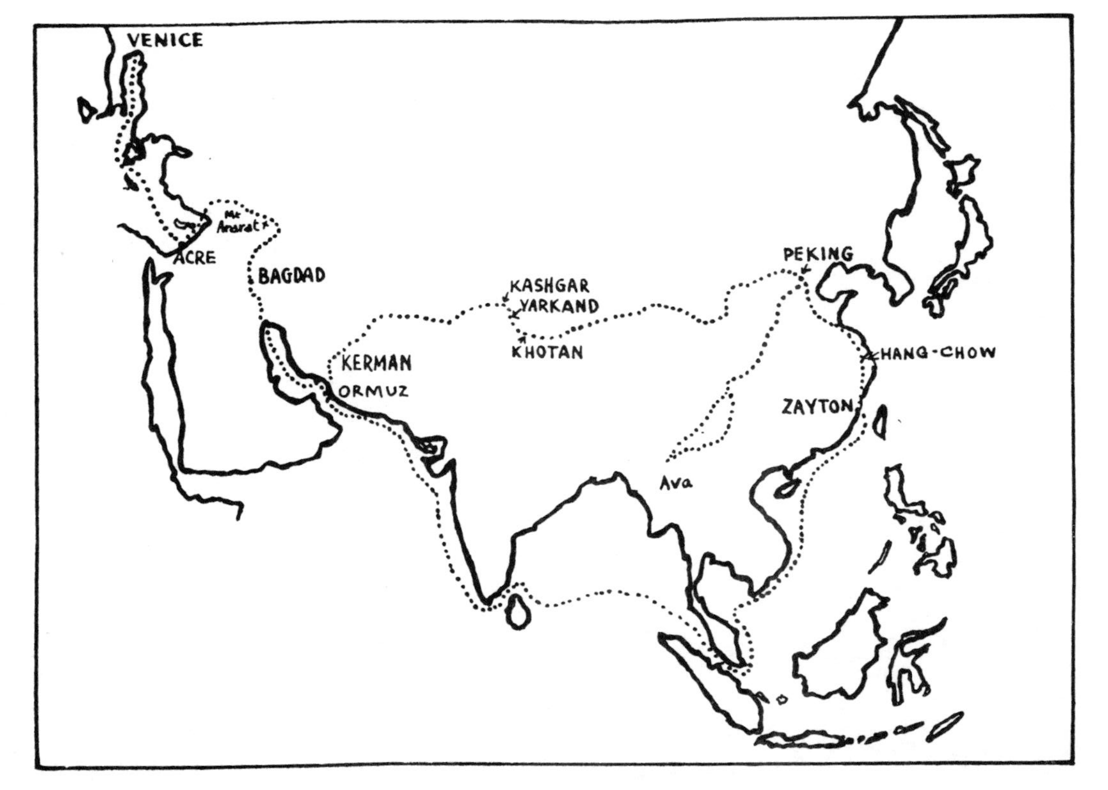

JOURNEYS OF MARCO POLO

journeying were unbearably brackish. They were worse: "Should even a drop of this water be swallowed, frequent calls of nature will be occasioned." They won beyond these inhospitable tracts, travelling at great haste on horseback, and reached the town of Khubeis, beyond the Lut Desert. They were expert metal-workers in Khubeis, Marco notes, ere belting himself for a further stretch of desert, north-north-eastward through Khorassan. Here was another desert of eight days' journey: beyond it, they came to the region of Damaghan, the ancient Hecatompylos, where Alexander had pursued the flying Persian king fifteen hundred years before.

There were still rumours of that flight and battle among the inhabitants, Marco tells. Relation of that rumour and a description of a marvellous plane-tree in that region which modern botany has failed to segregate complete his account of Damaghan, except that he found its men handsome and its women, in his opinion, "the most beautiful in the world". The speculative historian wonders, pondering that strictly impersonal chronicle, what this phrase covers. Was Marco as objective as usual, or did the "young gallant" lose his heart in Damaghan?

He seems to have occupied himself but a short time in the process, if at all. Recounting the tale of that Satanic malcontent, the Old Man of the Mountains who had proved so antipathetic to Moslem and Mongol alike, he and his father and uncle appear to have held by an almost eastwards course, through Jan-Jerm and Nishapur towards Balkh, in what is now northern Afghanistan. In this region of Khorassan they came upon a fresh desert, fortunately of no great extent: beyond it, and refreshingly, the country was a notable one in the production of large and succulent melons. Marco noted them with care and impressiveness in his mental tablets, and probably sampled them in like manner in a physical way.

So, at last, to Balkh, the ancient Bactria Regia of classical times. But it had lost its glories only a few years previously at the hands of Jenghis Khan, who in 1221 had ordered its inhabitants to be massacred and its walls to be razed. Probably there were no more than a few families of squatters in that "most ancient town in the world".

The surrounding country swarmed with bandits and broken

soldiery. There were great lions in the hills to the north of the city. Pushing eastwards through a starving country, the Polos carried provisions to see them beyond the range of hills, and in two days reached the "castle" of Taikan. It was a great corn-market, a town embowered in salt hills. The inhabitants of Taikan Marco found bloodthirsty and treacherous wild men, clad in the skins of wild animals, forerunners of the modern Afghan. Beyond Taikan came a land of scattered forts and waste plains where Marco tells that the porcupines—beasts of peculiar size and ferocity—had the habit, when hunters set their dogs at them, of "with great fury shooting out the quills or spines with which their skins are furnished, wounding both men and dogs". Probably the Polos themselves made no researches into these artillery practices. They came to a new tundra-waste, overshadowed by the Pamirs. Three days travelling through it brought them to the land of Badakshan.

In Badakshan, remote in the heart of Asia, Marco found a king who claimed descent from Alexander the Great. He had even the title *zul'Karnein* (the horned one)—the title which the Eastern folk had bestowed on Alexander fifteen hundred years before on account of the horns of Ammon displayed on the Macedonian's coins. The hills were reputed to be filled with precious stones ; the valleys bred good horses ; the men were fine sportsmen ; the air on the mountain-tops pure and salubrious.

Marco approved of this genial land. The Polos seem to have made some little halt here. The young gallant was suitably intrigued by the dress worn by the women of the upper class—trousers made as wide as possible in order to exaggerate the actual size of the hips. Decorative steatopygy was something new to the young Venetian.

Here, in Badakshan, Marco heard of various states and towns southwards, in India, across the Hindu Kush—of Peshawur, where the inhabitants were of evil disposition, worshipped idols, ate rice, and in other ways misconducted themselves ; Kashmir, also filled with devil-worshippers and magicians. Most of these accounts were gathered from the prejudiced mountaineers of Badakshan, Mohammedans to a man. But the account of Buddhist monks we know to be substantially true, as is the record of the food and drink and dress of those distant Indian communities.

How long the three travellers and their retainers halted in Badakhshan it is impossible to say. Perhaps they waited for the melting of the snows in the upland passes of the Pamirs. Perhaps it was on this occasion that Marco fell ill and was nursed to health again in those salubrious upland slopes. But that incident seems to belong to his future.

They set out at length, north-eastward through the passes of Pamir, "ascending mountain after mountain". On the high plateau of the Roof of the World they saw no birds and Marco noted how on these heights fires gave less heat and water took long to boil. There were no inhabitants to be met with for great distances in a land of snow and skyey crags. The Polos went laden with great quantities of provisions and doubtlessly wrapped warmly in winter robes purchased in Badakshan. Even so, it must have been a more than trying journey for those folk from the genial Mediterranean.

But at length, crossing the Kisil Mart, they reached the great city of Kashgar and a genial climate again. They passed through great cotton-fields in this land, flourishing plantations of flax and hemp. As usual, only man was vile—the Kashgari a "covetous, sordid race". Samarcand lay remotely in the west and Marco, either now or on a later journey actually visiting it, stops to give details of that great emporium of the East. They are scanty enough, being mostly devoted to the fable that Zagatai, one of the sons of Jenghis Khan, had there embraced Christianity, and, to prove his new and meek spirit, no doubt, robbed a Mohammedan mosque for a column with which to build a Christian church.

Marco greatly approved of Zagatai.

Probably the travellers held some debate as to what route they would now take to reach the court of the Grand Khan in China. At length they turned south-eastwards, towards Khotan, and appear to have reached that city and halted there, in the midst of a prosperous and fertile land "where the inhabitants were not good soldiers", awaiting the gathering of a caravan to cross the Takla Makan desert, in pursuit of the still-distant court of Kublai.

§ 7

North-eastwards from Khotan lay two great desert stretches to be traversed ere the travellers could reach Peking :

the nearer and smaller, that of the Takla Makan, the further, that of Gobi. It is unlikely that it will ever be settled what exact route they took, or whether the description applied by Marco to the desert of Lop should mean the small Takla Maran or the Great Shamo itself. The description of the desert crossing is itself vivid enough. A month was required for crossing this great waste, travelling from brackish water-hole to water-hole. Neither beasts nor birds were met with, "because there is no kind of food for them". It was an abode of evil spirits, prone to amuse travellers to their destruction. The Polos appear, nevertheless, to have crossed it without mishap. Perhaps at Khotan they had been met by envoys of the Grand Khan, sent to help them on their journey—for news of their approach throughout the last three years appears to have travelled far to China.

They reached Su-cheu, where abominable burial customs were observed, and probably halted there, refreshing themselves with food and water after their desert crossing, and also with gossip on the life and customs of the surrounding provinces. In Khamil the hospitable host, Marco heard, was in the habit of handing over his womenfolk to the entertainment of the casual stranger; in Chen-chen they mined an astounding substance "of the nature of the salamander, for when woven into cloth, and thrown into the fire, it remains incombustible". This is one of the earliest European mentions of asbestos; of the district of "Tanguth" (now impossible to identify with any certainty) "where the most excellent kind of rhubarb is produced"; of Kan-cheu, with its gigantic statues to the Buddha.

Reaching Kan-cheu, Marco and his father and uncle were detained there the space of a full year. In that narrative filled with great time-periods, with journeys of three and four years' duration, with casual visits which developed into stays of fourteen years or so, with voyages lasting an unhasting twenty-four months, this is one of the most remarkable entries. But Marco dismisses it as being on account of the fact that "the state of their concerns rendered it necessary". Possibly they were detained while news of their coming was forwarded to Kublai and his instructions awaited. If so, it appears to have been the only spot in the whole of the gigantic Mongol Empire in which their passage was stayed by authority.

Thereafter the route followed by the travellers till they did verily arrive at the Grand Khan's court at Peking is extremely doubtful. Marco's record is filled with details of the life and customs of the people of China and Mongolia, but that he then adventured up into those northern regions is unthinkable. It seems most probable that the three Venetians turned south-east again, crossed the Hoang-ho, and arrived at the city of Si-ning, whence they took the great Tibet-Peking road. It was a land of gigantic wild cattle, the yak of Thibet, and Marco was so impressed with the quality of the hair of those beasts that he purchased some of it, and, long years afterwards, carried it home to Venice. The inhabitants of Shen-si were in a mixed proportion "idolators" (Buddhists or Confucians), Mohammedans and Christians—strayed Christians of strayed Nestorian sects. In the north there still lingered the tradition of Prester John, that Christian Emperor of bloated fantasy and attenuated fact. Marco and his companions appear to have actually passed through a great stretch of Christian territory over-ruled by a direct descendant of Prester John.

Now at length they were drawing near Kublai's residence—apparently not Peking, but the city of Chang-tou, where the Grand Khan had recently erected a handsome palace. Messengers came to hasten their approach, and the much travailled travellers who had crossed half a world at length attained to the imperial presence. We should like to know more of this meeting than the scanty notes that Marco has left on the subject : we should like to know his feelings when he stared at last at this human fulfilment of a dream.

Upon their arrival they were honourably and graciously received by the Grand Khan, in a full assembly of his principal officers. When they drew nigh to his person they paid their respects by prostrating themselves on the floor. He immediately commanded them to rise, and relate to him the circumstances of their travels, with all that had taken place in their negotiation with his holiness the Pope. To their narrative, which they gave in the regular order of events, and delivered in perspicuous language, he listened with attentive silence. The letters and presents from Pope Gregory were then laid before him, and, upon hearing the former read, he bestowed much commendation on the fidelity, the zeal, and the diligence of his ambassadors ; and, receiving with due reverence the oil from the holy sepulchre, he gave directions that it should be preserved with religious care. Upon his observing Marco Polo, and inquiring who he was, Nicolo made answer, "This is your servant and my son"; upon which the Grand Khan replied, "He is welcome, and it pleases me much," and he caused him to be enrolled amongst his attendants of honour. And on account of their return he made a great feast and rejoicing; and as long as the said brothers and Marco remained in the court of the Grand Khan, they were honoured even above his own courtiers.

§ 8

That stay was of sufficient duration. Four thousand miles from Europe, every Spring the winds came down from Mongolia blowing fresh the sap in the young tree-shoots around Peking; Summers brought their intense heats upon the crowded Chinese lands, Autumns their harvesting and the great desert winds, Winters their shivering snows against the damascened palace walls. And for seventeen years, journeying hither and yon, on this and that mission of the Grand Khan's, the young Venetian Marco lived a life such as no European had ever thought possible. Sometimes, it is plain, all thought of ever returning to the familiar sight and smell of Christian countries faded from his mind. They were no more than a dream fringing the horizons of his nights—his nights when he lay down to rest from his toil on this and that business of his master.

With insatiable curiosity he gathered details of all that life surrounding him and the places into which he travelled, reconstructing, faultlessly enough in general, that medieval life of China and Indo-China. Often he himself did not visit the lands he described, and they lie outside the scope of this record.

But he himself, with unwearying feet, seems to traverse the greater part of Further Asia.

A favourite of Kublai's from the beginning he early learned (so his chronicle relates) "the manners of the Tartars, and acquired a proficiency in four different languages, which he became qualified to read and write". It has been greatly debated whether one of those languages was Chinese—and that language in particular denied the traveller because of its almost insuperable difficulties for the foreigner. But there is little reason to suppose that Marco, himself sent to govern a Chinese city, did not know the language of those he governed. He was in the springtime of his life and athirst for knowledge of all kinds.

Apparently his courtier-like protestations of willingness to serve were put to test by Kublai in a drastic fashion within a year or so of the young Venetian's arrival in Peking. He was despatched on a diplomatic mission to a region, Karazan, which is undoubtedly the Khorassan of modern geographers. He and his father and uncle had passed through this land in the course of their toilsome journey east—it lay remotely away in the west from China, a province of Persia.

If his heart failed him when that order was given, he makes no record of the fact, nor, indeed, any record at all of his journey thither. He went uncompanioned by the elder Polos: they pursued merchants' activities in and around the capital city.

Six months journey over the routes already traversed brought him to those Afghan heights where the air was so salubrious; and, here on his mission, Marco's health broke down and he abode a long year in those upland heights, recovering from his travels and noting ingenuously and undiscriminately everything of interest about him and above him and below him: he gathered tales of far countries and their peoples and manners, not only it seems for his own delectation, but for that of the Grand Khan, Kublai, a wonder-loving man.

Returning from this mission, Marco seems to have joined with his uncle and father in aiding Kublai in one of his warlike enterprises. This was the reduction of the Chinese city of Siang-yang (in the modern Hu-Kuang) which, after the conquest of the surrounding country by the Mongols, still held out obstinately. It held out, Marco tells, for a full three years, and "when the operations were reported to his majesty, he felt extremely hurt that this place alone should obstinately hold out, after all the rest of the country had been reduced to obedience". The wording is unintentionally humorous. The Polos appear to have conferred on the matter, and then approached Kublai and proposed the erection of great mangonels with which to bombard the recalcitrant city "by which the buildings might be destroyed and the inhabitants killed". This remarkable example of Western culture won the Grand Khan's instant interest. Nestorian mechanics laboured under the direction of the Venetians, and in a few days had the infernal machines completed. They were tried out in the presence of the Grand Khan, approved, and shipped south against Siang-yang. Siang-yang surrendered after the first bombardment, and the credit of the Polos was raised accordingly.

Perhaps it was in return for this aid that Kublai appointed Marco governor of the city of Yang-cheu-fu—a locum tenens only, though a satisfactory one. In this city of idolators and the makers of warlike instruments, Marco appears to have ruled with considerable discretion and success. But at the end of two years he was again recalled to Kublai's court and employed thereafter as a kind of envoy-at-large to distant provinces of that great sprawling anomalous thing, the Mongol Empire. He travelled far up the windings of the Yang-Tse-Kiang, which he computed the greatest river in the world. It was filled with shipping and active commerce, its banks crowded with rich cities. Seawards, in Kiu-Kiang of Kiang-si, Marco saw not fewer than "fifteen thousand vessels"—armadas undreamt of in Europe of that far Mediterranean he might never see again. In the city of Hang-cheu, diligently note-taking (it is the first time that he mentions his tablets) he found a second Venice, peopled by Buddhists who delighted in the arts and "looked upon soldiers and the profession of arms with a contemptuous disgust". They were among the most surprising phenomena observed by the ingenuous Marco, not excepting the magnificent residence of the last true Chinese Emperor, over which he was personally conducted by one of that lost monarch's servants.

He was not always free from bias nor (outside personal observations) easily ungullible. He records that the inhabitants of Fokien were cannibals—a statement of such staggering audacity as most modern commentators must pass over in silence, for the inhabitants of Fokien were among the most highly civilized of the ancient Chinese. His constant assertions that the people of this, that, and the next province were "savage and inhuman" becomes wearisome even in the midst of its naïvety: for in a subsequent paragraph or so he will go on to describe some atrocity of the Mongol troops with complacent commendation. He was Kublai's man, a naturalized Mongol, and Indians, Islanders and Chinese he regarded with cautious Tartar eyes. He lived before or beyond the days of democracy and the democratic vision: it was natural for him to see the peoples of every land as but the playthings, the chessmen on the boards, for the operations of their kings and rulers ; even so, there is surfeit of Eastern adulation of royalty and the royal act.

His lengthy descriptions of the court of Kublai have the fatuous irrelevance and nonsensical admiration-cry of a Mid-West child in Versailles. The reader misses the Marco of those earlier years voyaging down through Persia and across the Pamirs : it is almost, despite the impersonality of the record, as though we saw the callow and pleasant youth change slowly before our eyes, in those lush Chinese scenes, into the typical adventurer of his era—typical in all but his intelligence and his intense geographical curiosities, his faith in the Golden Ruler he had attained.

Frequently the mistakes he makes in his narrative suggest an imperfect acquaintance with the tongue of his particular informant of the moment. It is doubtful if he ever visited Amoy. Now, Amoy was noted for its artists, its portrait-painters. But in Marco's record these appear as tattooists—he tells that travellers came by sea from as far afield as India to have their skins tattooed by the craftsmen of Amoy. They came, we need hardly doubt, to have their portraits painted.

He was probably present at Kublai's port when the great and disastrous Mongol armada was launched against Cipangu (Japan), under the command of a Chinese and a Mongol General. The Generals fell out en route to the island, and much confusion resulted in the invasion. The first city captured, says Marco, was put to the sword : decapitation was the sentence pronounced upon the entire population, and carried out in all but the case of eight magicians, who had protected themselves with amulets and whom iron was incapable of either killing or wounding. Discovering this, the crafty Mongols beat them to death with a heavy wooden club ! . . . His further account of that invasion is much mixed with fable, yet tallies with the Japanese records in agreeing as to the complete failure of the enterprise. The Mongols were routed and enslaved, their generals escaping back to China and there being executed by order of the enraged Kublai. As a result, the young Venetian looked upon the Japanese with no favour, and records that their diabolical behaviour was unprintable ; also, as usual, they indulged in banquets of human flesh. . . .

Year after year went by on this mission and that for the

Grand Khan; the elder Polos are dim figures in the background—ghosts assiduously collecting gold. But for a chance of marriage and intrigue that presently arose it is probable that Marco, at least, would never have returned to Europe to amuse and instruct it with the tales of his golden pages and his gilded wanderings.

§ 9

In the last of those wanderings in Kublai's service, Marco appears to have been despatched on a voyage "with a few vessels under his orders", to some parts of the East Indies. Probably it was a voyage to Cochin-China and Annam, round to India, for debate and demand with some misty Hindu monarchs, and returning by way of the Philippines. He was probably the first European for fifteen hundred years to travel those seas that for Europe had neither existence nor rumour of existence, it is even possible, in some misfortune of wind and water, that he visited or sighted the Celebes and Moluccas, island groups unremote from Australia. In Cambodia, recently become tributary to the Grand Khan, he gathered that "no young woman could be given in marriage, until she had been first proved by the king". This over-worked monarch, when Marco saw him, had three hundred and twenty-six children. . . . We may long for news of other than these amorous activities, the great art and religious efflorescence of Cambodia at that time, some note of that civilizing influence that Cambodia sprayed eastwards and southwards and at last to the coast of the Americas. But beyond elephants and illegitimates, Marco's record finds that "no other circumstance requires particular mention".

He heard also on this voyage of Java and Borneo, though he mixed them and their products together, ascribing much gold to a Java that produces little or nothing of the metal. Presently, also, he heard the tale of the rich province of "Locha" which remains still unidentified. It may have been southern Cambodia—or, strange strayings of distant geographical data—it may even have been distant Papua. Most probable of all, it was the Fortunate Isle.

For, the first of our kind so to adventure, he had reached a region which trade and legend alike were later to credit with fantastic wealth and fantastic wisdom, islands of gold and spice and glamour, the bournes of all The Life Givers. He was to come again to those islands ; and strangest of searchers for the quest of this record, to tell nothing of the excitement he felt—surely he felt !

However that be, he returned from this mission at a time when the elder Polos seem to have wearied exceedingly of their enforced exile in those alien lands. Age was upon them, and they saw the same on the face and hair of the Grand Khan Kublai. They saw also, as all the Mongol Empire, watching, saw, that with the Grand Khan's death a wild confusion would fall upon his empire—a confusion in which his successor might have little time or inclination for protection of the pale-faced aliens from Europe. We may even suspect that they were not greatly loved among the Mongols and Chinese, those aliens whose sole gifts to China had consisted of mangonels out-tartaring the Tartar.

Nicolo Polo accordingly took an opportunity one day, when he observed the Grand Khan to be more than usually cheerful, of throwing himself at his feet and soliciting on behalf of himself and his family to be indulged with his majesty's gracious permission for their departure. But, far from showing himself disposed to comply with the request, he appeared hurt at the application, and asked what motive they could have for wishing to expose themselves to all the inconveniences and hazards of a journey in which they might probably lose their lives. If gain, he said, was their object, he was ready to give them the double of whatever they possessed, and to gratify them with honours to the extent of their desires ; but that, from the regard he bore to them, he must positively refuse their petition.

Here spoke the typical senile autocrat. That wealth and honours were barren things for men to expend and enjoy outside the range of their own country, with those sweetest of sauces, the applause and amazement of neighbours, was beyond his understanding. And the Polos seem to have shirked the explanation—very warrantably, for the Grand Khan's favour was a thing uncertain enough : behind that glitter of palace and court there is throughout Marco's pages a perpetual smell of the shambles and the torture-room. But fortunately an incident in the policy of Mongol inter-marriage was to provide them their release.

Arghun-Khan, the grandson of Hulagu, that excessively sanguinary Mongol soldier, had newly succeeded to the throne of Persia. A widower, he desired a wife from the family of the Grand Khan and despatched a mission, toilsomely, across Asia to China to ask for the hand of a Mongol princess. Kublai chose one of his innumerable progeny, the Lady Kutai, handed her over to the envoys, and allowed them to depart on the long homeward route to Persia. It proved more than lengthy. Eight months' slow travelling, princess-laden, they found themselves still remote from the borders of Persia. Transoxiana was in a ferment, warring Mongol princelet warring on warring Mongol princelet. The envoys turned about and retraced yet again their weary steps to the court of Kublai. The Lady Kutai remains a shadowy, if doubtlessly perspiringly travel-worn, figure throughout the history.

The re-arrival of the Persians coincided with Marco's return from his voyagings in the East Indies. Marco reported most of his travels in an open audience to the Grand Khan, stressing particularly the safety of navigation in those distant and barbarous seas. The Persian envoys heard and pondered. Presently they entered on a discreet intrigue with the Polos. They would petition the Grand Khan to allow them and the Lady Kutai to proceed to Persia by sea, if the Polos would accompany them. Then, beyond the immediate jurisdiction of Kublai, the Polos, having conveyed the Persians to Ormuz, could proceed to their own homes.

The plot was successful. Kublai consented, albeit reluctantly, to part with his prized Venetians, whom he probably regarded with the customary pride of a king of his day in strange oddities from distant lands. They were almost as unique as unicorns. They had been seventeen years in his court's employ : even so, he would not allow them to depart until they had sworn to return to China after they had visited their families. The Polos swore : with what intention in the oath it is needless to ponder at this late date. Circumstances were to free them from the necessity of foreswearing themselves, did they contemplate that.

At the same time preparations were made for the equipment of fourteen ships, each having four masts, and capable of being navigated with nine sails, the construction and rigging of which would admit of ample description ; but, to avoid prolixity, it is for the present omitted. Among these vessels there were at least four or five that had crews of two hundred and fifty to two hundred and sixty men. On them were embarked the ambassadors, together with Nicolo, Maffeo and Marco Polo, when they had first taken their leave of the Grand

Khan, who presented them with many rubies and other handsome jewels of great value. He also gave directions that the ships should be furnished with stores and provisions for two years.

§ 10

The sailing of this remarkable flotilla convoying the bride of Arghun-Khan is undated in Marco's record. But it was probably early in the year 1291. The ships were manned with a total of two thousand souls—envoys, courtiers, soldiers, sailors, slaves, women, the Princess, and the three Polos. Possibly Marco had the position of chief navigator: he may even have been in chief command of the expedition. They seem to have sailed with great cautiousness down the South China Seas, in equable weather though it was. Three months after quitting Pei-ho, they sighted the Malay Peninsula and Marco appears to have swung his flotilla round the point where Singapore now stands, and sailed it up the Malacca Straits. Here, however, they were halted for four months by contrary winds. The modern investigator knows those winds for the south-west monsoon, blowing down the Malacca Straits; he knows further that the month must have been May, and that the expedition with its clumsy ships must indeed have had to anchor until October, when the blowing of the monsoon changed to the north-east.

They seem to have anchored the ships in some minor bay in the north coast of Sumatra. They were so far south that the Pole Star was invisible—even the Plough invisible, tells Marco, but that is exaggeration. Knowing the time that must elapse ere they could sail, Marco had the entire party of two thousand disembark and establish a fortified camp on the shore.

This section of Sumatra was nominally under the Grand Khan's rule—great stretches of those eastern seas had heard of the name and fame of Kublai and sent him presents and vague promises. But Marco was suspicious of the natives "who seek for opportunities of seizing stragglers, putting them to death, and eating them". Accordingly, he

caused a large and deep ditch to be dug around on the land side, in such manner that each of its extremities terminated in the port where the shipping lay. The ditches he strengthened by erecting several block-houses or redoubts of wood . . . and, being defended by this kind of fortification, he kept the party in complete security during the five months of their residence.

The others secure, it seems that he himself was seized with his old, wandering restlessness. Sumatra at the time was divided into eight "kingdoms", and six of these, Marco tells, were then visited by him personally. There is no good reason to believe that it was not on this final expedition that the visiting was done. The armada lay in its bay, in boredom and idleness. The Lady Kutai turned soft Chinese eyes in weariness from the unending rocks of the barren shore. The sailors carried their sick to places where the wind might cool them to health. The Persian envoys, sick of strange foods, muttered and combed at their beards and peered into sunrises for sight of that never-coming wind. But the young alien, their commander, appears to have vanished into the interior of the island, indefatigably exploratory.

The territory on which they had encamped was that of Perlak—Mohammedans on the shore-lands, cannibals in the mountains. But the term cannibal in Marco's pages is little more than a term of abuse for those who refused clothes or kow-tow to the Grand Khan. Beyond it, interiorwards, lay Pase, filled with wild elephants and rhinoceroi—the latter the unicorns of contemporary European belief. Marco records a solemn warning that the popular European notion that a virgin may tame this beast is erroneous. He also unravelled, in good detective fashion, a remarkable example of fraudulent commercialism foisted upon the sage. In distant Europe trade brought to inquiring savants the mummified bodies of exceedingly miniature pygmies—a race supposed to live at the thither side of the earth. But the pygmies in question, Marco discovered, were merely monkeys (the orang or the gibbon) which the natives would catch, kill, shave, and embalm, despatching the resultant cadavers to distant ways of trade and travel in return for a small payment. In Europe those monstrosities sold for great sums. They took long years to reach that distant continent from the East Indies—as remarkable a comment on human folly as ever has been made!

Eastwards in Andraghiri, the natives devoured their dead according to peculiarly horrible rites which Marco cites in great detail. The account of this species of ceremonial cannibalism is much more credible than the almost universal anthropophagy which the Venetian delighted to foist upon those living on the fringe of the unknown—they ate their dead for religious reasons, not hunger.

Far in the south of the island he came to the kingdom of Jambi, a land of idolators and agriculturists. Here Marco, admiring the indigo plant and its uses for the purposes of dyeing, purchased seeds. Long afterwards, facing the frosty Venetian weather, those seeds refused to sprout. Jambi had "men with tails, a span in length, like those of a dog, but not covered with hair". Friendly commentators on Marco's narrative were wont to excuse this gross libel by suggesting that he had been deceived in glimpsing certain of the apes resembling the human species—in particular, the orang-outang. Unfortunately, the orang is as tailless as Homo Sapiens himself. . . .

He saw pith being dug from the "interior of a tree" and a "kind of meal" made therefrom. He tasted it and found it good. It was, as we now know, sago. He heard innumerable tales and reports, the Fortunate Isles gleaming unafar. But at length, we may conclude, October was drawing near. He retraced his steps to Perlak and embarked the weary armada.

Three or four hundred of that two thousand who had left the Pei-ho were perhaps already dead—victims to an unhealthy climate and an unwonted life. But still the Mongol Princess survived, and neither of the elder Polos appear to have taken hurt. The expedition launched out across the north Indian Ocean.

Midway, it seems to have halted at the Nicobar Islands, where Marco gazed disapprovingly upon the naked inhabitants —"little removed from the condition of beasts". Here, perhaps, he heard from some traders of islands even remoter, inhabited by dog-headed savages who killed and ate "every person they could lay their hands on". Those canine anthropophagists were undoubtedly the gentle Andamanese, stung into ferocity and madness through several centuries of raiding and murdering along their coasts carried out by Malays—just such adventurers as the Venetian's admired Mongols.

Marco gives with a fair accuracy the distance from the Andamans to Ceylon, so that it is possible that the squadron may have actually strayed as far north as the former islands. However that may have been, Ceylon at last was reached; and the fleet put in at a port—perhaps Colombo. It anchored here for some time, while Marco, indefatigably curious, observed the ways and customs of the Singhalese, their worship of Sogomon-barchan—a strange corruption of Sakya-Muniburchan, itself almost meaningless in its admixture of Hindustani and Mongol—the Divine Sage God. This was the Buddha. Marco, however, though he tells a twisted version of the Buddha legend, never heard of the great teacher by the name of Buddha, though he had encountered the Chinese variant, Fo. For him the followers of Buddha, as of all the Indian gods, were merely "idolators".

Thereafter the course of the armada is doubtful. Marco launches on an extensive description of the various Hindu states—lands of wonder and terror, gigantic idols and gigantic idolatries. Some passages in the text suggest a slow coasting to Coromandel and as far northwards as Masulipatam ("where good oysters are found)". Sailing south and calling at this port and that, or trading for provisions on the way, Marco gathered a considerable amount of information regarding the Indians. The stories of the Brahmins and the rites of their religion are greatly distorted—evidently Marco received a great part of his information from Mohammedans. Possibly, by the time he turned Cape Comorin, he had engaged Mohammedan pilots for braving the dangers of the Arabian Sea.

"Idolators" apart, he heard, what we now know to be true, of extensive Christian communities settled in India even in that early day—followers of that St. Thomas whom legend related had been martyred at Mailapur, where his tomb in Marco's time was still supposed to stand. Miracles were there performed daily, Marco heard, but he himself does not appear to have disembarked to investigate. Instead, rounding Cape Comorin, he remarks on the great monkeys which infested the land, and how tigers, leopards and lynxes everywhere abounded.

His pages are suddenly filled with description of interior states such as Delhi which he could not himself have visited personally, at least on that return expedition. Perhaps, however, he had done so while an envoy of the Grand Khan. Sailing northwards up the Indian coast, he sighted or heard of a variety of states and cities which have long since vanished from recognizability—Kambaia, Servanath, Kesmacoran. Beyond Bombay, the course of the squadron again grows doubtful, for the record commences a particular description of Socotro lying remotely across the Arabian Sea at the mouth of the Gulf of Aden.

It is not impossible that the squadron actually may have

coasted across to the Arabian shore, and from there Marco heard of those wondrous lands of "Great India" which he described in such detail—Abyssinia, Madagascar, and the like. In Madagascar he heard with gravity of

an extraordinary kind of bird, which they call a rukh, making its appearance from the southern region. In form it is said to resemble the eagle, but is incomparably greater in size; being so large and strong as to seize an elephant with its talons, and to lift it into the air, from whence it lets it fall to the ground, in order that when dead it may prey upon the carcase. Persons who have seen this bird assert that when the wings are spread they measure sixteen paces in extent, from point to point; and that the feathers are eight paces in length, and thick in proportion. Messer Marco Polo, conceiving these creatures might be griffins, such as are represented in painting, half-birds, half-lions, particularly questioned those who reported their having seen them as to this point; but they maintained that their shape was altogether that of birds, or, as it might be said, of the eagle.

Could the rukh have been the albatross?

He heard of Zanzibar with its authentic negroes, "having wide mouths, thick noses, and large eyes". "*Sed cooperiunt suam naturam; et faciunt magnum sensum quando eam cooperiunt, eo quod habent eam multum magnam et turpem, et horribilem ad videndum.*"

It is to be noted here how orthodox was Marco's conception of the Indian Ocean—as a kind of great inland lake, its shores the Indias, Great, Lesser, and Middle. This was a notion obtained from the classical geographers, but it was the most serious distortion introduced into the maps apparently confirmed by the tale of the Venetian. Yet, ending his account of those innumerable lands of Africa which he called Middle India he had a qualm of hesitation, casting back his mind to the East Indies and the tales he had heard there of innumerable other islands, inhabited and uninhabited—"twelve thousand seven hundred islands". Was this some rumour or notion of the vastness of outer Oceania?

At long last they came within sight of the shores of Persia, coasting up to the island of Ormuz, where the three Polos had descended from inner Persia to inspect the quality of the ships on their outward journey nearly twenty years before.

They had been eighteen months on the journey. Six hundred of the crew—"and others"—had died since they left the Pei-ho. But the Lady Kutai was still alive and the

Venetians, apparently toughened and hardened to any hardship, unharmed.

Landing in Ormuz, they heard the news that the prospective bridegroom, Arghun-Khan, had died some time before and that considerable confusion prevailed in Persia as a consequence, the regency having been assumed by the dead ruler's brother, Kai-khatu, to the exclusion of the heir, Chazan-Khan. In some perplexity they sent messengers to Kai-khatu, asking how they should dispose of the princess from Kublai's court. The answer of the uncle was that he was sure the nephew would desire the lady. The Polos were accordingly requested to convey her to Chazan-Khan's territory remotely in the north of Persia.

Undaunted, Marco and his father and uncle, and presumably the rest of the escort, set out through Persia, and at length reached Chazan's territory and disposed of the Lady Kutai there. Of how they were received there is no mention; of what subsequently happened to the princess herself we know nothing; of what happened to the remains of that great escort of Mongols that companioned her from China we can only speculate. The Polos appear to have dropped the matter from their minds as from their record. They turned westwards, seeking Armenia and Europe.

§ 11

Even yet, this tale of that first great explorer of the Eastern world does not dwindle to diminuendo. The roads to the Euxine were troubled and dangerous; at their request Kai-khatu provided them with passports and troops of horses, and they appear to have made slow but steady progress up through the Armenian lands till they reached Trebizond. From there, first touching at Constantinople and Negropont, they sailed home to Venice, arriving in that city long lost to their eyes some time in the year 1295. . . .

With their arrival they pass for a year into a wealth of fiction and fable.

It is told that they came to the Ca' Polo bearded and dark, in half-Tartar clothes, speaking a strange, half-Tartar speech. And their relatives looked out on the wild men and refused to recognize them, seeing little to identify them with those three, the middle-aged men and the gay young gallant, who had sailed for the East and there perished twenty years before. Thereat the three Polos ripped open their shabby garments and showed the interiors lined with jewels of great price, and the canny stay-at-home Polos fell upon their necks, recognized them, and embraced them. . . . If the fable be false, the allegory is true enough.

En route from the court of Kai-khatu, they had heard of the death of Kublai in remote Cathay. Their oath to return was foregone now, and we may imagine them (the elder Polos at least) renouncing wandering and settling to contentment and fur-lined robes and slow strolls along the Prado, amid the wheeling of the pigeons, blue, and grave debate and supper with grave friends. The East, that world beyond the Blanket of the Dark, had lifted for them for a magical glimpse, and very quickly and strangely memory of the picture in that glimpse faded from their minds, the long Chinese roads and the winding Chinese rivers, the clanging bells of the temples, the furred shores of the strange islands that looked out on the great Sea of the East, the beating drums in dark lands of idols and terrible fires as they camped by the straits of Malacca. . . . Some such picture we may build for ourselves of that after-life of Nicolo and Maffeo, for thereafter they sink from the record. They were never, we are aware, explorers in any sense, they seem to have traded with a single fidelity and obtuseness for little other purpose than trade. But for the fact of that nephew and son who travelled with them the glimpse might never have been recorded for the world to read.

It is doubtful if it would have been recorded at all but for the events of the year 1296. Venice and Genoa declared war. Even before the return of the three from Asia the Polo *gens* had been called upon to equip a galley for the coming sea-fight. Marco appears to have thrown himself into the task with zest. He was appointed commander of the Polo galley and perhaps sailed it with musings on tactics of sea-fight seen at the thither side of the world. Andrea Dandola commanded the Venetians; and the fleet sailed.

It met the Genoese off Curzoia on the 7th of September, 1296, and was routed with great ease. Marco Polo's galley was boarded and compelled to surrender, Marco himself being carried a prisoner to Genoa.

Nothing more fortunate could have happened to him from our point of view. But at first he must have found imprisonment, after his life of activity and interest, more than maddening. Apparently he was allowed to write letters to the Polos: it seems that Maffeo and Nicolo made desperate efforts to ransom him. But the Genoese were in revengeful mood, and refused ransom. Marco was left to loiter and brood in the free and easy captivity of that day, captivity that was yet exasperating enough for such active soul as his.

Then it appears that his room or cell was shared by a fellow-prisoner, a Pisan named Rustician. Marco, in boredom, talked of his travels and exploits. Rustician, a litterateur, was more than interested. There was food for great romance in this travel-talk of Messer Polo's.

Whatever the arrangement, Marco set about dictating the entire travels to his fellow-prisoner. It is uncertain even in what language they were dictated—the probability is that it was Italian, though the French is among the oldest of the surviving scripts. Marco must have procured from Venice his tablets, his notebook, or whatever it was in which he had been wont to jot his memoranda. And with those beside him, pacing up and down the cell day after day, he wandered forth again on those unending journeys by river and mountain and desert plain, up into the heights of Khorassan again, across the windy Roof of the World, down the highways of China, the sounding coasts of Cathay. . . . Names and dates had here and there blurred to an inextinguishable confusion in his mind. Sometimes his memory or his tablets betrayed him, so that he foisted upon Central China the habits of remote Borneo. But in the main, and in a mind that seems to have been as single-track as his soul, he remembered vividly and accurately all he had seen and heard.

He was in prison for three years. At the end of that time the gates opened, and he walked out of Genoa, and thereafter, so far as we are concerned, walked out of the pages of his colourful travels into the obscurity of private citizenship in Venice. He married a wife, Donata, of whom we know little; she bore to him three daughters, of whom we know less. He was wealthy and famous and ridiculous very soon, for the story of his travels had spread abroad in Venice, he himself, questioned, was probably the reverse of reticent, and the wits sneeringly dubbed him Il Milione—"the Thousander"—because of the constant recurrence of that word throughout his tales in his descriptions of mileage and jewel-splendour.

Copies of his book began to circulate. He sent a copy to a French noble. . . . And for twenty-five years thereafter he vanishes from our gaze.

But on January the 9th, 1324, he made his will, leaving the bulk of his estate to his wife and three daughters. Very shortly afterwards he died, the much-travelled and ridiculed and perhaps by then embittered, and was taken from the Ca' Polo and buried without the Church of San Lorenzo in Venice.

§ 12

While he lies and sleeps sound enough, long dust and ashes under the flagstones of San Lorenzo, we can assess him now with cooler minds than his contemporaries—whom he exasperated into derision—or the later centuries' commentators—whom he irritated into foolish admirations.

Fundamentally, his was the kinetic, not the poetic mind. This has been true of most explorers, but especially was it true of the Venetian. That his record lacks those personal touches that would make him—in the writer's phrase—live, is not apt : all that he writes on mountain and river and country and king is surface-observation of a limited quality. Ante-dating the days of careful measurement and calculation of route and road, his geographical records naturally had lacks and lacunae enough : what is more tragic is the essentially commonplace quality of the mind which viewed not only those geographical tracts but the peoples that dwelt therein, the imputations from tide and drift and wind.

It is hardly to be wondered at that until Behaim's time the maps remained unaltered despite the issue of his *Travels*. They were inconceivable in two senses—the geographical information was served planlessly, multitudinously, wearyingly and confusingly ; and the peoples of those distant lands of whom he wrote were verily inconceivable peoples, lacking every one of them both individuality and individuation. There is little essential difference between a town in northern Armenia and a town in the Straits of Malacca as Marco Polo depicts them—they are both filled with shadow-folk, in the flat, not the round, mechanically pacing a mechanical existence, whether as Christians or the unescapable "idolators".

He spent seventeen years in and around China ; yet he

never appears to have made any attempt to grasp the philosophy of those "idolators" by whom he was surrounded. He never appears to have heard of Confucius or Lao-Tze. Buddha was to him the idol of a god. He was incapable of identifying even the Singhalese Buddha and the Fo of remote Shen-so—though their similarities are so obvious. His command of four languages there is little reason to doubt, and their very possession is the more damning against him: with these as his tools he might indeed have brought a rich work of delineation and interpretation out of the East, beyond that painted veil that covered it from European eyes. But the soul-quality of the Venetian was unequal to the task.

Even so, his record remains one of the great travel records, the narrative of one of the earth's earliest true conquerors—in a sense indeed that Marco would have been incapable of apprehending. His book remains still authoritative—confirmed and re-confirmed as it has been by the modern world from other native scripts—on the life and being and surface appearance of that distant East.

Very slowly the ideas in his record spread and were apprehended by other eager and questing minds. Beyond the confines of Asia Minor was not merely India and a wild and deserted land, but Empires of wealth and high civilization, innumerable islands, lands of wonder stretching on and on, lit by strange suns, into the infinite, as it seemed to those early minds. . . . Lands innumerable, and of all most fascinating those Spice Islands of the Venetian's—surely the very Fortunate Isles of old.

A century and a half after muffled feet had carried Marco to his last rest in San Lorenzo, a child of the Italian enemy-city he had hated would sit long hours above his *Travels* and pore over the story of those islands.

IV

DON CHRISTÓBAL COLON AND THE EARTHLY PARADISE

§ I

SOMEWHERE remote in the Old Stone Age, perhaps ten thousand years before Christ, the hunting clans of the Yenisei in Siberia commenced a slow northwards and north-eastwards drift in pursuit of game or merely in happy-go-lucky migration. They were folk of mixed Mongol and Armenoid stock, tall and lank, perhaps without that gravity that later became a characteristic of their race; they were hunters and trappers, wielding chipped weapons and tools; they went naked and unashamed, men of the Golden Age, without culture or rigorous custom, without religion or superstition, kingship or classes, social problems or social convictions. As they moved north and north-eastward through hundreds of years they followed a gradual amelioration of the climate of that time: the earth was recovering from the rigours of the Fourth Ice Age. By the time they reached the vicinity of what is now the Bering Straits it is possible that they found those straits green and verdant, low swampy lands, sea-washed, stretching remotely into the hazes of sunrise. They went into that sunhaze and all unwitting their achievement crossed the landbridges from the Old World to a New Continent hitherto untrod by the feet of men.

This continent was America. Wandering south slow millennium on millennium, the hunters passed down the length and breadth of the Americas, reaching at last the remote forests of the Amazon and the chilly pampas of Tierra del Fuego. They split and differentiated into multitudinous language-groups, though not into nations, for nationhood was as unknown as culture or war. They hunted the beasts of this strange continent and made themselves shelters in caves and by breakwinds, fished in the seas of the Mexican Gulf, bathed in the waters of the Pacific, and lived and died in countless generations through that hard yet happy life that had been the life of all their species since first men climbed, by accident of arm and eye, to mankind's status.

They were in a continent geographically remote from the rest of the world, separated by long seas from the wandering incursions of other tribes of Old Stone Age folk. This till the accident of the discovery of civilization in the basin of the Nile led to the greatest revolution in human affairs.

For those kindred groups of the Old World discovered civilization. They originated agriculture : they spread abroad Europe and Asia in quest of Givers of Life. They invented boats, and by 500 B.C. wandering drifts of them, divinely led, were adventuring out into the waters of the Pacific. Culture and cruelty and economic security and slavery had come into the world ; but for long America remained untouched.

Yet, as we know now, beginning somewhere around the time of the birth of Christ in distant Syria, the first of those Archaic explorers, Proto-Polynesians or Chinese, reached the coasts of America in a stretch of a century or so, by half a dozen different routes. There they explored and settled and searched for metals and gems ; and wherever their feet trod some variant of the Archaic culture rose anew—a culture in America founded on the cultivation of the maize, a culture with dim gods that speedily became Americanized whatever their Asiatic ancestry. Then the stream of Polynesian-Chinese raiding and exploring appears to have dried up for a time.

But about the seventh Christian century there was a great cultural ferment in India and beyond in Cambodia and all the East Indies. Mariners of those countries sailed and traded remotely into the Pacific. They reached America—at Panama, along the Mexican coast, at Arica in Peru by way of Easter Island—bringing fresh cultural strains to the lowly Archaic civilization. From those fresh cultural impetuses grew up to considerable heights of achievement the notable civilizations of the Maya, the Nahua, the Inka and Pre-Inka. Then once again the changes of time and fortune cut adrift those communications across the Pacific : the Mongols of Kublai Khan had flung all Eastern Asia in a ferment and the cultural capital and the cultural leisure of Asia no longer sent forth its missionaries into that strange country of rumour and legend of which the Chinese Buddhists told, and which we now know to have been America.

CHRISTOPHER COLUMBUS

Remote in the north-east Leif the Lucky, as we have seen, came exploring in quest of the Fortunate Isles, and discovered them in the continent of North America. The tale of that discovery filtered back to Europe, there to mix inextricably through four centuries with the legend of the Fortunate Isles themselves, with—more concrete, yet kin—the story of the great Spice Islands of the East. Towards the close of the fourteenth century two Venetians, Nicolo and Antonio Zeno, sailed as far north as the Faröes, and there (according to a descendant) heard of Iceland and Greenland. Visiting these lands, they heard yet again of another country distant in the south, Estotiland, where the Norse were settled, and of a country, remoter yet, "where the inhabitants had a knowledge of gold and silver, lived in cities, erected splendid temples to idols, and sacrificed human victims to them".

Mythical or otherwise the Zeno's adventures, conviction grew stronger, century on century, in each imaginative European mind, that somewhere out in the dark Atlantic, did a man but steer far enough, he would come to a land of wonder, of strange gods and self-sown wheat, the Fortunate Isles, the Islands of Spice. Those spices, eastward brought, were authentic enough. And for hundreds of years the Atlantic European had found drift out of the west, in the accidents of storm and tide, strange things that confirmed his curiosities. Carved sticks and the trunks of trees came, the bodies of men of un-European, un-African race, this and that item of flotsam to keep wonder kindled. It is even possible—and indeed probable—that now and again a non-Norse ship in the North Atlantic, coasting north or south, was driven from its course across the whole wide stretch of the Atlantic and glimpsed strange alien shores, and returned with the tale of them, to be half-believed and disbelieved and remembered for a little and half-forgotten.

So, long before the publication of Marco Polo's *Travels*, telling of a thousand-islanded sea beyond Asia, there was belief in an islanded Atlantic. America, untrodden perhaps by all Europeans but the Norse, was nevertheless a land of definite and continuous rumour, known through meagre fact and abounding fantasy. The geographers of the fourteenth and fifteenth centuries dotted the remoter Atlantic with islands—"Antilia" the most popular—and it was regarded as a truism that if the sphere were the true form of the earth practice and theory might indeed be linked, and, sailing westwards from Europe, a man come in time to those islands of Brandan and Brazil, of Antilia, the Wineland of the Norseman—and beyond them to the Spice Islands and the unremote Cipangu of Marco Polo.

But it was also recognized that it would be a foolhardy and unprofitable venture because of the immense distances to be covered, the terrors and uncertainties of weeks at sea on an uncharted waste of water.

§ 2

The man who was to solve and annotate those puzzlings and affirmations of the European geographers was born in the city of Genoa in an uncertain year that was perhaps 1448. His father was a wool-carder, a cheesemonger and a publican—and but poorly equipped for all three professions, for he suffered from frequent bankruptcies. His mother is no more than a name—Suzanna Fontanarossa—though it may be from her that the young Columbus acquired his energy, his faith, his fluency. His mendacity—he was to develop into one of the world's great liars—was probably self-sown and reared and cultivated, shade and shelter for the cloudy surmisings and vague visionings of that poet's soul which was truly his.

He was apprenticed to the more stable of his father's trades—wool-carding—at the age of eleven; he ran errands about the Genoese streets, he touted cloth samples up and down the Italian roads . . . and in intervals of the press of existence read and pondered every one of the scanty books on which he could lay his hands. He learned Latin to aid that reading—the later Christopher of the booming mendacities was to affirm that he attended Pavia University to do that learning—and devoured tales innumerable: particularly tales with a background of geographical speculation. They kept him alive in the dust of the sweating card-room, the sweat of the dusty roads, those lands of mystery and imagination. Sometime, we may imagine him affirming, he himself would achieve their like—did he ever escape the draggled toil and poverty of Genoa.

He endured the life of a wool-carder for a long three years

and was then shipped to the Levant as tout in the employment of the great house of di Negro and Spinola. This was 1475. Next year he was despatched, in a convoy of Spinola ships, on a trading adventure to England. En route, the convoy was attacked, sacked, looted and half destroyed by a Gascon admiral-freebooter. Christopher narrowly escaped with his life—his ship was rescued by the Portuguese and sailed into the safety of Lisbon harbour. Refitting next year, it proceeded to England. . . .

Beyond that are three years of doubt and surmise. He was to affirm that thereafter he visited Iceland, that he traded down the Guinea coast, that he entered the employ of King René of Provence as a privateer captain. Mendaciously, unendingly, confusingly, he poured abroad this biography in later years that accepted it with a conviction it now fails to carry. For one who visited Iceland his ideas of the Atlantic remained singularly archaic: for a privateer captain his navigation singularly inefficient. Indeed, like Admiral Peary, there is no proof that he was ever a sailor or understood the handling of ships. Instead, we have picture throughout those years of a bookish young chapman dreaming vision on vision as he raised his eyes from the pages of this and that fantastic glomeration of fable—visions of the Fortunate Isles, the Earthly Paradise lying awaiting discovery a few days' journey westward there in the Atlantic sunset. . . .

Presently fortune sent him wandering to Lisbon, where his brother had taken up the trade of map-making.

Lisbon at the time was the centre for all the adventursome and skilful pilots of Europe. From Lisbon had been directed those grandiose explorations of the African coast which were to give Portugal such remarkable commercial ascendancy over the rest of Europe through two long centuries. In Lisbon, on the fringe of all this activity, were hosts of map-makers, geographers, and the like fauna. In Lisbon it is possible that the remarkable project to realize his dreams and sail directly westwards across the Atlantic first seized hold on the imagination of the youthful Columbus.

But there is excellent reason to believe that the project was not inspired until some four years later. Columbus settled to map-making: fantastically bad maps on which he let loose the products of his imagination in great monster hordes. He knew little of seamanship, less of the world, but much of the

Earthly Paradise. Had not the Northmen touched it, the Land of Wine, had not perhaps Marco il Milione glimpsed it in the islands beyond Cipangu? Cosmographically muddled, geographically out-dated, hampered by a poor education and lowly social status, Christopher clung to those convictions with the proud, pathetic tenacity of his unfortunate social compeers—the self-educated men—in all ages. Presently he was spreading his beliefs abroad in a social class other than his own.

Through some accident the map-maker had encountered the Perestrellos in Lisbon—Perestrello the Governor of Porto Santo, father of an attractive daughter, Filepa. They were nobles. A poet was noble as well. Christopher, in the hearing of astounded brother Bartholomew, invented himself a lineage on which even the Perestrellos looked with respect. He was descended from Colonius, the Roman commander who conquered Mithridates; his first cousins had been nobles and admirals—the admirals Casenove Coullon of Gascony, Columbus Pyrata Palæologus of Greece—witness the kinship of their names. And the sea was in his blood as well—witness his many voyagings.

Of some such fabric was self-woven the legend of Columbus. Tall, ruddy, ardent, blue-eyed, engaging, he captured the hearts and minds of his new friends. They liked his piety, his exploits, and his gentle birth. The first of these at least was authentic—it was to be the central drive behind the great quest of his life.

So the far-straying son of the Genoese wool-carder had presently wedded the gentle Donna Felipa, the daughter of the Portuguese navigator who had been made the first governor of Porto Santo. Presently they moved from Lisbon to Porto Santo itself, Columbus stepped into his father-in-law's shoes of property, if not of power, and set to earn himself a livelihood by the making of maps and charts in the approved custom of the time. He was on the high-road to the Africas, and the maps may have sold well to uncertain or doubtful navigators hastening south slave- and gold-raiding along the kingdoms of the blacks.

And there, at Madeira, it seems that a remarkable piece of good fortune was granted him. He encountered a nameless pilot (nameless to us) who had a strange story to tell. This man had been blown across the Atlantic in his ship in a great storm, and, after the storm had died down, had come on a litter of islands in that western sea. He had made no attempt to name or claim or explore them ; instead, had sailed back for Europe. Nameless and enigmatic, he sails away from Madeira, leaving to our imagination a kindled young man staring after him. No mere rumour or theoretical quibble of the geographers, no mere imagined land of faery, but *reality* whatever its reality, Cipangu, India, Antilia, the Earthly Paradise—there at the thither side of the world, awaiting discovery and conquest !

So it seems the great inspiration came on him. He made his first proposals for this deliberate adventure out into the Atlantic to the State of Genoa. But Genoa appears to have declined with singular brevity either to finance the expedition or grant Columbus the honours he adjudged fitting for that expedition's commander. He was still to the Genoese, if recognized at all, only the wool-carder's son. Nothing daunted, his vision shod with the solid shoes of fact, he next forwarded his scheme to King John the Second of Portugal. King John was engaged in the serious business of warfare but paid the project some attention. An amusing project. But Columbus's claims outrageous. Doubting, the King referred the matter to a committee of Portuguese geographical experts.

The committee was headed by the Bishop of Ceuta. Columbus presented himself personally to plead his case. The Bishop examined it in detail, demolished it with ease. Cipangu—Antilia distant only a few hundred miles ? Messer Colombo was perilously antiquated in his cosmographical notions (the Bishop was entirely in the right). Report to King John : a hare-brained scheme.

The king was unsatisfied : the project had intrigued his fancy. It was merely that he had balked from Columbus's astounding claims : the title of Grand Admiral, the title and power of viceroy of all new lands discovered, a ten per cent share in the trade with all such lands. Thereon the wily Bishop suggested that it might be a good idea not to send an expensive expedition out into the Atlantic under the command of the excitable young Italian but to despatch a single caravel to investigate the western seas. King John, somewhat faithlessly, acceded to the suggestion : a caravel was secretly despatched.

It returned in the space of a week or so. Frightened on the

verge of the great cliff of ocean up which, homeward-bound, their vessel would never be able to climb again, the sailors had refused the expedition and put back into Lisbon.

§ 3

It was 1484. Donna Felipa was dead. Columbus, disgusted at the treatment meted out to him by the Bishop of Ceuta, resolved to remove himself together with his son Diego to Spain. Meantime he appears to have made a compact with brother Bartholomew. The brother was to go to England and lay before Henry VII the same proposals as Columbus himself was to carry to the Spanish court.

That court was at Cordova, actively engaged in preparations for the last campaign against the Moors in Spain. Ferdinand and Isabella had other tasks in hand than to pay overwhelming attention even to the highly vouched-for proposals of the skilled Genoan pilot, Messer Colombo. For Messer Colombo, his piety his guerdon, had found friends very speedily in Spain—lay, noble and ecclesiastic. His poet's fiery vision passed readily to imaginative, impractical people of like calibre to himself. He persisted ; his friends persisted ; and the king and queen were at length led to summon a junta of cosmographers at Salamanca in 1487—a junta deputed to test the claims and pretensions of the Genoese.

Columbus appeared before this junta, but with no more success than he had appeared before the council in Lisbon. He was later to represent it as packed with the orthodox flat-earth fanatics to a man. More probably there was hardly a member of the junta that did not believe the earth round. What they balked at was not the planet's sphericity, but Columbus's unsubstantiated statements that India was distant but a few days' sail across the Atlantic. Hard though the old legend dies, it is plain that the junta did not regard the Genoese as a "round-earth irresponsible" but merely as a romancer and an incompetent. In both accounts they were as correct as they were mistaken in dismissing the romancing as inconsiderable.

They decided that the project was "vain and impossible, and that it did not belong to the majesty of such great princes to determine anything upon such weak grounds of information".

Columbus's counter-arguments are not recorded. It is probable that indeed they were not very convincing. For of all things it is plain that the pious young poet was as poor a theoretician as a seaman—his cosmographical ideas were medieval, long years behind those of the junta. He seems to have urged nothing more original than that to the west there lay great tracts of island and unknown country (the Madeira pilot had supplied him with proof); and perhaps backed up this statement by invoking the authority of that Marco Polo who had spoken of the many-islanded Pacific.

However, his persistence won from Ferdinand and Isabella the statement that they did not definitely reject his proposition. When the war was ended. . . .

From camp to camp and city to city, as the campaign progressed, Columbus pursued the court through a long five years of solicitation. He must have become a wearying figure in the sight of one at least of their majesties of Spain. Yet they were impressed: his poetic earnestness and devoutness impressed, if his cosmographical arguments seemed feeble. Various sums of money were granted him for his private expenses, he was billeted near the court as a public functionary. Ceaselessly he argued and intrigued, attempting to make influential friends, to obtain introductions here and encouragement there. Juan Perez de la Marchena, guardian of the monastery of La Rabida near the little town of Palos, became a close friend. Perez had once been the confessor of Queen Isabella. Now he agreed to take young Diego and educate him while tall, ruddy, mendacious, scoundrelly-poetic Christopher pursued his two loves—the courtship of the favour of the Queen, and the seduction, courtship and marriage—in that order—of the pious, complacent, and poverty-stricken Beatriz Enriquez de Arana. (Beatriz, wedded and bedded, was thereafter alternately maltreated and mislaid.)

But at length he left the court in complete despair, and repaired to Palos to fetch Diego. He had determined to depart to the French court and try his fortunes there—his brother had failed with singular completeness to impress the cautious-minded King of England. Arriving at Palos, he told of this project to Perez and the chief shipowner of Palos, one Martin Alonzo Pinzon. For different reasons they were dismayed—Pinzon also had transatlantic venturings in mind. Perez wrote to the queen begging her once again to pay heed to the suit of Columbus; and once again the kindly Isabella consented, remitting sufficient money to allow him to return to the court. Negotiations (as they might now be termed) were resumed.

They were speedily broken off. The cost of the expedition was negligible and easily raised: the personal claims of Columbus were considered outrageous. The dispassionate observer of later times can hardly fail to agree. Like most visionaries and poets, Columbus was as mercenary as he was mendacious. He believed very vividly he might attain the Earthly Paradise—failing it, Cipangu—by a westwards voyage of a few days' duration. And for such kingly attainment should there not be a kingly award? . . . Tall, ruddy, greying of hair, he would expound his sureties in the Palos monastery, in the Cordova Court, and believe them all very truly himself. But now and again, perhaps in the dead of night—he would wake up and stare a moment of bewildered fear at his true foundationings—the affirmations of a strayed sailor foisted upon the book-learnt visionings of a Genoan cloth-chapman. . . .

He set out a second time for France; piqued, Queen Isabella had him again recalled, and again opened negotiations. Ferdinand, the sardonic Ferdinand, kept apart from the negotiations. He seems to have had little liking and less respect for Columbus: he was merely another of Isabella's hare-brained paupers. . . . But now the negotiations proceeded apace. An agreement was drawn up and signed: an agreement which conceded Columbus all his demands, on the understanding that he himself was to pay an eighth of the cost of the expedition.

The total cost of that expedition, on which Columbus had spent seven years of debate and argument at the Spanish court, was less than £400. Wool-carder Colombo of Genoa rode down to Palos Admiral Cristóbal Colon.

Palos was ordered to provide two of the vessels, and a third one was chartered. The enrolling of crews proved a difficulty. Death by drowning was as little popular in that day as in this; and, whatever the imaginings of Isabella, seamen at least knew the Admiral no sailor. However, a proclamation of immunity from all civil and criminal processes was issued for all persons taking part in the expedition. As a result, the more desperate of the criminals and debtors of Spain flocked down to Palos. The Pinzon family proved active in providing men and materials: those friendly Pinzons whose friendship was to fail the test of the voyage.

None of the three vessels was of more than a hundred tons burden. Only one, the *Santa Maria*, in which the noble Don Cristóbal Colon himself took up residence, was decked throughout. For navigator and captain—he himself hardly capable of navigation—he chose one Juan de la Cosa. The other two ships, the *Pinta* and the *Niña*, were half-decked caravels under the commands of Martin Alonzo Pinzon and Vincente Yanez Pinzon. The total numbering of the expedition was a hundred and twenty souls, including an Irishman, William Herries, and an Englishman, Arthur Lake.

On the 4th of August, 1492, the expedition set sail from the Bar of Saltes, commissioned under the new admiral, not, as was afterwards told, to reach the coast of Asia, but "to discover and acquire certain islands and mainland in the Ocean".

§ 4

The Canaries were reached in the course of a few days. The weather was mild and beneficent. Yet the caravel *Pinta* had unshipped her rudder, apparently at the instigation of her commander, Martin Alonzo Pinzon, who had began to regret his share in the undertaking. Columbus, fuming, half scared perhaps already to be actually launched, must halt while the *Pinta* was repaired. News was brought him that three Portuguese ships were lying off the Canaries, Government vessels which intended to intercept the expedition, for Columbus was venturing out on *mare incognita* which was under the dominion of Portugal. The Admiral seems to have been little perturbed: with chance, tide, and the terror of navigation to face, what were a few Portuguese? The convoy again in order, he sailed from Gomera in the Canaries on the ninth of September.

Thereafter the tale of the voyage is largely an abridgment from that doubtful journal which only doubtfully can be ascribed to Columbus's own hand. Greatly helped by the north-east trade winds, he sailed on day after day, almost due west, into the unknown waters. Such was the speed of the vessels that Columbus—apparently with the complicity of his navigator, for he could not have done it alone—commenced a remarkable deception. This was the keeping of two logs—one for his own private record, one to deceive the sailors. In the sailors' log the distance was falsified and minimized as much as possible, in order that their unquenched fears of the Ocean might not overflow. (Such is the story: but what of the logs of the *Pinta* and the *Niña* under the hostile Pinzons?)

Still, unhastening but unceasing, the trade wind blew the three small ships westwards over that untenanted sea of great waves and dipping stars. September nights came down cool and quiet and unruffled over the mysterious flow and glow of the combers. On the evening of the 13th it was found that the compass needle had declined to the north-west. On the morning of the 14th the declination was abruptly to the north-east. It was the first time this variation had been noted by Europeans. On that 14th also the sailors on the *Niña* looked out and saw two great birds hovering in the sky—tropical birds such as were common to Africa, they thought, and never seen far from land. Land must be near.

In the evening of the next day a great meteor woke the twilight of the sky, flashing ensaffroned in the sea ahead. The sailors' fears received a stabbing poignancy. Was it a sign from God of His displeasure? Columbus paced his deck, apparently stolid and cool, inwardly probably the prey of acute fears. What now of his belief in the nearness of Antilia—what if there were *no* Antilia? He soothed his crews and the ships sailed on.

Next day, the 16th, they found themselves on the verge of a great plain of seaweed, stretching remotely to the horizons. In the morning light those plains rose and shook their strange forms, as though alive, and to the sailors it seemed they had come to a place neither land nor sea, but a swamp on the verge of the Abyss. All day the three small ships ploughed steadily westwards, still with the north-easter behind them, cutting through the clinging weeds of the Sargasso Sea. Night sank on the great green plains, unended. Next morning they found themselves still sailing the great weed-fringed lagoons. This morning they caught a crab, from which the admiral "inferred that they could not be more than eighty leagues from land"! His certainty had returned: he would lie himself to the ends of the Ocean.

His remarkable inference appears to have calmed his

companions. Next day many birds were seen in the sky and a great massing of clouds. Drizzling rains—land rains—came with nightfall. Land was certainly near.

But still there came no land. Columbus was made privy to a plot hatched on his own ship—"that it would be the best plan to throw him quietly into the sea, and say he unfortunately fell in while he stood absorbed in looking at the stars". He guarded himself accordingly, knowing that his companions' fears were like to mount into madness because of that very wind which drove them still steadily westwards. They had come to the conclusion that there were no winds on those seas to take them back to Spain.

But a contrary wind arose, calming this fear, and with lessened speed the three small ships beat forward into it. Drifting grass patched the sea. Far in the south-west arose a great shadow on the sky. Columbus altered his course to make it. Land was near.

But it was no land, only a cloud-shape that altered and melted as the *Santa Maria* drew nigh.

On the 3rd of October there were again signs of land, and the crew would have had Columbus stop and beat about in search of it. But he had been deceived too often. In later days he was to ascribe that determination to sail still further west to his determination to reach the "Indies". Rather we may be certain it was merely a confusion of his own uncertainties.

But now the crew of the *Santa Maria* at least was quite definitely mutinous, and Columbus had to set himself to pacifying them by as strange a collection of threats and promises and lies as ever the commander of an expedition addressed to his followers. What would happen to them in Spain should they indeed sail back without him—or against his orders? What would their women-folk say of them? Think of the riches of these lands in the west that awaited their conquest. . . . Day after day, and hour after hour, between the times of those nervous pacings of the deck, he argued and soothed the mutineers. But at last it seems that they refused the direct westwards course. Martin Alonzo Pinzon came from the *Pinta* and headed the mutineers. A compromise was arrived at. On the 7th of October the course of the vessels was altered to the south-west.

Four days later, and still the seas were untenanted. Then,

the thirty-third day of sailing from the Canaries, a "table-board" and a carved wand, the carving apparently wrought by "some metal instrument" were fished up over the side of the *Santa Maria*. (Or did the Admiral drop them over the side and then fish them up again ?) Sailors in one of the caravels about the same time saw a drifting branch "with berries fresh upon it". Land was certainly near.

§ 5

And at last, indeed, those fragments of flotsam and jetsam were justified. The afternoon passed with no sign of land ahead, but at night, near ten o'clock, while Columbus was pacing the poop he saw a light low in the west, and called Pedro Gutierrez to witness it. The two of them stood there and peered into the still night-smother, and again the light flashed and winked low down in the waters. . . . They make a fine and significant picture, those first of deliberate explorers from the Mediterranean, seeing that first gleam betokening human habitation in the unknown Americas.

They called the "overlooker" who had been deputed by the Spanish court to witness all the actions and transactions of Columbus, and Rodrigo Sanchez came slowly and unwillingly and stood between the Admiral and Gutierrez, and with them looked into the west. Once again the light flashed, and Columbus in some excitement drew Sanchez' attention to it. At first the cautious "overlooker" professed himself unable to see anything. But in a little even he could not deny the evidence of his eyes. Light it was—"it appeared like a candle that went up and down, and Don Christopher did not doubt that it was the true light, and that it was on land. And so it proved, for it came from people passing with lights from one hut to another."

There was no sleep on board the three vessels standing off with furled sails that night. Of Columbus's thoughts we may guess : What was this land—Antilia, Cipangu, Wineland, or (Mother of God ! he crossed himself in the dark) the Fortunate Isle, the Earthly Paradise itself. . . . And he, *he*, the non-sailor, the cloth-chapman of the Levant, had been guided by God to its shores. . . .

A reward of ten thousand maravedis had been promised

by the Queen to whosoever should first sight land. At two o'clock in the morning of the twelfth a sailor on the *Pinta*, one Rodrigo de Triana, called out that he saw land ahead; he was not mistaken. A low shore, tree-clad, was coming up out of the mists of dawn. The vessels stood in towards it and cast anchor.

It was the greatest moment in the life of that strange, ruddy, grey-haired, devout and scoundrelly poet who was the Admiral. He had the boats manned and himself clad in full armour and carrying in his hand the royal banner of Spain was rowed to the shore. The Pinzons, also banner-bearing, put out from the *Pinta* and the *Niña*. The armed crews blew on the lights of their match-locks and stared over the shoulders of the rowers at the nearing beach—no deserted beach at all, but one in the morning light crowded with a throng of men and women such as no Europeans had ever seen—tall and naked and staring their surprise in silence upon the newcomers.

Perhaps they gave back a little, those nude primitives, as the strangers landed. Columbus fell to his knees as soon as his foot touched the strand of the unknown country, and offered up thanks to his God for having so preserved him and justified him. All the rest of the Spaniards knelt as well, and then pressed round the Admiral, excitably, many of them in tears, to cry his pardon for their doubts of him and their threatened mutinies. It was an affecting moment, and no doubt the simple islanders, standing watching, thought it so as well. They little realized how prophetic it was—those tears shed by the first white men who came to their island.

The scene may be best seen through the eyes of the islanders of Guanahani—that island that is now Watling Island of the Bahamas. They had lived all their lives on that island, as their fathers before them through long millennia, a corner and outpost of the human drift, almost the last men of the Golden Age that survived in the Central Americas. They were without tools or weapons, classes or wars, gods or kings, simple and kindly children of the earth and sea, Natural Men as once were all our fathers. And up out of the morning had come sailing those strange beings, so strangely shrouded and clad, who were yet evidently men like themselves, albeit overmen as well. They saw the strange beings kneel and cry aloud in strange, harmful ways, as though in fear or pain, and drew a little nearer, helpfully. But the incantations were no more than the spoken words with which the Admiral was taking possession of the land in the names of their majesties the King and Queen of Spain.

The Spaniards saw they had nothing to fear from the natives who flocked about them in simple friendliness. By signs Columbus gathered that the name of the island was Guanahani. Calmly obliterating its name even as he had annexed its territory, he re-christened it San Salvador. The sun was shining and the air clear and sweet; and looking over the heads of the naked islanders he saw all their land behind them in "the likeness of a great garden". He looked at the children of this second Eden, and for perhaps a while saw them with strange clarity as the innocent and happy souls they were, paradisal folk whose paradise his coming was to end for ever. But that moment passed quickly enough:

> Because they had much friendship for us, and because I knew they were people that would deliver themselves better to the Christian faith, and be converted more through love than by force, I gave to some of them coloured caps and some strings of beads for their necks, and many other things of little value, with which they were delighted, and were so entirely ours that it was a marvel to see. The same afterwards came swimming to the ship's boats where we lay, and brought us parrots, and cotton threads in balls, and darts and many other things. These they bartered with us for things which we gave them, such as bells and small glass beads. In fine, they took and gave all of whatever they had with good will. But it appeared to me they were a people very poor in everything. They went totally naked, as naked as their mothers brought them into the world.

They were tall and red-skinned and handsome folk; they painted themselves, for amusement, agreeably; they knew nothing of arms or warlike practices—one took hold of a Spanish sword by the blade, and hurt himself. Even their darts were merely for the chase. "And I believe they would easily be converted to Christianity, for it appeared to me that they had no creed."

Even so, they had also an obvious independence and wildness that gnawed a little at the edge of this good opinion. It was the wildness and intractability of the free wild animal. Satisfied that their island contained nothing of note or worth, Columbus had the ships weigh anchor. All the surrounding seas they saw as they coasted slowly down Guanahani in the sun of that day, islanded unendingly. Columbus remembered back into his early readings. Could these, the islands of the Madeira pilot, be also the islands of Marco Polo ?

Five leagues from San Salvador, that re-christened Guanahani, they came to another island, which the Admiral named Concepcion. Here, even at such close quarters, he found a slightly different type of life than at Guanahani. Here the natives were cultivators of the Archaic Culture—that culture that was slowly seeping though the Americas from its focal points in Central America and Peru. It had been carried to the West Indies by the Caribs, who themselves had acquired it far up in the head-waters of the Amazon, where that river's tributaries rise in Peru. Raiders and head-hunters, the Caribs had settled here and there amidst the Golden Age peoples of the islands. Some islands—such as Guanahani—they had missed entirely ; some—as portions of that Cuba now undistant from the *Santa Maria's* course—they dominated entirely. Concepcion was in a midway condition : the state of happy, primal innocence had been lost, but it was still a benevolent thing, this new culture, ruled benevolently by its little sun-kings.

And now the Iron Age had come upon its world.

§ 6

In one of the Islands of Santa Maria de Concepcion the eyes of the Admiral and his crews feasted on the sight of some trivial golden ornaments which the natives wore. These were regarded by the folk of the Archaic civilization (we know) not as jewels or money, but as mystic Givers of Life. To Columbus's Spaniards gold also was a Giver of Life—but in no mystic sense at all. With eagerness they questioned the natives : where did the gold come from ? "From Cubanacan", was the answer, the natives pointing south.

Incredibly enough, Columbus took this word for a corruption of Kublai Khan—the great emperor of Marco Polo's journey, dead two hundred years. He hastily assembled his ships and coasted hurriedly southwards to the court of Cathay.

Island on island confirmed the tidings : southwards was the land of gold. Sometimes the name Cubanacan was varied greatly. But at length they came to the shores of the veritable El Dorado itself.

It was Cuba.

They coasted along the north-eastern part, questioning the natives who put out in canoes. Gold ?—gold came from the interior, from the mines of Ciboa.

The Admiral despatched two discoverers into that interior —one a Jew who spoke Hebrew, Chaldee and Arabic, and so would be able to converse with Kublai Khan on the terms of the utmost familiarity. The "discoverers" came on neither Mongols or gold ; instead, the first recorded Europeans to view the practice, they came on tribes which indulged in tobacco-smoking, an astounding and wizard-like practice. Everywhere in those clearings of the Archaic folk of the Americas they were treated with kindness and hospitality.

Meantime, in the vessels, things had gone not so well. Martin Alonzo Pinzon and the *Pinta* disappeared. Anchored off the territory of a chief called Guacanagari, Columbus had the *Santa Maria* wrecked in a shore-wind ; he and his crew decamped to the crowded *Niña*. Only one vessel was left with which he might return to Spain, and his crews, their enthusiasm considerably cooled, were becoming more and more insistent that he should set about that return. He resolved to establish a colony on Guacanagari's land. Still news of Kublai delayed.

Then the Jew returned : No Kublai, no golden city, nothing but leagues of bush had been encountered. The Admiral scolded him bitterly : the poet was fading to a ghost below the armour of the gold-seeker. . . . And now he might delay his return no longer.

The timbers of the *Santa Maria* were salvaged and the fort of La Navidad built. Forty men—including the Englishman and the Irishman—were left to garrison it. Then, on the 4th of January, 1493, the Admiral launched the *Niña* on her return voyage.

§ 7

Meantime Pinzon in the *Pinta*, deliberately separating himself from the company of the Admiral (whom he appears to have despised very thoroughly) had set out in search of the rumoured islands of gold. Several days' sailing the Cuban coasts had brought him no fabulous mines or cities, but

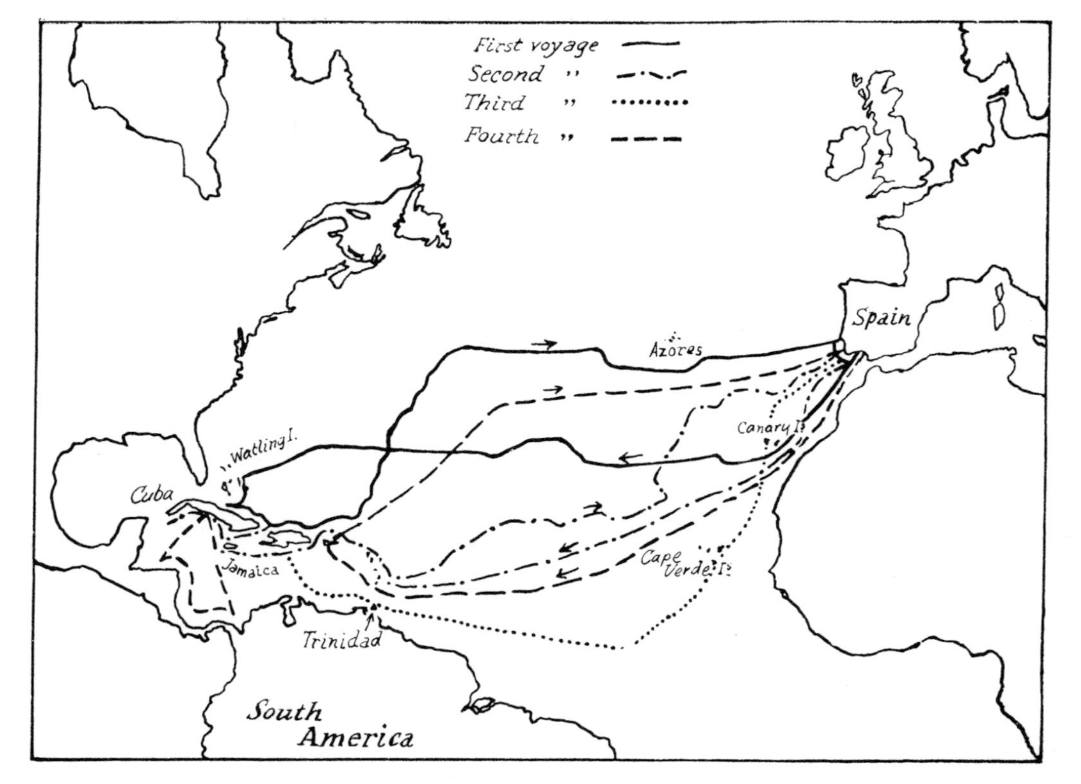

THE VOYAGES OF COLUMBUS

southwards, in an unknown bay, he had encountered natives who possessed the metal in considerable abundance. Probably they looked a sturdy breed, well able to defend themselves, not the unarmed and fenceless primitives of Guanahani. Instead of securing the gold by force Pinzon obtained a fairly large supply by barter, and turned the prow of the *Pinta* homeward.

It is a remote quarrel, that of Columbus and Pinzon, in which geographers for four hundred years have found it good to debate. Little sympathy has been given to Pinzon: he has been portrayed, unendingly, as a mean and evil personage sabotaging the schemes of the high-minded dreamer and planner who commanded the expedition. But we may see the matter with clearer eyes. Pinzon owned the *Pinta* and probably the *Niña*; it was at Pinzon's suggestion—or perhaps command—that the expedition had turned southwards on October the 7th and so come on land at all. Possibly he considered himself as well qualified as Columbus to claim the discoveries. And he had certainly more than the shadow of a case.

Unfortunately, homeward bound on the 6th of January, in the teeth of a head wind, his look-out sighted the *Niña*. Both ships, almost simultaneously, had to put about and shelter behind a headland, and Pinzon, to his chagrin, discovered the Admiral was on board the other caravel. He re-submitted himself with surly apologies to Columbus's command, though it does not seem that he shared out the gold with the second ship. Nor does it seem that Columbus pressed him hard in the matter. But discovering half a dozen natives in the *Pinta* whom Pinzon had abducted from an island, intending to carry them into slavery across the Atlantic, Columbus commanded that they be released. He refused, with a singular clear-eyedness, to disturb that harmony in which the natives had received them. The Indians who ultimately accompanied them back to Spain were volunteers.

Ten days later the head-wind abated. Coasting Hayti, the Admiral reluctantly abandoned further research along those alluring shores. The wind blew now for Spain.

But presently it died; they fought back in the teeth of adverse breezes. The *Pinta*, with her rudder uncertain as of old, retarded the passage. On the 12th of February they encountered the first of the great Atlantic storms. For three days it raged, the caravels scudding before it with bare poles. On the night of the fourteenth the signal-lights of the *Pinta* disappeared, and Columbus's own crew on the *Niña* gave up all hope of their own safety, relapsing into one of those sudden and easy despairs characteristic of their period and religion. But the ruddy, grey-haired, mendacious poet who commanded them lost neither his fortitude nor his faith. He commanded that they load the empty water-casks with sea-water, the better to ballast the caravel; and in a prayer swore that as soon as they sighted land he and his crew would walk barefoot, in penitential garments, to the first church dedicated to the Virgin. The Atlantic, soothed by this promise or restrained by the providential ballast, drove the *Niña* headlong eastwards, but declined to devour it.

Even so, the Admiral appears to have reflected that there were mischances between both of these powers which he had called to his aid. Accordingly, he wrote out a brief account of his voyage and discoveries, enclosed it in wax, sealed it in a small cask, and consigned it to the deep. Scarcely had he done so than the greater fury of the storm abated. The curling green monsters that had hurled them into the night had tamed by the morning of the 15th of February. Land was sighted—and almost instantly lost again in the smother. It was the Azores.

On the night of the seventeenth other islands were sighted, and the *Niña* lost an anchor in endeavouring to bring up under their coasts. But when the next morning came they succeeded in anchoring off the Portuguese island of St. Mary.

Here, landing in accordance with their vow, half of the crew, barefoot and clad in their shirts, were making pilgrimage to the chapel of St. Mary when they were ambushed by the Portuguese and taken prisoner. Breechless, they appear to have put up no resistance whatever. The Admiral, left on the *Niña* with only three sailors, had the anchor raised and beat away from St. Mary's. But presently his ardour and determination revived. It was impossible that the Portuguese should flout the royal warrant of Ferdinand and Isabel. He sailed back and held a parley with the governor of St. Mary's. Reluctantly that individual agreed that Spain and Portugal were at peace and that the seizure of the be-shirted crew had been unwarranted. They were restored to the *Niña*; Columbus steered for Spain.

More storms intervened to stay the voyage. The coasts of Europe were strewn with wrecks. But again, as that morning at Guanahani, it was Columbus's hour. He rode the *Niña* in triumph into the mouth of the Tagus on the 4th of March, 1493, after eight months absence from the shores of Spain.

§ 8

The Portuguese king proved more than friendly: he claimed that Columbus had acted as one of his own pilots. For was not all that stretch of the Ocean under the rule of Portugal? The Admiral declined to recognize the plea, and sailed for Palos.

On the 15th of March he sailed into the port where the expedition had been raised and staffed with the criminal off-scourings of the Spanish prisons. Two Pinzons he brought back, but the other, together with the rudderless *Pinta*, had apparently vanished in the troughs of the Atlantic. Columbus hastily indited letters to the king and queen, then at Barcelona, and prepared himself to set out for court.

But meantime Martin Alonzo Pinzon, undrowned, had succeeded in steering the damaged *Pinta* into Bayonne. From there, almost at the same day as Columbus reached Palos, he despatched letters to Barcelona describing his voyage and discoveries, and making no mention of Columbus. It seemed a neck and neck race: never did Columbus's fortunes hang so precariously in the balance. But the Court without any hesitation recognized their duly appointed commander: Pinzon received an order not to appear at court except in the train of the Admiral. Coupled with other ills suffered in steering the *Pinta* across the wild seas the news was too much for the Palos shipmaster. He lay dying in Bayonne on the day when Columbus marched in triumphal procession through the streets of Barcelona, his six Indians, parrot-laden in his train, staring their astonishment and disquiet upon this strange world in the maw of the sunrise.

Ferdinand and Isabella received him as a conquering prince. He was granted a coat of arms; the title Don was bestowed on him and his brothers and descendants for ever after. He was made a handsome allowance and was served at table as a grandee.

He was the most honoured man in all Spain, and the

most sought after. Sometimes, perhaps, he communed still at night with the Levantine chapman. Sometimes, drowning away from his own eyes all glory in his achievement, must have come memory of his mistreatment of the Pinzons, knowledge that though he had found new lands by the chances of luck and mislore he had still no notion what lands they were. Supposing one were the Earthly Paradise itself cravenly abandoned by him? . . . He would turn to prayer and new resolves for the new expedition.

His title of Viceroy of the new lands was confirmed, and he was appointed to command the new venture hastily prepared. For Portugal was laying serious claim to the discoveries. Ferdinand and Isabella, having finished with and finished the Moors, were eager to acquire new lands and convert fresh batches of the heathen. (Columbus's six natives were baptized with great enthusiasm, and one of them, dying shortly afterwards, was solemnly adjudged the "first of his race to enter Paradise".)

Seventeen ships were chartered or commandeered for the new expedition. Mattocks, spades, seeds, and plants were loaded aboard them for the colonization of the islands. Men flocked to volunteer for the new expedition—in the end the squadron sailed with a complement of more than fifteen hundred men. Among these were twelve priests, sent to convert the natives—the "Indians", as they were already called, for at last it had been decided by the cosmographers that the Admiral's discoveries had been in the neighbourhood of India.

The Admiral himself seems to have been less sure—he wavered in belief between Cipangu, India, and the outskirts of the Grand Khan's dominions. But for the urgings of the crew of the *Niña*, he gave it out, he might even have sailed into the harbours of golden Opir or scriptural Havilah. He had done no more, he affirmed, than touch on the outermost and barbarous fringe of a great and wealthy continent, where there was great treasure to be found and great hosts of souls to be saved.

In that conviction—and indeed, though in another sense, it was to be justified by the subsequent adventurings of his countrymen—he sailed west in command of the new expedition from the harbour of Cadiz on the 25th of September, 1493.

§9

They sailed a prosperous passage, untroubled but by one brief storm. Holding south of the route of the first expedition, on Sunday the 3rd of November they had their first sight of the New Lands. The island they came to was one of the Lesser Antilles, and christened Dominica by the pious Admiral from the fact of it being discovered on a Sunday. It was uninhabited. Cuba, with its colony and fort of La Navidad, he knew lay to the north-west, and cruised slowly along the Lesser Antilles group in that direction. The perfection of the weather held and with it the high spirits of the thousand and a half adventurers aboard. Their eyes were dazzled with the sheen of brilliant seas and brilliant vegetation, the colourful sunrises and sunsets of those sleeping sea-lands that verily seemed "islets of Paradise" to their ocean-weary eyes.

But landing at a new island, Guadaloupe, they discovered horror. The inhabitants were no simple primitives, but cannibal Caribs of a high scale of culture, with well-built huts and roads, and parcels of dried human flesh hung in those huts. Guadaloupe's menfolk were absent on some sea-raid, and the explorers saw only the women and children. They embarked after a hasty and horrified search and hastily sailed north.

Passing clusters of small islands on the way, they came to one lovely and large and fertile—St. John, as the Admiral named it, though it was afterwards re-named Porto Rico. In its loveliness, as in Guadaloupe, only man was vile: cannibalism was the mainstay of the Carib populace. Originally, as we of a later day know, this cannibalism had been religious and ceremonial in origin among the Carib tribes in the valley of the Amazon. But it had developed beyond that ceremonial usage. Large animals which could be used for food were scarce in the Lesser Antilles: anthropophagy, inaugurated by religious ritual, had become an economic way of salvation.

But the Spaniards knew nothing of these facts. To them it was a terrifying and disgusting practice, the mark of beasts, not men. It may be that it was in Porto Rico and in Guadaloupe that there developed that first savagery towards the West Indians which led to their ultimate extermination. That the primitives of the northern islands, the Bahamas, were neither Caribs nor cannibals mattered little to the Spaniard in pursuit of gold or slaves. He could salve his conscience and every murder by thinking of his victims as eaters of men.

The squadron coasted along Cuba and reached La Navidad. The fort had disappeared : it had been razed to the ground. The forty who had been left to man it had vanished—all but a few poor skeletons and rusting fragments of armour. While the dismayed Spaniards surveyed the ruins of the fort messengers came to them from Guacanagari with the tale of La Navidad's end. The forty whom Columbus had left to seal the friendship of Europe and America had from the beginning displayed an amazing insolence and licentiousness. They had wandered the island, taking what they would, interfering with the Indians, loud, braggart and boastful. Finally a neighbouring chief could bear with them no longer. He had raised an army and marched it against the fort, destroyed it, and killed the garrison. Guacanagari himself had been wounded in defence of the white men.

Such was the story. Possibly Guacanagari himself had played a less innocent part. Even so, it seemed even to the Admiral, remembering the quality of those he had left behind, that the chief might have been justified. It was plainly impossible to think of rebuilding La Navidad. The native Cubans had soured of the white men and their ways.

But a site and the building of a town were essential, for the overloaded convoy already groaned with sick and wearied men who cried for land, sight of the treasures which had drawn them from their homes in Spain. Columbus turned the squadron about and coasted down to Hayti. Ar Cape Haytien he anchored and set about disembarking stores and men on the jungly beach, there to rear the first European city of the New World, Isabella.

Isabella progressed but slowly. The men were tired and sick. But now the Admiral came out in less pleasing colours than in those days in Spain when he had been the gracious magnate receiving colleagues in a golden enterprise. He drew up regulations for labour, and enforced them ruthlessly, himself the while maintaining all the ceremonial state which he considered a viceroy's due. Isabella progressed amidst quarrels and dissensions. Provisions ran short ; medical supplies gave out, and it was soon obvious to Columbus that the financial strain of the colony would be very bitterly resented in Spain. Accordingly, he despatched an envoy to Ferdinand and Isabella with the proposal that the current expenses might be paid for by capturing hordes of the cannibal Indians and shipping them to Spain as slaves. This, he thought, "would be very good for their souls". . . .

He was a poet, with the ruthlessness and shiftiness of the poetic temperament. Like factors conditioned his greed —there was no strange and abrupt transformation of Paradise-seeker to slave-trader. He remained sincerely and righteously both—the slaves an economic necessity both for the quest of God's City on Earth and the maintenance in due state of the seeker God-appointed.

Slave hunting developed rapidly as a commercial activity among sea-parties despatched from Isabella. Specimens of the cattle were shipped to Spain. Meantime, the gold mines of Ciboa had been found and workings there had begun under the Spaniards, the natives having been violently dispossessed. Columbus concluded that the new settlement might be left to its own defences a while; and in mid-April himself put to sea in search of the golden land.

For five months he cruised to and fro the Jamaican seas, discovering Jamaica itself and a host of islets amidst which his squadron almost foundered. On this voyage it was that he came to an island off which a strange craft was seen—a canoe with sails, manned by cotton-clad canoemen. They gestured that they came from still further to the west, and the heart of Columbus, seeing their evident degree of civilization, rose high within him. What could they be but natives of Cathay?

However, he had no time to pursue investigations in that still unknown west. Isabella called him back. First cruising across the Lesser Antilles, he set his men slave-catching among the cannibals, then turned towards Hispaniola.

Hispaniola he found in confusion and turmoil. A gang of malcontents whom he had sent from Isabella to survey the country had roused all the Indians against them. Everywhere the enraged natives of the Archaic Civilization were rising against this new horror that the Iron Civilization had brought. One of their chiefs with a numerous array was marching on Isabella itself.

Columbus was down with fever when his squadron put in at Isabella. But at this news of the natives in arms he bestirred himself with a pious energy, confident that God would give the victory to His Christians. Brother Bartholomew had arrived from Spain. Leaving him in command of Isabella, the Admiral marched against the Indians.

It was a day of broiling heat and in the still air the corslets of the Spaniards were stiflingly hot. But they winked with a dreadful sheen in the eyes of the Indians with their stone-tipped spears and wicker shields. The natives charged with great bravery, and the Spaniards opened fire.

In a few minutes the fate of the battle was decided, the Indians flying in rout, hotly pursued by the Admiral's Christian bloodhounds. Four shiploads of slaves were captured, whipped back along the tracks to Isabella, and then despatched to Spain.

Caonabo, who had destroyed the fort of La Navidad, was also in arms. The Dons Bartolomeo and Cristóbal Colon marched against him with two hundred men, defeating him with great carnage. Everywhere the Indians were vanquished and those captured in arms enslaved. Caonabo himself was captured by treachery, and despatched to Spain for judgment as a "rebel". Maliciously he insisted on dying during the voyage, thus escaping the wheel or the stake, the first of the heroic native soldiers of the Americas who were to resist the invaders. His place is with Mochcovoh the Mayan, Quatemoc the Aztec, and the great "Stony-Face" of Peru.

Tribute was now imposed on the Indians of Hispaniola, and a general system of vassalage, land-slavery, implemented for those unfortunate denizens of the Utmost Americas. With a pious wish to save their souls and keep in being his correct number of footmen, the Admiral who four years before had spoken of the "free and simple folk" of Guanahani, now instituted a regular and unceasing trade in human flesh on a scale which would have made the cannibals of Guadaloupe blanch with horror.

But things in the colony itself went from bad to worse. They are hardly the concern of the record which deals with geographical quest not that pitiful tale of insult and blood and tears that has marched with colonial conquest. But their effects on the fortunes of the exploring Admiral were profound, if they left his strangely scoundrelly-idealistic nature unchanged.

In consequence of the complaints against Columbus's insufferable despotism a commissioner was despatched to Isabella by the King and Queen. He arrived in October of 1495, heard the evidence preferred against the Admiral, and drew up a report. There was no lack of evidence. Settlers and thieves, colonists and Indians, flocked to him with the terrible tale of the vivid injustices suffered under the rule of the devout Genoan, whose poetic soul was sorely vexed at the island's ingratitude. He resolved to return to Spain and justify himself before the court.

He boarded the *Niña*. At that Aquado, fearing lest his report might be forestalled, boarded another caravel. A passion for evacuation seized the Spaniards. Loaded caravels put out one after the other from Isabella, seeking the Atlantic loaded with misfortune and complaint. Bartholomew was left to misgovern Hispaniola.

Provisions grew scarce as the voyage proceeded. The ships were loaded with Indian slaves whom the crews threatened to kill and devour. It seemed that the Christians had become infected with anthropophagy as well. Columbus, heedful to the value of his cargoes, dissuaded them, and the starving convoy reached the Bay of Cadiz in safety.

Here, with that practical unimaginativeness that stamped his quality, Columbus decided on marching through the country in such triumphal procession as had witnessed his return from the first expedition. He proceeded towards the court in glittering garments, on horseback, followed by chain-gangs of Indians. But everywhere he was greeted with reproaches or derision, for news of these two years' failures was well known in Spain. Men shouted insults and women reproaches. Where were the gold mines of Havilah ? Where was the Earthly Paradise ? Was that Indian the Grand Khan —and that other—a Grander Khan ? Where were their husbands, their sons, lured across the seas by his promises, hanging roasted and dead in some cannibal hut ? . . . The reception accorded him by the King and Queen was courteously polite, no more. He was not placed on trial as Aguado and Bishop Fonseca would have liked. But his pleas for money for a further expedition were put aside into a limbo of innumerable delays.

He was a broken man. Some few of that great flock of imaginative mendacities he had unloosed upon the world had come home to roost. Here, to all seeming, ended both his quests and his discoveries.

§ 10

But behind that sanguine mask (that had acquired in his brief years of success a haughty pride) there was still indomitable if indefinite will, indomitable faith in his own fabrications and the romantic readings of the wool-carder chapman. If the Earthly Paradise sank a little from hope his cosmographical notions were still medieval. No less so were his historical notions. He was convinced that beyond those islands that had brought him little but false hope and disaster lay the golden lands of Ind or the pearly lands of Cathay. And it was his duty as a Christian to seek out those lands and win the inhabitants to the true faith—winning for himself a due pittance in wealth as reward.

For two years he badgered the court; and at length began to wear down the resistance of Ferdinand and Isabella, fundamentally kindly people, a pair who could not forget the vague glory that the Admiral's discoveries had attached to their names. It was true that except as a breeding-ground for criminals and a spawning-ground for a very ineffective kind of slave, the Indies as yet had proved of little value. But what if the Admiral were right in his further assertions—that as yet they had but touched the fringes of the great Western lands that might verily be the Eastern lands of rumour and wealth?

Indeed, it was now more than rumour that a great Western mainland existed. Sailing with English ships, Sebastian Cabot had set eyes on the North American continent and cruised along a wide section of its shore. Columbus, now that the king and queen had acceded to his fresh demand, determined to sail to the south, "well under the equinoctial line, for I believe that no one has ever traversed this way, and that this sea is nearly unknown".

(This sentence shows his uncertainty, his landsman's brief unfaiths in the dominant poet-prevaricator. For, as has been said, even before his first voyage all the western Mediterranean had been filled with rumours of the Atlantic lands.

And it was no impossibility that some such sailor as that Madeira pilot had indeed traversed these infra-equinoctial waters long before.)

With three ships he put out from the Cape Verde Islands on a voyage and in a spirit singularly reminiscent of that which characterized his first sailing. The trappings of viceroy were put by for the time. He was again the simple if inefficient commander of his ship, pacing the decks, staring at the bright Atlantic stars, shivering in the chill of a dense fog that fell on them on the 4th of July, 1498—a fog that "cut as with a knife". Presently the ships were again traversing those immense fields of shining seaweed—though now on their southern fringe. The wind died and a glassy calm came on the seas.

The ships moved slowly—as though some under-water current moved them, for the air was windless. To the Spaniards the eerie motion was terrifying. The heat grew stronger as the days went west, slowly, with limping feet, across the glassy stretches of water. Presently it became so dreadful that the crew refused to descend into the stench of the caravel's interior—even in order to succour their provisions and water. Men went mad and cried to God for relief from the burning intensity of the skies—a sky like a great inverted brazen bowl. Then at last, when it seemed that the expedition could endure no longer, a faint breeze rose and strengthened. It sent the scud flying and bellied out the heat-frayed sails of the ships. It drove them steadily west.

Three days later in the evening of the 22nd of July the look-outs saw great streaming flocks of birds against the sunset, homing towards the north-east. Land was again near, Columbus adjudged, despite the like portents on his first voyage which had betokened no land. Another week went by, bird-flights every evening dotting the signature of the sunset. Once a great albatross with wide-spreading wings came to rest on the rigging of the Admiral's own ship. Still there was no sight of land.

But on Thursday, the 31st of July, Columbus's outlook, Alonzo Perez, cast his eyes westwards from the mizzen and cried out that he saw land—far off, low down in the sea, three great peaks rising warmly coloured. It was that headland that later ages were to name Cape Cashepou, verily back-grounded by the three great peaks of Trinidad.

Columbus caused the vessels to cruise close in to the shore, but finding no suitable anchorage held on his course to the west. The shores of Trinidad unreeled before the staring eyes of the crews—shores with cultivated fields backgrounded by well-built huts. The Caribs ran and stared an even greater amazement than the Spaniards. Then darkness came down over the slow spread of Trinidad and the squadron kept on its cautious course still west.

Morning found them still coasting Trinidad. So much had the ships shrunk in the heat of the mid-Atlantic that they leaked like sieves and the Admiral scanned the coast with anxiety in search of a suitable harbourage for careening. Anchoring and taking in fresh water near Point Alcatraz, he obtained his first view of the coasts of the American continent—a long, low line of land with the running surf of the Orinoco a bright limning all along it. He took the continent for an island, and gave it the name of Zeta.

Coasting the richly cultivated and peopled coast, he entered the Gulf of Paria—entering it involuntarily through the high-ridged pressures of the Serpent's Mouth, where the autumn waters are caught betwixt Trinidad and the South American coasts and pour forth with impetuosity. The light ships of the Spaniards danced like corks, to the consternation of their crews. A canoe-full of Indians had put out from Trinidad that day to stare at the ship ; the Admiral, wishing to attract them, and doubtlessly abduct them, had his men play on a tambourine and dance on the poop. Recognizing these as indubitably warlike demonstrations, the Indians loosed a flight of arrows in reply and returned to the shore.

Inside the Serpent's Mouth, in the Gulf of Paria, the three ships cruised slowly up the American coast for several days finding the shores littered with heavily populated villages. Coming to the Paria Point, Columbus, repaying the natives their hospitality, abducted four of their number, and held on in search of Cipangu. At last they reached the second opening out of Paria, the Dragon's Mouth, and passed that in safety, coming again in the lie of the Lesser Antilles.

Asia and Havilah still delayed, but Margarita showed up the following day a blur upon the sea and sky. Columbus, albeit with absent-mindedness, reconnoitred its shores. But all the sailors, the soldiers, the pilots—and probably the cabin-boys—on board the three vessels had been confusing his never too-lucid mind from the moment they entered the Gulf of Paria. Sight of its raging waters—fresh water—had at first convinced the Admiral that what he had at first taken for an island was in reality a continent, and that continent of course Asia. He had proclaimed to the fleet that at last they had reached the richest land in the World. The fleet had been more than dubious. Some thought they had sailed round the shallow rim of the earth and were again near Africa. Some thought they were remote in the seas that fringe—of all places—Scotland . . . .

Columbus's mathematics collapsed under the strain of uncertainty. Desperately he resolved to sail at once and seek for Hispaniola—unless it also had vanished in some crinkle of the maps.

So Margarita was given but the most cursory of surveys; the Admiral fled northwards from his kingdoms of fantasy in search of recognizable geography.

§ II

For three years after reaching Hispaniola Columbus remained in control there. It was three years in which all that was best in Columbus—the visioning explorer, the attractive, if mendacious poet, the sincere, if fantastically romantic religious enthusiast—became obscured in the rôle of haughty governor and heaven-ordained viceroy. More darkly, they became obscured in the slave-trader. On the least pretext the miserable Indians of Hispaniola and the surrounding Islands were driven into rebellion, pursued with horses and bloodhounds, captured in hundreds and shipped to Spain for sale in the market of Seville.

At last this practice reached such limits that Ferdinand and Isabella—for their time enlightened rulers unless heretics were at hand—could bear with it no longer. They forbade a great sale in Seville and paid more attention to the constant stream of complaints that were launched against Columbus.

So serious were these and arriving in such volume that it was decided to despatch an investigator. He had no very definite orders, the Comendador Francisco de Bobadilla, but he was a fiery individual, and quite as egotistic as Columbus himself. Arriving in St. Domingo on the 23rd of

August, 1500, he took possession of the Admiral's house and summoned Columbus and his brothers to appear before him to answer innumerable charges.

News of this command flew abroad Hispaniola. The miserable Spanish colonists flocked to testify against their oppressor—the Genoan foreigner who had starved and bullied and beaten them while he himself lived in luxury surrounded by his brothers and favourites. These were the colonists. But some of the Catholic priests spoke for the Indians—Indians who had been left unbaptized in order that they might be enslaved, Indians on whom Columbus had raided and warred without cause or pretext till in the course of a short eight years he had transformed that sleepy garden of the Archaic Culture into a hell on earth. . . . Bobadilla, cold and contemptuous, heard the spluttered defence of the greying Admiral: and then ordered his arrest. His brothers were arrested at the same time, flung in chains, and shipped aboard a vessel bound for Spain.

With the chapman's plebeian theatricalism ousting the unauthentic aristocrat, Columbus insisted on wearing those chains even on board the vessel; he insisted that he would never have them removed except by royal command. The Spanish settlers crowded to watch him pass to the vessel and shout their execrations upon him. Flushed and haughty and tired, he walked through their midst without a glance.

News of the fashion in which he had arrived in Spain was carried to the court. The King and Queen, shocked at the arbitrary methods of Bobadilla, ordered him unchained and sent to the court in all honour.

Ferdinand, never the friend of the plausible, poetic Genoan, refused to grant him an audience. But Isabella received him semi-privately, and listened to his defence, and replied in words astounding enough in their reasonableness and humanity:

"Common report accuses you of acting with a degree of severity quite unsuitable for an infant colony, and likely to excite rebellion there. But the matter as to which I find it hardest to give you my pardon is your conduct in reducing to slavery a number of Indians who had done nothing to deserve such a fate. That was contrary to my express orders. As your ill fortune willed it, just at the time when I heard of this breach of my instructions, everybody was complaining against you, and no one spoke a word in your favour. . . . I cannot promise to reinstate you at once in your government. People are too much inflamed against you, and must have time to cool. As to your rank of admiral, I never intended to deprive you of it. But you must bide your time and trust in me."

Bide his time . . . when on the tip of his eager tongue was a great project to push still further west than the islands, on a fourth great expedition which would bring him, by way of a "strait" of which he had heard, to those dominions in Asia which the Portuguese, sailing eastwards, were already exploiting. . . . The Spanish rulers listened with some doubt to weary months of pleading, and at last and again surrendered. That golden tongue riddled every shield of sanity and reason opposed to it.

On the 9th of May be sailed from Cadiz with five ships.

He was strictly interdicted from putting in at Hispaniola or meddling at all in the affairs of the colonies. But was he not the Admiral ? On the pretext that one of his ships required repairs he determined to make Isabella En route, he looked at the skies and saw certain signs of the coming of one of the great Atlantic storms. Unless he found shelter for his squadron——

Ovando, the new governor who had superseded Bobadilla, refused to allow the squadron shelter in the harbour. He refused, equally, to delay the sailing of a great treasure-fleet loaded with gold from the mines of Ciboa. On board it sailed a cloud of the Spanish adventurers including Bobadilla. Two days out at sea a great tornado smote it. One ship escaped, having seen her companions whelmed in the great Atlantic mountains. Columbus had proved a true prophet.

Escaping the worst of that storm himself by sheltering under an unknown headland, he held on in the course of his fourth expedition of discovery. Jamaica was reached on the 14th of July, 1502. Still he held westwards. But presently the fleet almost foundered in the maze of cays and islets that littered those seas—islands flowering a rank green or glimmering rocky and inhospitable under the burning summer. The winds died away.

For over two months the worm-eaten, leaking ships tacked to and fro amidst those islets, seeking a wind to help them escape. Scurvy came on the crews, and men sickened from drinking the brackish waters of the islets. The summer was one of exceptional heat. Presently mutiny grew loud-voiced. Had the Genoese clown brought them here to perish in company with his idiot self? . . . Columbus paced the deck, now white-haired, but vision-rapt and unapproachable as ever, confident in the guidance of God and the sureties of his own mendacity.

At last an easterly wind sprang up. The caravels moved out into the Western Caribbean, hitherto unexplored. In the course of a day's steady sailing they sighted a small island. It was Guanaja, off the coast of Honduras. Columbus, giving it a cursory survey, for he had already seen the dark limning of the continental mass in the west, was about to sail on, turning towards the north but for an accidental encounter. This was with a boatload of Indians from the main-land—cotton-clad Indians, traders in flint arrow-heads and copper axes.

By signs the Admiral entered into communication with them. Their leader, an ancient of imposing mien, appeared to understand perfectly, though Spaniards and Indians had no word of common vocabulary between them. Columbus by signs inquired if Cathay and the court of the Grand Khan lay near? By equally impressive signs the ancient in command of the canoe signalled Yes!

Close at hand was the land the strangers sought—a land much frequented on the further shore by ships like the Admiral's own—and he would guide the Spaniards thither.

§ 12

Had Columbus steered north-west, as had been his first intention, he would have made Yucatan where the great Asiatic-inspired civilization of the Maya was slowly sinking into decay. But instead, under the guidance of the volubly sign-making Indian ancient, he steered southwards along the coast of Honduras, bright with tamarinds and the ferns of rocky headlands. This was the coast of the authentic Americas, but Columbus believed it merely another island, though one of great extent. Southwards, somewhere, lay the strait leading to the Grand Khan's dominions.

For three months, in a confusion of place-names that

have now vanished, he cruised up and down the Panama neck seeking the strait or the country of gold "frequented by great ships" of whom the Indian had told him. It is possible that the Indian had re-told a rumour of trading vessels from Asia seen on the Pacific side of the Isthmus. As we now know, Asia traded with America into remote historic times and there is nothing improbable in rumour of stranger ships in the Pacific having been noised abroad throughout Honduras. But that, at the best, had been beyond the reaches of the impassable Isthmus.

Mosquitos plagued the crews by night, heat by day. The rotting vessels made slow headway even with favourable winds. Once, anchored off a creek, Columbus was attacked by the Indians ; once, seated in conclave with them, still querying the whereabouts of Kublai, he observed the natives indulging in a soothing pipe, and was somewhat alarmed believing them magicians making spells against him. In early December came a great storm, the waves bursting over the leaking vessels in phosphorescent floods and driving Columbus back to the shelter of the coast which at last he would have abandoned.

Born of this minor mischance, however, came gold at last. They had anchored off the territory of a chief named Quibia—perhaps a heritor of the degenerate Coclè culture of Panama. Gold was everywhere evident. By barter and actual excavation large quantities of the ore were procured, and the Spaniards, changeable and as easily enheartened as downcast, were enthusiastic for remaining on those shores. A village of huts, Bethlehem, was built on the bank of a stream, and there the Admiral determined to leave a garrison of eighty men while he returned to Spain for supplies and reinforcements. Bartholomew was left in charge and the Admiral put out to sea.

Unfortunately, Quibia, maltreated by the Spaniards, had gathered his forces and prepared to attack the settlement. Braves crept forward under the cover of darkness and sank the few leaky boats left for the use of the colonists. A dozen Spaniards up the reaches of Bethlehem stream were massacred. Frightened, the settlers would have communicated with Columbus still lingering in sight of the shore and awaiting a favourable wind. But there was no means whereby to communicate.

In this strait they were aided by the uneasiness of Columbus himself, fancying that all was not well in the settlement. His own boats were incapable of making the three-mile passage to the shore, but the pilot Ledesma, the solitary hero of the expedition, leapt overboard and swam through the shark-infested waters till he reached Bartholomew. Columbus's ships were signalled shorewards again, and the expedition re-embarked.

Before they could sail again, however, a caravel, leaking too desperately, had to be abandoned to the winds and tides.

The ill-fated Bethlehem settlement hull down in the north west, Columbus coasted the Darien Peninsula for a short while longer; then, abandoning still another caravel, steered for Cuba towards the end of May. The sieve-like ships staggered drunkenly through the squalls of the Caribbean. In the mist of one night the two remaining ships collided head-on, and for a while were like to sink with all hands. Indomitably the Admiral had them re-patched. Hunger assailed the crews; land was lost for days. But at last, weary and forsaken, they sighted the southern coast of Cuba, where food was obtained from natives still hospitable enough to succour the needy, even though these might be the white devils from the sea.

With that coming to Cuba there ends the tale of Columbus the explorer, the seeker of the Earthly Paradise, even as there begins a long record of him as marooned mariner, cowardly courageous commander, and—persisting to the end—mendacious egomaniac. Behind him, westwards, the Americas drowsed in sleep, the war-rent lands of the great Maya civilizations with their scrolled temples and strange gods, the sun in its full splendour before sunset on the strange aberrant splendours of the Aztec genius in floriferation, the Inka confederacy dominating Peru and the surrounding lands, immense and seemingly impregnable; that, and the league-stretching plains of North America, the forested immensities of Amazonia, the little patches by river and mountain where still, as in the Bahamas, the last of the great groupings of Natural Man lived that free and happy and animal-like existence which was soon to end for ever as the tides of a newer and crueller civilization rolled eastwards in the track of the Genoan's chance discovery.

§ 13

But the shell of the poet-explorer cannot pass beyond our horizon without a glance of interest. From that southern anchorage at Cuba, Columbus, despairing of making Hispaniola, crossed the straits of Jamaica and ran his ships on shore, embedding them in the sand. Then he sat down and wrote letters to Ferdinand and the Governor of Hispaniola, asking for aid and describing the wonders of Panama in the usual terms of overflowing optimism and exaggeration.

These letters were carried by his lieutenant, Mendez, after numerous encounters and flights and fights and travails, to San Domingo. Months went by and no news of relief came to the two ships stranded off Jamaica. The natives grew less friendly, suffering from the depredations of a scoundrelly Spaniard, Porras, who had quarrelled with the Admiral. Porras finally decided to seize the ships for himself and his fellow-mutineers. He attacked from the woods and a pitched battle on the sands was witnessed by the asembled Indians. Porras was defeated and captured, mainly through the instrumentality of brother Bartholomew, and on the 28th of June two caravels arrived from San Domingo to carry the shipwrecked sailors from Jamaica. Columbus, with a happy disregard of the actual situation from which he had been rescued, sailed in apparent confidence that in Hispaniola Ovando the Governor would give way to the superior authority of the Viceroy.

Ovando displayed no such inclination. There followed a month of wrangling, the haughty and ageing Genoese opposed to the cool and dried Ovando, a typical Spanish Grandee. Then Columbus took ship from the Indies, and never saw them again.

Even on this last voyage misfortune dogged him. The Atlantic was swept with storms and great seas beat on the deck of his ship. Ill with a fever which came with gout, Columbus lay in his cabin and listened to the thunder of the weather and turned a weary head to seek rest again, disillusionment at last upon him.

Nor was that unwarranted. The court sent no summons for him to appear. He had wasted the fortunes of the fourth expedition, he returned with no news of the imagined strait or having penetrated to the elusive dominions of that elusive Kublai who had been sleeping the last sleep in dusty Peking two hundred years. Columbus was carried to his house in Seville, to the attentions of that devoted family which held by family feeling with a strong Italian tenacity. Had he been able to sink himself in the care of his neglected Beatriz or the devotion of his sons, Diego and Ferdinand, he might even then have escaped to life and health.

But such grace and greatness was beyond the Genoese, unabandoned still by his own febrific fabrications of fantasy. For him life had become the pursuit, ever westwards, of the golden kingdoms of myth and imagination. He was incapable of resting and taking his ease. Presently Diego was despatched to the court to plead his case. He had little time for effective pleading. Isabella, the only person likely to listen again to the Admiral, was dying. With her death on the 26th of November his last hope of receiving either reinstatement or funds for a new expedition vanished.

He lingered on two years more, white-haired, pain-racked, insatiable still of reinstatement. At Vallodolid in early May it became plain that his time was short. He had a priest summoned and received the offices of his Church with the same fervent devoutness as had characterized all his life ; he looked round at the faces of the family which encircled him, and forgot them, staring in spirit still westwards ; then his thoughts strayed from even that worldly longing. His last whisper was "Into Thy hands, Master, I commend my spirit."

And when that enigmatic spirit had sailed into the dim seas to its utmost bourne, surely his Earthly Paradise at last, they buried the strayed chapman of Genoa in the monastery of Las Cuevas of Seville.

§ 14

The consequences which followed the discovery of the sailing-route across the Atlantic focused on their discoverer more attention than has been paid to any other of the earth's conquerors. He has been viewed through innumerable works and innumerable eyes, from innumerable viewpoints. He has been acclaimed as the hero that son Ferdinand saw him; as the sly trickster whom Las Casas viewed. But his greatness has seldom been disputed. His feet may be feet of clay, heavy poet's feet splashed with the blood of human suffering, but they are planted certainly enough upon that "New World beyond the wave" which he gave to Castile and Leon.

Yet he was not the first European discoverer of America: Leif Ericcson, on a similar quest, had preceded him; the mythic Irish voyagers of the seventh and eight centuries may have preceded him; and—more seriously—the strayed pilot whom he met at Madeira had preceded him. His discovery was not of a New World—which all his life long he strenuously denied and disbelieved. His discovery was of the sailing route across the Atlantic.

Even so, it was great enough. It loosed upon the sparsely inhabited American continent the hungry hordes of over-populated Europe. It loosed new motifs in art and science and perhaps religion. It ended for ever those great and strange experiments in civilization on which the native Americans were employed. And for all Europe it meant a great lifting and widening of horizons, cultural and geographical.

It meant the vanishing from the minds of men for ever of the flat-earth hypothesis, did that hypothesis still lingeringly endure; it meant the breaking down of a great and elaborate synthesis of thought regarding the earth's origins, the origins of all men, the connection of the facts of ethnology and history with the Mosaic myths. Nothing has been so fruitful of discussion and discovery as the question of the origins of the Red Indians and their various strange cultures. America, where the last of the great masses of Natural Men—neither savage, barbarian, nor civilized—were encountered as a consequence of the establishment of the transatlantic route, influenced profoundly contemporary and subsequent political and politico-sociological thought. It may be said, indeed, with its influence upon Thomas More and Rousseau and the Encyclopædists, that Columbus fathered the French Revolution and modern humanitarianism. He was (a ruddy, horrified shade) the godfather of modern Rationalism, the Diffusionist School of History, the philosophy of Anarchism.

These were no more than undreamed consequences. His own stature was not great: it was as fantastically puny as his cosmography was fantastically irrelevant. Europe had despatched to the Far East in the person of Marco Polo a bright and hard young Venetian merchant-adventurer as its envoy to the Kingdom of Wonder; to the west it despatched in quest of the haunting Fortunate Isles which Leif had looked upon a dream-ridden, inefficient Genoese wool-carder who suffered from an inferiority complex and a congenital inability to refrain from prevarication. But beyond and above the pitiful clown with the numerous footmen in Haiti, the theatrical chains at Seville, there abides very essential and real the Explorer whose horizons the undiscovered West so vexed: there is the Columbus of the First Expedition who paced his decks and saw the falling star and was undaunted as that strange beacon of God beckoned him on the Americas, the light of whose native peoples he quenched.

V

CABEZA DE VACA'S QUEST FOR THE CITY OF GOD

§ I

BOTH of the great continents of North and South America had been discovered—or rediscovered—by Europeans before the year 1500. Thereafter followed, century on century, the penetration of those continents by explorers who seldom enough followed such flag of fantasy or single-minded faith as would bring them within the pages of this record. They explored for purposes of plunder and profit, seldom in the cause of divine perversity.

Even yet the task of exploring the Americas is incomplete: there are still little lost valleys in the northern crinkles of Canada on which the aviator gazes astounded; there are still great stretches in Brazil into which a Colonel Fawcett may disappear. But the main limnings of river and mountain and plain are now known: there remains little to be done but the filling in of the minor pieces of a giant mosaic.

In that late fifteenth and early sixteenth century it is curious to note how the main work of apprehending the geographical contours of the Americas paused and swirled about the confluences of the two continents for over thirty years. Central America, with Mexico, was the focus for European eyes and the background for European adventure. Only slowly did men strike north and south of the narrow Neck, into the illimitable plains of the north, into the illimitable forests of the south.

This for the best of reasons: Columbus's discoveries and settlements had been in the islands; at a short distance sail, westward, lay the Central Americas. And the traditional route of Atlantic exploration was due west, in search of either a passage through this mysterious land-mass to Asia, or in the belief that the land-mass itself was a portion of Asia. That tradition resulted in the discovery of Yucatan and its northwards coasting by Juan de Grijalva and others; it resulted in the discovery of the great congeries of Amerindian civilizations which in the modern mind link together under the name of Aztec ; and it resulted, finally and completely and disastrously, in the raiding expedition of the Spaniards against the Aztec Empire.

Captained by the slaver and planter, Hernando Cortes, a small force of Spaniards in 1511 landed in the region of the modern Vera Cruz, marched through an indifferent or hostile country, tributary to the High Chief of the Aztecs, Moctezhuoma, and reached that Moctezhuoma's capital, Tenochtitlan, with but little resistance offered them. They found Tenochtitlan a great lacustrine city, "finer than Seville", stone-built in great streets, with gigantic pyramidal structures the design of which had been imported from Cambodia long before, with gigantic and affrighting idols and religous rites which represented the driftage and seepage century on century across the Pacific of all the stray theological notions that had ever irritated the Asiatic mind. And they found this culture a golden culture : gold was as plentiful in the reality as it had been in the dreams of Columbus and his first fellow-adventurers.

The story of that murder of the Aztec civilization is not with this record : our conquest is of another kind. The Aztec Empire fell to pieces before the musket-volleys of the Spaniards and gold flowed into Spain in dazzling torrents, throwing the world financial market into such chaos as impoverished Spain for three long centuries. This was history's ironic commentary on the looting of Mexico's vast treasure-house; the geographical repercussions were no less ironic.

Spain, almost unchallenged, dominated intercourse with the New World across the Atlantic ; and to Spain, after the discovery of Mexico, that New World gradually betook itself from the shores of the Atlantic into the cloudy regions of myth and legend. Mexico : it was well known that Mexico was but a poverty-stricken parish in comparison with the rich and amazing kingdoms that yet awaited exploitation north and south of the devastated Empire. Indians had been captured with the tales of a Seven-Citied Kingdom of Golden-Doors, Indians had been tortured to the story of a king who daily annointed himself with gold-dust and nightly and negligently washed that dust from his person. . . . So, cloud-capped cities in a strange cloud-cuckooland, Ciboa and

ALVAR NUÑEZ CABEZA DE VACA

Manoa came to haunt the minds and desires of the poverty-stricken gentry and commons of Spain. Men sold all their worldly goods not to follow Christ, but to follow the beckoning star of wealth, easily achieved, easily looted, in the magic Americas. The Atlantic bore on every ship a host of greedy adventurers confident of a return to Spain and an endless life of wealth and pleasure on the barren home Peninsula, served on golden platters by the daughters of Amerindian princes.

As a result, the Americas were explored with an intensity and passion, if a staggering unintelligence, that for the moment clouds the achievements of our star-following earth-conquerors into insignificance. In that lust for gold around and about the year 1523 Alejo Garcia, a Portuguese marooned with a few companions on the Rio de la Plata in South America, gathered a force of Indians and marched north-westwards in quest of Manoa. Chartless and mapless, they plunged into land that is still posted on the maps as "terra incognita". They traversed unstayable the wild lands where Fawcett was to vanish four hundred years later, they crossed the green hell of the Gran Chaco and actually reached to the foot of the Andes, and touched there on the Spanish conquests coming from the Pacific. Somewhere on those desolate western slopes Garcia and his companions fought a great battle against a native community rich in silver, looted the community, and turned about, treasure-laden, to recross South America at its widest part and gain the Atlantic again. And that stupendous journey they again accomplished, only at the Paraguay to be killed and scattered by epidemic or war and all their loot lost. . . . Compared with the wild Odyssey of those cruel and competent and vigorous adventurers, the exploits of such star-followers as Leif and Christopher pale for a little into seeming insignificance.

But it is little more than seeming. They left few if any reliable guides to the countries they traversed, those plundering adventurers; Indians were for them soulless brutes of no distinct speeches or cultures—the abundance or lack of tribal gold the only distinction. They confused river and mountain and plain very thoroughly; their light upon the unknown scene is the flare of a beacon lighting a countryside doubtfully and presently quenched in blood. After them came the ploddings of the merchant-explorers, as they may be called, the phalanges of the commonplace who are also outside this record. And amid them is here and there a star-follower or two who kindles to our touch with authentic glow—of them all Cabeza de Vaca the most noteworthy.

He was neither the greatest nor the best; but the chances of his life gave him to a great venture into the wild lands of the North American Continent, one almost equally great in the tracks of that expedition of Garcia's which was whelmed by the Paraguay River. And on both of these ventures—as confused as Columbus, his search for the land of gold and his quest for the City of God inextricably mixed—he trod a unique track.

§ 2

Alvar Nuñez Cabeza de Vaca was born in Jerez in Southern Spain about the year 1492—the year of the discovery of the American sailing-route by Columbus, twenty years after the subjugation of the Canaries by his grandfather, Pedro de Vera.

His was a noble family, if the nobility in legend had been endowed it only a short three centuries. That legend led back to the year 1212 when a shepherd guided a Christian army across the Sierra Morena by a secret pass he had marked with the skull of a cow. For this service the Vera of that time was ennobled, his descendants using indifferently the honorific "Cowhead" (Cabeza de Vaca) or the family name, de Vera, with a happy improvidence greatly confusing to the historian but apparently undisturbing to themselves.

Little or nothing is known of early life of Alvar Nuñez. All Spain was aglow with rumour of great treasure and great fighting at that time; his grandfather, the conqueror of the Canaries, no doubt refought his battles over again in the presence of the young and impressionable lad. One builds up of him a portrait, modified from that self-painting of later days, of one cool and watchful—and even then oddly, quietly *doubtful*. That indeed was to become his dominating characteristic—a quiet, questioning doubt of everything affirmed or believed of this terrestrial scene. Only the celestial scene itself he was never to question; he grew to the devoutest of Catholics: his devoutness was to become of a quality almost comparable to that of St. Francis of Assisi.

Yet such devoutness was no bar to share in warfare:

it was indeed, in that society and reach of life into which Cabeza de Vaca was born, understood to be complementary to warfare. The brutish adventurers in the West Indies who, in the days of Cabeza de Vaca's childhood, would crucify a dozen Indians in a row in imitation of the Twelve Apostles were doubtlessly aberrant abominations from the true human norm, conditioned from early years to cruelty and neglect and ferocious disciplines ; but that cruelty was largely religious in origin. Christ and the saints if they did not openly delight in blood and torture welcomed an *auto-de-fé* of erring souls, sniffing the sweet savour of burning and tortured flesh. Human cruelty was the incensing of celestial sadism.

In 1511 war began in Italy between the Pope and the Italian princes ; Cabeza de Vaca sailed as a cadet in a Spanish contingent loaned to the Pope by Ferdinand of Castile and had speedy opportunity to put both his skill in arms and his devoutness to test.

The Papal Army and its allies marched against the Italian princes and their French allies. At Ravenna the two armies met and for a long and bloody day disputed the passage to Bologna. By nightfall the Papal forces were fleeing in bloody rout and the French themselves preparing to retreat from that Pyrrhic encounter. Here, for almost the first time in European warfare, the enormous destruction achievable by heavy firearms was obtrusive; a gasp of horror went up from all Europe. Cabeza de Vaca, a young man shaken and nervous from the sights of that horrific field, reached Naples with other sections of the rout, and there apparently succeeded in recovering his composure. For shortly afterwards we find him appointed governor of Gaeta near Naples, a considerable city where he was to remain a long twelve years that is for us a passing breath, if for him no doubt a flowing current of tribulation and happiness and dread and careless indifference in the minute ripplings of the river of life.

In 1513 there is a glimpse of him in the light, before he vanishes into the clash and glitter of the long years of civil war waged between the Spanish monarchy and the insurgent nobles, the Comuneros. Returning from Italy, he took service with the Duke of Medina Sidonia as a steward for that nobleman of Seville. Medina Sidonia was a monarchist ; Cabeza de Vaca followed him into the field against the nobles with what feelings or beliefs there is no knowing. He seems to have acquitted himself with no great distinction: one has already doubts if his heart was in this business of war.

At the least, when those wars ended, he passes into obscurity again, to Jerez and a life dull, if happy, a life of marriage with a woman whose very name we do not know. But it is fair to assume theirs a happy marriage, for in subsequent years she was to mortgage all her property on the ventures of the strange man who had left her side and vanished into the doubts and forays of the kingdoms beyond the Atlantic.

But that time came slowly. He seems to have moved to Seville, perhaps as retainer in some noble house; he seems to have had little interest in the tales that flooded the streets and quays of Seville—tales of conquest and discovery and conquest yet again, Cortes and his subjugation of Mexico, the voyagings of that Magellan who preceded him in venture but follows him in our record. It is as possible that he could have met and talked with Magellan as it is unlikely that he ever sought the opportunity. They were too fundamentally unalike in all passions but one—and that passion still unawakened in Alvar Nuñez.

But in 1526 he fell in with a remarkable visitant from the New World, one Panfilo de Narvaez, a dull and unscrupulous man who still laboured under the grievance that but for a night-sortie on the part of Cortes capturing and dispersing his rival raid on the Aztec Hegemony he himself might have attained the glory of the conquest of Tenochtitlan and the rich kingdoms of Mexico. Narvaez by then lacked an eye; but he came back to Spain filled with visions. To the north of Mexico—in the dim lands behind that Florida which Ponce de Leon had by now discovered—was a great and glorious kingdom where the streets of the cities were paved with gold and simple kings awaited conquest. He petitioned the right to conquer this great territory for Spain and, after long months of intrigue and question, had the right granted to him—he himself to equip the expedition and assume all responsibilities.

His treasurer the records display—astonishingly, considering his previous attitude towards such ventures—as Alvar Nuñez Cabeza de Vaca.

§ 3

The expedition sailed from San Lucar de Barrameda on the 17th of June, 1527. It consisted of five caravels, loaded with over six hundred men, crossbowmen and men-at-arms, ennobled adventurers and adventurous nobles. In their company went five Franciscan monks, deputed to preach the Gospel to such of the heathen as would survive their conquest of the northern Americas. Amongst the nobles was a Mexican cacique, Tetlahuehuetzquittzin, whom the Narvaez expedition had mercifully rechristened "Don Pedro" in the interests of brevity or loquacity. Cabeza de Vaca's duties included those of provost-marshal as well as treasurer; in that turbulent company it is unlikely that the office was a sinecure. The lash and half-drownings were the customary disciplinary tools of the time: and it is probable that Alvar Nuñez was a provost-marshal with no great heart in the work. The ships were overcrowded in the fashion to which men of the time were accustomed; to our day they would have much the same seeming as those loaded slavers that crossed that sad Atlantic so many times in the centuries to follow.

Early in August Narvaez' fleet put in to San Domingo, where over a hundred of the expedition promptly deserted, seeking native women and Cuban wealth rather than adventure further afield. Sailing on for Cuba, Narvaez attempted to recruit to a greater strength, and here it was that most of the expedition's horses were purchased. Cabeza de Vaca and another were sent south, forage-hunting, each in command of a vessel. A great storm came on, wrecking the vessels while the two commanders were ashore, and laying waste most of the southern half of the island. Terrified at this manifestation of the winter Atlantic, Narvaez determined to lay up the ships until the Spring should come. The three surviving vessels were sailed to the port of Jagua, beached and careened, and the expedition encamped in boredom and squalor and riotousness for a long three months of which we know little or nothing, though we can guess much. By mid-February Narvaez was convinced that his attempts at recruiting were fruitless. He sailed to the dimly known coasts of Florida with four hundred men and eighty horses. Already the expedition had lost a third of its complement.

Out of the shelter of the islands misfortunes commenced anew. Storms drove the little ships, loaded with seasick landsmen, to and fro amidst the drummling seas for nearly six weeks. Not until the 12th of April was the land of Florida sighted. But that sight was encouraging, the storms had cleared away and the low Florida beach glimmered in the green of its bright vegetation and the translucent sheen of its grey sands. Sailing cautiously northwards in search of good anchorage, they finally put in at a spot now known as The Jungle, and appropriately so known, lying a little north of the modern St. Petersburg.

Here Narvaez proceeded to disembark and set out on his conquest of the North American continent.

§ 4

Near at hand was an Indian village, visible above the low scrub that mantled the shores. It was strangely silent. Suspicious of ambush, the Spaniards advanced upon it cautiously, finding it entirely deserted. The small huts brooded in complete quietude around the central "long-houses"; there was little but domestic rubble to be found in the interiors as the disgusted Spaniards searched to and fro. Then, fatefully, a soldier found a golden rattle in one of the buildings—a trade-product from Mexico, perhaps, in the days before the coming of the white men to the American continent. It was hailed with glee, an obvious sign that the expedition was on the right track for the golden cities. Men remembered the poverty-stricken appearance of the coastal villages of Mexico: so here, inland also, lay the great cities of wealth.

Preparations were at once on hand for a march into the interior. On Easter Sunday a solemn mass was held on the beach; and on this day the first Indians were observed. They were doubtlessly the villagers who had fled from Gold-Rattle Village. They stood on the fringe of the jungle and gestured their aversion to the Spaniards—they gestured "go away". Solemnly the Spaniards knelt and disregarded the heathen.

Thereat there followed, in the usual fashion of these expeditions, weeks of delay and wrangling. There were two schools of thought among the leaders: one favoured embarking on a land expedition at once, the other, of which Cabeza de Vaca was champion, favoured the finding of a suitable anchorage for the fleet and a ready supply of food for the soldiers before betaking themselves on the search for Ciboa through the bright jungles of Florida. For food began to run short. Also as usual, an insufficient quantity had been shipped from Spain and insufficiently augmented at Cuba. Nor was there much supply to be encountered in this new land itself.

Raiding northwards, the Spaniards (who in Cabeza de Vaca's narrative are consistently, and with unintentional humour, referred to as "the Christians") had come on two native villages surrounded by minor plantations of corn and squash. These plantations they had duly despoiled, apparently aided rather than hindered by the inhabitants, mild and peaceable people in the same cultural stage as those Archaics whom the Spaniards had now almost exterminated in the Islands, in the Old Civilization stage, ruled by minor Children of the Sun, warfare known but seldom practised, tall and kindly men and women given over to the tilling of the ground and the reading of the sky for weather-portents, their lives absorbed in the worship and life-being of that Giver of Life, their ruler, their deaths evil things to be averted through the repetition of those propitiatory ceremonies which had crossed the Pacific to America fifteen hundred years before.

At length the quarrels of the expedition were ended by compromise. The ships would sail north questing a good harbour. The soldiers would also journey northwards, and at the first great opening in the land turn seawards, meeting the ships.

Northwards, as they had already gathered from the Timucua Indians of the neighbourhood, was veritably the land of gold—Apalachen. In that far day and long anterior to it it seems that the great Giver of Life had indeed been mined in some quantity by the Apalachee Indians of Northern Georgia—mined and exported or hidden away by barbaric, cultureless miners. But the Spaniards knew nothing of that. They believed that a second Tenochtitlan was close at hand.

On the 1st of May they marched northwestward into the interior.

§ 5

On the map that journey up and across the Suwanee River to the neighbourhood of the Ochlockonee looks of small import, a mere indentation on the familiar American coast-line. But to that exploring party it was an Odyssey of far travail in their gear of armour and stout leather, inadequate and poor food, in their crippled, diseased, gold-haunted mental equipment. Swamps and creeks and the bright shimmer of still more dripping swamps swam ahead their forward vision day on day. It was a land as trackless as it seemed uninhabited, there was no food to be gathered, no gold, nothing but foot-ache and weariness. Presently their high spirits began to evaporate very rapidly.

The shore remote and unseen far to the left, they came to the Withlacoochee, and swam it or ferried over their gear to the point where an Indian village at last uprose in the jungle. It was an agricultural settlement and they raided the fields, ravenously, weeping for gladness at the taste of fresh foods. The Amerindians regarded them with a stony wonder. Here they halted a little while, Cabeza de Vaca tells, while an expedition was sent down the river to look for the ships at its mouth. But there was no mouth : merely a long, flat echoing shoal of beach where no ship sailed, and remote on the horizon the tumbling waves of the Mexican Gulf playing under a hot sun.

They took to the trackless forests again, north-westwards, in search of golden Apalachen. Here and there villages rose from the forest depth: they were met by Indians of a different breed from any they had hitherto encountered—tall, cool men, musicians and warriors, for here the Archaic Civilization was in its third state of development : inter-tribal war had come on the scene with the death or decay of each tribal Sun Child rule. They regarded the Spaniards with a bright, brief interest, fed them, directed them northwards by signs, and, near the Suwanee, became bored by them, fired a flight of arrows at their drowsing camp one night, and then dis-appeared.

Six weeks after setting out from the coast the Spaniards came at last in view of the golden city of Apalachen, guided thereto by captured, and doubtlessly tortured, Indians. They attacked the town in a great cavalry charge, Cabeza de Vaca in command of the storming-party. No resistance was offered. Golden Apalachen had neither walls nor castellated points, neither armies nor embattlements. Instead, it was an ordinary-looking Indian agricultural village, deserted at the moment

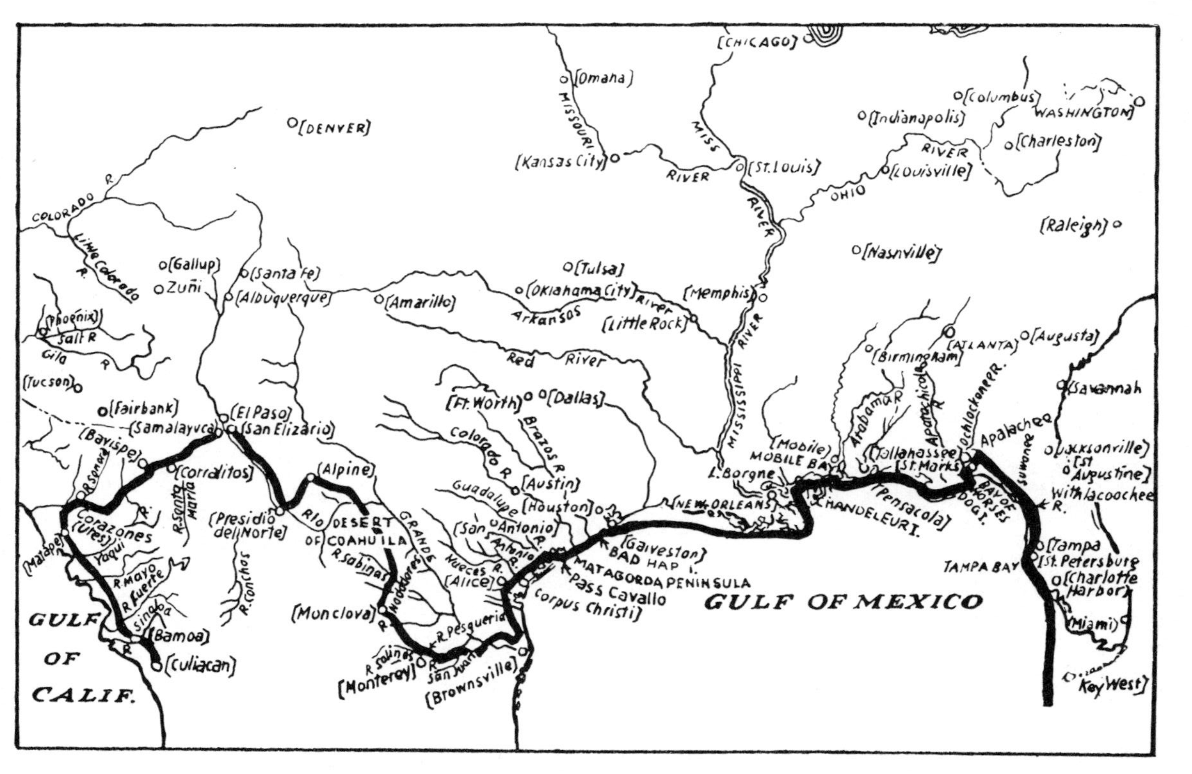

NORTH AMERICAN JOURNEY OF CABEZA DE VACA

the while its braves were on the warpath northwards. The disgusted and heartsick Spaniards looted and plunged amidst the huts and drove out the women and children: no gold, no treasure, yet they gathered that this was veritably Apalachen.

It was a lacustrine "city", Cabeza de Vaca tells: probably the lake was Lake Miccosukee in modern Jefferson County, in thickly wooded country that swarmed with wolves and bears and similar unkindly fauna, deer also, and that pouched animal, the humble oppossum, on which Cabeza de Vaca and Europe gazed astounded for the first time. But there was little peace for deer-hunting or the enjoyment of rest after the rigours of the march. The Indians were up.

Probably they were the returned braves of Apalachen itself. They laid a strange and effective siege to the town, pouring in volleys of arrows at dusk or dawn, harassing small parties of the disheartened Christians. The bow had come to this section of the Americas, a great, strong weapon wielded now with deadly effect. In a little it was to prove even more effective.

For three weeks the Spaniards endured Apalachen; then, in something like the panic that prefaces rout, abandoned that site and marched south in quest of a rumoured village, Aute on the sea-coast, plentifully supplied with provisions, if no gold. The Indians followed on their heels, attacking at fords and lake-crossing, great gaunt, painted bowmen wielding dreadful bows compared to which the Christians' crossbows seemed mere toys. Casques and plate-armour split and crackled under the impact of arrow-heads hardened in fire and water; the strayed Mexican cacique, "Don Pedro", was slain; so was a cavalier, Avellaneda. Cabeza de Vaca was wounded; and the rabble of the commonalty among the adventurers doubtlessly suffered even more. At night the insects of those jungle lands awoke in myriads and feasted upon the travailling whites; by day sun and Amerindians scourged their travailling march. Aute, attained at last, was found burned to the ground and the inhabitants fled.

A party under Cabeza de Vaca set out for the sea. That reached, they found it deserted, no ships in sight, a smoulder of stinking flats. They returned to Aute and reported. The hearts of the Spaniards sank within them. Nightly the woods echoed to the war-whoops of the great bowmen. In a long night attack the expedition was almost overwhelmed. Narvaez determined to march all his fever-stricken, gaunt and disheartened band down to the sea.

At the coast at last, the adventurers took counsel. The ships appeared to have vanished from the face of the earth. They could not make their way along that impossible coast. They must build boats and skirt the coastline down to Tampico where the northernmost Spanish settlement in Mexico was held.

They had neither tools, craftsmen, skill nor strength. They had neither food nor knowledge. But the barges were built after incredible pains and incredible labour the while the diseased and haggard Spaniards subsisted on their slain horses and meals raided from Indian villages. The Indians retaliated. Ten Spaniards were found transfixed through and through with the great Amerindian arrows. Night-times were times of terror, expecting massed attacks on their settlement where the limekilns glowed and the half-made barges lay in sprawling disarray on the sands.

At length the barges, great sogging hulks, were completed, equipped with clumsy oars, the shirts and underwear of the Spaniards hoisted as ineffective sails, and the flotilla prepared to depart. They believed Panuco of Tampico close at hand to the west. They had no vision of the long, creaming weariness of surf that stretched for almost immeasurable leagues between themselves and the harbour they hoped to gain.

§ 6

The journeyings of the Spaniards in those crazy boats were an odyssey in themselves, if no more than prelude to the sufferings and far wanderings of that dark and kindly and enigmatic soul, Cabeza de Vaca himself. For thirty days they ploughed and sweltered along that barren sun-smitten coast. By day the heat maddened them, equipped as they were with leaking water-bottles made of horse-hide; by night chill winds froze their uncovered, sore-scarred limbs. Finally, after dreadful privations for lack of water, they seem to have made Pensacola Bay, where an Indian settlement loomed shorewards. The Indians, gigantic men, welcomed them on the shore, gave them water to drink, and then attacked them—why it is difficult to say. All that night the fight raged on the shore, the majority of the Spaniards taking to their boats, though Cabeza de Vaca and the less wearied carried on the fight on the beach. By morning the Indians had fled: Alvar Nuñez had thirty of their canoes broken up and burned. Then the expedition sailed out in the Gulf waters again.

In Mobile Bay, where they put in for water, a negro and a Greek adventurer insisted on departing with the Indians who paddled out to view them; neither were ever seen again. Disintegration of discipline set in rapidly in the sweltering boats labouring along the low, flat coastline. Men dropped exhausted through heat and malaria, and with glazing eyes remembered Spain.

Of these Cabeza de Vaca was not one. Piloting his boat and apparently encouraging even his own commander, he seems to have been the first to sight the lip of a great river's mouth—wide and brown and tremendous, great-currented, wheeling down to that desolate shore. It was the Mississippi, at its mouth a fusion and confusion of islets amidst which the ragged flotilla swayed and ebbed, and, at length caught in the great current, drifted far out to sea. They lost sight of land for three days, and then coasted up to America again, seeing as darkness fell all the landline alight with great fires. But again contrary currents swung the flotilla round, to the open and unprotected Gulf, and Cabeza de Vaca's and another boat were lost or abandoned by the frightened Narvaez.

In the morning Cabeza de Vaca and the commanders of that other boat, Penalosa and Tellez, joined forces and held raggedly north-west. Storms hurled them across the Southern Texan shore: far off, in the cream of the breakers, they glimpsed the islanded coastline where New Orleans was to rise. After seven nights on an uncertain sea an equally uncertain night came down on the two boats. But near dawn Alvar Nuñez "heard the tumbling of the sea; for as the coast was low, it roared loudly". A wave in the darkness flung them up on this low shore, and the few who survived crawled out and waited chilledly for the dawn. They found themselves on an island—la Isla de Mal Hado, Bad Hap land, Cabeza de Vaca was to call it.

Bad Hap Island (an island off the modern Galveston) was inhabited by a race of lowly fishers and hunters, tall bowmen, who stared childlike wonder at the Spaniards, fed them and coddled them and doctored them in the true style of the Golden Age that was vanishing so quickly from that coastland as agriculture and science drifted up to it from the Aztec lands. To the Spaniards it was a land and a life of horror; few, even Cabeza de Vaca, realized at first the hospitality and childish simpleness of their hosts.

Winter was near. The wrecked party was joined by another from the same expedition—one that had foundered on the northern shores of Bad Hap land. The newcomers were as useless as the followers of Cabeza de Vaca in the procuring of food, and though the Indians continued to feed them with indefatigable generosity the whole business was a strain upon the economic resources of the island.

Presently a great storm came. For six days the Indians could neither fish nor dig up the shore-roots on which they lived. They endured the hunger with a placid stoicism. The Spaniards, being civilized, had less control. Some of them went mad. The Indians discovered their guests indulging in cannibalism, and put a stop to the practice with an angry indignation. It was the only occasion on which the Christians had seen those simple men of the Golden Age moved to anger.

As curious a comment as history and the historical processes have made anywhere may be noted in this connection. Within a hundred years the natives of those islands and the neighbouring mainland were ill-famed for their warlike manners and their cannibalism. Primitive man, simple and free-hearted, looked with an amazed and disgusted eye on quarrelsomeness and cannibalism: it needed the example of Christian Europe to teach him war and man-eating.

Disease worked its inroads throughout a bitter winter, when the winds from the Gulf blew chill through thin Indian shelters. Presently it was more than disease—a plague which left eighteen men surviving out of eighty and spread among the Indians themselves. Justifiably alarmed, the latter assembled and debated whether it would not be well to kill off the Spaniards as a sanitary precaution. Had they themselves been the guests of Spain, disease-carrying, *their* hosts would have carried discussion to decision speedily enough. Instead, the Indians assembled the Spaniards and heard their defence. Cabeza de Vaca, ragged and torn and dark and devout, said humbly that it was no work of theirs, they tried to heal themselves. The Indians admitted the justice of the pleas, and seeing that the Spaniards were useless in fishing, appointed the ragged survivors the healers for the island. Gradually the plague abated: the foulness of the white men was frozen from their flesh, though Cabeza de Vaca as usual was to assign the cause to the special intervention of Providence.

For those Spaniards it was an island of horror. They hated and loathed with a shuddering abhorrence the Indians who fed and tended them—all except Cabeza de Vaca himself, that perfection of the civilized man of his time, with his slow groping from cause to effect even in the agonies of his body's hunger. He saw his hosts generous and affectionate, loving to their children, children themselves, and wondered on the thing, muzzily, the while he laboured at digging roots. Such of the Spaniards as survived had been put to this task: even while reasonably fed they had shown an apathetic sloth of which the natives tired. Cabeza de Vaca was later to describe himself as a slave—albeit uneasily. He was at liberty to depart if he liked: if he stayed, decided his simple hosts, he must work for his living.

Spring came. The Indians crossed to the mainland on an annual trek. They took Cabeza de Vaca with them. Exactly a year before the proud expedition of Narvaez, now scattered and lost in jungle and swamp, had sailed from Cuba.

§ 7

Cabeza de Vaca's Indian tribe was the Coco or Cahoque. On the mainland it seems to have spent some six months or so every year, wandering to and fro in search of berries and shell-fish, hunting the shy beach deer, trading with the resident mainland tribes. And throughout the space of a year Cabeza de Vaca himself led this life.

At first it was probably one of despair. Then sickness came so that he lay ill in delirium for several weeks. In the space of that period the dozen or so other Spaniards who survived set out on a march along the coast, determined to come to that Panuco which they imagined to lie round the next headland or so. They gathered and looked on Alvar Nuñez before they departed. He was obviously too weak to accompany them. They left him to the mercy of the hunger-vexed Indians.

That mercy was not wanting. They seem to have fed and looked after this useless encumbrance who had come into their lives with that calm benignity that was an attribute of Natural Man. Cabeza de Vaca recovered, possibly living the next months or so, abandoned by his kind, in a stupor of despair. He lived the life of the Food-Gatherers themselves, troubled in his pride in his relationship to them, for he was unable to do any but women's work, unjust in his later account of them, for that status of his long rankled in his memory. In his account of that time he was to describe these Indians again as his masters, and he as their slave ; yet was to go on to confess that when he desired to leave them and pass on to another tribe on the mainland the Cahoques made no objection whatever.

His move to the mainland was accomplished in the character of a pedlar. He traded to and fro in suchlike articles as conch-shells from the beaches, skins from the woods and prairies. Winter came. He hibernated with a mainland tribe, the Charrucos, and endured the usual torments of insufficient food. Spring found him on the move, a dull if competent trader, already with some knowledge of the generic languages talked by the mainland folk.

Here definitely the Indians were tribal, hunters and agriculturists constantly at war. It is difficult to understand those wars around Galveston Bay as described in Cabeza de Vaca's record but as ceremonial wars. In a like measure a large part of their entire existence was regulated. There were ceremonial drinking feasts on a brew made from the *ilex vomitoria*—a brew which the communicants drank at intervals for three days on end, greatly to the Spaniard's astonishment. Sometimes a tribe would raid and massacre another tribe at whose lodges he had arrived. He himself was left unattacked : he was outside the ceremony.

He wandered a considerable distance inland through those stretches of treey America, and more than a hundred miles along the coast, southwards, without setting eyes on longed-for Panuco. He had dressed in skins and carried his trade goods in a deerhide pack. He was barefooted and haggard and greatly bearded. Externally and internally he was slowly altering and reshaping with the ready adaptability of a member of the earth's most adaptable species.

The single other Spaniard left in the vicinity was one Lope de Oviedo, on Bad Hap Island. Cabeza de Vaca tells that he tried again and again to persuade this timorous and reluctant soul to set out with him on a march to the south, in search of Christians. Each year Oviedo put him off with this excuse and that: he seems to have found the life of the Simple Men to his taste. But at last, in the early autumn of 1532, he consented to make the attempt in company with the trader.

For three weeks they plodded and tramped and swam the sandbars and creeks of the muddy Texan coastline. Somewhere near the modern Port O'Connor they fell in with an Indian tribe, the Quevenes, who had news of the dozen or so Spaniards who had set out to make Panuco three years before. All but three of these wanderers had died—two white men and a black-faced one. . . . It was a new and a bitter country into which Cabeza de Vaca and his companion Oviedo had come. The Quevenes were both truculent and cruel—perhaps the passing bands of Spaniards had misbehaved in the usual fashion, leaving a fury of resentment in the Amerindian breast. Cabeza de Vaca and Oviedo were pelted with mud, jeered at, threatened with bows. Oviedo looked at the scene and endured it for a little. Then he came to his simple conclusion. He had had no particular desire to leave Bad Hap land : and he was going back there.

So back he went, and passes from the record. Perhaps two hundred years later, when those Indians of that region were cannibals and ferocious warriors, they had amongst them those with the proud blood of Lope de Oviedo in their veins.

§ 8

Cabeza de Vaca escaped the Quevenes, holding south to Guadaloupe River. Here he fell in with a new tribe, the Mariames, who came every year feasting in the pecan groves of Guadaloupe. And here he met with the three survivors of the Spanish hijra—Andres Dorantes, Alonso del Castillo, and Dorantes' negro slave Estebanico. All three were held for service by the Indians, grinding the pecan nuts in hollow mortars ; they were treated with a bitter cruelty which makes strange reading. War had very quickly destroyed the morale of the simple men of the Americas.

In that period of enslavement by this inland tribe Cabeza de Vaca studied them closely enough and reports at length on their lives and habits. Some of his details are unconsciously humorous. The Mariames are described as "casting away their daughters at birth and causing them to be eaten by dogs". Women were raided from hostile tribes. Though one recognizes here a distorted version of the world-wide exogamic custom which went with the Archaic Civilization, the details sound improbable, especially as the chronicler goes on to say that the surrounding tribes did the same. A multitude of tribes without daughters must have found difficulties in procreation. But they were certainly a degenerate congeries of stocks, those seashore Amerindians. One of the most remarkable institutions of the Mariames was that of a third sex—the homosexual or the hermaphrodite was a common and tolerated phenomenon, with definite social duties, pleasures and responsibilities. This purely American evolution was indeed widely paralleled over the great plains and mountains far to the north in the America of that day and much later, though Cabeza de Vaca went unaware of the fact, thinking it only a loathsome local practice.

The Spaniards determined to escape as soon as the tribes moved on their annual migration to the great tuna (prickly pear) region in the south-west. Late in the summer of 1533 this migration began among the Mariames: the Spanish slaves carried loads like women, and like women bore the stripes. After a rough and hungry march they sighted the great region of the ripe tunas somewhere in the neighbourhood of the modern Corpus Christi; there, however, their plannings to escape were frustrated. Quarrels broke out among the tribes. Loaded with produce of the tuna country, Cabeza de Vaca trailed back to the Mariame squatting-places for another year's weary slavery. In this he was separated from Dorantes and the others but kept in touch with them by unchancy messengers, planning yet another escape when the prickly-pear season returned.

Summer of 1534 flaming its sunrises and its misty sunsets over the Texan wastes. Again the tribes assembled to drink of the sweet juice of the tuna; and again the three Spaniards and the wide-grinning Estebanico were united.

They fled in the dark of a moonless night and attained the shelter of the lodges of another race, perhaps the Coahuiltecans, gentle primitives whose habitat was somewhere in the region of the modern Alice.

The Coahuiltecans were in trek southwards to their permanent lands across the Great Sand Belt of Brooks. For five days the plodding tribe with the three gasping white men and the obscure negro made their way across those glittering lands. At last they reached regions of herbage and fruitage again. It was the Arroyo Colorado.

Late prickly-pears were in fruit ; water sang and gurgled. Scattering, the entire tribe sought food. Cabeza de Vaca wandering farther than most was lost for five miserable days ere he stumbled upon his hosts and companions again. He was fed and welcomed like a lost sheep.

Here, halting in the Colorado Arroyo, Cabeza de Vaca gradually acquired among the surrounding tribes the reputation of a miraculous healer. He and the other three refugees, asked if they could raise the dead and heal the sick, appear to have replied, in desperation, that they could. Cabeza de Vaca was led to a hut where a man lay dead—or apparently dead. Cabeza de Vaca prayed over the corpse, massaged it, and breathed upon it. A short while afterwards the cadaver got to its feet, smiled, and walked about.

Great kudos came to the Spaniards as a consequence : it was plainly a miracle wrought by God to prove them to the heathen. A later and more sceptical generation might ascribe it to convenient exhibitionism on the part of the unauthentic corpse.

Yet there was probably more in it than that. The grave and pious Alvar Nuñez from his ordeal in the wilderness had emerged with a burning faith in his own unworthiness preserved by God for some mysterious means. So possessed, it is likely he possessed some considerable degree of that physical magnetism that in modern times can still perform psychological miracles. The Indians believed so. The fame of their cures (for the others practised as well) spread far and wide among the simple food-gatherers. As that winter came on the refugees lived on their reputations as doctors, plus much backaching carting of wood to the great communal fires. The winds blew chill and famine came. Naked, the Spaniards shivered ever closer to the fires, longing for the Spring.

Spring came at last. A misty plan had matured in Cabeza de Vaca's mind—to press ever southwards, seeking Mexico. South-west lived a friendly food-gathering tribe, the Maliacones. Thither the refugees tramped, a long seven leagues. The Maliacones welcomed them and took them on yet another trek in search of mesquite and ebony beans. The region was found with the beans yet unripe ; the Maliacones turned back. But the Spaniards and the negro believed they might as well starve forward as in the rear. Killing two small dogs and eating them, they pressed on south-west through desolate country.

They lost their way. Rain in drenching torrents swept the tundras. In a forest they encountered two women and some youths who led them to the camping-ground of their tribe, the Cuchendados. Here Cabeza de Vaca practised the healer again, amidst great applause. They rested and fed themselves on their hosts' bounty for a fortnight, then held on to the south-west.

Still they were in land where the feet of other white men had never trod. And still there was no rumour of men like themselves. The stray tribes encountered fed them and fêted them ; they were fed on meal from the mesquite bean, that detestable flour, and found it delicious. It was a kinder country into which they had come now and the natives unspoiled primitives even at that late day. At length through country of thorn and scrub they were led by guides from a tribe, healer-denuded, to the banks of a great river that flowed wide and tremendous across the countryside—"wide as the Guadalquivir at Seville" says Cabeza de Vaca. It was the Rio Grande.

Probably they crossed it somewhere in the modern Hidalgo County, Texas. Still they were in the land of the food-gatherers. These simple folk convoyed them from village to village, honouring and fearing them, according to Cabeza de Vaca. But penetrating behind universal motive we may obtain another picture. The Spaniards were probably regarded joyfully and amusedly as astounding freaks come to relieve the monotony of life. Hundreds of years before, south in Mexico and west in California, similar freaks from Asia had landed, Children of the Sun, and been acclaimed and welcomed by the primitives of those regions, and left to debase the minds and hearts of those primitives the rituals of religion and kingship and shamanism. The Spaniards were in the tradition. Fed, they preached their creed to the natives, who gaped and yawned and laughed and were impressed.

Now they were in Northern Mexico, though they remained unaware of the fact. Escorts of Indians convoyed them onwards and their faith-healing, simple and often unefficacious, was greatly in demand. South-west they still marched, over thorny plains thinly inhabited by the Pintos, that strange, light-coloured race which suffered from ophthalmia and had possibly a European ancestry—it is possible they were descendants of pre-Columbian white settlers. What settlers?

But here at last their south-westwards progress was stayed. Far in the south in lines of battlements upon the sky appeared the crests of range upon range of mountains. The Spaniards stared at them troubled. How pass these—and what lay beyond? Mexico—or some unknown devil-land?

A great confusion as to compass-points, customary in that day, appears to have fallen upon them. They debated their next move and decided against turning east and seeking the sea-coast where they had been so starved and mishandled. Southwards the mountains appeared to bar their progress. Westwards the tribesmen told them was an uninhabited land, desert, where they would assuredly starve. There appeared only one practicable route. This was to turn north-west, through the Rio Grande tributaries, and skirt to the north the great desert of rumour. So at last they might hold through fertile lands till they again attained a favourable southwards passage remote over there in the horizons of the west.

> Moreover, we chose this course because in traversing the country we should learn many particulars of it, so that should God our Lord be pleased to take any of us thence, and lead us to the land of Christians, we might carry that information and news of it.

He was consciously at last what he had not been when he left Seville for the bright glamour of the unknown coasts of the west: an explorer.

They had been seven years in North America. Through those seven years they had worked a slow passage along the Gulf coast to a point roughly near where the modern Monterey stands. Now they set out on a journey that was to last a long two years, through the habitations of dim tribes that even now we may identify only dimly, over a trek that extended for more than two thousand miles.

§9

The Indians parted from them with tears and waving hands, refusing that unknown west. The Spaniards plodded on alone, uncompanioned, the windings of the Rio Grande remotely seen in the north. Presently the affirmation of their late hosts that the west was uninhabited proved false. Instead, the exploring Spaniards arrived in a village where they discovered the first true agricultural activity they had seen since leaving Apalachen seven years before. They were on the edge of settled agricultural communities again. Maize and squash and pumpkins grew in well-tended fields. Halting a night and a day now at this village, now that, the Spaniards with their reputations and practice as healers pressed on with some speed. A curious rite accompanied them. A hundred or so Indians from one village would march with them to the next and at that next village levy toll on all goods available. Then the taxed village would send on its escort to the next village and levy a retaliatory tax—it was playing over again the game of touch which Cabeza de Vaca had learned in Jerez as a boy.

Everywhere they went in this new land they were hailed as Children of the Sun, miraculous travellers from other lands bringing new gifts of healing and enchantment. Cabeza de Vaca believed his progress and reception unique; but much the same seems to have greeted Quetzalcoatl landing on the Pacific shore of Mexico some six hundred years before—a strayed Indonesian or Hindu also hailed as a Child of the Sun. All those agricultural lands were alive with tales of miraculous beings just such as the Spaniards who had proved the bane and blessing of remote generations—as indeed, legend apart, they had.

In one village they were presented with the sacred gourd rattles, marks of magicians, which accompanied them throughout the remainder of their journeyings, wielded by the black Estebanico. In another, remote up the slopes of the Sierra Madre, they encountered two aliens at a village—cotton-clad men who had a plenitude of copper—who presented Dorantes with a copper rattle. Where these two came from is still mysterious, but the Spaniards were stirred by the sight of the signs of pseudo-civilization as for eight years they had not been stirred. The wonder civilization that had led them from Spain—could it be near at last?

Northwards was the land of copper, said the strangers, and northwards the Spaniards turned through the confluents of the Rio Sabinas, a rich and fertile land where they were well entertained by the Archaics. Here, also, they encountered buffalo-hides for the first time. The buffalo-herds of North America roamed almost as far south as this. They were beyond the lean and starving coasts of Galveston. Hunters as well as farmers, these tribes lived well on deer-meat, rabbit, turkey, and fed their strange guests lavishly as the latter wandered north in their search for the Golden City. Sometimes they went accompanied by small escorts, sometimes with thousands of hangers-on and holiday-makers tagging out behind them, at night the glow of their camp-fires lighting up forest and plain like the bivouacs of an embattled army.

But presently tiring of that northwards stravaiging they turned north-west and so for a period passed out of fertile country into the grim tundra-stretches of the Coahuila Desert. Here the rattlesnake lurked, and hunger with him, and here their escorts thinned out. But still before them and about them in those sparse holdings flew the news of the coming of the Children of the Sun. Ragged, bearded, burnt black in the sunshine, the Spaniards with their slave marched now with unaching feet, tempered to travel by the long roads from Florida. Beyond desert at last, they came again to a great stream gushing between cañons, the upper reaches of that river, the Rio Grande, which they had crossed long months before far down in the west.

Somewhere in the Big Bend mountains trouble stayed them awhile. The tribe neighbouring the handsome agricultural mountaineers amidst which they sojourned was a warlike one : once again we are apprised of the being of raiding nomads, like those of Galveston, which hung on the fringe of the Archaic settlements. Those folk of the west were buffalo-hunters, fierce men. The mountaineers were determined that the Children of the Sun should not go among them.

They compromised and went south instead to another agricultural community somewhere in the neighbourhood of the modern Presidio del Norte, where the Rios Grande and Conchos join. Here they found well-built pueblos inhabited by the "most civilized" race they had yet encountered. They were received as usual as Children of the Sun, and implored to heal the sick and teach magic. The latter at least they did, learning the simple natives the sign of the cross and suchlike ritual gestures. Then they sat down to debate their forward route.

North-east would lead them far from Mexico. South they were told was broken, inhospitable territory. North-west was a starving land up the banks of the Rio Grande.

Incomprehensibly, they chose the Rio Grande route, and early in January 1536 resumed their trek into the unknown.

§ 10

It seems to have been a cool and pleasant march, that upwards journey along the banks of the Rio Grande, despite the constant hunger which gnawed below the breast-bones of the travellers. The Indians were starving: hospitably or fearfully they shared their scant food with the wanderers, mistaking them, as usual, for Children of the Sun. Without gratitude the food was accepted and the Spaniards hurried on. By this time it is evident that all three, if not the negro, were men mentally overwrought, half-believing in their own divinity while still ascribing the thaumaturgism of their occasional "miracles" of faith-healing to the kindly gods of their own lost and kindly Spain. They made swift passage: they ate little, even in a land where there was little to eat.

Seventeen days after setting out they crossed the Rio Grande again, somewhere near the modern El Paso, and so reached their furthest north in the course of their memorable journey. They were on the borders of New Mexico, swarming with tribes half-nomad, half-settled, including the skilled pueblo-dwellers of remote Zuñi, the most highly civilized race north of the wanderings the three Spaniards had involuntarily undertaken.

But they had heard of waterholes at intervals to quench the thirst of those who crossed the desert. West accordingly in the track of the sunset they turned their bare and toil-hardened feet, through the sandhills of Medanos, by the salt-lake of the Salado, by trails age-old in that ageless continent, roads and routes tracked by the Amerindians of those regions since the coming of the first civilization to the first Americas fifteen hundred years before. Near Samalayuca they turned south-west, and through mountain and desert passed with hasting feet, their convoys of attendants from village to village still at their heels, into country that grew gradually more fertile, that gradually gave evidence of a more settled and orderly existence. Finally, penetrating the Sierra Madre to a village that appears to have stood somewhere on the Yaqui River in Sonora, they found fields waving green with maize, plantations of pumpkins and squash, a cotton-clad agricultural people who bore jewelled arrow-heads in their ceremonial dances, kindly folk who welcomed the frayed Children of the Sun with kindness, and even, it would seem, washed their garments for them. . . . It was a new glimpse of the diversity of races and cultures in even a fragment of the great continent they had almost crossed.

But they were not quite to accomplish that crossing. Cabeza de Vaca's exploratory spirit was for the moment broken, the rumoured Golden City impossible of achievement. He longed as passionately as his companions to escape these regions of staring admirers, decently cotton-clad though they might be, covering "their shameful parts" in seemly fashion, not naked and unashamed like the coast-dwellers of Bad Hap land. Wars sometimes raged in these regions ; but news of the coming of the Children of the Sun led to truce. Cabeza de Vaca and his companions, unhindered, marched from village to village, southwards, finally descending the Sonora Valley almost within smell of the Pacific to an Indian town, adobe-built, somewhere by the site of present-day Ures.

Here they heard again of the Zuñi wealth and power far in the north, and perhaps hesitated, thinking of a raid up into those remote regions, themselves to catch sight of the golden cities of Ciboa. But they were in no case for any such expedition. They turned definitely south.

The sea, the Pacific, was less than a hundred miles away, but they had had enough experience already of the hard life of Amerindian fishers and seafolk to have any hankering to visit its coasts. Marching parallel with that unglimpsed ocean they passed by the modern Matape, forded the flooded Yaqui River, and came on an Indian wearing a necklace of which a sword-belt buckle was part of the decoration. . . . So they learned of the nearness of their kind at last—an expedition that had raided up as remotely north as this, killing, plundering, raping in the usual Spanish fashion ; till the Indians had gathered in a great body and exterminated it near the Rio Fuente.

But they levelled none of the blame on the foot-weary

travellers. Instead, they lodged them and fed them and sped them on their southwards search.

Presently Alvar Nuñez and his companions found that southwards search giving ample proof of the presence or nearness of Christians. Gutted villages, rotting corpses by the side of the trail, trees decorated with fleshless skeletons—all showed that Spanish raiding-parties had passed. Cabeza de Vaca records his joy to know of nearness to his kind ; but also a wild compassion stirred in his heart, seeing the wilderness his kind were making. Perhaps his mind went back to the unhampered journeyings of the last two thousand miles, the kindliness and gratitude with which he had been received, the simple men of Bad Hap land who had shared their last mouthful with the wanderers, all the incidents of trail and trek that had shown these heathens of the great lost continent kinder than Christians, heathen though they were. As though penetrating wall on wall of prejudice and fear and gross and bestial superstition, that knowledge of a common kinship of humanity reached down to the heart of Cabeza de Vaca and never again, it would seem, quite left it.

The lands devastated by the slave-raiders drew nearer. Dorantes and Cabeza de Vaca in one party, Castillo and the negro Estebanico in another, they set out in search of the Christians. Burning homesteads marked the nearness of those followers of the Prince of Peace. The Pacific littoral reeked with tales of their cruelties ; whole tribes had abandoned their fertile fields and fled to the safety of the hills. At length, early in March of the year 1536 Cabeza de Vaca emerged from the bush near the River Sinaloa into the sight of four halted horsemen. They stared their surprise at his almost naked figure, his matted beard, and then cried out and ran towards him as he called to them, weeping, in broken Spanish.

§ 11

It was a slave-raiding band of Diego de Alcaraz, an under-captain of Culiacan, that they had encountered. The slaver was delighted, casting eyes on the six hundred or so Indians who had come in escort of the Children of the Sun. Promptly he fell on their camp and enslaved them. Castillo, Dorantes and (though his opinion was of no account) the negro Este-

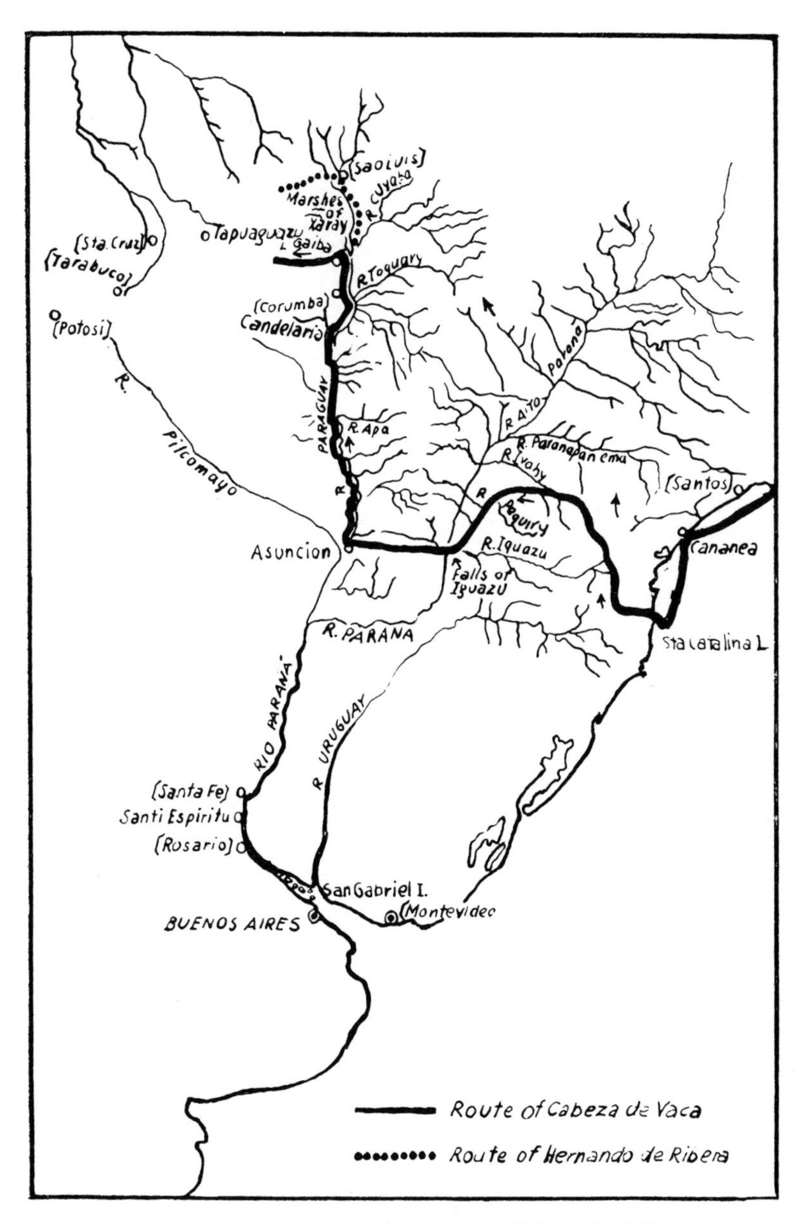

SOUTH AMERICAN JOURNEYS OF CABEZA DE VACA

banico appear to have looked on with considerable complacence. It was what Indians were for.

But Cabeza de Vaca, that devout, dreaming soul, was of different calibre. He was moved to a passionate shame that this should befall the followers of the Children of the Sun. Straightway he set out for Culiacan and there lodged his protest with the governor of the district, one Melchior Diaz. So doing, he passes out of that eight years of wandering and exploring—involuntary and voluntary—which have brought him to the pages of this record.

But we may note with brevity his life in that long hiatus of years before he set out again adventuring through the unknown lands of the New World. Diaz upheld his claim and had his escort released by Alcazar; that accomplished, Cabeza de Vaca and his companions journeyed down to Mexico City and attained at last Christian food and company and soul-comfort, Cabeza de Vaca a wild and ragged figure astounding the hidalgos with his appearance and the tale of his incredible Odyssey.

But one incident in it was credited readily enough—the rumour of the golden cities of Ciboa (which was founded on the rumour of the distant Zuñi pueblos in New Mexico). Would Cabeza de Vaca join an expedition against that northern El Dorado?

He would not. He had other plans. Another Golden City, never seen on sea or land, had enslaved the vision of Cabeza de Vaca. Probably he did not confide his plans to the Mexican Viceroy, Antonio de Mendoza. They were daring enough. He had ascertained that the grant of the lands of Florida to Narvaez had never been rescinded or supplanted. Now Narvaez was dead and he himself, as he knew, the only worthy survivor to take his place. He sailed for Spain determined to obtain the concession of all the lands of the modern United States to his governorship. And when he himself was governor——

It is probable that his intentions towards those natives among whom he had sojourned were kindly enough, though his altruism has been distortedly magnified by later commentators. He planned to found a great northern colony where the Indian would not be enslaved but suitably (and no doubt forcibly) Christianized under due supervision. And in the so doing the Golden Cities of Ciboa would be discovered and suitably annexed to the king's domains, and ruled by the Church for the glory of God.

After various misadventures of encounter, flight and fight by the way—for the seas swarmed with French privateers—Cabeza de Vaca's vessel put in at Lisbon on the 9th of August 1537. Here he heard (from his point of view) appalling news. A golden kingdom in the Americas had indeed been discovered—that of Peru, in South America. Pizarro had subdued it. Adventurers were flocking back loaded with the loot of the most glorious civilization of the Amerindians, that civilization carried across the Pacific in the early days of the Christian era, that civilization compounded so skilfully of so many alien fragments—Indian ritual and Polynesian myth and Egyptian culture, and even stray fragments of Greek philosophy. . . . But of these facts the Spanish conquistadores, robbing temples and murdering nobles, had had no cognizance and would have been little interested if they had. The most notable among their returned number was a certain Hernando de Soto from whom the king had borrowed money, and who in return had obtained from His Majesty a grant to occupy and colonize all the lands known as Florida. . . .

It was a bitter blow, and for a little it seems that Cabeza de Vaca sank under it. He went home to Jerez, to the greeting of that dim wife on whose face the light of history shines hardly at all, whose voice we hear only once, and that faintly, giving her husband an account of how she behaved as steward of his property while he was in the "Indies". She had behaved commendably. Perhaps it was she who urged him to go to court and lay his case before the king, seeking to have the de Soto grant rescinded.

En route, he halted in Seville and conferred with Hernando de Soto. The latter offered to make him lieutenant of his expedition. But this was not good enough for the grave-faced, taciturn man who dreamed of himself as the Ruler and Protector of all the Northern Indians. He journeyed on, seeking the court. King Charles was in Monzon. Cabeza de Vaca obtained an interview with him; the king listened kindly. He fully agreed as to the barbarity of the methods by which the Indians had been entreated. He himself (and this was no lie) was strongly opposed to enslaving the Indians. But he could not cancel de Soto's grant. Cabeza de Vaca must wait on the Council of the Indies for employment on some other and suitable expedition connected with the West.

The summer faded from the grey walls of Saragosa ; winter came howling down the bleak passes of the mountains ; and still, shiveringly, Cabeza de Vaca besieged the court for employment. Spring came, another summer, another year, and we see him dimly through the dust and squabble of those years, his purpose still firm in his mind, if heartsick for fulfilment. Who but he had a right to seek out new golden lands, carrying the teaching of Christ ?—himself, a Child of the Sun in Indian eyes.

And in September of 1539 his patience and his dogged badgering of the Council of the Indies was rewarded. The Spanish colonies on the Rio de la Plata in South America were in sad case, crying for help, fever-ridden, Indian-attacked, badly governed. Cabeza de Vaca was appointed the new governor, his territory extending from the borders of Peru to the Straits of Magellan.

In October 1540 he sailed for Paraguay with two ships and two hundred and forty expeditionaries.

§ 12

Juan de Ayolas had been governor of the Plate River settlements. As noted before, an expedition had pushed through the trackless Chaco from those settlements, reached the Andes, looted there a mysterious silver-rich native state, and marched back to the Paraguay where the Spanish murdering adventurers were in return murdered by the natives. Fired by the news of this feat, Ayolas had had a numerous convoy row for long weeks up the Parana and Paraguay till he came to Candelaria. There he had split his forces, instructed Domingo Martinez de Irala to hold the base camp, and himself launched out into the wilds in search of the silver city. With him he had taken two score conscripted Indians : Indians of much the same stage of civilization as those Cabeza de Vaca had encountered around the headwaters of the Rio Grande, agriculturists, shy, strong men, friendly but suspicious.

Irala had awaited the return of his commander only a few months, then had sailed down river and established Asunción. His brutalities in charge of the colony had led the River Plate Spaniards to send to Spain the request for a new governor.

There was an important codicil in Cabeza de Vaca's appointment. If Ayolas should return from his expedition into the bush, and still prove sane, Cabeza de Vaca must surrender the governorship to him, and serve under him.

The squadron meandered across the Atlantic in the easy-going sailing of those days. Almost they ran aground on rocks off the coast of Brazil—and so would have done but for a cricket aboard which chirped loudly at the suspected nearness of land. Finally they put in at an island which rose wooded off the Brazilian shore. It was Santa Catalina island, inhabited by shy Indians whom Cabeza de Vaca had lured from the woods "and entreated with kindliness". The rest of the Spaniards stared. Was this their new commander's method of dealing with such ordure ?

It was. And at first it proved successful. From the shy simple men of Santa Catalina he heard of two Franciscans, relicts of a previous expedition, living on the mainland. He had them brought to his ships and questioned on the affairs of the River Plate colony. Of those they knew little. But soon additional information came to hand with a boatload of deserters from the Buenos Aires garrison far to the south. Ayolas was reported dead, killed by the Indians of the Paraguay. Irala was acting governor back in Asunción, deep in the bush, surrounded by tribes every day growing the more bitterly hostile.

How long would it take the expedition to reach Asunción, sailing up the Parana and Paraguay ?

Perhaps a year. Perhaps longer. And by that time it was very likely that Irala and his expeditionaries would be dead.

Cabeza de Vaca then came to a decision that was to enlist him on the second great exploring expedition of his life. Instead of coasting down to Buenos Aires and sailing with pain and trouble up the rivers to remote Asunción and its threatened garrison, he would land an expedition and march across country.

His companions attempted, with growing hostility, to dissuade him. The country was wild and barbarous, filled with cannibals, savages who lived off the flesh of men, wild beasts scarcely less ferocious than the men. Cabeza de Vaca was unimpressed. He had encountered both before.

Landing a hundred men under one Pedro Dorantes, he ordered them to scout ahead to the west as to the practicality of a route. Reluctantly they marched off into the green day-night of the Brazilian jungle, adventured and rested and plodded ahead there for a long three months, crossed a hilly stretch of country, encountered no hostile natives, and appeared at last in view of Santa Catalina island whole and unharmed. The route was practicable, if the stretch of country so enormous as to defy courage.

Cabeza de Vaca's courage was unimpaired. On the 15th of October, 1541, he had two hundred and fifty men landed at the mouth of the Tapucu River, fifty miles to the north of the island. There he exercised them, examined their arms and equipment, and on the 22nd of November marched off at their head into the interior of Brazil.

§ 13

At first the going was by forest paths, deep in detritus, green and a glare in the hot sunshine. The men behind the governor, lightly clad, plodded on stoically but uninspirited. They were given no licence to loot and rape and rob in the Indian villages encountered. Was this the fashion for a commander to treat his conquering army ?

At length came the beginnings of the hills, cold and barren. They ploughed through their sulphurous passes into the strange Brazilian sunsets. Nineteen days after leaving the coast they came in sight of great plantations of maize and cassava. The cultivators were Guaranis, cannibals and fowlkeepers. Cabeza de Vaca bargained for food with them, paid for what was delivered, and kept a tight rein on the looting propensities of his followers. Murmuring grew ever louder in the Spanish ranks.

On through the unending, unbegun forests again. Five days from the first village they came to a great river, the Iguazú flowing through the woods westwards. Here Cabeza de Vaca appears to have built a bridge to transport his foot-sore expedition across the water, and then marched on along the Iguazú banks. Lured by the tale of the white man's friendliness, the Indians of the forests flocked to meet them and feed them. Maize, honey, birds, deer were readily obtainable and the expedition feasted, but grumblingly, for Cabeza de Vaca ordered them each night to camp at a distance from the Indian villages. Nor would he allow them to trade directly with the Indians but only through his personal lieutenants and other intermediaries. This fact was yet to be remembered against him.

Instead of holding their march down the Iguazú-Parana and reaching the Paraguay, the expedition crossed the river and plunged again into the forests beyond. It was the true Brazilian jungle, choked with creepers, the air bright with the flash of insect-wings, great monkeys screaming from the trees as the soldiers passed underneath, lazy alligators opening a languid eye by this creek and that to stare at the passing feet of the Spaniards. Presently the cultivated clearings of the Guaranis were left behind. The forest thinned out on the fringe of a range of barren mountains, never properly explored to this day. They climbed them gasping in air that seemed thin after the coagulated flow of air-currents in the corridors of the forests. Westwards, they saw jungle rise again.

Cabeza de Vaca walked ahead of the expedition, barefoot by now, the Indian guides trotting beside him, glancing round now and again at the haughty, contemptuous faces of the mounted hidalgos, or the sweating countenances of the Spanish rank and file trailing despondently west. So thick grew the undergrowth that a score of men at a time went forward to hack out a way for the labouring expedition. With night came clouds of insects that might only be endured with the lighting of great fires which glimmered far and bright through the wastes of the forests. Reclining to rest, some Spanish soldier would give an ejaculation of alarm as a bright snake glided away ; or, peering into the darkness beyond the encampment, see slinking, tawny forms turning towards the firelight bright golden eyes. Were they completely lost ? Was there any end to this forest ?

At last they came to a great village and a clearing. Here, famished, the Spaniards ate so that all the next morning were troubled with stomach-ache—all except Cabeza de Vaca himself. He gave orders for the forward march despite a wail of protest. March they could not : half of them were sick ! To this he answered that those who stayed behind would stay permanently. He set forth with the guides, and after him, stragglingly, belly-gripping, came the expedition. Presently they had walked off the effects of the feast, as Cabeza de Vaca had foreseen.

The forest avenues seemed endless. Wild boars scuttled across the choked trails: they saw the strange armadillo and in dark depths heard the sloth cry his strange eerie plaint. Crossing themselves, they followed on at the heels of the untiring Cowhead. He had gone mad again, they sneered, again imagined himself a God as in North America, and was searching for Indios to worship him.

December passed. With the new year the forests again thinned out, and again came uplands sparsely clothed in bamboo scrub. By now the provisions they had carried were exhausted. They split the bamboo canes and ate the weevils that nested within them, and drank of the brackish waters of those curious slopes. Then the bamboo brakes were left behind: in the west they saw the flow and glow of a river. Next morning they found themselves in a rich riverine land, watered by nameless tributaries of the Paraguay, haunted by great droves of deer and peccary and wild boar. They hunted the boar with their crossbows and halted and ate flesh after a long fast.

Here the two Franciscans quarrelled with Cowhead and disappeared into the forest ahead with a hundred followers, mostly Indians. They vanish from the record for a while, but for incidental mention of the fact that they plundered stores of food here and there, and slept with great numbers of Indian women. The Indians seem to have been complaisant. Cabeza de Vaca was less so. He had a formal indictment of the Franciscans drawn up by his notary.

Rumours had come to him that Asunción was now undistant. At a spot which he ascertained was a tributary of the Paraguay, Cabeza de Vaca despatched two Indians, by river, to bear the news of their whereabouts to Asunción, and asking for two luggers to be sent down the Parana to convoy them upstream. The two Indians set out on their journey, and Alvar Nuñez and his following took to the forests once more.

Presently they came again on the banks of a great water. It was the Iguazú, met anew after long wanderings. Here it seemed broad as (that unfailing comparison) "the Guadalquivir". Cabeza de Vaca determined to descend it, hoping to meet with the rescuing luggers from Asunción. Instead, as the canoes purchased from the natives swung half of the expedition around wide bends, and the other half plodded along the shore, they heard the distant thunder of falls. So that day they came, the first of their kind, to the foam and fall of the great Iguazú falls, very terrifying and lovely, a play against the evening light. Here they had to disembark and set about a long and difficult portage. Arriving exhausted at the foot of the falls, and hoping for rest and food, they discovered neither.

Instead an army of Guaranis, strong bowmen, had assembled to resist the passage of the invaders.

Cabeza de Vaca had neither doubts nor hesitations. He remembered the road to Culiacan and the Indians who had greeted him as a Child of the Sun when he walked among them fearlessly. He did so now, carrying gifts. Grumbling and shame-faced, the Indians lowered their bows. Instead of massacring the weary expedition they soothed and petted and fêted it, and guided it across the Iguazú, to resume, luggerless, its seemingly endless march.

But now the forest had been left behind. They had come to the thinly wooded, rolling llanos of Paraguay, rich and fragrant in flowers at that season, so that the Spaniards stared astounded at such loveliness in this dark continent. The natives guided them on, trek after trek, with friendliness because of the appearance and acts of the dark-faced, devout leader. February passed, and the rumour of the river drew near. With rumour came at least an emissary from Ascunción itself, to guide them to the town.

So, at nine o'clock in the morning, on the 11th of March, 1542, the expedition of the new governor marched into Asunción, having walked a thousand miles from the coast through land never before trodden by white men and previously considered impenetrable.

§ 14

Asunción Alvar Nuñez found under the temporary governorship of Domingo de Irala, a typical Spanish soldier of the time, courteous, cruel, courageous and domineering. With a poor grace Irala surrendered up the governorship to the newcomer, and that newcomer proceeded to astound and mortify Asunción. He commanded that the Indian slaves be freed: he forbade unnecessary wars and raids against the dark tribes of the forest: he planned the building of a City of God in the heart of the dark, half trodden Americas; and (seeing no incompatibility of one vision with the other) he set about organizing a great expedition to penetrate north and north-westward to the Golden City of Manoa.

That northwards road had been ascended twice before. But no such detailed account of it comes to us as from the expedition that Cabeza de Vaca led. Both he and his enemies left voluminous accounts of that most pathetic of all the attempts to reach the Golden City of the interior—that Golden City which Colonel Fawcett set out to find less than a decade ago.

Wherever the Spaniards penetrated from the Atlantic seaboard into South America they were met by rumours of a land of great wealth, ruled by kingly dignitaries, magicians, godlike men, which lay long days travelling into the west. Its centre was a city where gold was so common that it was used for "the most shameful" of domestic utensils. Beside this city was a great lake with templed islands in the midst thereof. Its ruler was a Child of the Sun.

The modern investigator in that haze of inaccurate documentation that details the rumours and legends and wanderings of the time is faced with two alternatives, and generally selects unhesitatingly. Either this persistent rumour of a secret city which has haunted South America from that day to this was and is no more than a transfiguration of the legend of the power and wealth of the great Peruvian native civilizations, or there actually was some other region remote in the Brazilian bush where the Archaic Civilization flowered forth even such strange bloom of culture and attainment as was encountered by Europeans in the flourishing metropolis of Cuzco or remembered in the ruins of Tiawanako.

Even yet the second alternative has not been definitely disproved: we are as far from certainty in that matter as Cabeza de Vaca was, though we lack either his optimism or his urge. That such a civilization could have grown to maturity in the dense riverine jungle is not impossible: civilizations root for almost every reason but sound economic ones. But that it should still survive undiscovered is, to say the least, improbable. Even so, there may yet be explorers who will come on the ruins of some pueblo in that bush and know they have found Manoa at last.

Cabeza de Vaca seems to have had little doubt of the success of the expedition he launched from Asunción six months after his arrival there. With ten luggers and four hundred Spaniards, besides a force of Indian auxiliaries, he ascended the Paraguay through the droughts and heats of a long summer. Sometimes they had to land and make portage; sometimes they rowed and stumbled through long leagues of marsh. The Indians flocked down to the shores to stare on them: Indians generally hostile in encounter, though speedily pacified by the tactics of Alvar Nuñez. He might be on a raid against the great Indian city of treasure and legend, but he would allow no robbing of the roosts and riverine plantations by his grumbling, fever-stricken followers.

In a month they had reached as far up the river as that spot where Juan de Ayolas, the earlier governor, had died. This was Candelaria. It was on the border of Gran Chaco, the Green Hell of modern nomenclature. Alvar Nuñez halted, parleyed with the Indians, antagonized them in an unfortunate speech, and had to set about the penetration of that wildest stretch of the American bush unaided.

Mosquitoes descended in stinging droves upon the adventurers as they fought on northwards through weary days and nights; vampire bats sucked their blood while they slept—Cabeza de Vaca himself had a "slice of his toe" bitten off. Then, on the right, they found the great converging mouths of the Taquary pouring their slime-green waters into the attenuating flood of the Paraguay. Caymans lifted lazy eyes from the mudbank to stare at the labouring advance of the luggers: great anthills towered offshore. At night, tying up the luggers, they would hear far off the wail of the sloth, the howl of the hunting jaguar.

They reached the broad mouths of the Cuyaba. Down this stream, into the Paraguay, the Portuguese from Brazil had penetrated once before, turning west in search of the Golden City. So Alvar Nuñez heard, and himself turned west in their tracks, coming at last to a spot where he erected a permanent base, Los Reyes on Lake Gaiba. Here a great Indian village was encountered: Alvar Nuñez entered into friendly relations with those ceremonial cannibals, the great-eared cultivators of that forest, men who worshipped the devil in some contentment and happiness. Alvar Nuñez had them sternly warned against this practice, instructing them to listen to the teaching of the Christian friars, who would acquaint them with the terrors of hell. Impressed and grateful, the Indians promised to bring supplies of food to the base.

As November came in Cabeza de Vaca completed his preparations for the march on Manoa. Quite definitely it lay due west : some Indians said twenty days' march, some thirty. He left a fourth of his men to guard Los Reyes, and took the trackless jungle track into the west.

Indians guided them. Presently even the accustomed guides were at fault in that dense tangle of flowering undergrowth and giant cane-brake. Cabeza de Vaca had men walk ahead with cutlasses cutting a passage for the labouring advance of the main body. Horses floundered fetlock-deep in the viscid mud of the treey corridors, and the Spaniards, who had learned no lessons of dress or accoutrement from all their years in the Americas, cursed under the weight of heavy clothes and heavier armour. But Cabeza de Vaca was undepressed looking at the sunset colours in gold and blood as he took to his bed each night. Strangely, devout and ascetic though he was, he had a fine camp-bed carried into those jungle tracks for his use. Muttering and cursing, sweating men swore to remember that bed.

But that light in the sunset boded no good. Four days after the commencement of the march the rain began to fall—the great tropic rains of the interior. Presently the jungle paths became quagmires. An Indian sent forward to a rumoured village had to crawl half the way there and back. Yes, he reported, the Indians of the forward village confirmed that there was inhabited land even further west—at a distance of sixteen days' journey, a rocky hill uprising from the forest.

Sixteen days ! Alvar Nuñez had his hopes rekindled. But his following boiled over. Sixteen days of crawling on hands and knees along the littered, choked, and dripping trails ? Carrying the governor's bed the while ? . . . They voted an instant return to Los Reyes.

§ 15

There was nothing else for it. Reluctantly, with that bright vision of Manoa remote in the bush to haunt all the remaining years of his life, Cabeza de Vaca gave the order for the expedition to turn about. So turning, he ended the last of his ventures in unknown America.

Los Reyes he found in desperate straits. The surrounding Indians had revolted and refused to bring food to the needy Christians. Cabeza de Vaca sent expeditions up and down the river in search of friendly natives and food. Some of the expeditionaries perished of fever, some under the clubs of the cannibal Guaranis. But one, led by a Captain Hernando de Ribera, sailed up the Paraguay for twenty-three days and returned with a strange tale. At the end of that twenty-three days' voyage, beyond the leagues-stretching marshes of Xaray, they had come on a great town of the Indians, neat and reed-built, where the ruling chief presented Ribera with a great bar of gold and a crown of silver. Near at hand, he had told, was the country of the Amazons, the breastless women, who might be raided by the Spaniards if they desired more wealth.

The Spaniards did so desire. Abandoning their boats somewhere near the site of the modern San Luis, they had marched off west into the slither and pelt of the jungle rainy season. It was a land of miasmic swamps. They waded knee-deep hour on hour, day on day. By night they collected drifting wood and piled it on sandbanks and kindled unchancy fires. By day they slipped and staggered and stumbled into the beckoning west where the breastless women were reputed to be "very hot and very rich". For fifteen days this fantastic march endured. Then higher land came. The Spaniards climbed out on it, dripping, to be met by dejected groups of starving Indians. Ribera gestured questions: Where was the country of the Amazons?

In another month's travel, beyond the westward floods, he would come to that land of heart's desire, the Indians replied, staring a lacklustre unsurprise at the draggled adventurers.

Ribera and his Spaniards cursed them, their country, the distant Amazons, all the soaking, reeking planet, and turned back to flounder through the lagoons to San Luis. That attained, they sailed down the Paraguay again and came to Los Reyes, where Cabeza de Vaca, wearied and dispirited, lay deep in fever the while mutiny and a violent distaste for the governor and all his ways seethed throughout the colony.

§ 16

Beyond that point the saga of Cabeza de Vaca, that strangest admixture of devoutness and monomania, gentleness and arrogance, sinks into the turgid waters of plot and counterplot, battle, murder and sudden death, an epitome of early Spanish-American colonization. He returned down-river to Asunción a sick and beaten man. The colonists revolted, imprisoned him, threatened him with death, and finally shipped him to Spain with a load of accusations against him—some of them read curiously unreal in this later day, some of them have an authentic ring. So, for the last time, in a day in March 1545, peering from the tiny porthole in the tiny cabin where he lay chained, Alvar Nuñez looked back on that continent that had given him so much of fantastic dream and fantastic adventure, and saw its shores glide off into evening, and lowered weary eyes from the sight. . . .

En route to Spain his captors attempted to poison him. But by then he had recovered much of his old strength of will. He refused the food, lived half-starved, and at last, in December, reached Spain. Then began a course of trial and imprisonment that lasted many years.

He is a dim figure amid that squalid squabble of accusation and counter-accusation. He is not only a dim but a tiring figure. It was well-nigh impossible to adjudicate between him and the Paraguayan colonists, though the Spanish court at length did so, finding him three years after he landed guilty of all the charges brought against him. This was in March 1551. He was removed definitely from the governorship of the Rio de la Plata, forbidden to visit the Americas again, and ordered to serve as a horseman in Barbary in the King of Spain's army.

Old and poverty-stricken, he was still kept in close custody, despite the later proviso of the court's finding. But six months later the sentence was modified. He need not go to Barbary. He was released from prison. All Spain was very bored with him and his case. It hoped he would keep quiet in future.

It was mistaken. He continued to make appeal on appeal, impoverishing himself and his family in those vain pursuits. We hear dimly of his wife, old and impoverished as himself, assisting him loyally. But at length all his money was spent. In 1556 he fell very ill and appealed direct to the king for aid. Incomprehensibly, the king relented and made a substantial grant in September of that year to Alvar Nuñez "that he might be cured of his illness".

Thereafter the records are silent. Probably no cure was affected, though he may have lingered on a few years more. History had passed beyond him, history and exploration alike, the Americas resounding, north and south, to the tread of the feet of following adventurers on those trails he had beaten through wild leagues of bush and swamp while he sought the golden cities of mirage, the unknown lands where he would win wealth and many souls to God.

So the Child of the Sun passed to a last eclipse.

§ 17

The final chapter in the history of American exploration was not, as we have noted, written by Cabeza de Vaca. Indeed, that final chapter is still unwritten. But his service was a real and a great one. For his era he was among the most acute and penetrating of explorers; he had a close interest in mountain and bluff, tribe and tribal weapon, the setting places of the sun, the appearances of the sky in rainy seasons, all the good land-hunger in another sense. Equally, his deficiencies were largely those of his time: his insistence upon regarding all the ceremonial of the Indian's religion as directly inspired of the devil, his practice of foisting upon all that mass of observance pseudo-Christian or Satanic meanings, his hunger for the ease and security that successful gold-thieving would bring.

But his two great journeys as no others opened the eyes of men to the wide and wild diversity of culture and custom that dominated the Americas. Here at last, Europe began to realize, was no stray fragment of Asia, but verily a New World, with new and strange peoples—a world thinly populated, conquerable. Europe belted on its armour and sailed west; where before there was scarcely a ship but a Spanish ship, France and England now sailed their fleets to conquest. And if that conquest the unprejudiced may hardly write on the credit side of Cabeza de Vaca's achievement, yet he left for us much that would otherwise have been lost. His pen was one of the least prejudiced in recording the life and being of the Amerindians, of customs ranging from those of the Simple Men who entreated him so kindly to those of the Archaic Civilization, raiders and freebooters, kindly human beings like himself distorted from the human norm under the influences of civilization and its misbeliefs.

VI

FERNÃO DE MAGALHÃES AND THE FORTUNATE ISLES

§ 1

COLUMBUS had set out Westward, on the trail of a dozen rumours, and encountered, like Leif Ericsson, the great Barrier of the Americas. That barrier Cabeza de Vaca and a score of others had explored and traversed, convincing themselves that between Europe and the Far East was a new world, an unimagined and greatly unimaginable continent. Was there any passage or strait that led through this continent to the sea beyond, to a westward route by which men might attain the islands of wealth and perfume and spice and legend ?

Here the chronicles achieve a fine confusion of names and dates. By the beginning of the sixteenth century the English and French had already commenced a northwards search for that passage-way ; southwards, along the coast of the South Americas, it is possible that lone Spanish traders (in not officially recognized ships or expeditions), had penetrated as far as Cape Horn, or perhaps passed entirely through that strait that was later to be christened with the name of the remarkable individual who dominates the scene in this section. For few of those traders and voyageurs who put out southwards from Buenos Aires were explorers in any sense at all. Their objects were speedy enrichment by trade, and return to Spain. The globes of Schöner, issued in 1515 and 1520, suggest that the passage south of South America was already known ; and that possibility summons up a vision of a lone and secretive trader slipping through that passage-way and penetrating across the unknown Pacific to trade with the distant East even while Ferdinand Magellan was attempting to din home his plan, unwitting his lateness, at the courts of Portugal and Castile.

But this is only a possibility, and a remote one. The geographers of that age were armchair men greatly given to armchair daring, what of the breadth and extent of the area of the planet confirmed by the voyages of Columbus and his successors. Schöner in his globes may well have been doing no more than exercising his imagination on the Americas as he did on Terra Australis—that immense southwards continent he postulated as a geographical necessity around the South Pole and extending far into Antarctic and Pacific waters.

Slowly the sea-route to the Far East, round the coast of Africa, was being mapped out by the indefatigable Portuguese, brown men, bearded, greedy and cruel and strangely inhuman to our alien eyes. They were adventurers in the geographical unknown of as shoddy a quality as was ever known. Few had vision or selflessness in any degree; they were most of them the wealth-haunted, ghoul-haunted men of their time and class, so that even Vasco da Gama is not for this record, he lacked both that impersonality and that pitiful heroic perversity which characterized men like Columbus and Cabeza de Vaca, men like that youth, Fernão de Magalhães, who sailed with da Gama's great expedition of 1497.

§ 2

Magellan was born some time about the year 1480 at the family seat of Sabrosa, near Chaves in Traz-os-Montes. He was of ancient and haughty and much blood-letting Portuguese descent, a noble, the oldest of a family of three sisters and two brothers. Very early there was instilled into him the arrogance and pride and self-possession of his blood. The Magalhães were not of towering lineage, and their province, the only inland province in Portugal, was of no great moment or import in those stirring days when Portugal had awakened and looked seawards. But Magellan considered himself of a blood and descent equal to that of any in the land; he seems to have had few doubts or disbeliefs in either himself or the established order of things. A dark-faced, heavy louring boy in the trunks and hose of his period he wandered around the great odoriferous, rambling family residence at Sabrosa, perpetually covered in the moist Portuguese dust, crowded with innumerable uncles and cousins, retainers, cooks, page-boys, mules, donkeys, offal, and all the litter, animate, inanimate and in between that characterized the domestic economy of a house of his time and class. But he did not envisage those things as either fulfilling his life or his destiny. He had early made up his mind to seek the court and recognition there; he hated with a very deep passion the squalor and dull indignity of his ancestral estate.

So, growing up amidst the safe solemnities of life at Sabrosa, he seems to have found the mountains perpetually vexing his horizon, in wonder on what lay beyond, what they did and wore and said at Lisbon, how the king looked, how a great captain felt sailing his treasure-ships up the Tagus? Treasure-ships from the East, ships from the dim and distant and strange West discovered and claimed for Spain by the vile-born Genoan merchant, the Colombo. . . . A mere merchant! If a noble should essay such voyages what glory might he not attain!

He would stare, in the hot silence of the long afternoons, at the ancestral arms carved above the great wide door at Sabrosa while the urchins peered out at him from the rambling shacks of the servitors. To add fresh glory to those arms! . . . And turn away, to regret his own youth and look forward to the time when, as promised him by that indefinite father of his whose name, if it was not Pedro, was either Ruy or Gil, he might ride out of this sleeping valley with its hot smell of goats and peasants, its droop of unintoxicating vines—on the road to Lisbon, to life in Lisbon. . . . Years afterwards men were to come riding down the valley at the king's command and hack that coat of arms away in crumbling flakes; but that was no vision of the heavy-jowled boy staring across the hills.

At last, at the age of sixteen or seventeen, the time came. A certain shyness seems to have come over Fernão at that coming. But father Ruy-Gil-Pedro and mother Mesquita Impenta treated his shyness with a brusque disregard. There was no other way of advancement for a gentleman than to go to court and there win to favour, secure command in the army, a place on the council, or the like honour. Their vision did not, as their son's, extend to those seas in unceasing play flinging up the long questing Atlantic rollers against the coasts of Portugal.

§ 3

He found the Portuguese court agog with the news of the great voyage of Vasco da Gama—the voyage which had carried the Europeans around Africa, the first circumnavigation since the days of King Necho, to the Indian Ocean and so across to India itself. Calicut had been reached, rich in wealth from the spice-trade, and its rumours of even richer lands beyond—Ceylon with its cinnamon, Malacca with its cloves, Malaya with its great tin mines. For a little while it seemed to the court at Lisbon, listening to the account of that amazing voyage of 24,000 miles, that the expedition of the Genoan across the Atlantic had been foolish and unnecessary. Here was the Land of Spice—that necessary commodity in the keeping and eating of the meats of the day—brought in contact by the reasonable and secure eastwards passage. Magellan, nineteen years of age, heavily built, haughty, courteous, listened and pondered, as he learned his duties as a Gentleman of the Household. The eastwards route might be the most obvious route—but what of those lands that the Genoan had discovered out there in the Atlantic ? What connection had they with those distant lands of rumour of which da Gama had heard—the Spice Islands, the Moluccas ?

In such speculations and his ordinary duties he vanishes from our eyes for five long years. Throughout that period the far-sailing Portuguese continued to extend their influence and enlarge their trade about the coasts of India. Relations with the Indian potentates—especially with those who harboured Moslems—remained unsatisfactory. Portuguese were upon occasion murdered with a fine, almost Christian brutality, and their ships confiscated. And still the sea-route remained uncertain in great stretches down the half-known African coast, out in the wilds of the Indian Ocean. A second official voyage was required.

Vasco da Gama was commissioned to it in 1504. He was to take an Armada of fourteen ships, re-traverse the route of his great voyage, establish the Portuguese power firmly in India, and leave Francisco de Almeida there as Viceroy.

Innumerable Portuguese flocked down to Lisbon to volunteer for service in the expedition. The great Admiral, the cruellest and least magnanimous of men, a Portuguese Catholic

Puritan, had a heavy task in choosing between the service of this and that ragged but competent shipmaster, this and that incompetent noble who was nevertheless a good man with sword and harquebus. Disliked by his fellow-countrymen, sneered at as a prig and a proselytizing clown, the Admiral's task would have seemed hopeless to any other.

But with a chilling severity, refusing here, accepting there, da Gama manned his Armada. Presently the ships were in trim, loaded with provisions and guns and trade goods. Solemn mass was said, and the sins of the voyageurs commuted in invocation of that peaceful God whose name they were to spread abroad the Far East till the most obscenely cruel and treacherous of easterners were to shudder with a sickened horror at mention of the Christians' God. Vasco da Gama had his company confessed and embarked. In the ship stores was a supply of oil, capable of being boiled and used for the questioning of recalcitrant natives.

Among the common sailors was Fernão de Magalhães, a volunteer, a dark-faced, louring, squat court gallant who had abandoned the court, its dogs, its flirtations, its heavy spices and its chill meals in quest of—what ? Honour and glory, he would have answered, even as his mind strayed off unceasingly on that question ?—Columbus's Cuba—how did it lie in relation to the Moluccas ?

§ 4

Long years were to pass before he was even to attempt the answer to that question—years in which he endured the blister of suns on hot decks in the reel and sway and excrement-smell of sea-fights, years in which he hasted up and down this and that Indian street that ran with the blood of massacre, years of pillage and cruelty and a sordid avariciousness beyond the concepts of home-staying Europe. With Albuquerque he fought at Diu in that great sea-battle where the power of the Moslems in India went down before the superior strategy and artillery of the Christians ; with Albuquerque he was at the siege of Goa when the town was captured, coldly considered, and then carefully and serenely given over to rape and massacre, so that not one man, woman or child escaped. . . . He seems to have taken it all with a surly dispassion. There are tales

FERDINAND MAGELLAN

of his heroism and his escapes, conventional tales, showing him the conventionally cruel and savagely courageous Portuguese of his age and class. But the essential Magellan remains hidden away while slowly the Portuguese power crept down the Indian coasts.

Ceylon had been reached in 1507. In 1508, after Goa's fall, an expedition was despatched to Malacca where centuries before the homeward-sailing ships of Marco Polo had waited the monsoon long months. Malacca was seized and a fleet under Antonio d'Abrei despatched to discover the Islands even more distant, the islands of cloves and nutmegs.

Magellan sailed with that expedition, into those strange seas and about those stranger islands, down by Java, to Sumarat, where he captured a slave who was to help him much in his subsequent voyagings—and repay his enslavement by a royal revenge. Perhaps the slave was no Sumatran native—he told Magellan much of the seas and tides down there in the uncertain east. Magellan discoursed on these with his friend Francisco Serrano. Serrano's objects in these voyagings and adventurings were sane and Portuguese: he wished to make money, to capture women and sleep with them, to return to Portugal. But Magellan had become an uneasy quantity among these islands. An old question had come haunting his mind: which of them was Cuba, the island discovered by the Genoan?

To Magellan and the men of his time there was nothing more likely than that some Indonesian island was Cuba. The vast extent of the hemisphere of water was not realized. That the earth was indeed a sphere had not been proved by actual circumnavigation: it was merely an article of faith. Cuba and the surrounding islands—the American continent itself was accounted a cluster of islands—were held, quite falsely, to be no more than remote, detached lands on the fringe of the Grand Khan's dominions. In a fashion, knowing as we now do how much of their cultural capital the early American civilizations drew from Asia, we can acknowledge this as true: the early Spanish explorers in the Central Americas who thought so much of the life and ritual and decoration of those countries repeated the East were not mistaken. But of the immense distances which those early Asiatic colonizers, civilizing America, had crossed, there was no concept. Somewhere beyond Cuba, beyond Panama, beyond

Florida, a short distance sail, was Asia and the Asiatic islands. . . .

So Magellan believed, and so a project appears to have slowly matured in his mind. Perhaps he gathered from his slave and others in the Moluccas rumours of the still more distant islands of Polynesia, inhabited by a simple and child-like people—undoubtedly such hospitable innocents as the natives of the West Indies who had vexed the Spaniards "because the hardness of their heads blunted good swords". Sailing south-west beyond Cuba one might pass amidst those islands and a new, swift route to the Moluccas.

In 1517 he sailed for home, coming to Lisbon, and there apparently immersing himself in a sudden and unexpected study—that of navigation. It was an essential part of education among the cultured of the day—ladies studied navigation, lispingly, in the Portuguese veiled rooms—but its genteel and unintelligent application was not sufficient for him who had sailed from Portugal as a common sailor with Vasco da Gama. He had suddenly glimpsed light and reason for making of himself the master-navigator of his age.

His parents were dead—he seems to have heard of their death in those years of war and wandering in the far east—and Sabrosa of no interest to him. He had grown tall, though still burly, with dark hair and brows that met in an austere frown across a beaked nose and heavy-lidded eyes. In Lisbon he studied his navigation ; and, turning eyes and ears westwards, heard of all those voyages extending the supposed "islands" of the Americas into the great continent that men now realized it was—the voyages of de Solis, of Amerigo Vespucci, of the two Cabots—voyages defining ever more clearly the extent and nature of that gigantic westwards barrier which uprose between Asia and Europe. . . .

If so it did uprise. For there could, even now, be moments of doubt. What if there were verily no terrestrial globe, but some twisted surface of no geometrical name ? So that no voyage could ever be made westwards, reaching Asia and those islands where he had captured his slave . . . He put the fantasy from him impatiently. Somewhere, somewhere remotely south of the furthest journeyings of the Spaniards, was surely an opening.

It is possible that this was more than a mere hypothesis in his mind. With his return to Portugal it seems he was made free to search amidst the innumerable charts and maps of the Americas which, since Columbus's day, had drifted into the great repository of the King of Portugal's treasury. They were maps and charts of a muzzy uncertainty in coastline and latitude, many of them. Beyond the limits of his own exploration the explorer would draw the figures of a man-eating savage, a hypogriff, a sea-monster. But certain of them were as cold and accurate as Magellan himself; and, long after his voyage, it was stated that among those charts he discovered one which showed clearly the mouth of the strait that was afterwards to bear his name.

Whether or not that was so, he was presently, with the persuasive and learned aid of a geographer of the time, one Ruy Faliero, engaged in soliciting the attention and patronage of the King of Portugal for this expedition he planned. It must be a great expedition—the greatest of all expeditions—for it would give to Portugal not only wealth to discover a westwards passage to the Spice Islands, but honour and glory beyond that known to the rest of Christendom. There must certainly be a passage to the south of the American lands, Magellan persuaded—with his mind's eye, according to later and hostile commentators, on that chart of Martin of Bohemia which reposed, neglected, in the royal treasury.

King Manoel appears to have listened with little attention. He was a lively and volatile monarch, quick and airy and cruel and light-hearted, and he appears to have detested Magellan almost from the moment he set eyes on him. In the intervals of study, Magellan had crossed to Africa to take part in the war against the Moors. Wounded, he returned without permission and took to badgering the king for support of his project to sail beyond America. King Manoel was more interested in questioning his breach of discipline; presently the royal nerves could be badly frayed at mere sight of the limping figure of the navigator, dour and obsequious. Manoel disliked his appearance, his record, his mode of address, his code of life, and everything that appertained to the rough-bearded, heavy-eyed adventurer from the Moluccas. His plans and his theories were accorded a brusque disregard. Magellan found himself treated in a fashion he had little looked for.

He appears to have awakened with a haughty rage. He had no small idea of his own importance, his powers of navigation, his faith in himself as the ideal leader for a conquering armada. After an obscure but vicious squabble in the year 1518, he rode out from Lisbon in company with Ruy Faliero, to an unknown destination.

It was not long unknown. News came to Lisbon that Magellan had ridden to the court of Spain, had there offered his services, and been accepted as captain of a great westwards-sailing expedition to add fresh wealth to the treasury and fresh glory to the name of the Spanish king.

§ 5

He was received by Charles V with a fine Spanish courtesy which presently gave way to interest and enthusiasm as Magellan's plans were unfolded. He was plainly, with his geographic notions, his experience of the Moluccas, and his widely reputed skill as a navigator, the commander Spain had been long awaiting. An expedition of indefinite intention, under the command of one Estefano Gomez, had been preparing for some time. Its object no longer indefinite, Magellan was appointed to command it, superseding Gomez. A charter of instruction and exhortation was drawn up, carefully and politely guarding the rights of Portugal:

> Firstly you are to go with good luck to discover the part of the ocean within our limits and demarcation. . . . Also you may discover in any of those parts what has not yet been discovered, so that you do not discover nor do anything in the demarcation and limits of the most serene King of Portugal . . . nor to his prejudice but only within the limits of our demarcation.

This should have satisfied Manoel. But the latter, unreasonably, was filled with fury. Magellan was outlawed by Portugal and down through the valley of the transmontane province rode the emissaries of the court to dusty Sabrosa, there to deface the coat of arms above the doorway on which the boy Fernão had gazed often and oft in the days before he went a page to court. . . . Magellan heard the news with indifference, his whole attention engaged in reorganizing and staffing the expedition of Spain.

Or almost his whole attention. For in those unhasting days one learns with little surprise that the work of reorganization took nearly two years; and in some pause of it Magellan loved and married that Beatriz Barbosa of whom little or nothing is known, except that her alliance with the Portuguese was "a love affair of passion and splendour". Magellan was certainly capable of both, if in other devotions than to women; and presumably the woman who drew such storm of regard upon herself was of other quality than the usual languid Spanish harim-women of the day. She came to live with Magellan at Seville; their son Rodrigo was born there in March of the year 1519, and Magellan drew up a new and careful will in his favour. . . . He visioned not only the achieving of the Spice Islands, but the founding of a noble family in Spain.

But while the Guadalquivir near their house in Seville was astir morning and night with the coming and going of seamen and officials and ship-chandlers and long trains of provision-laden mules, panting and raising up the slow little dust-clouds, Magellan was slowly realizing how deeply all Spain that was not of Royal blood resented his coming, his command, and his pretensions. Estefano Gomez proved a trouble-maker from the first. Magellan had appointed him second-in-command—a move he was deeply to regret—but that did not stay his hostility. Hatred and distrust of the Portuguese may be said to have affected the expedition adversely from the beginning. Magellan was not a tolerant man, haughty and uncommunicative, with the glare of his inner vision—*beyond Cuba!* —under the beetling brows, and the Spaniards regarded him with a passionate distaste. What was the object of this extraordinary voyage, where did the Portuguese hope to steer?

For it seems that he kept the expedition in doubt of his route, if not of his ultimate aim, as his devoted chronicler tells with the usual rhapsodic adulation:

> The Captain-General, Ferdinand Magellan, had resolved on undertaking a long voyage over the ocean, where the winds blow with violence, and storms are very frequent. He had also determined on taking a course as yet unexplored by any navigator. But this bold attempt he was cautious of disclosing, lest any one should strive to dissuade him from it by magnifying the risk he would have to encounter, and thus dishearten his crew. To the perils naturally incident to the voyage was joined the unfavourable circumstance of the four other vessels he commanded, beside his own, being under the direction of captains who were inimical to himself, merely on account of his being a Portuguese, they themselves being Spaniards.

Magellan's caution in disclosing his route to the Spaniards he allowed to lapse very early in his intercourse with the expedition's geographer-historian, the Italian Antonio Pigafetta. From the first (and perhaps in consequence) Magellan for Pigafetta was the hero who could do no wrong. His chronicle is Magellan's apologia, and no poor one. To our later eyes it seems reasonable enough that the Italian amidst a host of Spaniards should turn in admiration to the single other foreigner among the men of note who manned the expedition: they were both in a measure outcasts, barbaroi, dreaming men, visionaries, shifty and untrustworthy, among the hard, contemptuous Spaniards. But Pigafetta's admiration was deeper: it long survived Magellan's patronage, and indeed, Magellan himself.

Five caravellas, each from a hundred to a hundred and fifty tons burden, were outfitted on the Guadalquivir. The caravella was oddly reminiscent in shape and rigging of a Chinese junk, clumsy but strong, hard to steer and hard to destroy. The flagship chosen by the louring Portuguese was the *Trinidad*, the largest of them all; and no sooner had this been done than Magellan proceeded to lay down rules of unexampled severity in discipline. Men on board ship must do thus and so, saluting here, assembling there, sleeping in selected places, awakening at stated hours. . . . It sounded appalling to Spanish ears, accustomed to the easy perennial state of disorderly half-mutiny characterizing all the westwards-sailing crews. But Magellan was of other mettle than Columbus. He had no fancy for venturing those immensities of sea-space in company with the unruled and the readily insubordinate. He planned and was to enforce an elaborate code of signals for the purpose of keeping the flotilla together, by night as well as by day. Columbus's experiences with the *Niña* should not be his.

So at last all things were in readiness. "On Monday morning, the 10th of August, 1519, the squadron having everything requisite on board, and a complement of two hundred and thirty-seven men, its departure was announced by a discharge of artillery, and the foresail was set." This according to Pigafetta: the expedition streamed down the river from Seville, only, however, in the absurd anti-climax beloved of the times, to cast anchor immediately afterwards at the port of San Lucar, and proceed, solemnly (forgetting it had set out fully equipped) to "lay in a stock of provisions".

Through August and well into September, with a bored laggardness, Spain provisioned the ships. The crews lay stewing and fuming, cursing the delay and the foreign commander, sneering at his piety and his regulations alike. Wait till they had him well out in the Atlantic. . . .

Before he sailed, Beatriz was again with child. Knowledge of the fact must have stiffened Magellan's resolution to achieve both fame and worldly success—somewhere, beyond the Americas. And on the 20th of September, 1519, that expedition which had charmed his vision for ten long years sailed out into the Atlantic on its first lap of one of the greatest voyages of all recorded history.

§6

One very dark night this light appeared to us like a brilliant flambeau on the summit of a large tree, and thus remained for the space of two hours, which was a matter of exceeding consolation to us during the tempest. At the instant of its disappearing it diffused such a resplendent blaze of light as almost blinded us. We gave ourselves up for lost, but the wind ceased instantaneously.

Thus Pigafetta on the meteoric lights that played about the mastheads in the storms beyond Teneriffe. His is a chronicle rich in wonders, by sea or land. Presently, the storm abating, the sailors looked out and saw "birds of many kinds. Some appeared to have no rump ; others made no nests for want of feet, but the female lays and hatches her eggs on the back of the male, in the midst of the sea". Those unnatural fowls presently disappeared as the fleet went hull-down on its weary voyaging west.

The ships, "very old and patched up" had not benefited with the storm encountered beyond Teneriffe. There ensued unending days of contrary winds which drove the ships hither and thither about the Line "until fair weather came". Not until two months had passed did the battered and heat-frayed flotilla arrive at Rio de Janeiro and proceed to load up with fresh supplies of vegetables. Magellan had as yet had little trouble with his subordinates. But that trouble was unremote.

Loaded with potatoes and sugar-cane, the flotilla coasted slowly down Brazil. Reaching the mouth of the Rio de la Plata,

Magellan, with a dour disinterest, proceeded to quash the rumour that the immense estuary of that river might lead to some unknown strait. He sailed up the estuary and had buckets lowered from the *Trinidad* and the water tested. It was fresh. Here could be no channel to the Western Sea.

For five months of which there survive but the barest records of sailing and close-reefing and anchoring, the Portuguese coasted modern Argentine, searching each bay and inlet with scrupulous care to see if it might qualify as the expected channel. Magellan's caution and care seem the best disproval of the rumour that he followed definite information of a channel in these regions. Winter (but in those latitudes a winter of summer weather) went by in such pursuits and the weary crews grew ripe for mutiny. Where was this outcast from his own country leading the chivalry of Spain?

Towards the end of March 1520 they put in at an excellent harbour in lat. 49° 30′ S, the harbour that was to be christened Port San Julian. Winter—when it should have been summer!—was coming on with some intensity, and Magellan determined to await the passing of the storms that had begun to lash the desolate coasts of Patagonia with great breakers. That coast haunted the halted ships—desolate and deserted, with the tall pampas scrub wilting under the coming of winter. The Admiral brooded alone over those charts he was reported to have stolen from Lisbon: the crews yawned and gossiped and stared over the sides of the vessels, remembering Spain and the long, hot days of a spring month there.

April went by: the storms ran their long foaming currents past the mouth of Port San Julian: birds drove before them in great numbers. The sky was a scudding desolation, like the shore. May followed it, and still Magellan refused to move. But suddenly the boredom on board the ships was broken. The sailors crowded anew to stare at the shore.

A man of gigantic stature presented himself before us. He capered almost naked on the sands, and was singing and dancing, at the same time casting dust on his head. The captain sent one of our seamen on shore with orders to make similar gestures, as a token of friendship and peace, which were well understood, and the giant suffered himself to be quietly led to a small island where the captain had landed. I likewise went on shore there with many others. He testified great surprise on seeing us, and, holding up his finger, undoubtedly signified to us that he thought us descended from heaven.

Those gigantic primitives of remote South America, but slightly tinged with the spread of the Archaic Culture from Peru, had nevertheless their memories of Sun Children, as almost everywhere on the New Continent. Magellan's men were credited with like origins. Magellan himself stared under his scowling penthouse brows at the gigantic *patagones* of the native—the fur-shoes worn to protect the feet from the stubble of the pampas—and christened the country on that—in several senses—understanding.

The giant was allowed to depart in search of companions. Presently he brought back men and women of his tribe to stare at the Spaniards, to gesticulate to heaven, and to astound the sailors with their unvaryingly gigantic stature. Here were the ogres of the world's end. Magellan cautiously decided to carry away a couple as specimens: they would amuse the Spanish court, might even breed there, and astound future generations: nay, what beasts of burden they would make!

He had two of the men enticed on board by a trick, and manacled. They howled loudly, great and astounded and weeping children in the hands of the gods. The Spaniards thrust them below to stay their cries, and went ashore in a furtive endeavour to capture two of the women, those future breeders of the solution of Spain's transport problems. But the alarm had spread. The Patagonians fled into the scrub pursued by the enraged Spaniards. If they could not have them alive, it was sport to shoot at the gigantic leaping figures. Unfortunately, one of the Patagonians was also a keen sportsman. He hid behind a bush with a bow or blowgun and waited till the Spanish pursuit came up. The nearest Spaniard, an arrow in his thigh, called out loudly that he was wounded. He was mistaken: in a moment he was dead. The arrow had been poisoned.

Daunted, and indignant at this heathen abomination, the Christians sorrowfully halted the pursuit, gathered up the body of their companion and retreated to the shore, on the way burning down the shelters of the Patagonians that these barbarians might realize the superiority of Christian moral and ethic.

Magellan had the men-captives kept in chains. Breedless or not, they would amuse Spain when he presented them at court. But presently he gathered intelligence which made it unlikely that he himself would ever see Spain.

§ 7

This was a plot, slowly maturing throughout those months of idleness among the ship-commanders, to murder Magellan himself and sail back the flotilla to Seville. But at the last moment the hearts of some of the conspirators misgave them. News was brought to the Portuguese, and he acted promptly, diplomatically, murderously. Omitting the ship commanders, he had Juan of Cartagena, the vehador; Luiz de Mendoza, the treasurer; Antonio Cocca, the Paymaster; and Gaspar de Casada arrested and tried. The remainder looked on with a sullen irresolution.

Magellan acted according to his nature and the brutish times. Juan of Cartagena was ordered to be skinned alive. He was taken ashore and this atrocious punishment carried into effect with a refined and deadly cruelty which the expedition was not to forget. Mendoza was stabbed to the heart; Cocca left in chains. In his treatment of Gaspar de Casada, Magellan showed, as his companions viewed it, the cloven hoof of the treacherous Portuguese. At first pretending to pardon this officer, whose life he dare not attempt (he having been directly appointed by the King of Spain), the Admiral next had him marooned on shore in company with a priest. The Patagonians, he calculated, would soon return and settle Casada's problem out of hand.

Even in Pigafetta's chronicle, so meticulously adulatory of Magellan, these read cruel and cowardly deeds on the part of Magellan: that skinless body which squirmed and screamed on the shore till it died haunts us still. But had the mutineers succeeded in their objective they would have killed not only Magellan; they would have killed that on which he had set his heart and soul—the reaching of those Moluccas he believed with a visionary's strength lay somewhere beyond this land of Patagonia. He displayed a fanatic's ferocity in his treatment of the mutineers—unfortunately amended with an unfanatical diplomacy that denigrates even that excuse.

Misfortune had not ended its play of dark happenings over the expedition on the Patagonian coast. One of the caravellas, the *St. Iago*, had been sent southwards to explore the coastline as the weather lightened. It was wrecked and the crew scrambled ashore. Presently two of their number, having walked overland, appeared weary and limping at the harbour of San Julian. Magellan had to set about organizing a relief expedition. Not only must the men be rescued but all the provisions and stores brought overland from their ship.

June and July passed by in this unprofitable trade. Summer had come in these remote lands. At length all was ready. The pious commander had a cross erected on the summit of a neighbouring mountain, the Monte Christo, and sailed from Port San Julian on the 21st of August.

In lat. 50° 40′ S, however, such a storm arose as almost wrecked the squadron. Magellan put in to shore, into a bay he named Santa Cruz, and cast anchor, awaiting the subsidence of the storm. Wood and water were plentiful, and fishing good. The ships restocked with fresh provisions. Magellan appears to have decided that his move in August had been too hasty; he halted in Santa Cruz for a couple of months, preparing, say his chroniclers, to face with healthy and contented crews the dangers of the unknown south.

But those inconstant lingerings and plannings read queerly to this later day. It seems more likely that a faintness of heart had come on Magellan, a cold uncertainty in which he mislaid for a while, in doubt and some measure of despair, that urgent vision that had been his since his days as a page-boy in Lisbon, since his days in the Moluccas. How could he ever achieve that channel—if it did exist? How hope for success with those who hated him?

But at length, after having the crews confessed, he ordered the anchors to be weighed and put out from Santa Cruz. On the 21st of October a great rightwards opening in the rugged coastline was discerned. Precipices towered on either side, and as the squadron sailed in through the opening at the Admiral's signal they saw open out in front of them what appeared to be merely another great bay, land-locked by beetling crags and mountains that lifted in glacial scaurs of snow their crests far into unhappy skies. The waters boiled round the rocks that sheltered under the crags and the Spaniards stared their dismay. Was this where the Portuguese planned to destroy them?

Mutiny again raised its head. But no actual engagement ensued. Magellan stirred to a virile activity, commanding and directing and suddenly inspiring. He despatched the *San Antonio* and *La Concepcion* to examine the westwards end of the bay and determine its nature; *La Trinidad* and *La Vittoria* anchored close inshore. Raising their heads, the Spaniards saw the wheel and dip of immense clouds racing up from the south.

That night a great storm came on, and raged through all the night and all the next day. The two detached ships vanished from sight in the great walls of spray that boiled across the surface of the apparent bay. On the second day, while murmurs arose that the ships had been sent to their destruction without reason or warrant, smoke was seen arising far in the west. This could mean but one thing. A ship had been wrecked and survivors were signalling from the shore.

But on the fourth day, with flags flying and guns firing, the two ships returned, and signalled their success. They had discovered and penetrated through a narrow gut leading from this present bay into another. Leading from that other they had discerned while they fought the storm yet another channel vanishing into the west.

§ 8

Magellan had the *Trinidad's* anchors weighed and sailed for the third bay. Herein he found not one outlet but two, cliff-surrounded, with the foaming tides pouring down dark canyons south-east and south-west. The *San Antonio* and *La Concepcion* were despatched down the south-east gut; the Admiral on the *Trinidad*, with the *Vittoria* in attendance, attempted the south-western channel.

It broadened and narrowed and broadened yet again, retreating into the hazes of the west. Finally they came to the mouth of a river and cast anchor in uncertainty. Here the sailors found abundance of "small fish like sardines" and from here Magellan despatched a boatload of men to explore the coast round the great cape that rose westward. The boat put in to shore and the seamen climbed the heights of the cape. So doing, they saw the western outlet of the channel, perhaps the first Europeans ever to see it, and beyond that, "another sea, which is called the peaceful sea".

When news of this was brought to Magellan on the *Trinidad* he broke down and wept, to the astonishment of the sardonic Spaniards. At last—visions fulfilled! He paced the decks and stared with a stirring heart at the towering moun-

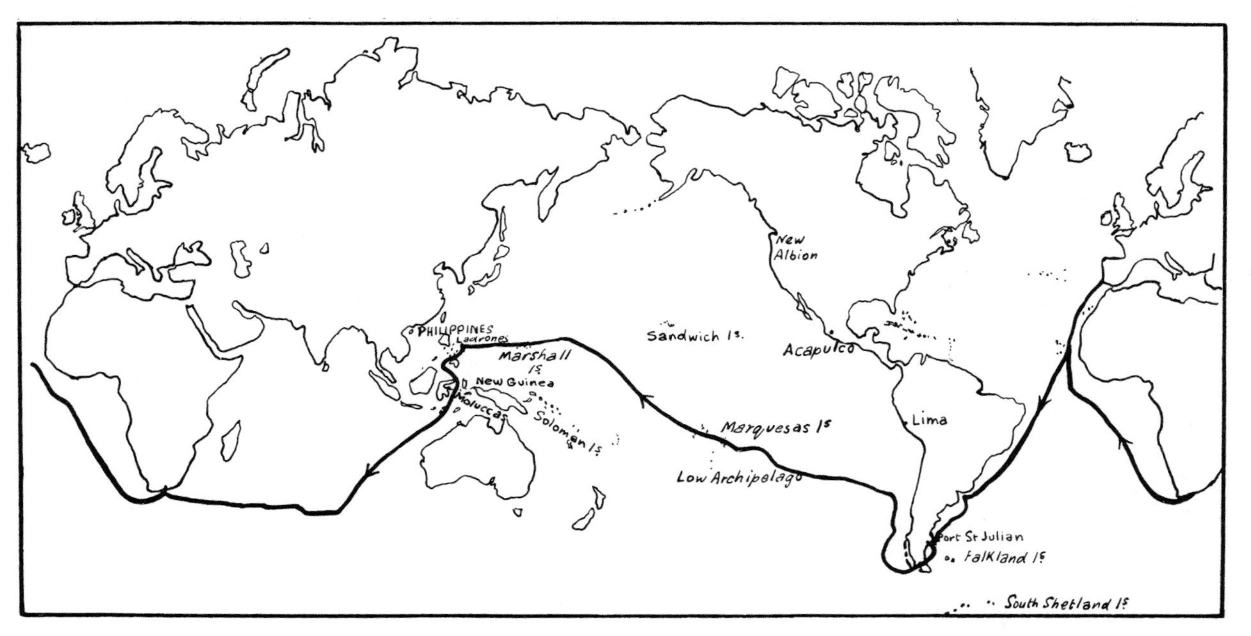

VOYAGE OF MAGELLAN

tains to north and south, the precipitous cliffs that shielded the Old World from the Far East, and knew then, perhaps, such joy and fulfilment as he was never to know again in his life.

For one of the officers on the *San Antonio*, which had sailed to investigate the south-eastwards channel, was that Gomez whom Magellan had superseded in command of the expedition outfitting on the banks of the Guadalquivir. He conceived, and correctly, that his opportunity had arrived. He and the other officers on guard attacked and overcame the captain of the *San Antonio*, put him in irons, and, clapping on a press of canvas, turned about and made for the eastwards outlet. That attained, they turned north, put in at San Julian, rescued Casada and his priest from the Patagonian shore and made for Spain.

Unaware of this defection, Magellan, rejoined by the *Concepcion*, set about searching dreary mile on mile of strait and inlet for sign of the missing vessel. Finally he conceived it impracticable to remain longer; and, leaving signals on "islands and promontories to guide the wayward vessel" he turned to the adventure of braving the perils of the Peaceful Sea.

Summer had come. There were only three hours of night in those southern latitudes and Magellan occupied the days as well as he might in re-outfitting the diminished squadron for his attempt on the Moluccas. Southwards, in the rugged islands, there would gleam far away as the day waned pin-points of fire; and the Spaniards would cross themselves as they watched those enigmatic signals upon the darkness in that bleak unknown country, Tierra del Fuego, the Land of Fire. We know those fires to have been but the cooking fires of one of the last races of true primitives left in the Americas, the Fuegans, strange, naked happy savages living amidst snow and ice without fears or houses or gods or culture, without even knowledge of the Children of the Sun. They had been in their time the world's greatest explorers—descendants of men who had traversed all northern Asia and held south through all the Americas till they came to the last island where land ceased and their wanderings with it. Perhaps ten thousand years before Magellan stared at their craggy land under his pent-house brows they had come to that land. But their Golden Age was something remote from the concept of the seeker of the Golden Isles.

A long delay was dangerous. Magellan had only three ships left, who had started from Spain with five. Of the complement of 237 men only 183 remained. Provisions were running low and despite his anxiety over the *San Antonio* she must be left to her fate. On the 18th of November, 1520, a year and two months after his departure from Spain, the Portuguese Admiral raised anchor and headed west. . . .

About the same day the *San Antonio*, homewards bound, was crossing the Line and committing to the sea, unceremoniously, the gigantic, wasted body of one of the Patagonian ogres.

§ 9

> They were the first that ever burst
> Into that silent sea.

Magellan had the *Trinidad* steered north-westwards along the coast for a little while. Then, taking his bearings, he determined to attempt the great stretch of the Pacific without base or support. The weather remained calm and still, upon the sea the flying fishes scudded before pursuing birds, a mild breeze blew up the colourful clouds of sunset in the face of the little squadron trimming its sails. No ships, no men, no cultivation or sign of cities in all that wide stretch behind. In front . . .

Day on day they sailed north and north-west, the land long lost behind them, the trade-wind following at their heels. Presently they were aware of strange skies above their heads, of a vanished Polar star.

> The Antarctic has not the same stars as the Arctic Pole; but here are seen two clusters of small, nebulous stars which look like small clouds, and are but little distant one from the other. In the midst of these clusters of small stars two are distinguished, very large and very brilliant, but of which the motion is scarcely apparent; these indicate the Antarctic Pole.

So they looked, the first of their race, on the nebulæ of Magellan's Clouds. Near it they saw gape the Coal-Sack, an apparent hole in the sky, unstarred and untenanted; and beyond, in the Pacific night, the glory of the one Christian constellation, the Southern Cross. To them it seemed near and friendly, sign of the eternal verities of their faith, a friendly thing in that alien night with its coloured candles lighted across the great arcing candelabrum of the Milky Way.

Day followed day and still there came no sign of land, Magellan pacing his poop with grim eyes below the heavy brows, the sailors yawning and laggard at brace and clew, the spindrift gleaming fading in the wake of each ship. Days lapsed into weeks, weeks into first one month, then another, and still there came no sign of land. Steering north-west by west, they crossed the Line after traversing some twelve thousand geograpical miles. No land was seen, no storms encountered even as now a more westerly route was steered. Magellan's self-imposed route had a mathematical directness; but it took him far from the Pacific Islands and their verdure and hospitality.

Water and food grew scarce; disease and unease increased in the stifling constriction of the small vessels.

> The biscuit we were eating no longer deserved the name of bread, it was nothing but dust and worms, which had consumed the substance, and what was more, it smelled intolerably, being impregnated with the urine of mice. The water we were obliged to drink was equally putrid and offensive. We were even so far reduced, that we might not die of hunger, to eat pieces of the leather with which the mainyard was covered to prevent it from wearing the rope. These pieces of leather, constantly exposed to the water, sun, and wind, were so hard that they required being soaked four or five days in the sea in order to render them supple; after this we boiled them to eat. Frequently, indeed, were we obliged to subsist on sawdust; and even mice, a food so disgusting, were sought after with such avidity that they sold for half a ducat apiece. . . .
>
> Nor was this all. Our greatest misfortune was being attacked by a malady in which the gums swelled so as to hide the teeth, as well in the upper as in the lower jaw, whence those afflicted thus were incapable of chewing their food. Nineteen of our number died of this complaint, among whom was the Patagonian giant and a Brazilian, whom we had brought with us from his own country. Besides those who died we had from twenty-five to thirty sailors ill, who suffered dreadful pains in the arms, legs and other parts of the body, but these, all of them, recovered. . . .
>
> And during the whole of these three months and twenty days we went in an open sea while we ran fully four thousand leagues in the Pacific sea. This was well named Pacific, for during this same time we met with no storm, and saw no land except two small uninhabited islands.

These "small, uninhabited islands" sighted on January the 24th, 1521, have been identified with Puka-Puka in the Paumotu Archipelago. Magellan made no attempt to examine them in detail, but pushed on in hope of shortly encountering the Spice Islands. Skilled navigator though he was, however, he was out of his reckoning. Not until March 6th did land appear on the bow, and then not of the Spice Islands.

It was, instead, Guam of the Mariannes. Putting in to shore in search of vegetables and fresh water, the first Europeans to cross the Pacific encountered the remote Polynesians who inhabited those islands, tall and olive-brown and almost naked, a people without gods or kings or even images to worship, primitives who had been but slightly touched by the passing fringes of the Archaic Civilization long centuries before. Yet they remembered sufficient of that raiding passage, and remembered war, and the evils then wrought upon them. As a result, they set about stealing everything of the strangers on which they could lay their hands.

They stole weapons, caps, dirks; they stole the skiff hanging astern of the *Trinidad*; had they had the time and experience, they would probably have stolen the entire flotilla and left the Spaniards gasping in the sea. . . . Magellan had had enough. He knew how to treat these men abandoned of God. Landing with forty men, he burned down the nearest village, stove in all the boats he could see, killed seven of the disgusting non-idolators who had not had the address to flee, and, leaving behind him these marks of the coming of a superior civilization, took to his ship and steered due west. He christened the islands the Ladrones, the Islands of Thieves; what the inhabitants christened Magellan history leaves unrecorded.

Again the interminable ocean. Not even a sea-bird marred the desolation, the chronicler tells, and voices had a startling sound in that sea-waste. What if there were no Spice Islands to be found on this track—no complete globe to round? . . . But at sunrise on the 16th of March the Admiral lifted his fanatic eyes and saw far ahead, shining in the dawn, the peaks of a high country. Slowly it drew nearer and they were aware of an island covered with luxurious vegetation. One of the Spice Islands at last?

It was Samar of the Philippines. But Magellan and his men knew nothing of that; they cruised doubtfully off-shore for a little, then put in at a convenient bay. Magellan landed with armed boatloads of men and surveyed the near beach. No natives, hostile or friendly. He gave orders for the crew to disembark and bring the sick on shore.

But next morning a vessel was observed in the bay beyond the ships—a "vessel of superior build". It was hovering doubtfully off-shore and at sight of that hesitation, the Admiral, in a fever to discover his whereabouts, gave orders that no Spaniard was to make the least move, hostile or otherwise. They waited, breathless. The boat came nearer. The Europeans stared their relief.

It was filled with men in rich but outlandish garb—men it was plain with rulers and gods, devils and beliefs and afflictions like themselves. They had reached civilization again.

§ 10

Pantomimic gestures of questioning and welcome were exchanged between the Spaniards and the boatload of civilized islanders. Off-shore, the Spaniards discovered, was a native fishing fleet; and a rapid trade sprang up between the Filipinos and the Europeans. Here, for the first time, the latter set eyes on bananas—"a fig a foot long" as the impressed chronicler avers. Finally, the natives gave the crews to understand, in expressive pantomime, that they had no other trade goods at hand; but would sail to their own homes and return in four days' time with other articles.

Four days later, true to their word, they returned, bringing—surety at last that the Spice Islands were near—pepper, cinnamon, cloves, nutmegs. Much more to the point, gold appeared plentiful. Painted chiefs wore bracelets and armlets of gold; pepitos of gold were used as a kind of currency. And still more to the west, the natives gestured, was a land of gold.

It was the familiar device of all such people for getting rid of over-pressing guests. Magellan and his Spaniards swallowed the bait with great simplicity, and raised anchor and held west—firing, as they did so, a parting salute which threw the Filipinos into a terrified confusion.

Magellan's personal slave, captured long before in Sumatra, had survived the voyage; now it struck Magellan for the first time that he might soon be able to put this dependant's linguistics to use. Eight days after leaving Humumu he put in to the bay of one of the islands, and had his slave stand by his side as a boatload of men approached. These hailed the ships in some doubt, but were a little reassured when the much-travelled Sumatran cried down to them words of peace and amity—words which they apparently understood. The slave begins to emerge into prominence for the first time in the record: he is not to retreat from that position.

The Filipinos paddled away and the Spaniards waited until the next morning, when Henry the Sumatran was sent ashore to negotiate with the "reigning prince". This mission he appears to have carried out with considerable skill and diplomacy, assuring the island chief that the unpleasant-seeming foreigners were not bent on rape, loot and conquest, but were voyaging these seas for pleasure. Probably anxious to view such curiosities at closer hand and tell the tale of them to his grandchildren in the future, the "reigning prince" came aboard the *Trinidad*, embraced Magellan, and "presented him with three porcelain vases full of rice". In return the heavy-browed Portuguese treated the native potentate to breakfast and then an exhibition of the armaments and armour of the expedition. The Filipino was impressed. If not gods, these foreigners were evidently devils. Impressed by the weight of his own reasoning, he invited Magellan to send two of his people to examine the country.

Pigafetta and another were given the task; they landed and spent the night in wassail and admiration; of the country, complacently, they saw nothing, believing it like all such countries full of uncouthness and heathen abomination. But in the morning, returning to the ships, they were accompanied by no less a personage than the chief of the neighbouring island of Mindanoa—a tall and handsome individual covered with golden ornaments. He was also an unrestrained talker. Gold, he told, was so plentiful on his island that they made the baser utensils "of the bed-chamber" of that precious metal. The Spaniards listened with a loose-mouthed avariciousness. Where—and at once—was this Mindanoa, ruled over by this silk-clad heathen who gave his barbarous title and name as that of the Raja Siagu?

But Magellan, pious as ever, delayed departure in search of the islanded El Dorado in order to celebrate Easter Mass on shore. The natives crowded to stare their surprise. The service finished, Magellan had a large cross erected on a neighbouring height, informing the Raja Siagu that this was

> the standard confided to him by the emperor his master to plant wherever he landed; and that in consequence he should erect it on the island, to which this symbol would, moreover, be auspicious, as all European ships which would in future visit it would know, on seeing the cross, that we had been received as friends, and would refrain from any violence to the persons and property of their (the Filipino chiefs') subjects; and should any be taken prisoners, they would only have to make the sign of it to gain their liberty.

Thus Pigafetta; the reactions of the Raja Siagu are not recorded. Possibly an attitude of fixed and unwavering diplomacy with these strange sea-raiders had been decided upon. Pigafetta noted with disgust the habit of the common people of going almost naked and chewing betel-nut: it was evident that they were not so civilized as at first had been assumed. But the upper classes, with their silks and porcelain, trade-goods obtained in contact with the Chinese, were evidently wealthy and important beings of a wealthy and important archipelago. Magellan, slowly collating reports of the whole group, gathered that there were three principal islands: Leite, Mindanao, and Sebu. Sebu was the greatest of these.

The Admiral determined to steer for Sebu, obtain its Raja's submission to the authority of Spain, trade the shoddy goods in the ships to the simple inhabitants in exchange for solid gold; and then, with such bright offering to lay at the feet of Charles V, seek out the genuine Spice Islands and return at once to Europe and the empty arms of Doña Beatriz. . . .

They were empty enough. The second child had been still-born; and even as Magellan was steering his ships into the port of Sebu, his son Rodrigo lay dying in Seville.

§ 11

On April the 7th, 1521, Magellan's squadron entered the port of Sebu with flags flying and a "general discharge of ordnance". This last, according to the chronicler, was intended as a general salute. But the scared inhabitants of Sebu, rich and civilized bourgeois, fled into the interior streets of that important town, and the Admiral, anchoring, looked in some doubt at an all but deserted sea-front.

An envoy, together with Henry, the invaluable Sumatran, was sent ashore to interview the Raja. That dignitary was discovered in the market-place surrounded by the terrified inhabitants. With the hauteur of the badly scared he suggested to the envoy that his master would do well to enter foreign harbours more quietly: but, now that he had entered, did he know he was subject to the usual harbour-duties?

Somewhat staggered, the envoy had the Sumatran slave reply that the Admiral Magellan was the messenger of the earth's greatest king, one who paid tribute nowhere. If Sebu would prefer an invader rather than a friendly visitor, let it say so.

Fortunately, Sebu was advised by a merchant present in the market-place, a wandering Arab or Malay who had seen something of the devastation wrought by the Portuguese at Goa or in the East Indies. He strongly advised Sebu to put on as cheerful a face on things as it might, for these foreigners were undoubtedly devils without bowels of compassion.

Sebu took to a day's meditation on this cheering counsel. Then the Raja Humabon entered into cautious negotiations with Magellan's envoys. He would give presents to the strangers—providing the strangers gave presents to him. This naïve summarizing of all royal gift-giving impressed Magellan as sensible. But he made the further condition that the Raja must acknowledge the suzerainty of the King of Spain, and this, according to the chronicler, Humabon did—probably with various mental reservations.

Direct negotiations were then established between Admiral and Raja. Permission was given to open a storehouse on the shore, and down to this store flocked the whole of Sebu to trade, bartering nuggets of pure gold in exchange for articles not worth half a ducat. There was great cry and commotion on the ships because of the orders issued by the Portuguese regarding the necessity of caution in bargaining, "lest the natives believe that we hanker unduly after gold". The common sailors were of the opinion that Admiral and officers were doing well in the trade; why might not they also? As night fell over the warm Philippines they would slip ashore and trade rings, beads, knives, caps and cloaks for the precious metal, conceal it about their persons, and steal back to the ships to dream of ease and rest and long cool drinks on the long-lost patios of Spain. Everyone traded: gold was here, after so many disappointments of the Americas, easy to obtain from the heathen.

But meanwhile state and religion awoke. The priests accompanying the expedition insisted on the conversion of the inhabitants to Christianity, and were aided in this pious project by a miracle. The Raja's brother, dying, confessed himself a Christian. He promptly recovered, burned all the images of his gods, and proclaimed the new faith far and wide. Sebu heard, saw, and was conquered. Within a fortnight the entire population embraced Christianity, casting out its native devils in favour of the foreign ones. . . .

Such at least is Pigafetta's account. Subtracting nine-tenths of the account as either the result of palm-wine potations or genteel propaganda, there was probably some basis of truth to foundation the tale. Looking at that face with the gloomy penthouse brows, Humabon may have confessed as formal a Christianity as he confessed the Spanish King his suzerain. . . . That second confession was now to bear its fruit.

Acknowledging the King of Spain his overlord, Humabon had done it on the understanding that he himself be recognized as ruler over all Sebu and the neighbouring Isle of Matan. Magellan had agreed. Now there came news from Matan that one of the two chiefs there refused to acknowledge either Humabon or the King of Spain. At this news Humabon demanded the assistance of a boatload of Spaniards in subduing the recalcitrant Matani.

Magellan consented, and himself determined to captain the boat. It was a splendid opportunity, he conceived, for displaying his power and prowess before the natives, friendly and hostile. He envisaged a short, sharp engagement, the rout and destruction of the Matani forces, the burning of their villages, the rape and massacre of their women. Probably there would be gold. . . . He had sunk considerably from that stern dreamer who had left the Guadalquivir with the route to the Spice Islands, Atlantic-crossing, his vision. The Spice Islands he now knew to be close at hand; and, in other aspects of character no different from the men of his class and times he looked forward to loot and wealth and a return to Spain as his worthy objectives. He himself would command the boat.

His captains, little love though they had for the Portuguese, tried to dissuade him: he had proved too valuable a commander for them to allow him to imperil his life unnecessarily. "We entreated him not to hazard his person on this adventure, but he answered that, as a good pastor, he ought not to be away from his flock."

So he took the fateful decision, and with a boatload of sixty picked men, in helmets and cuirasses, armed with muskets, swords, shields and lances, set out for Matan. Thirty boatloads of native auxiliaries accompanied the invading expedition.

§ 12

Magellan's forces arrived off the coast of Matan three hours before daylight, seeing the ghostly shine of the beach under the heavy Indonesian stars. The Admiral had a message sent ashore warning the Matani to submit, for he came with steel lances to enforce that submission. Nothing daunted, the Matani returned the answer that they also had lances, though only of bamboo, stakes hardened in fire. But they knew how to use them, and had their country to defend. It was a gallant reply: in other times and circumstances it might have moved a classical historian to grave approval of those island Laconians.

They were Greek in their subtlety as well. With the returning messenger they sent the request that they be not attacked till daylight—*as they were expecting reinforcements with daylight!* Pondering this naïvety, Magellan came to the conclusion—correctly, as events were to prove—that the Matani hoped this message would lead to the Spaniards attacking while it was still dark, and so find themselves entrapped by some stratagem. Indeed, this was the Matanis hope: they had dug covered pitfalls between the beach and their encampment.

The boats waited off-shore as the stars slowly paled and went out and a quiet breeze arose and blew in the dim foliage of the shoreward trees. Then Magellan commanded his men to the attack, forty-nine of his men. The rest were left in charge of the boat. Raja Humabon and his Filipinos were forbidden to take part in the engagement: Magellan desired them to lie off and watch the fashion in which Spain dealt with rebels.

This grim request was complied with. The morning rose very still, cocks crowing far inland. Rowing inshore, the Spaniards with their dark-browed Portuguese commander saw the islanders, brown, naked men with bamboo lances, assemble in great force. The shore approach was shallow and the Spaniards had to jump from the boat and wade through the water waist-deep, musketeers to the right, crossbowmen to the left.

Attaining the beach, they were forming up and firing into the brown of the natives when the undaunted Matani charged. A desperate fight broke out then along a wide stretch of the beach, the Matani mown down by the fire of the European archers and harquebusiers, the Spaniards pressed back and like to break under the weight of the sheer number of naked spearmen. It was a miniature Marathon, the Spaniards the Persians, the Matani making up in courage and agility what they lacked of Miltiades's men in the way of weapons. Wielding small shields, the natives flung themselves on the ground as each ponderous weapon was discharged at them, then leapt up afresh to renew the combat. Nevertheless, the slaughter in their ranks was terrible, and they gradually drew back.

Beyond the pits they brought their own archers into play on the hesitating line of invaders. These archers were wielders of the blowgun, shooting poisoned arrows which rattled harmlessly off the Spanish mail like hailstones. Observing this, the Matani aimed lower, at the unshielded legs of the white men, and Magellan, much vexed, ordered a sortie rightwards against the straw-built village, with the command to set it on fire, so that the natives might be drawn off to stay the conflagration, and the invaders attain their boat again.

The sortie succeeded. Presently Matan village was in flames, lighting up the struggle on the beach. But its effect was the reverse of Magellan's expectation. Howling, the Matani fell on the Spaniards with renewed ferocity. Two of the seamen were killed in the village as the party was driven back to the beach, and here the struggle grew ever more grim. Islanders tore stones from the ground and hurled them in the Spaniard's faces, hurled earth and sticks and lances in a frenzy of valour so that here and there, stabbed or overwhelmed under sheer numbers, a Spaniard went down. Seeing that the day was lost while yet hardly begun, Magellan ordered retreat upon the boat.

At that moment a poisoned arrow lodged in his leg, and he staggered and almost fell. But, recovering instantly, he motioned his companions back towards the water, and, himself facing the enemy, began to retreat.

Seeing that the day was lost, the majority of the Spaniards turned about and reached the water, squattering and swimming towards the boats. Curse the Portuguese! Let him fend for himself.

But some seven or eight still fought by Magellan's side, among them the faithful Pigafetta. Magellan was now staggering and weak with the poison in his blood, and found himself singled out for the especial fury of the natives. They had recognized him by his rich armour.

> This combat, so unequal, lasted more than an hour. An islander at length succeeded in thrusting the end of his lance through the bars of his helmet and wounding the captain in the forehead, who, irritated by its effects, immediately ran the assailant through the body with his lance, the lance remaining in the wound. He now attempted to draw his sword, but was unable, owing to his right arm being grievously wounded. The Indians, who perceived this, pressed in crowds upon him; and one of them having given him a violent cut with a sword on the left leg, he fell on his face. While falling, and seeing himself surrounded by the enemy he turned towards us several times, as if to know if we had been able to save ourselves. As there was not one of those who remained with him but was wounded, and as we were, consequently, in no condition either to afford him succour or avenge his death, we instantly made for our boats, which were on the point of putting off. To our captain, indeed, did we owe our deliverance, as the instant he fell all the islanders rushed towards the spot where he lay. Thus perished our guide, our light, and our support; but the glory of Magellan will survive him. He was adorned with every virtue; in the midst of the greatest adversity he constantly possessed an immovable firmness. At sea he subjected himself to the same privations as his men. Better skilled than any one in the knowledge of nautical charts, he was a perfect master of navigation, as he proved in making the tour of the world, an attempt which none before him had ventured.

§ 13

So fell the boy from the far-off estate in the Portuguese hills who had wondered on the whereabouts of the land beyond

Cuba. With him there fell eight of the Spaniards. The boats made back in haste, in company with the silent Raja Humabon. He had looked on white men in battle, and had been unimpressed. And the great captain was dead.

Another was conscious of that as the greatest happening his life had known—Henry, the Sumatran slave, whom Magellan had seized years before and put to the question regarding the seas beyond the Moluccas. He went ashore and conferred with the Raja, and together they made their plot.

It was almost completely successful. Juan Serano, the new commander of the expedition, was invited ashore together with the other commanders "to receive a great present from the Raja ere they should sail for the Moluccas". And somewhere up in that dark welter of native streets, under the decorated Chinese cornices, Serano and his score of leaders were done to death, very bloodily and probably very slowly and ingeniously. Their cries of agony and for help ring painfully down four centuries from Pigafetta's pages, obscured only in the cries of that man who was skinned alive on the Patagonian shore.

The survivors made for a lonely island remote from the main group, revictualled there, emptied *La Concepcion*, burned her, and steered the single surviving ship again east. The weary seas resumed their still glare. Then, on the 6th of November, 1521, after an absence from Spain of two years and three months, they sighted at last the Moluccas which Magellan had sought with such persistence and valour and bloody tenacity.

But Magellan himself was dead, and the remainder of the tale of that voyage comes down the years in diminuendo. Ultimately harried by the hostile and unforgiving Portuguese authorities from the East Indies all about the Cape of Good Hope and up the African coast, only the *Vittoria* reached home to San Lucar, with its Spaniards having circumnavigated the globe for the first time in human history. On board it bore the faithful and voluble Pigafetta, he who wrote the story of the expedition's wanderings and loved Magellan, and presented that story to Charles V of Spain, and then vanished from our sight.

So, in its broader effects, the lure of the Spice Islands that had haunted European seamen of so many races to so many ventures, found at last its greatest triumph. That triumph opened up innumerable other seas and untraversed lands to the explorer ; but the greatest of the feats had been accomplished—the circumnavigation of the globe from a fixed point of departure.

Doña Beatriz died when she heard the story of her husband's death.

Spain gained little from the expedition but glory, not unmerited, we may think, and it preserved in some state the annals of the voyage.

While it did so it is probable that Magellan's corpse, hoisted on a stake, bleached and bleached through long years in the sight of the villagers of Matan, till the flesh fell from the bones, and the bones themselves apart, vanishing away even these, the last mementoes of a life lived sternly and cruelly, tempered with a thin-pointed flame of resolve, and wasted at the end on such cruel, small folly as that of a boy seeking to kill a bird for vanity and meeting in the act with a tiger in its lair.

VII

VITUS BERING'S SEARCH FOR AMERICA AND GOLDEN GAMA LAND

§ I

WITH Vitus Bering and his two great ventures we turn to a new trail in that quest of the Fortunate Isles that Magellan abandoned with the spears of the Matani Filipinos in his throat. The Pacific was mapped and charted and greatly sailed throughout the next two centuries. Drake voyaged around the world, the first of the commercial explorers, seeking very definite gains in loot and wealth, no magic islands of escape from his age or himself. Michael Drayton's doggerel embodies the creed and intentions of such with a fine explicitness :

> A thousand kingdoms we will seek from far,
> And many nations waste with civil war. . . .
> And those unchristened countries call our own,
> Where scarce the name of England hath been known.

Even in search for the rumoured great continent of the South Seas—Terra Australia Nondum Cognita—his attitude was more that of a company promoter of a doubtful mine than of one who was haunted by the sound of the nameless sea on the undiscovered isle. The voyages of Pedro Fernandez de Quiros in 1605 were of like kind, charting the Low Archipelago, the New Hebrides, New Guinea. Schouten, Le Maire, and Willam Janszoon (the first recorded discoverer of Australia) were bronzed Dutch chapmen slightly astray from their ledgers and warehouses ; the great Abel Tasman of 1642 was the same chapman bitterly urgent for solid new spheres and routes of trade. The sixteenth and seventeenth century explorers of the South Pacific suffered and achieved terribly and commendably ; but they are outside this record.

The North Pacific remained a region of myth and legend.

Betaking itself from the coasts of Africa, from the Indian shores, from the Spice Islands (so long its home) the Fortunate Land went north and hid in the mists of the unexplored Pacific in the lee of the long north-western coasts of America, the equally unknown coasts of opposing Asia. From the death of Magellan onwards there had developed a fairly regular intercourse with Japan on the part of the Portuguese and Dutch; and outside the sailing routes of trade rumour and the speculative geographers studded the seas with islands of gold and good fortune as of old—Gama Land, that the Spaniards were said to have discovered, the Staten Landt and Compagnies Landt of the Dutch navigators Vries and Schaep.

Myth flowered from legend and sometimes from lies, as in the case of the remarkable Juan de Fuca who claimed that in 1592 he had been outfitted by the Spanish government in Mexico and sent northwards to explore the coasts; and had found a great channel driving north-eastwards into the American continent—undoubtedly the North-West passage; and had returned to Mexico and been treated with neglect and opprobium, finally setting out for Europe and sympathetic gossip in his old age. . . . The tale enlivened a great portion of the seventeenth century, exhilarating and confusing men's minds. But the urge to explore the North Pacific remained faint and negligible, despite the chance of brisk loot in golden Gama Land, the certainty of brisk trade and quick profits if a North-West passage were charted from the Atlantic to the Pacific. Sensibly, commercial enthusiasm considered it better to follow the ordinary trade-routes than to freeze in the icy seas off northern Canada.

But in Northern Asia itself events had begun to develop, to sketch in the background to those ventures that were to push back the bounds of shadowy Gama Land, the lost Fortunate Isle, into the Arctic Circle itself. This was the Russian invasion and conquest of Siberia, a long and bloody tale of robbing Cossacks crossing the Urals, seizing Tartar kingdoms and attaining recognition from the Tsar on sending him gifts of furs. The Tartar kingdom of the Obi fell in 1577 and in the track of the invading forces came Russian traders and trappers in great numbers, into a thinly-populated, uncheerful land, bright with flowers and crops in the summer, in winter an unmapped chaos of snow and desolation.

Tobolsk, a trading post, was built. Tomsk was reared to

VITUS BERING

dominate the upper valley of the Obi. Town followed town, the disorganized Tartar tribes making unwilling submission, European geography following with notebook and sphere the eastwards press of bloody-heeled soldiers and bloody-handed traders. Men reached the Delta of the Lena, unwitting the gold below the frozen surface, staring out in winter at the great berg mountains that shadowed the coasts. They followed the Lena up towards its source, by the Aldan and the Maia. Finally, through great mountain valleys, the Uruk took the Russians to the Sea, the Sea of Okhotsk that the Kuriles and Kamchatka enclose from the North Pacific itself. . . . This mastering of Northern Asia was one of the great feats of mass trade-exploration, greater than that achieved by any other white people after the rise of the Second Civilization.

The Okhotsk was reached in 1640. Four years later a determined trader, one Michaelo Staduchin, accomplished a marvellous journey. Trekking along the Arctic shore through Yukahi he reached the outlet of the Kolyma river where Kolymsk now stands. There for another five years exploration halted. Then in 1649 the adventurer Deshnef led a party of sable-hunters into the Anadyr peninsula.

Abruptly exploration halted. The Anadyr, the furthest outreach of Asia as we now know it, was inhabited by an excitable, valiant, stone-using people of the Archaic Civilization, the Chukchi, of very different quality from the class- and religion-oppressed Tartars whom the Russians had subdued with comparative ease throughout the length and breadth of Siberia. The Chukchis bitterly resented the appearance of the hunters. They were unimpressed by the Second Civilization. War broke out, the Russians retreated, cold and the ferocity of the regrettably manful natives compelling the retreat. Between the Anadyr and the Kolyma was still *terra incognita* triumphant.

The news of the Russian feat slowly penetrated to Europe and slow geographers, with many a pause and many a mistake, filled in the outlines of this great new campaign in the conquest of the earth. At Kolyma, like the Russians, the geographers halted. And here, having nothing to go upon in fact at this furthest point of Asia, faith came in as knowledge went out, that naïve faith that had haunted civilized man since the first Egyptian pondered on the dead beyond Nile Bank. North of the Kolyma, beyond the Anadyr sources—what was there but the Fortunate Isles, the Wells of the Waters of Youth, the

Land of Gama rich in spices and gold and great wealth for the taking? . . .

Some, as always, doubted the land. It was questioned if it was a separate land at all, surely rather an extension of the coast of America meeting at last with Asia, this Gama Land, the ultimate point between the two continents, rich accordingly. It was the obvious bourne of future exploration.

But that exploration delayed for long. Russia busied herself in the fur-looting of the kindlier parts of Siberia, this new treasure-house so easily come into her hands. It was purely as a fur-bearing, a sable-bearing state, that for a long century Siberia was regarded, ruled over in each province not by a governor, but by a Voivode, a Chief Factor, whose duties were to collect the tribute on furs and enrich firstly and officially Russia and secondly and unofficially himself. Humanlike, he often reversed the order of enrichment. Wars were waged against the tribes, not in order to Russianize them or Christiansize them, but to exterminate the furless. The fur flew all over Asia, as the light-hearted historian might comment. But the north-eastwards ultimate peninsula, filled with a dreadful cold in winter and the equally dreadful Chukchis all the year round, was left to a severe solitude while decade followed decade.

Till, towards the end of the seventeenth century, Europe turned to watch with an admixture of amazement and amusement the rise of Peter the Great.

§ 2

Vitus Bering Svendsen was born at Horsens in Jutland some time in the summer of 1681, the son of a patient and unfortunate man, a trader, Jonas Svendsen, with whom the gods had dealt meanly and unjustly all his life. Even in marrying Anna Bering he had but little bettered his fortune, though the Berings had been distinguished souls for centuries. Trade gaped and fled when Jonas appeared on the scene; Anna's sister May married two successive mayors of Horsens, and did from behind the mayoral chair what little she could for the unfortunate Anna and her spouse. But Jonas was a man predestined to trouble as the smoke flies upward, and the appearance of Vitus on the scene appears to have been the copingstone to a great piling of misfortunate phenomena.

He had an immense family which had eaten up his earnings like locusts. He had a wicked son, who sailed away and returned and got in trouble at Horsens, and vexed Jonas's respectable soul. . . . It was probably an anxious and careworn and overcrowded home amidst the flat midlands of Jutland where Vitus came to school age and calligraphy and a hurried flitting home of night through dark unlanterned wynds, the salt of the North Sea in his nostrils, the glimmer of the candle in his mother's room to light the way to the lowly and unfortunate house. There is no picture or portrait of Vitus of those days —his later biographers perforce built it up from the limnings his Russian colleagues were to make of him long afterwards: tall and ruddy and darkly bearded, grave and competent and, up to a point—a far point—fanatically energetic, fanatically visionary. Then, at that point, would come a sudden falling from resolve, a sudden and querulous timorousness, a disposition to turn and run. . . . Father Jonas had passed on his troubles, if not his nature, at a very early date to young Vitus, it would seem.

But these later lapses were as yet inapparent. Young, he was of the daring and resourceful nature that found little to hope for in fortune from the shops or warehouses of Horsens. He showed some skill and aptitude at school—especially in mathematics: he showed even more in haunting the sea front at Horsens, in sailing out the wide-bottomed Jutland boats and running with a flagging sail up the long flat coasts into the spray of the wintry North Sea. He resolved to seek, by shipping as apprentice on an East India trader, more of the world's goods than Jonas had ever been able to accrue.

He vanished into that life, perhaps at the age of sixteen, perhaps even earlier, and there is little record of what he did or thought for several years. He sailed to the East Indies, he developed into "an able seaman"—which surely had hardly the present-day connotation of the term; and in 1703 at the age of twenty-two he made the acquaintance in Amsterdam of that remarkable soul, Cornelius Cruys.

A Norwegian, Cruys had risen to the post of assistant master of ordnance in the Dutch navy, and might have risen even higher but for the eruption on the European scene of that remarkable barbarian, Peter the Great of Russia. Peter wanted a navy: native Russians were incapable of either building, directing or sailing a navy. Scandinavians were navy people by inclination and instinct. Ergo, Scandinavians he must have.

The result was that Cruys passed to his service, Peter Sievers passed to his service, Skeving, Grib, Dan Wilster. High pay and quick promotion were promised to all. Cruys in Amsterdam was a kind of roving recruiter on the outlook for likely young men : he looked on the twenty-two-year-old Vitus and found him good. Probably there was only the resolution and the energy notable then : he was a hasting and sincere and serene young man, little of a disciplinarian, but with large ideas, brave and perhaps somewhat rash Cruys heard. . . . He spoke with Bering to considerable purpose.

The result was that a few months later Vitus Bering had joined the Russian fleet as a sub-lieutenant.

What Jonas and Anna thought of the happening—not to mention that great horde of brothers and sisters that are always a vague limning in the background of Vitus's life—is not recorded. Vitus himself again disappears into incidental mention in diaries and the like for several years. He was appointed to a Baltic ship. War broke out, Charles of Sweden like a destroying fiend assailing with a fine impartiality Denmark, Norway, Russia, and any other competitor who chanced to near the lists. Peter's fleet was chased, or sunk and bombarded from one hiding-hole to the next. In that grim struggle Bering learned, with a score of others, seamanship and a rigid and cold obstinacy against the risk and disaster of tide and night and the frozen seas of the winter Baltic.

§ 3

It was more than the Baltic. Presently, as the Russian fleet scattered and reassembled through chaotic years, Bering was sailing swiftly round Europe to the Black Sea, to the Sea of Azov, dumping stores and ammunition, creeping back through the Bosphorus with other stores, running gauntlet of Turk and Swede before he reached safety again in the Baltic. Some of his exploits fame now questions—especially the renowned running of the gauntlet through the Bosphorus in 1711; with Peter Bredal and Simon Skop perhaps belongs the myth. But he emerged from those years with something of a reputation, he was known to Tsar Peter—"Ivan Ivanovitch", he called him, refusing the "Vitus" and acknowledging in the patronymic royalty's only cognizance of the unfortunate Jonas, he was known to Western Europe. His was hardly fame, some element in his nature denied him that, but the Russian navy commanders appear to have noted him with some emphasis.

His character is almost as dim and uncertain in those years as his voyagings. Possibly he had both the outward and inward seeming of a good officer, addicted to the somewhat insanitary amusements and intemperances of his time and class when he was not actually on duty, accumulating by open or discreet peculation the customary fortune collected with a fine assiduity by the flock of Norse ravens which Peter had brought with his navy to assist in dismembering the carcase of the Russian sheep. He was steadily and conscientiously promoted, a lieutenant-captain by 1710; five years later captain of the *Selafail*, a new ship; in 1720 a commodore. Then in 1721 the disastrous Peace of Nystaad descended on the Baltic scene. In the ensuing furling of the battle-flags Bering discovered his steady course of promotion interrupted. He was overlooked in promotion—deliberately, he thought. Perhaps some intrigue at the court of the semi-insane Peter had worked against him, perhaps he was genuinely believed incapable of holding higher rank. The act seems to have staggered him considerably.

He resigned from the Russian navy. He had a house in Finland, at Viborg, in a Scandinavian colony there, and to Viborg he retired. Perhaps he married then. If so, his wife (according to her own declaration of age in 1744, when she affirmed she was 39 years old) could have been a bare sixteen years of age. It is probable enough. She was a haughty, ambitious, bitterly pugnacious female, probably alternately teasing and petting the kindly Vitus. If he found some delight in her arms it is possible that he found little peace, and sometimes sighed for the sea and a ship again.

No word of how the promotion-dispute fared emerges out of the darkness of three long years. No doubt Bering, the wheels of intrigue in working against those hypothetical enemies of his at court, found the shore and the comforts garnered from navy peculation a bore and a weariness to the flesh very speedily, hungering for a return of work and responsibility and that sense of righteous fitness interwoven in his nature in the twenty years or so since Cruys enlisted him at

Amsterdam. But of this there emerges not a whisper from the records of the past : he was a man in many (we suppose) of his most intriguing moods and stances and characteristics one whom history has left entirely unchronicled.

Instead, history turns a new page to the failing years of the Divine Peter, the Beard-Cutter, the Crazed Loon of Europe, half savage, half moron. Western Europe had never forgotten the blank in the map of further Asia. Steadily such blanks elsewhere were being filled in as the new century advanced, and geographers began to question Russia on its abilities to deal with that unknown further point. Surely Russia under a cultured and progressive Emperor would not allow the question of the north-east land to remain long unanswered ?

The Barbarian of the Neva was flattered. Especially was he flattered at the discreet and kindly reproachings of the French Academy. It is probable that his own vision of the planet was palæolithic, his vision of human destiny neo-Sumerian, his outlook upon science one of gaping, unintelligent misapprehension. But flattery could pierce the thick skull where other weapons failed. He was pleased to be considered civilized, scientific : he had records of those explorations eighty years before unearthed and read to him, and presently, fired by the notion of looting the Land of Gama, the Fortunate Isle, and acquiring notoriety and French praise in the doing of it, he resolved on an expedition to Kamchatka and the Anadyr.

He sent off a preliminary one, to spy out conditions in Kamchatka and the Kuriles. It came to grief, but returned with a report. This was sufficient to strengthen the then failing Peter in his resolve to investigate further. He looked around for a competent commander, a man accustomed to command, but not too large commands, a sure and earnest and trustworthy man.

The name of Vitus Bering was brought to his memory.

§ 4

Bering was in his forty-fourth year, greying at the temples, when he received news of his recall and promotion to the rank of Full Captain. He was noted for his kindness and consideration towards his inferiors, qualities so little to the taste of the country and age that they survive surprised in history. When Jonas had died in 1719 and left his lugubrious will, signed by himself and Mother Anna:

> We are old, miserable and decrepit people, in no way able to help ourselves. Our property consists of the old, dilapidated house and the furniture thereto belonging, which is of but little value,

it is recorded that son Vitus passed on the 140 rigsdaler, which was his share, to the poor of Horsens. So strangely and uniquely commingled of these uneighteenth-century virtues, Bering found himself in charge of the great expedition to the North-East.

He seems to have studied the maps and supposings of the time with some care. Gama Land lay in the quarter he sought, a Golden Land. Some said that between it and America lay the Strait of Anian—a strait as mendaciously fathered on geography as the exploits of Juan de Fuca. Hondius's map, with a pleasing regularity, showed Eastern Siberia and Alaska balancing each other neatly, each side of Anian Strait, in the shape of perfected triangles. . . . Rumour said a multitude of things with no uncertain tongue—or rather, with a multitude of tongues. The failing Peter himself jotted down instructions for the expedition in that hazy and spasmodic manner characteristic of him:

> I. At Kamchatka or somewhere else two decked boats are to be built. II. With these you are to sail northward along the coast, and as the end of the coast is not known, this land is undoubtedly America. III. For this reason you are to enquire where the American coast begins, and go to some European colony; and when European ships are seen you are to ask what the coast is called, note it down, make a landing, obtain reliable information, and then, after having charted the coast, return.

This fine mixed bag of instructions tied about his neck, Bering set about organizing his expedition. The year wore on to its close while sailors, carpenters, mechanics were enlisted, officers appointed, and Bering made acquainted with his two principal lieutenants, Martin Spangberg and Alexei Chirikoff. Chirikoff was second in command, a sailor himself, haughty and efficient and intelligent. He was appointed to lead the van in the journey across Siberia.

Winter was the time appointed for departure, while the snow still lay thick and frozen and sledge-trekking would cover great distances till the boats and portages of the Siberian rivers were reached. On the 24th of January, 1725, Chirikoff and his long line of sledge-teams, in a cloud of snow-dust from the steel runners, passed out of St. Petersburg on their long journey across Asia to the Pacific.

Four days later Tsar Peter died.

His passing was to slow down not the tempo of the expedition, but the speed of assistance loaned it by all officials thereafter. The terrible Peter was dead, thought the Voivodes of Siberia, and they might yawn away a day and a night and turn again to a drowsy consideration of the needs and requests of this alien, Bering, with his plans to explore for Gama Land. Bering had lost his best prop in the passing of a man who was both his cultural and moral inferior.

But of that, starting out with the second half of the expedition on the 5th of March, he had no foreseeing. The snow held well and the long line of sledges, drawn by shaggy, half-wild ponies, passed in quick day treks over the Dvina, through the passes of the Urals, south-east to Kai on the Kama, and thence by Tyumen to the banks of the Tobol. There they found Spring in the air and Chirikoff and the advance guard awaiting their arrival. From Tobolsk they were to proceed by river.

Boats and barges in great confusion and number had been chartered for the expedition, Bering himself superintending the embarkation with a quiet serenity and authority. The desolate Siberian countryside was thawing under the coming of a slow sun as the boats held up the Irtish, northwards, with their motley crews. Snipe were calling in long marshes to right and left, and the Siberian bear snuffled in this and that thicket and paused to peer beady-eyed at the long train of river-craft that bore Bering's expedition and hope. So far, not a single hitch.

Junction with the Obi was made at Samarovsk, and they turned up the Obi against the strong current, running bright and turgid and swollen with the waters of Spring. Here oars had to be manned to back-breaking toil league on league. The mixed expedition crew murmured and sweated, but took to a manful toil under the eyes of the Dane, 'a real captain', kindly and considerate in all difficulties, reasonable, grave and

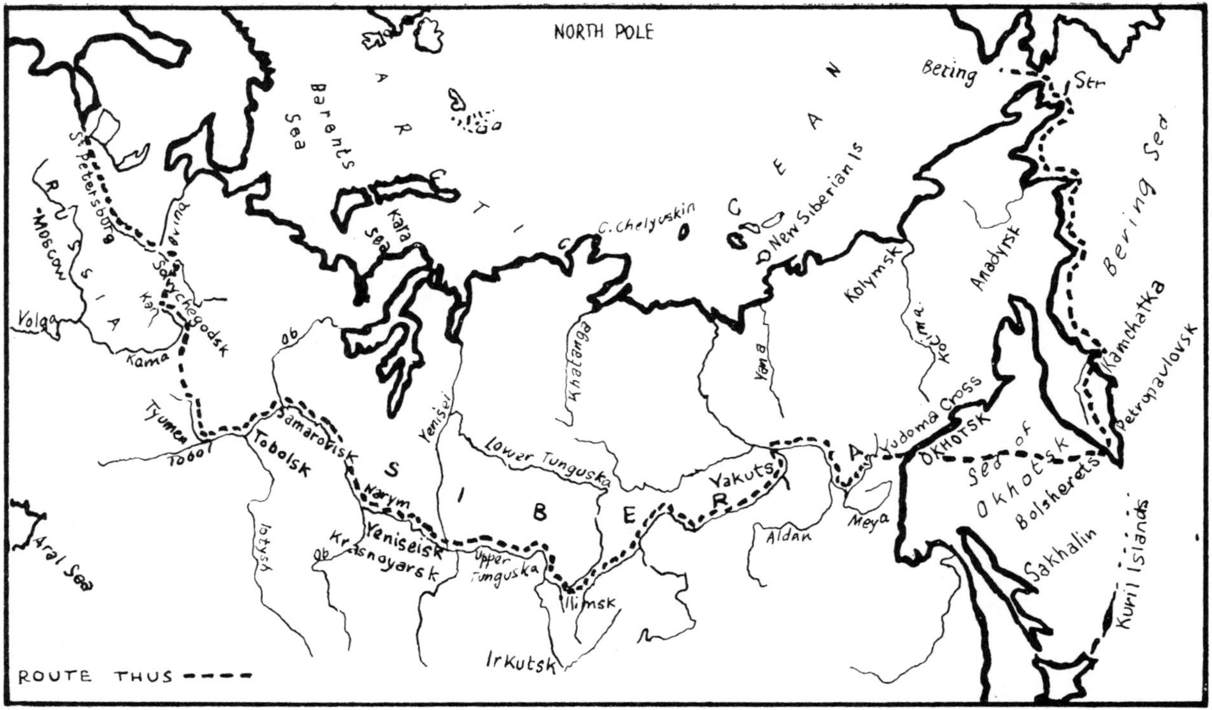

FIRST EXPLORATION OF VITUS BERING

thoughtful. Nights they tied up the barges against the flow of the current and the glow of their cooking-fires lighted up the waste banks long miles around, while Bering wrote up his diaries and stared eastward into the darkness, ceaselessly calculating and planning for yet another and another day's trek in that illimitable journey across the world's greatest continent.

Beyond Makofska Ostrog on the Ketya was a forty miles portage to the Yenesei. How might that be accomplished?

§ 5

It was done. They toiled and tripped and swore, bearded and ragged, the expedition's crews, as they loaded guns and gear and stores of food in rough country carts, on mule-back, on man-back, for the portage through the sodden tracks. Chirikoff proved a jewel of the first water, sardonic, efficient, competent to a degree, an admirable lieutenant. And at last, beyond the portage, the Yenisei came in sight. After long wrangling and delay, fresh water-transport was wrung from the district Voivode of Yeniseisk.

June came with the heats of Siberia sweating the expedition as the boats were poled into the entrance to the Tunguska, the great eastern tributary of the Yenisei. Here the current ran swifter and stronger than in any river they had yet fought; and as the days went by in slow rowing against the stream the boats creaked and split in the heat, food sometimes grew scarce, sometimes for long hours they paused in enforced siesta or drowsy stare on a land that glowed bright green and brittle beyond the river-banks, waving hot and fertile in the hot sunshine, deer-haunted, a land for the trapper and hunter. They saw little of humankind for day on day as that fight against the Tunguska went on, and June passed and July came in. Still the expedition, salted now, and with strong, if straining sinews, held on without mishap.

In August, far up the Tunguska, the waters began to fail. Brown rocks rose boiling from the low river-bed, and long stretching miles of sandbank over which the boats had to be poled and pushed and urged and cursed. Sometimes a boat stuck fast, gored as by a bull, and there were delays and halts in patching and mending : then again to the river's battle.

On the 30th of September Ilenisk on the Ilin was reached. Winter was near, a rapid winter with but little Autumn preceding it here in the heart of Asia. Bering resolved to go into Winter-camp for the rest of the year.

Of that Winter and the work in it there exists only a record of bare and necessary detail. Spangberg was sent overland eastward to the Kut, the nearest tributary of the Lena, there to build fresh boats and barges against the coming of the Spring. In strong huts and tents throughout the Winter the expedition suffered but little. Bering himself took to sledge journeys out and around Ilenisk, at last far south to Irkutsk itself on Lake Baikal, well out of the expedition's route, but a handy place to learn all there was to be learned about the necessities of the journey ahead. It was a mere trading post, Irkutsk, as were all the Russian so-called towns in that region so remotely east from St. Petersburg. . . . Returning from Irkutsk, Bering found Spangberg also returned.

The boats were ready.

They awaited the Spring. Beyond were the easy reaches of the voyage down the Lena to Yakutsk, and from there the dreaded land journey across the Stanovoi Range, half-known, uninhabited, to the shores of the Pacific at Okhotsk.

§ 6

Yakutsk was reached in June, after an easy voyage down the Lena. It was a small and odoriferous village, equipped with a surly Voivode whom Bering with a serene confidence overbore into helpfulness. Then, having rested for re-equipment and supplies, he set about the task of reaching Okhotsk.

He divided the expedition into two forces, one to proceed on the boats by way of the multitude of intersecting rivers. This was placed under the command of Spangberg and his route lined out for him—by way of the Aldan, the Maya, and the Uruk, up foaming rivers and through desolate passes, a hazardous attempt. But scarcely less hazardous was the passage which Bering planned for himself—a forced march across the mountains with two hundred laden pack-horses. Both he and Spangberg must hasten, for the Winter was close—the hasting Winter of those latitudes that knew no Autumn. On the 7th of July Spangberg sailed.

In mid-August Bering marched out his land-expedition to take the trail across six hundred and eighty-five miles of trailless country. It is one of the great marches in history. Exactly forty-five days afterwards, on the 1st of October, one of the dozen or so Russian fishermen who made up the population of Okhotsk looked out and saw a long train of laden horse descending towards the shore. It was Bering, who had lost only a few horses on the way. But at Okhotsk was bad news—no news. There was no sign or knowledge of Spangberg.

Nor as October and November went by did any news come of the river expedition. Meantime Bering had set his men to building houses against the rigours of the Winter. These came speedily, howling winds sweeping landwards out of the sea of Okhotsk, frosts that chilled the ragged and toil-worn men brought from St. Petersburg. But by mid-December they were warmly housed ; more than that, the carpenters and seamen had a ship on the stocks which was nearing completion. If only Spangberg would come——

In mid-December a toil-worn messenger appeared out of the desolate encompassing mountains. The river-expedition, overtaken by the winter, had abandoned its boats two hundred and fifty miles away—but abandoned them under guard. They were now on their way to the coast on foot.

They met hardship in plenty on that march, eating the dead horses they found littering Bering's trail (which they fortunately stumbled upon), suffering from frost-bite and famine and the fear of mountain-devils. Bering despatched a sledge expedition to their relief, and at last, on the 6th of January, they staggered down to the new-built huts at Okhotsk beach.

Winter closed down work on the *Fortuna*, the new ship, but early in Spring it was resumed, and an older vessel found and reconditioned. The plan of Bering's was now divulged. Northwards lay the peninsula of Kamchatka, half explored. On its northern coast was the river Kamchatka. They would spend the Summer in sailing the loads of gear and equipment from Okhotsk across the six hundred miles of uncertain sea to southern Kamchatka, unload the gear there, carry it across the peninsula to the Kamchatka river, sail down that river in boats to the open sea : and there set about building new vessels with which to explore northwards towards the inhospitable land of the Chukchis !

It was an astounding programme on which with such labour and sweat they wasted that year. The southern Kamchatkan shore proved too shallow for the *Fortuna* to draw near : goods had to be unloaded on boats and barges and rowed to the shore. Then began the trek across the desolate peninsula to the Kamchatka River. Midway that trek the Winter overtook them with stinging gales of sleet and such deeps of temperature as hitherto they had seldom encountered. Many died,- to the worriment of the kindly Bering. The trek was loaded down with canvas, ropes, nails, iron—all the equipment necessary, when they reached the Northern Kamchatkan shore, to build the new ship. If they ever reached it. . . .

They struggled through that Winter like men possessed, and at last attained their objective. If Bering's crossing to Okhotsk is one of the great journeys of exploration, his crossing of the Kamchatkan peninsula is one of the most farcical. Had the *Fortuna* sailed round Point Lopatka of Kamchatka she could have made the journey in comparative safety in a month or so. It took Bering six months to do it overland, at ruinous cost in men and materials, and at the end of the journey there was still another ship to be built. . . .

It is one of the two principal incidents that have led him to be denied the title of a great explorer. Yet it need not lead us to deny him a title in this record. That sudden access of timidity that made him refuse the Lopatka passage to the *Fortuna* was part of his nature—inheritance from the nature of old Jonas, now happed in earth where the wicked ceased from troubling under the rains of Horsens' graveyard. Knowledge of the value of men and gear, hatred to set them unnecessary risks, hatred of the thought of suffering in vainglory, these were the elements in the compound of timidity, hardly personal fear at all. He was, in truth, a searcher for the Fortunate Isle, that Gama Land that loomed ahead of the new ship's voyage, who doubted not the Island but only if the Waters of Life were worth the price of others' lives.

§ 7

Over three years had passed, he reflected, as that next Spring came in, without anything of moment having been discovered, any of the puzzles of the geographers solved, any glimpse caught of Gama Land's shores. This year——

The expedition on board the new ship, the little *Gabriel*, sailed from Kamchatka on the 13th of July amidst the cheers and shouts of the shore-party. A good wind drove them northwards : looking back, they saw Kamchatka's flat shape toy-like in the afternoon. Forward loomed the rugged and unknown coast pelted unceasingly by the North Pacific combers.

For seven days that voyage went on with a good following wind driving them further and further north along the uninhabited coasts of Utmost Asia. They crossed the Parallel of 60°. Fog and rain blew squallily upon the little vessel as it lurched into August. Fresh water became scarce and no suitable anchorage was sighted. But on the 6th of August, Transfiguration Bay hove in view, green and gracious and welcoming. The *Gabriel* put in and cast anchor.

They drank the fresh water and explored the shore and came on an abandoned Chukchi hut. Next morning some Chukchis themselves appeared : one swam out to the ship and told the news. Gama Land ? He had never heard of it. Islands of a sort there were to the north, with Chukchis on them, the Russians would be pleased to hear. Concealing their pleasure without visible strain, the Russians provided him with a few metallic toys and watched him swim back through the chilly waters to the neolithic shore of his native land.

They had passed the mouth of the Anadyr River. Presently they were doubling Cape Chukotski, and two days later an island was sighted. It was St. Lawrence's Day and Bering christened the uninviting fragment in the ocean after the Saint. Head winds arose, pounding the prow of the *Gabriel*, and long dark fogs seeped out from the Siberian coast as they still held northward again, keeping that coast in view. Though they were unaware of the fact—for no sign of land was seen to the east—they were passing through that Strait which has separated the Old and the New Worlds for several thousand years, that Strait that is now known by the name of the grave-eyed Dane who captained the *Gabriel*.

But presently, as the Asiatic shore was seen fading away into the Arctic west, a conviction of some moment came on Bering, believer in Gama Land though he might be. *There* Asia terminated, with no unknown land breaching the passage between it and America—or no land within close communication. Between Asia and America stretched this gulf of waters in which the *Gabriel* still held steadily north.

Where, then, was Gama Land? Where was America? In the geography of the time it was possible to imagine them both a thousand miles away in the east. No land was to be seen to the north, Asia had vanished, there was no longer purpose in keeping the course. So, on the 16th of August, Bering gave orders for the *Gabriel* to be turned about. This was in latitude 67° 18′ North.

There was probably some discontent at the decision, though no record of it survives. Bering was determined not to risk his crew in these seas now that Summer was gone, now that Winter—that haunting Winter—would soon be upon them. To sail only a few days eastward in search of the Fortunate Isle or America is a vision that seems one of obvious prompting to us: to Bering it was obvious that another and larger expedition must sail to seek those lands of repute in the apparently unlanded east.

So they passed back through the Strait, still uncertain that it was a strait, and beyond it the storms caught them, tearing the sails in shreds, tearing away the anchor, so that when they arrived at the Kamchatkan harbour the stout *Gabriel* leaked like a sieve. They seem to have sailed midway down the great Northern strait—at its narrowest only thirty-nine miles wide, with both Asiatic and American shores to be discerned on clear days. But fog, rain and storm blotted out sight of the eastward coast from their eyes.

Winter settled down over the Kamchatkan Peninsula. Bering had his men in snug quarters, but himself was in some unease, haunted by a vague knowledge of that mysterious eastward land. That it was near he was convinced, the Fortunate Island, Gama Land itself, or—less attractive—the north-west point of America. Wandering down by the Winter shore in the stinging sleet winds from the Sea that was to be called by his own name, he noted how

the driftwood did not indicate the flora of eastern Asia, and the depth of the sea grew less towards the north; the east wind brought drift ice to the mouth of the river after three days, the north wind on the other hand after five days . . . the reports of the natives corroborated his inferences. . . . In the year 1715 a man had stranded there who said that his native land was far to the east and had large rivers and forests and very high trees. All this led Bering to believe that a large country lay towards the north-west at no very great distance.

§ 8

1729. It was four years since he had left St. Petersburg, and he had news at last to carry there. South of 67° North, Asia and America were nowhere connected. Nor was it possible that they could be connected yet further north, he considered. He had discovered at least the termination of Asia, if not the populous countries postulated beyond.

Yet in the summer of 1729 he had one last fling at that discovery, taking the *Gabriel* with sudden recklessness out in a storm which battered its sturdy advancing shape through three long days, then swung it about so that they were forced to double Lopatka Point and seek shelter in Okhotsk, thus finally proving the peninsularity of Kamchatka itself. At Okhotsk Bering determined to delay no longer. He gave orders for the maintenance and care of the *Gabriel* and *Fortuna*, left guards over the stores and shipyards, and set out across the mountains on the long trail to St. Petersburg.

Of that long journey—as triumphant in essence as the journey of Columbus it should have been—there is little note in the histories. But it was no journey of triumph. Instead, Bering was regarded with indifference as he hastened across the Winter-gripped continent, finally reaching St. Petersburg on the 1st of March, the first of the great Russian explorers come to claim recognition from his adopted country.

It was not in his nature to be bombastic or over-forward. But recognition was his due. He had his maps and charts, the record of his voyagings, the witness of his two lieutenants.

Hardly pausing to embrace his wife at Viborg, he hastened to present his credentials at court.

And there, more formidable than the Arctic seas and the bitter storms about the Kuriles, he encountered the Russian Academy of Science.

§ 9

There followed three years of the most fantastic arguings in the history of exploration. The Academy of Science, staffed principally by young German and French pseudo-savants, not greatly honoured in their own country but welcomed to

Russia with a pathetic eagerness in the Russian belief that their coming meant culture and high western civilization, would have none of Bering. For his discoveries squared neither with the theories of the ancients—those remarkable ancients who limned the world for all time from a study in Athens or Alexandria—nor the explorations of the great da Gama or the equally "great" Martin de Vries.

Two Academicians, Gerhard Fr. Müller and Joseph Nicolas de L'Isle, were particularly bitter in their defence of the Fortunate Isle which Bering's voyagings seemed to deny. They altered their lovely maps not a jot, declaring Bering drunk, incapable or merely maudlin in his assertions. Neither of them had ever visited Siberia; but, enthroned on the pinnacles of their erudition, they were in no mood to be displaced therefrom through the crude notions and affirmations of a heavy Danish seaman, a cautious and uncultured man who preferred to waste time and energy on the health of his crews rather than seek out Gama Land—so the rumours went.

They must have been unhappy enough years in Bering's life. He stuck to his maps with a dour determination, neither exaggerating nor retracting his first statements. And gradually that dourness of affirmation began to have its effects. The restless and capable and amoral Anna Ivonovna liked Bering. Exploration and the thought of it thrilled her agreeably. And westwards lay Germany and France, still looking on Russia as barbarian and uncultured. It was decided that Russia "should show them".

Gradually an immense expedition was drawn together—an expedition of naturalists, metallurgists, geographers, astronomers, physicists, zoologists—and probably astrologers, milliners and deep-sea divers to make ballast. These learned men were instructed to investigate Siberia from all angles and in all the range of the sciences. The Pacific Coast was to be reached and charted fully and completely down to the shores of China, horses and cattle were to be conveyed to Okhotsk, the wilderness was to be set a-blowing with the flower of civilization—and all Europe was to gape with astonishment. . . .

Tagged to the end of this command and plan came instructions for prosecution of the search "for America or the intervening land".

Bering was appointed in command of the new expedition. It must have resembled rather a trek from the tower of Babel

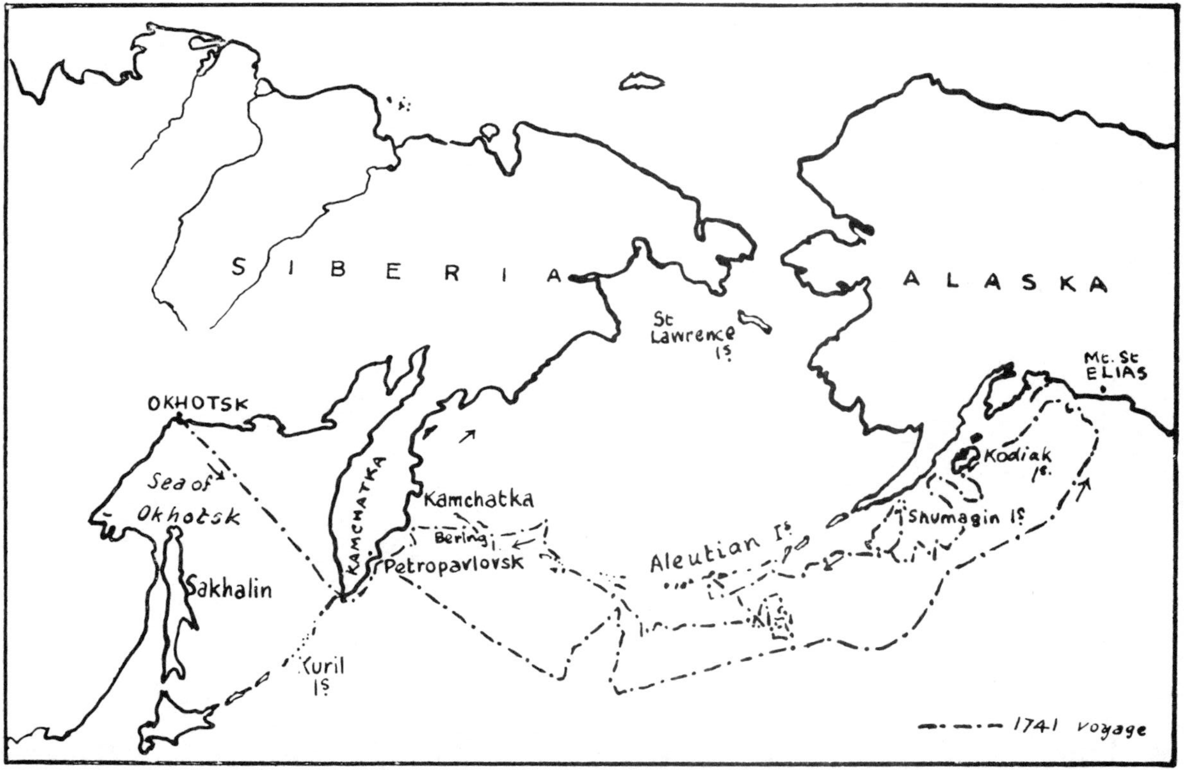

VITUS BERING DISCOVERS AMERICA

than the outgoing of any explorer's train that ever yet took the trail. The savants could not bear to be separated from their families—so the families and household gods went with them; Madame Bering found the possibility of a further long separation from Ivan Ivanovitch too tragic to be borne. Also, it would be agreeable to figure in the wilds as the wife of the expedition's commander. . . . So a sledge had to be found for Madame Bering. . . . Sledges were piled with the goods and chattels of men and women who were never to reach the Yenisei. Money was poured out in streams to feed and house and marshal the host even before it had crossed the Urals. Nearly six hundred men were under Bering's largely nominal command, including the invaluable Chirikoff, the equally helpful Spangberg, a host of subsidiary lieutenants, doctors, priests and the like unhelpful beings. In May 1734, the main body, minus various stragglers, reached Tobolsk.

Instead of pressing on to the real objective of his journey—the search for America or the Debatable Land—Bering had to pause here and see to the construction of a boat, the *Tobol*. This was despatched down the Obi to explore the river reaches and the lands about the Gulf; and so doing vanishes out of Bering's story. Rid of it, he pressed on over the seemingly unending Siberian ways to Yakutsk, the designed far-eastern base of the expedition.

Here two other ships were built, to descend the Lena, explore its Delta; and one then to hold westward, seeking Yenisei mouth, the other eastward, to round the Asian coast, sail down the Bering Strait and come to rest in Kamchatka harbour. These were launched a year afterwards, in June of 1735. The eastern Siberian coast was not rounded until a century and a half later.

Then began the enormous task of transporting the goods and gear of the expedition—all the gear and tools for the building of two ships, for Bering refused to rely on the long-abandoned *Fortuna* or *Gabriel*—over the seven hundred odd miles of way to Okhotsk. Summer fled. Winter came, with its howling storms and cessation of activity. Then Spring, rank and green in the Siberian wastelands as the long trails of mules and horses staggered through mountain passes laden down with packages of nails and cordage and iron staples. Autumn, a brief blink before the next winter, then again the long dark. So on and on, month after month, the costs of the expedition piling to marvellous proportions, deaths from exposure and hardships common, and all the weight and responsibility, blame for every delay, every calculation that went amiss, laid on the shoulders of the ageing, kindly, visionary Dane.

Meantime Madame Bering in Yakutsk had tired of the venture, of Bering and of Siberia. She had fallen out extensively with most of her friends and neighbours, indulged in a little mild crime, and in general contributed but little to the popularity of the Bering name. She resolved to return to Viborg : en route she was stopped and her baggage searched for smuggled furs. She flamed into long letters of hysterical upbraiding. . . .

At last, in the Summer of 1757, shipbuilding was commenced at Okhotsk. But the new Winter came before much could be done, with its coming there was a cessation of provisions from Yakutsk. The shipbuilders and sailors and naturalists had to cease from their hammering at the shipstocks and betake themselves to hunting and fishing for the earnest purpose of surviving until Spring. Meantime, though no food came from Yakutsk, messengers—Government messengers—succeeded in penetrating the mountains. Why had not Bering accomplished his explorations ? demanded St. Petersburg ; for what rhyme or reason had three hundred thousand roubles already been expended at his whim ?

He seems to have given little evidence of discouragement or bitterness, alone and apart, one of the loneliest figures in the conquest of the earth, never forgetting that consideration for the care of others that was of his life quality. He went about energetic and calm, reproached by his Government, a thousand cares on his shoulder as the New Year, 1739, passed rapidly away, and a new Winter came to halt activities. Then at last :

> In June, 1740, two ships were launched. Each measured eighty by twenty by nine feet, brig-rigged, two masts, and bearing fourteen small cannon. On the 4th of September the *St. Peter* and *St. Paul*, accompanied by two others [probably the old *Fortuna* and *Gabriel*] carrying provisions left Okhotsk.

After a delay of nine years the second exploration had commenced.

§ 10

The *St. Paul* and *St. Peter* rounded Lopatka Point and put in for the Winter at the new Kamchatkan port of Avatcha. By then it was September. They cast out Winter anchors and waited for the Spring, Bering meantime having all the equipment overhauled and the ships thoroughly prepared for the perils of North Pacific exploration.

So a tenth Winter went by. In the Spring two savants came to join the expedition—one Steller, a naturalist and geographer, a haughty, adventurous, skilful and daring man, the antitype of Bering ; the other the astronomer Delisle de la Croyère. The fortunes of both were to be closely linked with the two arms of the expedition.

They waited through a burgeoning slow Spring and the coming of Summer for a favourable wind. And at last, on the 4th of June, 1741, that wind came, and they sailed, Bering with Steller in the *St. Peter*, Chirikoff with de la Croyère in the *St. Paul*. South-east, went the rumour, lay Gama Land, and for eight days they held that course into an unknown, unislanded sea.

No sign of the Golden Land came in view even at the latitude of 46° 09′. Bering resolved to seek America.

The course was now due east. Day followed day without sighting land, over a glassy and Summer-stilled sea. But on the morning of the 20th wind and fog came down on the scene : presently a gale, shrieking through the rigging, pitching and twirling the small vessels in its hand. Night descended as they drove before the storm. When dawn came over the storming waters Chirikoff looked out from the *St. Paul* and saw the *St. Peter* nowhere about.

For three days he searched the unknown, uncharted seas for Bering's ship. Then, believing it either sunk or put back to Kamchatka, he resolved to prosecute himself the search for America. The storm had died : he held the course due east again.

Day on day, week on week, while water grew scarce and in the Northern heat the dry food from the ship larder almost choked in scurvy-touched mouths. Still no sign of land. June vanished and July came in, and the waste of the ocean was still about them. Then, when Chirikoff was almost resolute to abandon the search, driftwood was sighted and they heard the honking of sea-birds. Land must be near. On the 14th of July the crew of the *St. Paul* strained their eyes eastward all day; on the 15th, and at last, for the first time in recorded history, the northern coasts of America were sighted by Europeans.

It was coast somewhere between Cape Addington and Bartholomew. A rocky and inhospitable shore rose backgrounded by snow-covered mountains, dark in their uplands with forests of pine, blue on their crests with unmelting snows. For two days the *St. Paul* cruised northwards in search of an anchorage where they could put in for fresh water; and on the seventeenth anchored in a bay about 58° N.

Then followed two strange incidents. The pilot, Dementief, was ordered to take a boat and ten armed sailors up a near-by opening, land, investigate the beach, fill a number of casks with fresh water, and return. He was watched depart. Night came. He did not return. No sign of his presence rose from the shore. No sign the next day or the next or the next, while Chirikoff grew ever more uneasy. At last the boatswain was sent with a party in the remaining boat in search of Dementief. He too vanished within the channel. That night the twinkle of fires was seen far up the opening, smoke lay on the foreshore the next dawn. But neither Dementief nor the boatswain nor their men returned. They were never seen again.

Chirikoff was in an anomalous position: it was impossible to land, for he had no boats; equally impossible it seemed at first to abandon his fellow-explorers. But lack of water and scurvy drove him to it. On the 26th of July he weighed anchor and sailed for Kamchatka.

Unexpected storms and unknown tides beat the little ship about on the voyage throughout August; then fogs came, blinding the seaway. On the 9th of September islands—the Aleutian Islands—were sighted. Natives came off in their kayaks to view the sick and scurvy-stricken Russians: they were unimpressed. Illness and scurvy were increasing among the crew. Chirikoff himself was down with scurvy.

So was the astronomer, de la Croyère. The latter had worked out a system of keeping alive as unusual as it seemed efficacious: he remained permanently intoxicated in his cabin. At length, on the 8th of October, Kamchatka was sighted and the *St. Paul* entered the harbour of Petropavlovsk.

Chirikoff, very ill, was taken ashore. De la Croyère also

demanded to be carried to land. He expired in the fresh air almost immediately.

So ended the remarkable trip of the *St. Paul*, the first Russian or European ship to cross the spaces of the North Pacific and sight the continent of America.

And Bering?

§ 11

That story was to be told by the naturalist Steller, Bering's admirer, calumniator, assistant and ill-wisher. Bering's *St. Peter*, like Chirikoff's *St. Paul*, had cruised about for days in search of its sister ship. Then Bering came to the same conclusion as Chirikoff had come to: that he must abandon this search and proceed with the actual work of exploration.

He turned the *St. Peter* eastward—north-eastward, and it sailed through days of rain and fog, but in general with a good following sea. No islands were sighted, no land, it was a repetition of the fortunes of Chirikoff, with fresh water scarce, though food was more plentiful and of better quality than on the *St. Paul*. Also, the staff of the expedition in this ship was of higher quality, trained naturalists and savants, men very ready to brave discomfort in the service of that young infant of the Renaissance miscalled Science.

And night and day, on an empty sea, they peered east for the Fortunate Isle.

The coast of America was sighted on the 16th of July, exactly one day after Chirikoff, far in the south, had sighted the same coast. But here it was in latitude 58° 14′ N, a coast-line dominated by a single towering dark peak against an immense range of snow-capped hills. That peak was Mount St. Elias. Strong winds blew, and they might not anchor and land. But four days afterwards Kayak Island, just off the coast, hove in view. Here an anchorage, safe enough, was secured off a lee shore. The *St. Peter* was jubilant.

All but the commander. He had lain in bed ill, with incipient scurvy as it afterwards transpired, and when news of the land was brought to him in the dark and stuffy cabin where he lay he questioned the messengers. Yes, they did not doubt it was America. Their felicitations. He had won undying fame—and so forth, politely and enthusiastically, in the fashion of the time. For answer Bering turned his face to the wall.

Something, at that ultimate point in the expedition, seems to have gone out of him. It was as though a dynamic machine slowed down and stopped with a jar. Land at last—the land he had been sent to discover, the land that had obsessed his thoughts, his days and nights, for a dozen years. . . . And he was ill and weary and felt no joy. He struggled out of his sickness to dress and gain the deck and look with lacklustre eyes at the points of Kayak Island, the rugged heights of unknown America.

Those heights and their desolation suddenly terrified him :

> We think we have now discovered everything, but we do not stop to think where we are, how far we are still from home, and what may yet happen. Who knows but perhaps contrary winds will come up and prevent us from returning ? We do not know this country, nor have we provisions enough for wintering here.

It was the voice of defeat. His officers looked in amazement on the illness-wasted face of the ageing Dane, suddenly so peevish and fretful and—cowardly. Steller did more than look. He had but little respect for Bering, then or later : and he had not come to a new continent to hear grandmotherly complaints against its inhospitality. He was determined to go ashore and explore.

Go ashore he did, defying Bering. It was a dim and forbidding island, but Steller looked on it interestedly with a naturalist's eye, plant-collecting in company with a fellow-enthusiast, finally stumbling on an underground eirde, earth-house, where he found smoked salmon, bows and arrows, a fire-drill, all the marks of a Stone Age cult. He collected all the implements that seemed of interest, deposited an iron kettle and a Chinese pipe in their place, decided (in company with modern historians) that the marks of this cult showed strong kinship with the Asiatic and proof of Asiatic intercourse, and was proceeding indefatigably to other researches when the repeated firing of a cannon from the *St. Peter* warned him, as darkness drew down, that something was amiss. He returned reluctantly to the ship and the fuming reproaches of the sick man in command of the expedition.

But next morning Bering roused from his sickness sufficiently to order the next move and that a decisive one. He would linger no longer on this ill coast, so long sought, now dust and ashes in his wearied, years-jaundiced sight. Provisions were scarce and the season late. They would sail for Siberia.

The whole ship protested, Steller with frantic anger. But Bering would not be moved from his decision. To Steller it seemed that the commander of the expedition was crumbling away before his very eyes, no longer a man but a mere simulacrum :

> The only reason for this is stupid obstinacy, fear of a handful of natives, and pusillanimous homesickness.

It is the one definite and biting phrase that survives out of that day of ceaseless arguing and bitter comment, Steller's remark to the commander himself. Once they seem to have been friends : but Steller had as little comprehension and imagination in human relationships as he had them in great abundance in the wider matters of science and research. He saw nothing of the wearied and defeated Titan in the heavy Dane, the man overburdened with the cares of half a continent through year on year of reproach and blame and thanklessness, the man who had seen his life work shrivel up as the great glaciers of Mount St. Elias pierced the forward sky, the strangest and kindliest of the earth conquerors. To Steller the retreat from Alaska was merely farcical cowardice :

> For ten years Bering had equipped himself for the great enterprise. The exploration lasted ten hours !

§ 12

As if to close in his last days with the reproaches of the outraged seas, raped of their secrets at last, the secrets wherein the Fortunate Isle had lain in men's minds, if never in actual terrestrial latitude, the elements wove their garments of storm and cloud about the outward passage of the *St. Peter*. By the end of July they were still off the Alaskan coast, glimpsed now and again through sliding banks of fog and wavering sheets of sleet. Presently they were lost and entangled in a maze of islands, seeking to turn south and south-west, beaten back by contrary tides and winds, puzzled by the eruption of the

Aleutians out of the seething seas. Once or twice they succeeded in landing from desolate anchorages and filling the water-casks. But the scurvy spread ever quicker among them.

For two months the ship fought the seas off the American coasts before it won free to attempt the passage across the Pacific. By this time the moody and taciturn Bering, ill with scurvy, had virtually relinquished the command of the ship into the hands of two of his lieutenants, Waxel and Khitroff. A following wind at last drew them near Asia. The northernmost Kuriles were sighted. Then a mistake due to the fantastic incompetence of navigational science in that day decided the fate of three-quarters of the ship's crew.

This was a miscalculation of the nearness of Kamchatka. Their observations gave the parallel of 56° when it was nearer 54°. Land was sighted and the *St. Peter* steered towards it—low-lying land, treeless, spume-swept, a great low bank of sand and flying spindrift in the dim October day. A channel was sighted and the vessel steered into its entrance.

Scarcely were they within this channel than it was realized that this was not Avatcha channel. As anxious to leave as they had been to enter, Waxel and Khitroff awaited the lifting of the darkness. But next day it hardly lifted at all, for a great storm had arisen, fog came with it, and the little ship, pitching in the gale, sprung its mast so badly as to render it useless. Below, Bering lay semi-conscious in that torpor of sickness that had been upon him for two long months, hearing overhead the hurried tramp and scurry of the crew, the flail of sail and cordage, the crash of the breaking seas. Through dim ports he caught glimpses of the frothing waters of a racing tide. At last they brought the news to him. It was useless to attempt sailing out the *St. Peter* this season. They must winter here.

He roused himself—his last rousing—to object. If this, as they swore, was Kamchatkan coast, let them seek Petropavlovsk at all hazards. They declined, briefly, and left him. Three-quarters of the crew was down with scurvy. They must winter in this unknown Kamchatkan channel.

Only slowly did the realization come upon them that it was unknown because it was not in Kamchatka. Instead, they had landed upon a previously unseen island—that island of the Commander Group which is now called Bering Island. Kamchatka was ninety miles distant, the island, a great stretch of many miles, had neither trees nor inhabitants. Inland, scrub and game were plentiful, but at first sight it seemed merely an abode of seamews and the unceasing winds.

They could remain no longer on the ship. The lieutenants proceeded to disembark the crews in the biting November winds. Many died of exposure as they lay on the bleak hill-sides above the reach of the tides while Steller and the lieutenants strove with the aid of a half-dozen sailors to erect shelters and breakwinds of canvas and driftwood. In three months over thirty of the crew of seventy-seven had died, in spite of the fact that by the end of that time the indefatigable Steller had had pits dug in the ground where the expedition could shelter from the worst of the winter storms.

Bering was brought from his cabin and taken to a dugout next to Steller's. The latter's enmity had curiously subsided against his old commander. He looked at the explorer who had grown an old man, and saw that the end was not far off:

> His sixty years of age, his heavy build, the trials and tribulations he had experienced, his subdued courage, and his disposition to quiet and inactivity all tended to aggravate the disease. . . . Without doubt he would have recovered if he had gotten back to Avatcha, where he could have obtained proper nourishment and enjoyed the comfort of a warm room. In a sandpit on the coast of Bering Island, his condition was hopeless. For blubber, the only medicine at hand, he had an unconquerable loathing. Nor were the frightful sufferings he saw about him, his chagrin caused by the fate of the expedition, and his anxiety for the future of his men at all calculated to check his disease.

So we have this last picture of Steller, as he enters this record, assiduous in nursing, still cool and critical, coming in from his hunting and exploring of the low, mist-hung island—it swarmed with game, Steller killed animals with ease and rapidity, for they knew not men—to look at the still face and closed eyes of the old commander who had adventured so far from Jonas's house in Jutland. Perhaps in that adventure he had plumbed some deeps of the human spirit unknown to others who went before him in the conquest of the earth, the search for the Fortunate Isles—that pessimism of hope and outlook, that human frailty at last in the jaws of defeat. His was perhaps an essential type to complete the gallery, more human if less gallant than others, pity a strange ingredient in such a life as his, and weariness at last swamping all.

Perhaps as he lay there and they brought him the news that this land on which they had come was an island, a faint smile touched his lips—this was Gama Land, this the Fortunate Isle! Or perhaps even the humour of that might not touch him, beyond everything but the unease of his own body, the weariness of his own spirit.

He died on the 8th of December, 1741, two hours before daybreak.

He was buried in the sand beyond the huts, five thousand miles from Horsens. Presently the Winter snows covered his grave deeply. With Spring the survivors of the *St. Peter* built a new boat and departed from the island (which has remained uninhabited to this day) leaving the earth conqueror together with his conquest in the rains and tides.

§ 13

Steller, the lieutenants, and the forty-six survivors succeeded in making the Kamchatkan coast on the 27th of August, bringing (ultimately to Russia itself) news of Bering's death and the discovery of America.

More important from the viewpoint of trade, it brought news of the Aleutian Archipelago. Restraining its desire to appear civilized and western, Russia suppressed almost all information regarding the voyages and set about the exploitation of the islands and of Alaska.

Bering's (and Chirikov's) voyages solved the greater problems of the North Pacific, dislodged Gama Land from the maps, and sent the Fortunate Isle to hunt a new home in space and time, abandoning its insularity for the folds of continental obscurity, betaking itself to the depths of Asia, the Poles, and—remote and curiosity-stirring—Africa.

VIII

MUNGO PARK ATTAINS THE NIGER AND PASSES TIMBUCTOO

§ 1

IN that hasting conquest of the earth's surface which began in the eleventh century and continued campaign on campaign till to our remoter vision the surface of the planet seems tracked like a spider-web, interior Africa for long remained uninvaded. Before Columbus, the Portuguese in the service of Henry the Navigator had coasted the Western shores slow year on year, each year penetrating a little further south along those coasts that they named "of Guinea" and "of Gold". They traded with the shoreward natives, fought them, stole them, shipped great numbers of them to Portugal as slaves. They noted how below a certain line of the coast—the mouth of the Gambia—the Africans changed from indeterminate brown to black—they passed beyond the region of the Arabized Moor and came to the territories of the true Negroes. And at last, after long years of sailing and debating that have mention elsewhere in this record, they rounded the Cape of Good Hope, attained Zanzibar, and made the passage to India.

They were followed by the ships of other maritime nations—the Dutch, the Spaniards, the English. The former landed in South Africa and took to an adolescent plundering and planting that in maturity evolved its colonization. The Portuguese, from Angola, penetrated far to South-Central Africa, and erected strange "kingdoms" in indefinite localities before the close of the seventeenth century—kingdoms which presently crumbled to dust with the decay of the Portuguese power at home. Africa remained in its great northward bulking, despite those incursions from river and coast, an unknown country.

Deep in the heart of that unknown country Europe had long been apprised of the rumour of the Niger, a great river draining the forests and mountains, a river rivalling the Nile, a river on the banks of which stood fabulous Timbuctoo.

Rumour of this river had haunted the Mediterranean lands from earliest historic times. The Egyptians of late Dynastic days had sent an expedition in search of it—an expedition which actually appears to have reached the Niger's banks somewhere in the region of Lake Chad. With the coming of the outbreak of Islam upon the world communication or dream of communication with that distant river was cut apart—until the Arabs themselves evolved light and learning in travel and geographical curiosities. In advance of those curiosities mixed drifts of Libyan-Berber-Arabs crossed the Sahara in the ninth century and came in contact with the barbaric Negro states of the Archaic culture on the upper waters of the Niger. From that contact presently arose the great Negroid kingdoms of Songhay and Bornu, to astound the Arab geographers who came exploring south from Morocco in the eleventh and twelfth centuries.

Strangely, discovering the Niger, those geographers remained in considerable uncertainty regarding two matters of ancient debate. Where did it rise ?—In the Nile, according to the map of Ibn Mohammed al Idrisi, published in 1153 ; in Unknown Land, according to Ibn Batuta, most famous of the Arabs, who paid a visit to Timbuctoo in 1353. Where did it set ?—in the Atlantic, according to al Idrisi ; in the "sands of the interior" according to Ibn Batuta.

But, with the slave raidings of Portuguese, French, and English down the West African coast in the seventeenth and eighteenth centuries, that coast became so well known and mapped that it seemed no longer possible to assume that an unknown river, of such immensity as the Niger in debouchure, had its outlet on the Atlantic. All the great river mouths—the Gambia, the Congo—were known. Could the Congo be the Niger under another name ?

In 1778 the English African Association was formed under the presidency of Sir Joseph Banks for the encouragement of the Scientific Exploration of Africa.

Within five years of its foundation the Association had despatched three explorers into Africa in pursuit of the Niger. The first, Ledyard, an American marine, had some idea of tackling the problem from Libya. But he died in Cairo ere his mission was well begun. Lucas, the second man selected, had once been a slave in Morocco. He proposed to travel to the Niger country across the Sahara, and actually set out on that

MUNGO PARK

mission from Tripoli. But, after five days travel, he turned back his caravan, having come into collision with "revolting Arabs" (he referred to their political activities). The next selection of the Association was Major Houghton, fort-major at Goree, where the great French aerodrome is now built, a man of singular courage and address, in the phrase of the time, and well acquainted with Arabic.

Houghton's venture progressed further than that of either Ledyard or Lucas. With assistance and co-operation from a white slaver on the Gambia, one Dr. Laidley of Pisania, Houghton passed through the negro "kingdoms" of Woolli, Kasson, and Kaarta. Beyond Kaarta was Ludamar, a "kingdom" of half-breed Arabs—"Moors" as they were dubbed in the nomenclature of the times. Jarra was the border town and Houghton wrote from there his last and characteristic letter to Laidley five hundred miles away :

Major Houghton's compliments to Dr. Laidley ; is in good health, on his way to Timbuctoo ; robbed of all his goods by Kend Bular's son.

With this last cryptic message, Houghton disappeared into Ludamar, was again robbed, crawled on his hands and knees to a Moorish village, was there refused food, and either allowed to starve to death or knocked on the head and his body dragged into the woods.

News of the catastrophe filtered down to the coast with the slave caravans, and Laidley sent it on to the African Association in London. The third venture had not been lucky. Banks and the others looked about for someone to take the place of the unfortunate Houghton.

§ 2

The remarkable individual chosen for that fourth attempt upon the Niger had been born in a Scottish farmhouse near Selkirk in 1771. He was one of thirteen children, his father a peasant-farmer, his mother a handsome and competent woman of that exclusive and surprising breed which tills the land in Scotland. It was a family neither very poor nor affluent : they kept one servant, the Parks, though sight of the small whinstone house of Fowlshiels might lead the modern investigator to doubt the fact. Mungo's father was deeply religious, a stern and dour man ; his mother appears intellectually to have been of a like barrenness, if fecund physically. Mungo's brothers and sisters were ordinary and kindly and uninspired folk. He himself, through the play of innumerable small chances, grew up differently to his strange destiny precipitated by the death of Houghton in far-off Ludamar.

He was a tall and handsome and shy youth, with brown hair and a small mouth, and a very pious mind. His shyness is the thing most frequently commented on in his early days : it persisted, but little modified, all through his life. That modification was the assumption of an appearance of extreme coldness and reserve. Mungo below that mask was possibly such a warring civil insurrection as we may never penetrate and chart.

He was educated at the Grammar School at Selkirk, a very competent and model scholar, one who read books and books and still more books as he tramped the muddy Scots roads evening and morning in search of the much-prized Scots education. He read much of the Border poetry of that time, novels and religious tracts, and very early seems to have been moved by the wonder of plants and plant-life. It was possibly this incipient passion for botany that moulded his whole life in the ultimate shape it took. He refused the Church and elected to study medicine, to the great disappointment of his parents.

This was in 1786. He was apprenticed to a neighbouring practitioner, in the fashion of those days, and rode the district in company with his master, dosing the ailing and assisting at unique and bloody operations. He seems to have acquired no great love of his profession ; but he was a difficult youth either to know or to love. By 1789, when he went to Edinburgh to matriculate, he appears almost as mature as he ever became—coldly devout in the Presbyterian fashion, self-centred, controlled, occasionally very eager with friends and kindly with the unfortunate.

But even when he was a full and formal doctor, he seems to have paused in doubt of the next step. He was only twenty-one years of age, but considered that he was wasting his own time and the Lord's very seriously in not settling down to a profession—his own profession or some other. He confided those doubts to a friend of his brother-in-law, James Dickson. So doing, he made yet another contact with an outpost of destiny.

Sir Joseph Banks, a man of many concerns and projects, was interested in the dour young Scot, sympathized with his unwillingness to spend his life in the dreariness of a Scottish general practitioner's round, and at last found him more congenial occupation. This was to act as surgeon on an East Indiaman, the *Worcester*, sailing for Bencoolen in Sumatra.

Mungo sailed with the ship into a year of which we know little or nothing. He seems to have enjoyed the voyage and to have botanized considerably in Sumatra. He wrote a paper for the Linnean Society describing eight new and hitherto unchristened fishes. He spent sweating hours in the fo'c'sle, doctoring the ills of the sailors with a cool dispassion, long nights staring at the homeward stars as the *Worcester* at last turned about to seek England. They rounded the Cape of Good Hope in good weather, and he saw for long weeks, dark in the east, the bulking of that strangest of continents vexing his horizon. Wonder—the explorer's wonder—awoke in him. What lay within ? What man of his colour would first attain the gates of Golden Timbuctoo ? . . . Perhaps, like Hanno, he looked out on that distant shore some night and saw its fires lighting up the darkness.

The *Worcester* reached England. Mungo, paid off and unemployed, took up residence with his brother-in-law in London and looked about him for work. More determinedly than ever, he was not to become a general practitioner. On the other hand, long sea-voyaging wearied him excessively. It was an impasse.

It was an impasse which the news of Houghton's death, received by the English African Association, speedily ended. The Association, comfortably unfrightened (as it well might be) at the fates which had befallen its various explorers, determined to despatch yet another in search of the Niger's source and outlet ; and it looked around for a suitable person—"educated and trustworthy"—to take up the task.

Mungo's name was again brought to the attention of Sir Joseph Banks by the indefatigable brother-in-law. Sir Joseph remembered. Sir Joseph was interested. He spoke to his fellow-members of the African Association.

Mr. Park sounded suitable.

Mr. Park was summoned to an interview. He was cool and

eager and respectful, a young man with a face still faintly browned by the suns of Sumatra. There was nothing he would like better than to take up the search for the Niger, he declared, "for the unravelling of the secrets of those strange lands profoundly fascinated me".

He was formally commissioned, and sailed for Africa in May 1795, directed, in his own words

> on landing in Africa to pass on to the River Niger, either by way of Bambouk, or by such other route as should be found most convenient. That I should ascertain the course, and, if possible, the rise and termination of that river. That I should use my utmost exertions to visit the principal towns or cities in its neighbourhood, particularly Timbuctoo and Boussa; and that I should be afterwards at liberty to return to Europe, either by the way of the Gambia, or by such other route as, under all the then existing circumstances of my situation and prospects, should appear to me most advisable.

§ 3

Mungo's first meeting with Africa in speech and person was at Jillifri, a port on the northern bank of the Gambia. Here his ship put in to trade in beeswax and ivory, and here he began to collect his information regarding that inland country through which he purposed to travel in search of the legendary Niger.

It was a country of small negro and pseudo-negro kingdoms, some pagan, some recently Islamized. Coastwards, the prevalent and prevailing negro type was the Mandingo, heavy, tall men, good traders, "a mild, sociable and pleasing people". Their chief magistrate was the "caid", their tribal conferences were "palavers"—a word which showed an antique Portuguese influence. They cultivated maize and rice and cotton, exported slaves, taxed alien slavers, and were in general a barbaric people slowly moving from their ancient orientation in contact with the Europeans.

Interspersed with them were the warlike Jaloffs, an aristocracy on horseback, Moors in Mungo's phraseology, and the wild hinterlands Negroes, the Feloops, unsociable souls who cut the throats of slavers and lived in remote jungles. These Feloops, we may guess (for in this later day they have been long merged in other groupings) were the original Golden Age Negroes moved to those unrestraints of conduct and ethic which contact with the cultured has ever wrought in primitive men.

It was a swampy, wet and uncertain land that which lay into the sunrise, Mungo gathered. And he would do well to learn Mandingo, the lingua franca, before he adventured its unknown perils.

He had now reached Pisania, last Gambia station of the white slave-traders, and put up at the residence of Laidley, the obscure medico and slaver-philanthropist who had befriended Houghton. The Gambia was close at hand ; so were the rains. Disregarding both, the solemn young Scotsman sat down hour on hour, with word-lists and native teachers, to plod through the mysteries of Mandingo.

Slavers would come and look at the young man, and tell him tales of the interior ; he disregarded most of these with a placid suspicion. He was indifferent to the slaver's trade but distrustful of his veracity. By the end of July he considered himself equipped for the journey ahead, and would have set out then but that he caught a chill while observing, genteelly, an eclipse of the moon. Next day he was down with fever.

For three weary months this fever kept him prostrate. The rains—the tremendous gushing rains of the African coast—had come on, swashing across the Gambia, burying all activity in their silvery pelt. The Gambia rose and rose, and Mungo found little sleep o' nights in the chorusing of the African frogs. He took the matter with a cool, priggish philosophy : he was at least being inoculated against the fevers of the interior.

Slowly the fever abated. He resumed his studies of Mandingo, and questioned Laidley on the obtaining of servants and horses. Laidley—he liked Mungo—very obligingly loaned him a young Negro slave, Demba, a cheerful and happy and garrulous individual, who was promised his freedom on Mungo's safe return to the coast ; also, he hired for the young Scotsman's use an older native, one Johnson, who had been a West Indian slave and appears to have learned little to strengthen either his morale or morals in the plantations of English Jamaica. Asses to carry Mungo's small quantity of luggage and trade-goods were purchased, as well as a "small and hardy horse" to bear Mungo himself into the dark interior of Africa.

At last his fever had passed. He felt well and strong again. On the 2nd of December, 1795, he set out eastwards accompanied by Laidley and two other white slavers. Besides these was a small caravan—two negro merchants, Johnson, Demba, and a couple of interior natives returning to their homes from working on the Gambia. Mungo carried with him on the horse an "umbrella, a pocket sextant, a thermometer, two compasses, and a few changes of linen".

That night they reached an inland village, Jindey. Here they slept, and here, the next morning, the three white men bade Mungo good-bye, never expecting to see him again. Several miraculous chances were to disprove their expectations. But we gather from Mungo's chronicle that for a moment he himself felt very young and dispirited and lonely as he watched those men of his own blood and breed turn about and ride into the westwards forest. He looked about him at the broad, dark, alien faces, thick-lipped, round-eyed, of the strange people among whom he had come, and felt no lightening of heart. Then—already in his mind a faint bugle-call the very name—he remembered the Niger, and rode briskly forward.

§4

He was now in the "kingdom" of Walli. Walli, at its frontier, proceeded to tax him heavily. Seeing that the tax-gatherers were in too great number to be shot down or ridden down, the young Scotsman submitted to the imposition, and rode on. It was a flat and fertile land. But jungle waved in the south ; forward were great stretches of forest.

Three days of riding amidst little villages brought them out of Walli into Woolli. No one as yet had hindered Mungo greatly, or helped him either. He was still in lands close to the coast, and the white man a phenomenon looked upon without astounded gape. On the 5th of December, however, he reached Medina, the capital of Woolli, a sunshine land, with the mud-built "city" set amidst wooded hills and gentle declivities. Here he was hospitably entertained by the negro "king", one Jatta, who had previously entertained Houghton. Houghton's name, indeed, was constantly on the negro's lips. Did Mungo know what had happened to Houghton ? Mungo shook his head at this rhetorical remark : he desired information. He had it. Houghton had been murdered by the Moors !

Mungo tried to look as shocked and surprised as possible. He was always scrupulously polite and respectful in his dealings with African potentates. Jatta regarded him with a sorrowful eye, and said it was evident that nothing would stop him. He would pray for the white man.

On the 8th, still in Woolli, and still travelling undisturbed, Mungo and his small caravan, considerably scratched and jaded, arrived at a town that is famous in story and controversy. It was Kolor : out of that town Mungo was to bring the first account to Europe of a negro ritual to enrich our vocabulary. Kolor was the home of Mumbo-Jumbo. When the goodman of Kolor arrived at the conclusion that one of his wives was in need of correction he did not hale her before the magistrates or hit her in the jaw : he proceeded outside the village gates where hung a suit made from the bark of a tree. Getting within this suit and closing down the visor of the mask, the negro would wait until the fall of dusk and then enter the village, uttering loud cries. Hearing these, the entire population would assemble around the village bentang—a tree in the midst of each plaza. Orations and singings would take place : finally, Mumbo-Jumbo would point to the recalcitrant female for whom, she unknowing, all this ritual had been prepared, and would have her dragged to his feet. Then he would beat her unmercifully with a stick amidst the loud rejoicings of all the other women.

Mungo appears to have been a personal witness of this custom in operation. He regarded it with genteel disapproval and resumed his journey. Soon he had passed beyond the last stretches of country trodden by white men—except by the unfortunate Houghton, the news of whose fate continued to haunt his track. Crossing the borders of Woolli and Bondou, he found himself, beyond the village of Koojar, on the verge of a great forest, the true African jungle. The trees towered tall and dark green, a seemingly impenetrable wall. Wild beasts and bandits lorded over this tract in disgusting harmony. Mungo's servants, tremblingly, sacrificed to the gods of ways and means, and Mungo pushed the caravan forward into the treey depths.

For two days they traversed this unkindly region at considerable speed, still holding due east, feasting at this hospitable village, fasting at another. In places Mungo found himself an object of enthusiastic regard ; in others—such as in the village encountered towards midday of the 19th of that month—he was persecuted by the ravenous curiosities stirred in the African breast at sight of the young alien from

Scotland. Women manifested an astounded amaze and a desire to ascertain whether or not Mungo could be really human in those portions of his anatomy which the other sex regarded as of paramount proof. Mungo, gasping, mounted his horse and fled in horror, followed by his grinning caravan.

So far, so gently. But these days of peaceful penetration were numbered. The forests ceased. Fertile cultivated land appeared with ant-gangs of slaves at work in the fields. Crossing the Falemè river, they reached Fatteconda, the capital of Bondou. This was Foulah domain, not Negro, land of the browny men from the Saharan fringe. Some of these invaders, surprisingly, seem to have shed their Mohammedanism in their southwards progress: Bondou's ruler, Almani, was a pagan. He was also a thief. An hour after Mungo's arrival in the capital, he was summoned to court.

Court proved to be in an open field. Almani questioned the traveller suspiciously: why did he wander so far afield, if not to acquire gold and Givers of Life? Out of curiosity, said Mungo. Almani sniffed suspiciously, and dismissed him till next day.

That next day brought disaster. Again interviewing the unauthentic monarch, that individual indicated that he would consider Mungo's new blue coat, with brass buttons, a suitable gift. Boiling with inward rage, but outwardly preserving a calm appearance, Mungo took the garment off and handed it over. Noblesse oblige. Almani, somewhat shamefaced, said that Mungo could now proceed out of Bondou duty-free.

After an interview of somewhat embarrassing intimacy with several of Almani's harem, Mungo rode out of Fatteconda with his escort on the morning of the 22nd. It was again a land of bandits, nearing the borders of Bondou and Kajaaga. The heat beat down with restless intensity, and Mungo sweated under his beaver tile. It grew too hot for daylight marching. They halted at a village, waiting for moonrise.

With the rising of the moon they set out eastward through the forests. Beasts howled and the long moonbeams danced and played down remote corridors of the trees. Dawn brought the borders of Kajaaga, and midday of Christmas Eve brought them to Joag in that state.

Joag evinced the first definite marks of African hostility. As Mungo rested under the bentang tree of the town plaza that night a band of horsemen came seeking him. They had been sent by Batcheri, King of Kajaaga, an indignant monarch. Why had Mungo not visited him at his capital, Maana? Mungo replied that he had had no time. All night he and the raiders argued around the bentang tree. Finally, losing patience, the horsemen seized his luggage, broke it open, stole what goods they desired, and departed with the dawn.

All next day Mungo sat hungry under the bentang tree, wondering what would happen next. He had still some gold and amber concealed on his person, but dare not reveal the fact in case the horsemen of Batcheri should return and relieve him of those valuables as well. His attendants were very thoroughly frightened. But towards night an old woman gave them food, and with the coming of that night came further succour.

This was in the person of a nephew of the king of Kasson, the next native state through which Mungo must pass in his quest for the Niger. This minor royalty had been visiting in Kajaaga, and heard of Mungo's plight. He was polite and assiduous. Let Mungo accompany him to Kasson, that civilized state, and all would be well.

Thankfully, Mungo accepted the invitation. Next morning, after sacrificing a cock to the denizens of the jungle, the joint expedition set out from Joag through the healthiest and most fertile African country that Mungo had yet seen. The forests towered green and tenebrous far in the hills of the north. But the lowlands were closely cultivated and nearing harvest. Far off they caught a glimpse of the Senegal. This they must cross to enter Kasson.

§ 5

They forded the Senegal. The horses were seized and hurled over a cliff and bade to swim to the promised land. The nephew of the king of Kasson kept a hospitable eye on Mungo during the crossing. But his hospitality was of base metal. No sooner had they landed in Kasson than he demanded a present. Mungo, probably feeling politely murderous, handed over "fourteen shillingsworth of amber and some tobacco".

The nearest town was Teesee. Here dwelt the father of Mungo's "deliverer", a negro of the name of Tiggity Sego. He was a sour ancient. Regarding Mungo with a dull eye, he dismissed him without demanding a present. Mungo hoped to push on unmolested.

He was mistaken. Borrowing Mungo's horse, Tiggity's son rode off on a mission to the north. For eight days, wearied, Mungo, though unmolested, wandered the streets of Teesee, mud-walled, heat-smitten, in the throes of a war-scare. War was about to burst on and around all this grouping of little kingdoms. Pagan Teesee lived in fear of the nearby "Moors" of Foota-Torra and Gadumah: while Mungo was there Foota Torra sent an embassy with the demand that Teesee acknowledge the Prophet: otherwise Foota Torra would come down and exterminate the unbelievers. With a touching unanimity the inhabitants promptly declared their conversion to the tenets of Islam.

At length Tiggity Sego's son returned from his wanderings, bringing Mungo's horse. Mungo prepared to depart, as unostentatiously as possible, from Teesee. The ruling powers demanded again, and indignantly, where were his manners? Falling upon his luggage, they gutted the bundles. Plus the similar robbery which had taken place in Kajaaga, three-quarters of the young Scot's original baggage had now disappeared.

But even yet he was not disheartened; cold, calm, priggish and composed, he rode out from Teesee with his following and held on for several days through Kasson. At a village, Soolo, he encountered a negro slave-trader who was in debt to Laidley in Pisania, and who had been instructed to pay the debt to Mungo. This he was proceeding to do readily enough when more of the minor royalties of Kasson appeared on the scene and demanded that Mungo ride at once to the capital, Kooniakary. Distrustfully, he collected his small caravan. What new robbery was to take place?

Demba Sego Jalla, however, proved unexpectedly honest, a happy prince but for the fact that he had scarcely set eyes on Mungo than he began to ask if the latter knew what had happened to Houghton—Mungo was more than tired of Houghton by now. He replied that he knew of the latter's fate. Blearily and kindly, the king dismissed the explorer.

His forward route lay through Kaarta. But Kaarta was about to engage in war with a yet more distant principality, Bambarra—Bambarra where Mungo now heard the Great River itself was to be seen. The king advised Mungo to avoid the war-threatened lands and hold north by Fooladoo. This he determined to do, and returned to Soolo to collect the debt from the slave-trader and refresh himself before attempting the trackless north-eastwards lands.

On the 1st of February word came from the king that the route into Kaarta was still practicable, and Mungo could travel that way if he chose. He did choose. Mounting his horse, and accompanied now only by Demba the slave and Johnson the servant, he rode across a tributary of the Senegal and found himself on the disturbed Kaartan borders. Streams of fugitives were pouring into Kasson, for Bambarra, as usual, was expected to win in the coming war with Kaarta.

It was a land of hills, matted with vegetation, sparsely, so that they reminded Mungo, with a sudden qualm of homesickness, of his own Border country. Beyond those hills lay a stretch of desert. This they succeeded in crossing in one night, halting at a watering hole and being hospitably entertained by some shepherds. Hospitality was not general. At the next village, Feesurah, the landlord overcharged him outrageously: surprisingly, he was supported in this outrage by Mungo's own slave and servant. Cold and imperturbable Mungo surveyed the situation, paid the exorbitant charges, and pressed on westwards through more forested country. Becoming separted from his attendants while all three were berry-picking, he met a ludicrous adventure. This was in the persons of two mounted blacks, encountered in a forest track, men who had never before set eyes on a white man. They uttered moans of horror, covered their eyes, put spurs to their horses, and galloped away.

Rejoining his companions, Mungo rode on and came to a wide plain in the midst of which, in mud and stench, squatted Kemmoo, the capital of war-threatened Kaarta. Its ruler was the Desi Koorabarri, a heroic warrior and a kindly soul. This unusual combination of qualities listened to Mungo, thought it nothing unusual that an intelligent man should want to view far lands, promised him every support in his venture, and dismissed him with presents. Rather staggered, Mungo slept the night in Kemmoo, and in the morning sent his pistols to the Desi as a return present.

The black king acknowledged them and sent back an escort to help Mungo reach the borders of Ludamar, the northwards kingdom of the Moors. There Houghton had been killed, a dangerous and fanatical land. But war had now broken out between Kaarta and Bambarra, and it was impossible to press on directly into the latter country.

The young Scot rode northwards with his escort through Lotus-land; here the lotus berry was gathered as a commercial product. He tasted it and found it mildly appetizing. But all the while his mind was vexed with a disquieting question: how would the Moors of Ludamar greet his mission?

§6

He came to Funingkedy, the last of the Kaartan towns to the east. Already he was passing beyond the round-shaped negro huts, walled with stakes. Funingkedy had a "Moorish" appearance. It lived in constant terror of raids from the horsemen of the north. Mungo halted here a day and night while a caravan gathered to proceed to Ludamar.

It was resolved to travel at night to evade the bandits. In great fright and at great speed the strange convoy stumbled northwards, hour after hour, Mungo and Demba and Johnson at the tail of it. At daybreak on the 18th of February rocky hills came through the mists and began to serrate all the north. It was a land of streams, with wild horses disporting by the banks. Under those hills showed a walled town. Unhalting, the scared caravan pressed on; at noon Mungo entered his first Moorish town, Jarra.

Laidley had given him an order for money on a slaver who dwelt even as distantly as this. The slaver received Mungo and his blacks kindly: he was the only soul in Jarra who did so. They were stared at aggressively by the haughty horsemen who clattered through the streets. The negroes, here a subservient, helot populace, could lend them no aid. Mungo sent off a present to the ruler of Ludamar, the Emir Ali, asking permission to skirt through the border-lands down into Bambarra.

A fortnight went by—a fortnight of black looks from the Moors and frightened looks from the blacks. Both Demba and Johnson made it clear to Mungo that they would refuse to adventure forth into Ludamar. At last one of the Emir Ali's slaves arrived to guide Mungo on his way eastward. At that Demba relented, and joined forces with his master.

They had gained the southern fringe of the Sahara, waste sandy land wherein they made but slow and heat-hazed progress for several days. Infrequent villages would erupt upon the horizon—villages where the travellers were stared at askance by the negroes. The first of March brought the considerable Moorish town of Deena. Here Mungo lodged with a scared if hospitable black; but soon the news of his arrival had spread abroad. The Moors came flocking in droves to gaze on the Christian, to spit at him; finally, they broke open his luggage, stole what they desired, and departed.

Mungo resolved to escape in the early dawn. He and Demba fled eastwards through a misty morning wherein lions howled. Day brought heat and thirst and a long stretch of parched ground. Once they halted and would have ventured a near-by well but that, even nearer, they heard the cough of a lion apparently as thirsty as themselves. They slept that night, uneasily, in a hut of some Foulah shepherds.

But next day, as they swung south towards Bambarra, forest came again, interspersed with cultivated land. Here for three days they journeyed unmolested, Mungo noting with a cool interest the effect of the passing of a cloud of locusts and the equally surprising effects produced by the native manufacture of gunpowder. They came to the village of Dallu, and rested there the night. It was almost the last town in Ludamar, and Mungo confident that he would now escape from the land of the Moors, robbed, indeed, but unharmed.

But even while he sat so thinking a band of Moors entered the hut. They were a party of the Emir Ali's horsemen, sent to fetch him to the Moorish capital, Benowm, there to gratify the curiosity of Ali's wife, Fatima, who had never yet gazed upon that horrific animal, the Christian.

§ 7

This was disaster, and Mungo knew it. He begged to be left alone, he offered all his goods to the Moors, he must have seemed—that moment while his mask dropped—a very young and frightened alien indeed. The Moors soothed him, sardonically. Ali wished him well: but Fatima also wished to see him.

Back along the dusty roads to Deena, where he had been maltreated a few days before. Here a son of Ali's was in residence. This son, a genuine foretaste of the father, interviewed them, threatened them, and so frightened them that

that night Demba attempted to escape. He was frustrated and thrust back into the hut. Mungo slept with a cool wisdom.

Next day they reached Benowm in the Southern Sahara—no town of Arabs, but a great encampment of black tents. Benowm gave a yell of surprise at the appearance of Mungo, abandoned all its worldly goods and flocked to follow him. He was led to the presence of the Emir Ali, a venerable scoundrel who looked on him coldly and then determined on an acute psychological test. It was evident that the Christian was starving. Good. Christians ate pigs. Also good. A pig was brought and offered to Mungo, in the hope that he would eat it and thus openly prove his uncleanness.

Suavely, Mungo declined the gift, affirming that pork was abhorrent to his palate. Somewhat dashed, Ali considered a moment and was then struck by a bright notion. He commanded that the pig be loosed in the hope that it would attack Mungo.

Instead, carefully excepting Mungo, the pig attacked everyone within range. It was secured and led captive away. So were Mungo and Demba to a hut where all night the guards kept thrusting in their faces torches of lighted grass to see that their captives were still unfled. They were given a little food and water, and slept uneasily.

Next morning they were led to a hut. Here Mungo was commanded to take off his clothes so that the Moors might examine them. They were especially amazed at the appearance of his feet. They had expected extremities departing from the true Moorish norm of *homo sapiens*. Obsequiously, Mungo disrobed and re-robed through a long, stifling day. Night brought little rest. The pig of the previous venture had been tethered to the ridge-pole of the hut. All the hut lay in sleep. But in the dark Mungo awoke with the consciousness that someone was creeping upon him. Thereon he jumped to his feet. Discovered, the intruder turned to flee. Fleeing, he stumbled over Demba and pitched head-foremost on the pro-Christian pig. The pig yelled and then bit the Moor in the arm. Pandemonium ensued, only dying down as dawn neared.

Day succeeded day of maddening captivity. Ali would neither release him nor promise a date of release until Fatima arrived. Bored and hungry, Mungo stared out at the life of unbearable Benowm and dreamed of the Niger and templed Timbuctoo, and listened to the plaints of Demba. Ali had messengers take away all his possessions except one compass which he managed to secrete on his person. Not contented with that, the Emir decided to put the talents of the Christian to direct use. He appointed him court barber and ordered him to shave the head of one of the harem boys. Slyly, Mungo nicked the young Moor's head till the blood gushed. He was at once relegated to the lists of the unemployed. But the captivity went on.

Page on page in his chronicle tells of that strange arid life in the sands that fringe the Sahara. Fever struck him and he crept out to the coolness of a grove of trees. The Moors pursued him and threatened to shoot him unless he returned at once to the stifling hut. He returned. Health came back with a break in the weather. The break brought a deputation from Ali's harem—a deputation of giggling women wishing to inspect Mungo's genital organ, to see whether or not Christians were mere uncircumcised pagans. With a dour geniality the priggish young Scot said that he would be pleased to give an ample demonstration to one of the number (pointing to the prettiest) if the others departed. The women laughed, and went away laughing, sending him a gift of meal and milk. . . . Women of Africa favoured Mungo.

He was taken on a round of the harems. The women treated him to coffee, sniffs, and looks of amazement. Bored with his company, the riders of Ludamar, returning from the visit, used him for impotent target practice: they poised the young intruder in the middle of an open space and whirled about him, lance-brandishing. He endured it all with a stony face. When would he be released?

Two travellers, Moslem merchants, came to Benowm. They had acquired tolerance in their wanderings. Lodged in the same hut as Mungo, they watched him starve and imparted information to him. Timbuctoo? Mungo could never journey there. The inhabitants were the most fanatical of all the Southern Sahara, and would assuredly cut his throat. As for the Niger, the Joliba, he would come on that in the lands of Bambarra.

It seemed to Mungo in those sweating days that never would he obtain his release to make that attempt. But the warlike events in the south affected Ludamar. News came that Mansong, king of (for Mungo) the still unknown state of Bambarra, was about to invade Ali's principality. That venerable scoundrel was stirred to considerable fright. He gave order for the camp at Benowm to be struck and a move made northwards, to another site, Bubaker. Arriving there through the dust and smell of desert travelling, Mungo at last was introduced into the presence of the woman responsible for his captivity.

Queen Fatima proved fat, respectable, comfortable and cretinaceous. She looked on Mungo with an affected disgust, then relented slightly, and, as a compensation for the maltreatment of the past two months, presented him with a bowl of milk. Unbelievably, it seems he felt gratitude. But it waned in the ensuing days. Bubaker was an even more disastrous place than unbearable Benowm. It was now the middle of the hot season. Water was very scarce. Night and day the wells and the troughs surrounding them were besieged by hordes of maddened cattle trampling each other in search of the precious fluid. The Moors, by scrupulous rationing, had enough to drink: their rationing scheme did not include comforts for the Christian or his slave. Demba and Mungo gasped with parched throats through long hours. Did Demba attempt to approach the wells, he was beaten off. They begged a little water now and then from the slaves of the Moors.

Mungo entered into long periods of delirium, seeing in dreams the placid waters of Yarrow, sweet and grey and crystal-clear, and himself go scrambling down its banks from the grey homely lour of the biggings of Fowlshiels—down and down to drink there and lave there and forget the dream of the Great River he sought. Sobbing, he would come from sleep in the stifling dark, alone, a captive, in the hot dark only the tormented breath of his slave-boy, Demba.

One midnight, the fever upon him, he resolved to try his own fortune at the wells. They lay at a distance of about half a mile from the city of black tents. He set out, staggering with weariness. It was pitch dark, moonless, with a shimmer of stars. Beyond the woods he stood in doubt, and then was guided towards the wells by the lowing of the heat-maddened thirsty cattle. Even at this hour the shepherds were toiling there, filling the troughs in the light of great torches. By that the approach of the Christian was descried. The Moors paused in curiosity to hear his request, and then drove him away with curses and abuse.

But Mungo had sharpened his spirit to a steel-like point on humiliation and insult. Beaten away from one well, he would try another. So the thirsting hours wore on, with the dawn near. At last he came to a well where an old man and two boys drew the water. Hearing his request, the old man readily acceded and drew him up a bucket of water. Mungo was about to take it in his hands, when superstition suddenly overcame the old Moor's kindness. He recollected that this was a Christian, and his touch polluting. Turning round, he poured the water into a nearby trough, where three cows already drank, and indicated to Mungo that he could share with these beasts.

So the son of Mungo Park of Fowlshiels, that cold prim youth who had landed neatly clad and composed on the Gambia beaches six months before, knelt down in rags and filth among the kine, and drank and slobbered in their trough, crying with delight and fever as he drank.

But now the worst of the hot season was waning. Winds arose and whirled the desert sands icily about the encampment. Clouds came flooding up from the south, dimming the flare of the midday sky, and with them, presently, the flow of sheet-lightning unending upon the African horizon. The rainy season was near at hand. To Mungo this presented a new terror. The Moors were accustomed to retreat further out into the desert to escape the rains of the jungle belt. Would they take him with them ?

But a fortunate accident prevented this. The Desi, the heroic king of Kaarta, having beaten the Bambarrans and his own rebels, threatened Jarra, the frontier town on the Ludamar-Kaarta line. In Jarra were several hundred refugee and rebel Kaartans. They sent an embassy to the Emir Ali to hire a couple of hundred of his horsemen as mercenaries with which to assail the Desi, and Ali resolved to set out and treat with them in person. If only he would take his Christian captive as far as Jarra. . . .

Mungo begged the intercession of Queen Fatima. Surprisingly, intercede she did. Some of his clothes were returned to him, together with his horse, saddle and bridle. Then he and Demba were ordered to accompany Ali on his southwards march.

It was the 26th of May when the cavalcade set out from Bubaker. Mungo was worn to a mere shadow: but now a monomaniac, the Niger and the thought of reaching it haunted his days and nights, dispelling the knowledge of the little vexations of the hour. Even the news brought to him the first night they camped—that Ali had stolen Demba and had sent him back to Bubaker—moved him only a little. He swore to himself to obtain Demba's redemption when he had found the Niger. Till then . . .

Jarra was entered on the 2nd of June, and Mungo made his way to the house of the slave-merchant. Here he obtained food and apparently some money. He sat down to plot an escape from Ali.

Events aided him. The Desi of Kaarta was on the march against Ludamar, his army unafar from Jarra. Ali promptly mislaid his warlike intentions and retreated hastily up country again. Apparently he had forgotten Mungo's existence. Now was the time to escape and prosecute his search to the south-east.

Johnson promised to accompany him.

§ 8

On the forenoon of the 27th the Jarran sentinels gave the alarm: the enemy were descried from the walls. Wiltingly Jarra evacuated. Mungo and Johnson rode out east through a crowded confusion of flying negroes. The heat was intense and great dust-clouds overhung the perspiring flight of the fugitives. The Moors had long before ridden north.

For two days, east and south-east, that flight appears to have pursued a breakneck speed along the borders of northern Ludamar. Then the tempo slackened. The Desi would not penetrate thus far. Mungo was in the best of spirits. Now it seemed that he had definitely escaped the detested Ali. Resting at a village, Queira, he took stock of his position, and gathered information on the best routes into Bambarra.

But that afternoon—the 1st of July—he was apprised that he was still unforgotten of Ali. A party of Moors rode into Queira, questioning the inhabitants as to his whereabouts. The inhabitants seem to have lied magnificently. Very well, said the Moors, they would seek out the Christian to-morrow. Yawning, they went to bed.

Mungo, in a sweat of fear, gathered together his scanty wardrobe, waiting till stillness fell on Queira. That was towards morning. In the grey chill of the false dawn Johnson came and whispered that the Moors were asleep. He himself refused to accompany Mungo, but rendered this last service. So they parted, Mungo riding east. He never saw or heard of Johnson again.

Beyond the watering-place of Queira he was recognized by some shepherds. These set up a loud howl of distaste. Mungo rode on with a beating heart. Presently he heard behind him a loud cry to halt, and looked back. Three mounted Moors were pursuing him. This was the end: he was the captive of Ali's men.

Surprisingly, it proved quite otherwise. The three Moors seized his bundle of clothes, inspected it, stole the cloak, clapped spurs to their horses, and rode away. They were merely engaged in a little private robbery. Mungo beat his jaded mount to some pace and rode away again.

East-south-east all that day he rode through a desolate land of sand and cactus-clumps. Here and there he saw herds of goats feeding, but dared not approach, lest he be apprehended by the Moorish shepherds. By afternoon he was fainting for lack of water; he dismounted from his horse, unsaddled the beast with a curious compassion, and clapped it on the flank to encourage it to desert him. There was no need for it to perish as well as himself. Then he fainted.

When he came to the cold night air had revived him; the horse stood patiently near at hand. Refreshed, he saddled the beast again, but did not mount it. Instead, driving it before him, he stumbled on through the night.

That night was to prove one of the most terrifying in the journey. Alone, lost and unaided in the heart of Africa, suffering agonies from thirst and hunger, chance guided his steps so that he did not stray in the usual circle but held his route still evenly. Yet in the pitch darkness he could see hardly a hand's-breadth in front of his face; his horse was almost as weak as himself. Thunder growled overhead and once he imagined he heard the patter of coming rain. He raised his face, with open mouth, to the skies. Instantly his mouth was filled with sand: it was a sandstorm.

Later that night real rain came. He tore off his clothes and spread them to soak and wrung off the water into his mouth. Blessedly refreshed, he clad himself and tramped forward again.

At midnight avoiding a village he found himself in thin

forested country again, descending some trail he could hardly see. A slow dawn filtered down through the tree-tops: he heard the croaking of frogs at a near-by pool and sought out that pool and drank and climbed a tree to spy out the land. Far in the south-east he saw a pillar of smoke.

About noon he came to it, a Foulah village where he obtained some food and sleep. But presently, outside the walls of his hut, he heard some of the villagers planning to tie him up and send him to Ali. At that he made his way out of the village, sleep weighing so heavily on his eyelids that he could hardly see the forest track ahead of him. Riding a few miles, he dismounted, lay down under a tree, and was instantly asleep again. Roused from that by two Foulahs who imagined he had overslept the afternoon prayer, he yawned at them hazily, mounted the weary horse, and held on south-east again.

The Sahara fringe was left behind. It was country thinly wooded, deep in lush grass. Presently a forest-track led Mungo's horse to a pool beside which he determined, foodless though he was, to pass the night. Mosquitoes came in multitudes to sting him; hyenas snarled about his encampment; far off a lion roared. But the young Scot, lost, forsaken, exhausted, slept the sleep of the tired.

Riding next forenoon, desperately hungry, he achieved the passage of some low, hilly country and came to a village where Foulahs entertained him hospitably. He was now on the borders of Bambarra. Dense woods sheltered those borders. Towards twilight he mounted and rode towards them. Narrowly escaping a roving band of blacks, he held on in search of a pool beside which he might sleep. About midnight he came on such a pool, and spent an uneasy night beside it, continually disturbed by the wurring circling of a band of wolves.

Dawn found him, weary and haggard, pressing down the dense forest tracks towards Bambarra. Somewhere in those early hours he passed from Ludamar into Bambarra at last. Early forenoon brought him to a high-walled town, Wawra, where the headman, once a Gambia slaver, had considerable respect for the white men. He entertained Mungo hospitably, expecting presents in return. Mungo blandly left him in the expectation, eating and resting through a long and blessed day of ease.

In Bambarra: and the Niger flows through Bambarra.

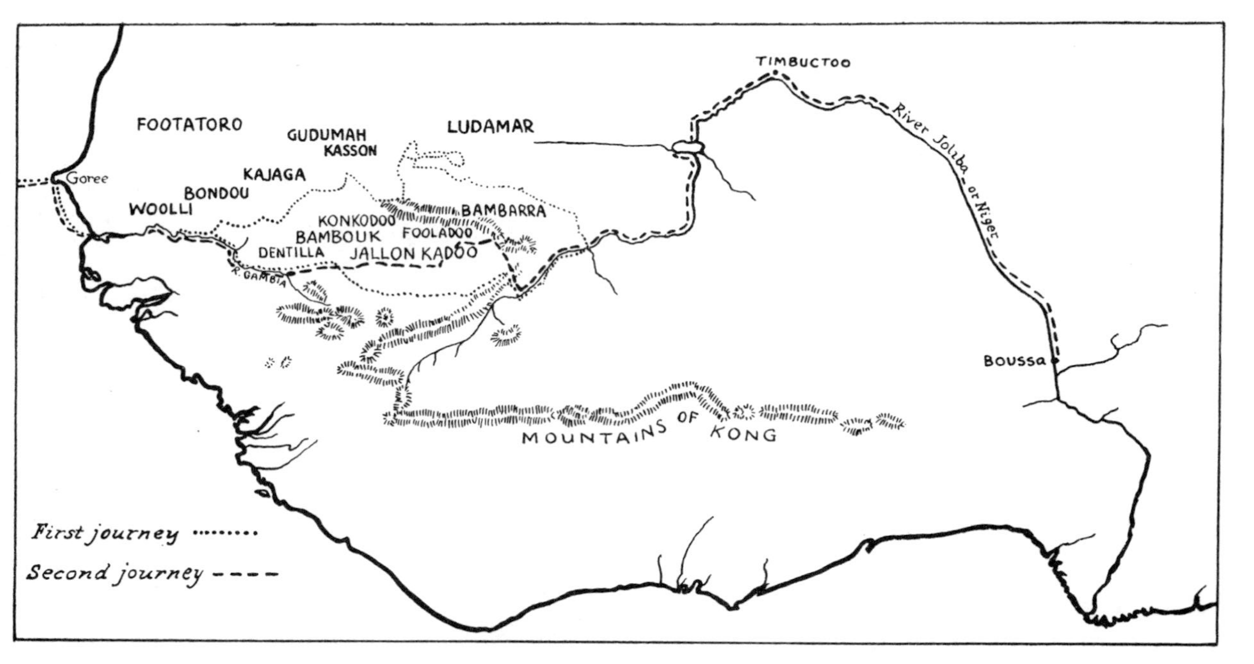

EXPLORATIONS OF MUNGO PARK

§ 9

The slaver dismissed him, shortly, from Wawra next morning, and he rode to a village called Dingyee, where he found a Foulah ancient willing to be hospitable in return for a definite favour. This was a cropping of Mungo's hair. With the hair in his possession, the Foulah planned to pound it to a paste, eat it, and thus acquire the wisdom of the white men. They exchanged food and hair, mutually gleeful, and Mungo pressed on to the next village, Wassiboo. Probably the Foulah died in convulsions.

Beyond Wassiboo was a dense forest, trackless, impossible to attempt without guides. Mungo halted for several days, assisting the villagers in their tasks, easily treated and carrying himself with a polite ease. By then he was beginning to recover his outward equanimity after the horrors of Benowm and Bubaker.

On the 12th of July a small caravan of Kaartans, bound for the capital of Bambarra, offered to guide the white man through the forest. It was a journey of several days' duration. In between patches of the great ocean of trees were tracts of fertile land, surrounding small and hospitable villages. But as they drew nearer to the Bambarran capital the land grew less fertile, the inhabitants less welcoming. Also, Mungo's horse staggered wearily in the rear of the Kaartans' caravan. Bored, they finally gave him up and pressed on themselves.

Wet weather had come, a foretaste of the great seasonal rains of interior Africa. Squelching through the mud, driving his horse, on the forenoon of the 19th of July Mungo met his first slave-caravan, coming from Sego, Bambarra's capital, and bound for Morocco, five months' march across the Sahara. He turned cold, sickened eyes from the appearance of the shackled slaves, and went on his way, unmolested.

Sometimes, in this and that haggard little village, he hungered, refused all sustenance but a drink of water. But now he looked too poor to rob, and, that apart, was apparently in the midst of a pagan people, who, outside the normal press of living, had no particular desire to rob anyone. The white man passed before their busied gaze, strange as a unicorn, and they stopped and stared a little in surprise, giggled and then let him go. Not in the whole course of his journey did he encounter savages: he never penetrated to the wild cannibal kingdoms of Benin far down the Niger.

But now Bambarra was coming very close. The inhabitants were becoming cultured, citified folk. They grinned at sight of Mungo, ragged, shoeless, plodding behind his gaunt mount. Wits offered to purchase the beast as a zoo curiosity. Mungo declined meekly, pressing on south-east.

He arrived at a village towards the end of July in company with two shamefaced negro travellers—shamefaced in that they must travel with this white scarecrow. That night Mungo, what of the news he heard, could hardly sleep. Morning found him with his horse already saddled, impatiently awaiting the opening of the village gates. Out of these he rode in company with the negroes, shortly afterwards overtaking the Kaartans who had deserted him earlier on the trail. Somewhat ashamed of themselves, these refugees now promised to introduce him to Mansong, the king of Bambarra, as soon as they arrived at the capital, Sego.

The road led by the verge of a marsh, though beyond that and all around the country was trim and well cultivated. Presently one of the negroes beside the Scotsman pointed ahead—see the water!

Mungo looked, gasped, took a long breath, the first of his European kind to see the sight. There, "broad as the Thames at Westminster", *and flowing to the east*, was the Niger.

§ 10

It was one of the greatest feats in exploration he had accomplished, but he was impatient to accomplish more. Flowing to the east—then did the great river indeed lose itself in the sands of the interior? And where, along its banks, stood the Golden City, Timbuctoo? He resolved to seek an audience with the King of Bambarra, obtain—somehow, by some miraculous chance—supplies from him, purchase a canoe, and set off down the Great River.

He descended to the water-front at Sego. Mansong was reputed to live on the southern bank. Ferries plied continually from one shore to the other, but Mungo was refused passage for the excellent reason that he had no money to pay it—money he found to be cowrie-shells. He sat down and waited patiently, the Kaartans having disappeared.

Presently a messenger arrived from Mansong. He had heard of the coming of the white man with a superstitious disquiet. Not under any circumstances must Mungo cross the river without permission.

Weary and again dispirited, Mungo sought out a village further up the bank. The day he spent in hunger and sun-glare, without food or water. But at night an old peasant woman took compassion on him, invited him into her hut, fed him with fish, gave him a bed, and sang him to sleep—one of the great and nameless heroines of all time had she her just due, for her feat was equivalent to that of an English or American villager inviting a ragged and scrofulous negro to share a single-roomed cabin. For three days Mungo waited in her hut, sending messages to Mansong, imploring help.

On the forenoon of the 22nd of July, a messenger arrived from the king. Provided that Mungo would set about leaving the neighbourhood of Bambarra, here was a present for him. Mungo opened the bag which contained the present, and found five thousand cowries.

It was a sum sufficient to take him well on his road back to the coast. But he planned quite otherwise. Purchasing some food, he set off eastwards along Niger-bank.

It was rich and well-cultivated land, the inhabitants busy and indifferent to his passage, Bambarran negroes, pagan and practical. But two days later he reached Sansanding, a considerable riverine port, with Moors, mosques and mulishness. The Moors assembled to threaten Mungo, to demand that he acknowledge the Prophet, and to watch him eat raw eggs. He endured the threats with a still, dour face, declined to either acknowledge or repudiate the Prophet, and let it be known that the story that white men lived exclusively on human flesh and raw eggs had been somewhat exaggerated. Finally, the negro headman rescued him from his tormentors and saw him on his way along Niger-bank.

Four days of constant though slow progress brought him to the village of Modiboo. The countryside through which he had passed was renowned lion-country: on one occasion he and his horse, both too tired to attempt escape, passed within a few feet of a couchant lion. The woods that fringed the Niger from Sego onwards thinned out around Modiboo. The Niger had broadened greatly, he saw, fed by the swamps and invisible streams. Midway the river were islets where the herdsmen pastured their cattle without fear of raiding lions.

But Modiboo itself was the beginning of the end of his exploration. Waking the morning after his arrival there, he found himself ill with fever: the swamp-mosquitoes had stung him greatly. Modiboo's headman, looking on him in alarm, refused to give him shelter a further night. Reeling with fever and weakness, Mungo and his horse both, they set out for the nearest village, Kea.

En route, the horse collapsed. Mungo removed its bridle and saddle, patted it, left a tussock of grass in front of it, and went on through the dim forest tracks, fever-hazed, completely alone.

Kea refused him shelter. He found a boat which took him diagonally across the river to the utmost town, Silla, that he was to see that year. Beyond Silla, into a dim haze of names and lands flowed the Great River, past Timbuctoo the sought, into the lands of the Houssa, into man-eating Maniana. . . . So he heard, sitting in a leaking hut in Silla. But he himself, he realized, was incapable of further journeying. Meagre though he considered the information he could bear back to the African Company, much though those unseen mysteries of the Lower River beckoned him on, he must turn and make the coast.

§ 11

It was the 30th of July. He had himself rowed across the Niger, gained the northern bank, and set out on his return tramp to the coast five hundred miles away, himself ragged, shoeless, weak with fever, in his possession only a few thousand cowries which would not act as currency beyond the boundaries of Bambarra.

And now even within Bambarra he found enemies arising. The Moorish shereefs who acted as Mansong's counsellors in Sego had prevailed on him to believe that the white man was a spy. Hearing that he had turned about and was retracing his footsteps, Mansong gave orders that he should be arrested. Strangely, his subjects showed no particular eagerness to arrest the polite and obsequious beggar. They avoided him, cursed him from their doors, but let him pass.

He had recovered his horse, tended and revived by a village headman; but the beast proved more a care than a help. Continuously the rains streamed from a grey African sky. His fever mounted and lessened and sometimes departed for a day or so, only to return with greater virulence. Holding north of Sego and avoiding Bambarran officialdom as much as possible, he tried to work out an essayable route to the coast.

By way of Ludamar he could not venture ; the Kaartan borders were still disturbed ; southwards, across the Niger, was the kingdom of Kong, a land of mountains, impossible because of language and other difficulties. He must attempt a passage along Niger-bank as far as possible, then strike on westwards through Manding and Fooladoo.

Begging at villages en route—here repulsed, here kindly entertained—he pressed on through the rains. His fever lessened. By mid-August he was deep in the land of the Niger floods—great tracts of country seasonally swamped by the burst banks of the Niger. At Koolikorro he earned a night's keep by writing charms for the headman on a board. This the headman washed from the board into a calabash, and drank down with many prayers. He probably needed them. Everywhere Mungo now halted the natives warned him it was impossible to escape the Niger floods in this season. He must halt a good three months ere they subsided.

But he could not halt. He was without food, clothing other than the rags he wore, or money—for the Bambarran cowries had long been spent. Still the rains held on. But for a while, towards the third week in August, he found himself dragging his weary horse through high and hilly country, pleasant to the touch after the squelch and slither of the flooded lowlands. Here, at Kooma, a lost Utopian valley of refugee blacks, he was kindly entertained and pressed on westwards with a gladder heart.

His gladness was premature. That day he was halted by a gang of robbers, stripped, robbed of everything he possessed but his hat and a pair of trousers, and so left "completely abandoned, naked and alone ; surrounded by savage animals and men still more savage".

§ 12

At that moment, so he tells in his *Travels*, he saw growing near at hand a small flower. Could God, who reared this flower for his own delight in the wilderness, abandon to perish of hunger a creature made in His own image ? God could and did. The bones of slave caravans were raddled in uncountable tracks from the heart of Africa to the utmost seas. But to Mungo the rhetorical question had only one reply : surely not !

Refreshed, he pushed on to the next village. There he met with a kindly reception. The headman promised to attempt the capture of the robbers. Mungo thanked him and hasted on into the west.

A week later, while he rested at a hunger-stricken village, two messengers overtook him. They drove in front of them the horse ; on its back was loaded some of the scanty belongings which had been stolen from him. Mungo gazed at the horse forlornly. It was more an encumbrance than an aid, he feared. His fear was justified. Next morning it fell down a well and took the united efforts of the villagers to retrieve it. Disgusted, he presented the beast to the village headman, obtained a spear and sandals in exchange, and resumed his journey to the coast.

The rains had resumed their seemingly endless pelt, the country swam in front of his eyes, a surge of green vegetable life, rain washed. He twisted his ankle and rested starving days in the village of Nemacoo. Slightly recovered, he plodded on again. But relief was near at hand. Crossing the slopes of a mountain he came to a town, Kamalia, a centre of the slave trade and also a centre of gold-mining. Here he fell in with a slaver, Karfa Taura, who was preparing an expedition to the coast. If Mungo chose to delay his departure till the next year, and would pay to Karfa the price of a slave when they reached the coast, Karfa in return would feed him and lodge him and bear him with the Gambia-wards caravan.

§ 13

With a cold serenity the haggard young alien tendered his thanks and acceptance.

Mungo never forgot that kindness of Karfa's. In all his subsequent dealings with the slavers, in all his subsequent comments on slavery, that memory lingers, sometimes uneasily, at the back of his mind. He was weak and shelterless and indeed had developed fever again. Karfa nursed him, fed him, gave him a hut for his own use, and in general acted the Good Samaritan.

Meantime, and slowly through the dripping weather, the caravan bound for the distant Gambia began to assemble. Recovering from his fever Mungo went and inspected arrivals. Sometimes he was hailed and recognized by pitiful slaves who had been haughty freemen far to the north in those days when he journeyed through Kasson and Kaarta.

Mid-December came. The rains ceased. A dry and parching seasonal wind blew from the north-east. Mungo gradually recovered his strength, watching the flames of the grass-burning light the night-time sky. Soon impatience succeeded lethargy. Still the days dragged by. They faded into weeks. Would the caravan never start for the coast ?

Yet this at length, on the 19th of April, 1797, the caravan did, a total of 73 human beings. Many of the slaves had been in irons for years, awaiting this move. Africa gossiped ; Africa yawned ; even on this march it insisted on halting every few miles to fire muskets and make speeches. Politely impatient, Mungo plodded in the rear.

Soon they came to the border of a great wilderness, the wilderness of Jallonkadoo. Within it for a stretch of several days there would be no villages for rest or shelter. Having dawdled so far, Karfa's caravan now decided on a forced march. It plunged into the wilderness at breakneck speed.

Perspiring as he limped along in his fraying sandals, the cold young Scot looked about him, seeing no wilderness, but well-wooded land of hill and glen alive with game. It had remained unsettled because of tribal wars. That night they camped in a place where wild beasts prowled, making the night hideous. Next day at noon a hive of wild bees attacked the caravan and put it to flight over a wide area. One of the slaves, a woman, proved recalcitrant and Mungo listened with sickened heart to the sound of the lash on her bee-stung flesh.

Still the wilderness continued, in spite of forced marching. The woman again proving recalcitrant, or incapable of keeping up with the march, was stripped and left to be devoured by wild beasts. Pressing on through great thickets of bamboo the caravan arrived at a village, Sooseeta, having crossed the Jallonkadoo at its narrowest point, a distance of a hundred miles.

Jallonka, the "kingdom" through which they were now travelling, was the home and abiding place of great bands of bandits. Avoiding these by stealth and stratagem, the caravan crept on towards the coast. On the 30th of April they reached the village of Tinkingtang. Ahead rose mountains, serrating all the western sky.

Next day they crossed those mountains. Now they were in lands not unremote from the coast, and Mungo began to feel again a stir of cold joy in his heart. If he could only last the pace of the march!

More mountains and craggy trails, the slaves groaning under their burdens. But on the 12th of May they crossed the Falemè river, south of a point where Mungo on his eastern journey had crossed it long months before. They were now in fertile, well-cultivated land, under better governance than Jallonka, Negro-land, far south of the Arab and his afflictions. A new wilderness, Tenda, a ragged stretch of forests and bamboo-clumps, was crossed without casualties, if with feet-aching weariness. Town after town, where white men had been heard of and this poor, strayed specimen (he was generally taken for a half-breed Moor, however) occasioned little surprise. Village on village while the west drew steadily nearer. At last, on the 1st of June, 1797, Mungo Park lifted his face and looked on the Gambia again. It was eighteen months since he had last seen it.

§ 14

They came to the capital of Woolli, Medina, on the 4th of June. Here it was that Mungo had been so hospitably entertained by the ancient chief, Jatta, in the course of his outward journey. Jatta, the explorer heard, was ill, but the caravan pressed on before he could make inquiries. Probably he had little urge—as always human beings meant little to the young Scot. On the sixth Jindey was reached, on the ninth Tendacunda, a village close to that Pisania from where Mungo had commenced his journey.

Here he heard the news and gossip of the coast. Neither Demba nor Johnson had returned. Everywhere it was presumed that Mungo himself had perished in the interior. The natives stared at him unbelievingly: this could not be the white youth of eighteen months before. Nor, indeed, was it.

Next day one of the white traders at Pisania rode through the woods to greet Mungo, and he himself mounted a horse again and took his way to the coast, to white faces and food and clothes and the blessedness of a razor again—astounding

Karfa, when shaved, with his appearance of a "mere boy". Laidley paid the sum Mungo had agreed with Karfa in distant Kamalia, and Mungo waited anxiously for a ship to take him home.

But it was no season of ships: no ships were expected for several months. Fortune proved kind, however, an American slaver, the *Charlestown*, appeared on the Gambia, and Mungo shipped a passage via the West Indies.

The ship sailed on the 17th of June, slave-laden. It was leaky and rotten. Soon the ship doctor was down with fever and Mungo had to take over his work. They halted long weeks at Goree, up the coast, under the broiling autumnal suns, awaiting provisions and new shipments of slaves, Mungo staring a sick distaste at the heat-hazed African shore.

Yet at length the *Charlestown* turned from it, putting out across a sullen Atlantic. Steadily the ship leaked. Slaves were brought up to man the pumps. Mungo toiled in a hell of disease and filth and fever. In the neighbourhood of the West Indies it became obvious that the ship would never make America. They put into Antigua.

Here Mungo disembarked and found a ship to take him to England. He reached it on the 22nd of December, after an absence of two years and seven months of such journeying as few had ever encompassed.

Shivering in the cold blow of the winter winds, he arrived in London in a sleeting dawn and went to walk in the gardens of the British Museum till the day should lighten and he could search out acquaintances. So walking, he was met by his own brother-in-law, Dickson—the same who had procured him his commission to search for the Niger.

Dickson stared as though at a ghost.

The African Association was to stare in similar fashion. All presumed him to have perished. Rumour of his travels and discoveries spread abroad London, Mungo himself closeted with the Association members and drawing up a hasty abstract of his journeys. It was published and his full account awaited with some eagerness. He went to Scotland to write it.

So he came back to the farmhouse where he had been born, and found changes enough there, a strange place to one whose eyes were still blinded with the sun-shimmer of the Niger country. He could not forget that even a day, even while he was falling in love with Ailie Anderson, the daughter of that general practitioner to whom he had been apprenticed. He would write his travels, marry Ailie, get him a new commission to seek out the Niger's source, find Timbuctoo, and live happily ever after.

§ 15

So he planned, but his plans went agley in many ways. His *Travels* were published, much read, much discussed, much attacked—principally by the Abolitionists. Then, and gradually, he was forgotten. The Government had more pressing business on hand than equip for the Niger the kind of expedition that the cold, haughty Scotsman demanded. He turned from them, sick at heart, to seek out work as a doctor in his native Scotland.

He had married his Ailie: they remained lovers and friends all their short married life. They moved to Peebles, where Mungo practised his profession, and was wearied to the verge of insanity, riding the barren hills attending the ills of the ploughmen and crofters. He had made friends with that writer who was then Mr. Walter Scott, and with him at least found a suitable companionship to discourse unendingly the questions of the Niger: where did it rise, what was its outlet: where stood Timbuctoo?

Tormented by a dyspepsia—the result of many a horrific African meal—bored and disgusted with an uncongenial profession, he endured a long five years. Slowly the dream of again seeking the Niger faded from his mind. Then events awoke it. Presently it was no dream, but an intention and a pan.

The British Government had awakened to the advantages that might accrue to British trade with a survey of the West Coast interior. Mungo was summoned to London and questioned as to whether he would captain such an expedition. He replied that he would.

Innumerable delays followed. But gradually the expedition's personnel was assembled: Mungo himself to command, his brother-in-law, Alexander Anderson, to act as lieutenant, and a Scots acquaintance, George Scott, to be general assistant. They would sail for Goree, enlist there a guard from the British garrison, strike across country to the Niger at Sego, build a fleet of boats, and sail the Niger to its outlet—either into the Atlantic itself or into the sands of the interior.

On the 30th of January, 1805, again in quest of the Niger, he and his companions sailed from Southampton.

§ 16

From the first this second and more ambitious expedition met with halts and disasters. The ship took nearly a month and a half to make the Cape Verde Islands from Portsmouth. Here Mungo and his companions landed and purchased a great number of asses to serve as pack-animals. Then they sailed for Goree.

There soldiers to the number of thirty-five were enlisted, enticed to the service by the offer of double pay and discharge from the army at the end of the Expedition. Two sailors came from the *Squirrel* frigate—future boat-builders for the fleet which Mungo was to sail down the Niger. An artillery officer, Martyn, also volunteered. Captain Mungo Park, tall and cool and cold, had the expedition embarked for Kayee on the Gambia.

But here another long delay took place while they attempted to enlist native aid. Laidley was dead at Pisania; the free blacks, for some reason that Mungo could not fathom, were chary this season venturing the interior. Nevertheless, he succeeded in enlisting the services of a Mandingo "priest", Isaaco, to act as his guide, and on the 26th of April the expedition set out on its march, a long array of donkeys and soldiers in stifling red coats—soldiers who jested blithely as they tramped forward into the waiting east.

Mungo planned to reach the Niger by much the same route as he had taken in returning from it ten years before. This he believed he could do in six weeks or so. But now, with the approach of the rainy season, the weather grew ever more hot, the air more stifling as the soldiers plodded white-faced down the forest-tracks. Theirs was not the stuff to make explorers, poorly fed, of indifferent physique, like all of the English working class of their day. Presently two men fell ill of dysentery: Mungo came to a swift decision, a decision that was to rule all his subsequent ruthlessness on the march. He had the men abandoned at a village and pressed on.

They passed through Medina, while the weather still retained its sultry stillness. On the 29th of May, reaching the village of Badoo, Mungo halted to write his last letters before he should reach the Niger. In those letters he told of the complete health of the expedition, their luck and happiness so far, and his conviction that they would reach the Niger in less than a month. . . . Some of the statements in the letters are deliberate falsehoods, some—true or false—now read with a pitiful flavour of old tragedy. It seems as though Mungo turned his face against the obvious facts louring behind the rain-clouds in the east.

For beyond Badoo they found the forests wilting under the great tornadoes that heralded the seasonal rains. Long before then the expedition should have passed through that countryside, attaining the shelter of Bambarra. Instead, they tramped down wind-blown forest-paths into early June, when the hesitating rain finally came. It came in long swathes of water athwart the dripping lines of men and animals.

Presently the paths were tracks of mud. Soldiers began to fall out in the increase of fever and dysentery. Mungo had them left at this village and that, and pressed on, aided by Scott and his brother-in-law, Anderson. They came, turning northwards to avoid the Jallonka wilderness, to the wild mountains of Dindikoo, now shapes of quartz serrating all the forward sky. Through and under the ledges of these they tramped as June wore on. Each night they halted and lighted fires, seeking to dry garments soaked with the rains of the day. The soldiers would shiver in cold and other dreads as around the villages and encampments with the coming of the dark they heard the cough of prowling lions or the howling of wolf-packs, hungry in the rains.

The rivers had swollen, sweeping away the native fords. The hired porters stole what they would, and vanished. At one river a crocodile almost ended the life of the guide, Isaaco; because he could not proceed with a guide lacking, Mungo doctored the black with such patience as he had paid to none of the dying soldiers. In early August they neared the Bambarran borders.

Soldiers lay down and died in the forests; Mungo left them to die, himself carrying out the work of a score, tireless, his vision ever forward on the unseen Niger. But beyond the Bambarran borders his brother-in-law, Alexander Anderson, fell ill, and him Mungo found he could not abandon. Despite the consequent delays to the expedition, he mounted Anderson on his own horse and walked beside him, holding the fainting man in the saddle. Once, so walking, they encountered three lions. Mungo fired at them with a musket, and walked towards the beasts standing astounded but unhurt. They growled their displeasure and took to the bush as the dour Scot plodded past. He had no time to waste on lions.

The weather cleared as they came to a village, Koomikoomi. They believed that the worst of the rainy season was over. Instead, it was scarcely begun. Recommencing, the rains recommenced the decimation of the soldier-guard from Goree. By the 19th of August scarcely more than half a dozen survived. But that day, as they climbed through mountains, Mungo halted his stride and stared, and gave a long sigh. Far off, flowing through the forests down to Sego, he saw the Niger again.

§ 17

There followed interminable discussions and arguings with the envoys of King Mansong, now from this village, now that, on Niger-bank. For the expedition was not allowed to descend to Sego itself. Mansong was willing to take presents and to promise canoes, but laggard in fulfilling his promises. Finally, early in September, he gave permission for Mungo and his people to descend to Samee, there to await the canoes.

Mungo had his ailing brother-in-law put in a canoe (Scott had died back in the last forests) and ordered the other survivors to march along the bank under the command of the mutinous Lieutenant Martyn. He himself sat down beside Alexander, and they were rowed down through rainy weather to the shelter of a village at least a little nearer the end of his journey. Soon the great canoes promised by Mansong would follow them, and then——

The river ran full and deep and strong, in flood. Still the canoes did not come. Then Mungo obtained permission to hold on to Sansanding (where, ten years before, he had been offered raw eggs to eat), and there dispose of his trade goods. He set up a shop and Sansanding flocked to purchase. Cheerful, Mungo proved an admirable shopkeeper, every now and then running out to look for the promised canoes, to glance into the hut where Ailie's brother lay.

At length the promised canoes arrived—two rotten and heat-frayed hulks. Mungo stared at them aghast. But there would be no others forthcoming. He stared at his small store of tools and then resolved on the impossible. He and the one sane, unsick soldier who still survived, a man named Bolton, must saw the two canoes in half and make of them one trustworthy boat.

It was impossible. But it was done. They laboured through sweating days at the river-front of Sansanding while the waters slowly sank. As steadily, Alexander Anderson did the same. On the morning of October the 28th he died while Mungo stood beside his bed. For a moment that occurrence wrung his heart. Then he turned to his canoe-building again.

At length all was ready. He had engaged a fresh guide, Amadi Fatoumi, to go with them as far as the Houssa lands. The canoe was loaded with the two surviving soldiers, Mungo, Martyn, the guide, and a slave purchased for paddle-work. They embarked on the Niger on the 19th of November, 1805, and the current rapidly swung them east and south.

§ 18

Thereafter, day on day, it is a record of battle, murder, and sudden death. Mungo had resolved to land at no point unless he was pressed for lack of provisions. Gone was his desire to walk the streets of templed Timbuctoo, the outlet of the Niger now his single concern. Again and again, deep in the country of the Moors, canoe-loads of bowmen and spearmen attempted to stay their passage. Mungo appears to have made no parley. He ordered his companions to fire into the brown of the natives, and this they did, beating a way through. At Dibbie this happened, at Kabara, the port of Timbuctoo. Then the river swung southwards. They were now on a river not only never before sailed by white men, but beyond the utmost rumours of Europe.

Day on day the canoe swept down the Niger, through low scrub land, through desert, through tracts where thin forests sentinelled the shore. Sometimes they stopped and purchased food. At the least sign of hostility the muskets were used, always effectively. Finally, they found themselves in the Houssa country. Here the guide Fatoumi must turn back.

Mungo landed him at the village of Yaour, neglecting to send presents to the king of that country. The king, enraged, resolved on an ambush. He despatched an expedition across a "bend" in the land to lie in wait for the canoe of the white men at the rapids of Boussa.

So the saga, the strangest and most terrible in many ways in all the history of exploration, came to its end. The canoe approached the rapids, sighted the waiting natives, and presently the battle opened. But the aim of the white men was uncertain on that dancing tide above which the currents foamed. Presently the canoe grounded. At that Mungo and Martyn consulted. Then each seized a soldier—the two remaining soldiers could not swim—and jumped into the water, striking out for the distant banks.

They were never seen again.

§ 19

News of Mungo Park's death at the Boussa rapids took several years to filter back to Europe. A son of his went in search of him, and died ; another relief expedition came on the guide Amadi Fatoumi and learned, doubtingly, his version of the tragedy. Even now it is doubtful what part treachery and betrayal played towards the enactment of that last scene at the Boussa rapids.

Neither of the two heroic journeys settled the question of the Niger's outlet ; but they pointed definitely enough towards that solution which Richard Lander carried out in 1830, when he trekked from the Guinea coast to Boussa, embarked there and sailed down the river to the spraying outlets of the great Niger delta. Masked in that Delta it was that the Niger for long centuries had attained the Atlantic, no great and visible outrush of waters.

If his life and death contributed greatly towards the solving of that supreme mystery of West-central Africa, his chronicles carried to Europe from the gossip of Benowm tidings no less startling, if disillusioning, regarding fabled Timbuctoo. No city of magic and mystery, but a decaying, dusty mart, mud-built, odoriferous, squalid. . . . And in such likeness indeed Major Laing found it in 1822 when he journeyed there from Tripoli.

Cool, impassioned, cowardly courageous, imperturbable, Mungo Park's character in analysis after a hundred and forty years disintegrates into fragments seemingly irreconcilable enough. The fire that integrated them was the Niger, Timbuctoo, search of the mystery river to the mystery city ; and when knowledge of both was in his grasp the fire burned through from its dark shrine and destroyed him.

IX

RICHARD BURTON AND THE FORBIDDEN CITIES

§ 1

WITH the exploits of Mungo Park and those explorers who followed at his heels, Timbuctoo vanished from the minds of men as either a Golden City or a geographical refuge of wonder. The Fortunate Isles, long divorced from the seas, betook themselves to those great tracts of Africa still untouched and unexplored. The nineteenth century was the great century of their quest in the African scene, Africa the last of the great inhabited and unexploited continents.

In the beginning the great Central regions, apart from such uncertain uplightings of their *terrae incognitae* as that achieved by Mungo Park, were still completely in darkness, the sources of the Nile undiscovered, the great Lake District unknown except through uncertain rumour. Abyssinia, despite the Portuguese, was still a land of myth and rumour, the upper reaches of the Congo a dark breeding place of tenebrous tribes of cannibals, strange animals, and stranger legends. Beyond the eastern sea-front lay somewhere the rumoured Mountains of the Moon, lay—it was impossible to know what lay there, except by actual search, and the nineteenth century set itself to the task with a commendable vigour.

Out of the multitudes of names associated with Africa in that century, the selection for this record of Richard Burton as the explorer elect is inevitable, in spite of his overshadowed reputation. Livingstone, who opened up such great areas of Central Africa, followed by Stanley, who rescued him and discovered even more, are both outside the count for reasons of taste, character, and sentiment. The one was a missionary-reformer-zealot led into exploration for the strangest variety of reasons, but never for that essential that we glimpse as the earth conqueror's supreme compulsion. Stanley, of a darker and baser persuasion, is outside the picture almost at once.

With him commerce, commendation, and the acquirement of decorations were the main urges. . . .

Schweinfurth, the great German naturalist, is one who competes in every particular except the last and the least important; but an essential one. This was lack of success, his mis-identification of the Welle, after those long years of research and triumphant genius in delineation which marked his explorations of the Upper Nile. In every other way he might be Burton's supplanter. Speke has claims, the unfortunate Speke, the true discoverer of the Nile's sources, Burton's enemy and ungenerous friend. . . . So has Keith Johnston. But none of that multitude of hardy and strong and gifted men who opened up the continent of Africa from the darkness of black barbarism to the new and spreading darkness of White exploitation and industrialism possessed that driving unease of curiosity on the geographically unknown to such force and urge as Burton, questing the ancient Fortunate Isles with a wry sneer of disdain, pursuing them out of Africa and abroad four continents, and escaping the sound of them at last in denial of their existence.

§ 2

Richard Francis Burton was born at "9.30 p.m. on the 19th of March, 1821, at Barham House, Herts, and I suppose I was baptized in due course at the village church".

Many of his contemporaries would have suggested that the baptismal font must have been left unsanctified. He himself was to leave, through various biographers, accounts of his childhood and its exploits which would set him in the picture of youthful gambollings with the more objectionable carnivores. All his life there was something of both the hyena and the jackal about him: beasts assiduously cultivated.

His childhood he occupied in the more egregious and unpraiseworthy of practical jokes, in forming gangs of youths of a like temper, in teasing governesses, climbing tall rocks, and playing the devil generally in the company of his brother Edward. His father, Lieutenant-Colonel Burton, a retired Anglo-Indian, pious, pettish, and weakly pugnacious, suffered hideously from asthma. Asthma haunted his life and the Burton household. Abruptly its twinges would descend on the Anglo-Indian; thereat he would root up his life of the moment and fly abroad—or from abroad back to England—seeking sanctuary from his ailments. A uxorious soul he insisted that each of these pilgrimages in search of his Giver of Life should also be a complete exodus. The Burtons were led captive about the Continent and educated with a haphazard efficiency.

Small, dark, black-eyed, insolent of bearing, young Richard was learning Greek at the age of three, Latin at the age of four, some twist of the play of chance in his brain had made it unusually receptive and attentive to the twist and play of meanings in alien vocables, he was all his life to be a great language-learner and language-user. They were means to curiosity, ways of escape from that sense of frustration that haunted very early the real Richard Burton behind the smooth façade of ruffian chin and godlike brow. For one so ready in the garnering of knowledge one might almost see the quest of the Fortunate Isles—in whatever disguise—as pre-ordained. And in his lifetime there was still left to European curiosity sufficient of an unexplored earth to set that quest on its ancient geographical tracks—for him, for a time.

Barham, Richmond, Tours, Richmond, Blois, Sorrento, Pau—marched the tale of his places of residence as a boy, language-learning, learning fencing with great joy and skill, a brutal, quick and destructive boy as he would have later ages believe. The belief is difficult. There was throughout his life an astounding harsh tenderness with the wronged, the distressful, that gives the lie to the clownings of the young hobbledehoy. His personality was then even less integrated than later, he had early encountered opposition and misapprehension, and then as later he acceded with a dark glee to the imputation of scoundrelism, worked on it and played on it, and almost achieved the imaginary likeness he had acquired in the eyes of spectator adults.

From Pisa he went, a boy, climbing Vesuvius. The fumes twisting slow wreathings of smoke far below his feet intrigued him considerably. He had himself lowered by a rope to investigate and was almost suffocated. The family moved on to Pau; here he fell in love. It was probably calf-love, shy adoration, that commingling of boyish idiocy and heartbreaking tenderness that is first love. . . . But the contemporaries of that adult who had been the boy at Pau found such an explanation incredible. Burton dead, they made him entice, desire, and fully, completely and satisfyingly seduce that dim early figure at Pau of whom he would talk. Burton would have approved his biographers and added masochistic details.

This wandering half-education about the countries of Europe in company with his sister and his brother Edward finally came to an end in 1840. Not yet twenty years of age, he was sent to Oxford, to Trinity College, in company with brother Edward. Both were intended for the Church by the asthmatic colonel; both were shocked at the idea. Trinity bored, infuriated, and amused Burton. He purchased a fowling-piece and would lean from the windows of his room and shoot rooks above the donnish garden-parties. Astounded learned gentlemen would raise their heads from gossip as blood-dripping bird-carcases fell amidst them. . . . Burton took to rowing, to more fencing, to anything but lectures, dry stuff out of books delivered by old men who also appeared to have emerged, incompletely, from books or dusty wine-bins. . . . He set about learning Arabic.

He rambled and explored the Oxford countryside, fell in with a tribe of Gipsies—the Burtons—who claimed family relationship, for he had their name and their dark look and restlessness, and that outward ruthlessness that companions the average muddled, kindly Gipsy. He was as Anglo-Saxon as he well might have been. But in that later, self- and sedulously-acquired scoundrelism that was his, he boasted the Gipsy strain he did not possess. It was a tribute to the one god of the Victorian hierarchy—the Christian Devil—for whom he had the compassion roused in him by most beings bullied and misunderstood of the bourgeoisie.

Long Vacation came and he went down, and saw the Colonel, and begged to be taken away from Oxford. He wanted to be a soldier, even though there was no hope of the Guards with its expensive commission. A line regiment would do . . . But the retired Anglo-Indian was obdurate. Richard was to study for the Church. Was not his father's miserable existence a sufficient warning of the life and fate of a soldier?

Burton went back to Oxford, brooded on the subject, went to forbidden races very carefully and ostentatiously, and was duly rusticated as he had planned. Packing cheerfully his books on Arabic, he went home. Father Burton, with no other option, set about the purchase of a commission for him in the East India Company's private army, which still governed India.

The commission was obtained; and now he could set out to the search for that life of wonder that lay beyond the borders of England, this country he detested, known and clipped, with its pale pudding faces and pale pudding morals. He acquired the sketchy military outfit of the time, embarked, endured boring days of heat and stench and monotony on the journey round the Cape, and landed in India on the 28th of October, 1842.

§ 3

There followed ten years of preparation in the making of that essential Burton that found him admittance to the company of the great earth-wanderers, the great explorers in the restricted sense that this record knows them. He learned Hindustani; he learned Gajurati, he learned Persian, he learned (on a holiday at Goa) Portuguese. He learned, unceasingly and avidly, languages, manners, customs, the ways that strange peoples looked on the world and fate and time, the manner and being of their gods and morals, the twists of hope and fear that spun their little mists in alien brain-tracks.

He was not popular among his fellow-officers. He came back to England in 1853 with a nickname that stuck to him throughout the rest of his life—that of Ruffian Dick. Ruffian Dick had been overbearing, brutal, unmannerly, uninterested greatly in wine and dicing and the vacuous gossip of the mess; instead, much to be found wandering odoriferous native bazaars, more often than not himself in the garb of a native, unclean and unashamed. He had even been admitted to a native order of mystics as a Master-Sufi; he was an atheist; and, very properly, he had been forbidden active service.

He returned to England for a long furlough, a somewhat disappointed youth, though still unembittered. Had they allowed him, he might have done so much! Instead—well, there was instead that second urge and obsession that haunted all his life—to write, prolifically, endlessly, staggeringly, on all he had seen, felt, believed, and conceived should be altered. He set about writing a book on falconry, he wrote one on the valley of the Indus, he wrote one on Portuguese Goa. And he wrote a Manual of Bayonet Exercise. They read extraordinarily affected and ineffective to later times, he suffered from the décor and decorativeness of his era in those early books.

RICHARD BURTON

But they have a freshness—even the bayonet exercises—much to our taste, if little to that of his contemporaries.

Still recuperating, he went holidaying in Boulogne, and there encountered that remarkable woman, Isabel Arundel, who was so greatly to influence his subsequent life. The encounter was as sentimentally romantic as only the Victorian age might devise : Casting his eyes upon the girl and her companion met on a chance walk, Burton wrote in the sand, "When can I see you again ?" Isabel fell in love with him from that moment. But he was penniless, disreputable, and an altogether impossible suitor from the viewpoint of the Arundels, this Ruffian Dick with the Gipsy face and the scoundrelly eyes and the scornful look that masked his impatience and his shy awareness of an unenviable reputation. Besides, what had he ever done—apart from ever made ?

He set about preparing an answer to that sneer. The plan had been in his mind since those days at Oxford when he vexed the dons on the question of learning Arabic. South Arabia was still—though not entirely—unexplored country from the viewpoint of the European. Mecca and Medinah existed, they had been visited by such great pioneers as G. A. Wallin and Burkhardt, but the lie of the country around, the real nature of the ceremonies at the Kabba, that focus and shrine of Al-Islam, were still uncertain. If not the Fortunate Isle for which to search, Mecca was at least the Forbidden City. He resolved to make the attempt of a pilgrimage disguised as a Moslem—a Persian Moslem.

He applied for and obtained a further year's furlough, had his skin stained with walnut juice, obtained the services of a halfwitted but devoted Mohammedan servant, and sailed from Southampton early in April of 1853, duly registered on the books of the P. & O. vessel as one, Mirza Abdullah of Bushiri, on pilgrimage to Mecca and the Holy Cities of Arabia.

§ 4

The ship landed him and his scanty chattels at Alexandria. He went to Cairo by river-boat, in a crowded tangle of other pilgrims, performing the ceremonial genuflections night and morning, discoursing briefly and piously with such as spoke to him—but discoursing not too loquaciously, perfecting his Arabic accent and his knowledge of the minutiæ of Moslem affairs. He reached Cairo with his disguise unpenetrated and there went into retreat with a Mohammedan friend, a retreat in which he trained as rigorously in the knowledge of Mohammedan ceremonial as he had done in the grammatical mazes of the Arabic language. His dark and heavy face looked well with its walnut stain, he had little of the European to vex his disguise and when at last he sailed on a pilgrim boat from Suez he did so with complete confidence in both himself and the venture.

Nor was the confidence misplaced. The boat disgorged the pilgrims, seasick, odoriferous, pious and pilfering, at Yambu ; a caravan was formed ; Burton mounted on a camel ; and they trekked into Arabia, into days of thirst and sunglare, over tracks not entirely untrod by the European. Burton was a success as a pilgrim, they called him the Father of Moustaches, and brought him their worst sores and boils to lance and cure. Beyond El Hamra the caravan was attacked by Bedouins. After a sharp engagement they were beaten off. Burton, mentally indefatigably note-taking, behaved with a sardonic composure during that comic warfare. But the ways were boring and seemed almost unending.

June had gone : Arabia burned in the heats of July, the long fall and flow of sand-nullahs unending upon the skyline. But at last, on the 24th, Medina was sighted by the dusty caravan with loud cries of praise from parched throats. It was a parched and unpleasing village. Burton found a shelter and increased his ostensible piety to wearying proportions. The caravan had dispersed, awaiting the arrival of fresh pilgrims.

By the end of August a great concourse was ready for its march on the Holy City. They marched on the 1st of September, an uneventful journey of ten days inland towards the holiest spot in Arabia, whence the Prophet had issued those admixtures of stern admonition and hysteric invective that founded a religion. And there at last, shining white and dirty in the sunlight, rode Mecca itself. Burton's heart rose high at the sight.

The caravan entered the town of pious robbers and put up at the caravanserais. Here, more than ever before, Burton had to exercise skill and patience in his character of pilgrim, to sleep with scores of the unwashed and diseased and untended, to keep company with his skin-vermin with a pleased benignity, to live the Arab as completely as it was possible for any alien to do. And he seems to have done it very completely. Long afterwards, when he was dead, the story was spread abroad that his companions—indeed, all Mecca of that pilgrimage year—were aware of his identity, but allowed him to pass on the understanding that he was a sincere English Mohammedan. If this were the case he was left singularly to himself, unstared at and undisturbed : had he been known as an English Mohammedan he would certainly have drawn in Mecca as great crowds of sightseers as a unicorn in Canterbury.

There followed days of pilgrimage to this and that site throughout the Holy City, culminating in the visit to the Kaaba, that centre of Islam, older than Islam itself, with the sacred black stone much be-kissed and be-slobbered by the crowding pilgrims. Burton, when it came his turn, knelt and kissed with an equal piety but a sharp eye. He noted the texture and appearance of the stone, decided that it was an aerolite, stored the fact away in his mind for future use, and passed on with praying lips and hooded eyes. . . .

But he was haunted now that he had seen the final thing with a knowledge of the strain upon him, that some night, some hour, his veil would slip aside, he would betray by alien gesture or motion that un-Islamic soul of his. The succeeding days were a torment of straining nerves while he awaited the slow gathering-together of a caravan seeking the homeward road from Mecca. Slowly the Jeddah pilgrims gathered.

Burton looked back and saw Mecca shine "like a pearl" in the after-horizon.

He reached Jeddah and the blessed peace and ease of the British consulate there a man subtly transformed : the transformation was to mask his life. Some of the kindliness had gone : and there was in him thereafter, reflex of those terrible days of which he was to write with a cool skill and contempt, a deep and enduring hatred for the savage, the Bedouin, the Moslems of the blood-feuds and fleas among whom he had passed those months of deliriously straining temper. If that was the alternative to civilization, then, after all, he was civilization's child. . . . Memories of little indignities suffered on the Mecca pilgrimage haunted that sensitive mind till its possessor began to bear truly enough in outward act and demeanour a fit likeness to the Ruffian Dick of contemporary reputation.

Meantime—one Forbidden City the less !

§ 5

He went back to service in India ; he wrote a book on his Mecca pilgrimage ; he wrote letters to his Isabel ; and he became very bored before more than a few months were passed. He had a hatred of civilization and discipline which were sometimes frantic. His exploit in penetrating Arabia had gained him some notoriety ; it even forced its way into recognition in the slow brains of the British overlords of India. For some time —over a score and a half of years, indeed—the Indian Government had toyed with the idea of the exploration of Eastern Africa, particularly Somaliland. The African and Indian connections existed from the days of Pliny when Somaliland itself was conceived to join on to India and the Pacific to be no more than an Indian lake. Curiously, this tradition of continuity of interest and association had grown up with the Honourable East India Company. But it was averse to risks and responsibilities : it wished to know the population of those regions, their habits and appearances, it wished to know the exact locale of the mysterious forbidden city of Harar, far inland ; it wished to ascertain the possibilities of establishing suzerainty in the south-Abyssinian borders.

Various adventurers—Cruttenden the most notable—had landed and investigated and suffered from fevers and native hostility, and received little or no support from the cautious and unimaginative souls who ruled the Indian destinies. . . . Now the latter wakened to receipt of a fresh communication from a fresh restless fool, this Burton whose fellow-officers had nicknamed Ruffian Dick, this swashbuckling outsider who had penetrated, somewhat indecently, to Mecca on pilgrimage.

Burton's proposal was that he be landed on the East African shore, with suitable provisions and money, and in company with two others. Thence he would march across country, visit mysterious Harar, pass on to Gananah, and so reach Zanzibar. Lieutenants Herne and Stocks had volunteered to accompany him.

The Bombay Council recommended the expedition in a letter to the Court of Directors of the East India Company : Burton, impatient of a reply, sailed to his base, Aden, in company with Herne, Stroyan and Speke, all Indian Army officers seconded for service with him in this attempt to penetrate East Africa.

Aden greeted them with jeers. Penetrate the country of the fierce and insolent Somalis, achieve, what no other had ever done, Harar, the Last Golden City, with its own language, its own coinage, its own army? . . . Ruffian Dick swaggered through Aden, greatly cheered. Harar sounded more fascinating than ever.

As a Haji, one who had made the pilgrimage to Mecca, Burton considered that he could travel in the disguise of an Arab merchant and reach the notorious city with comparative ease. He would take none of his companions from India: instead, he now proceeded to scatter them up and down the East African coast at various points of vantage where, returning from Harar, he might debouch. They were instructed to conciliate the natives, study the local flora and fauna, and keep a sharp eye upon the west.

On the 29th of October, 1854, Ruffian Dick sailed from Aden, his henchmen two Arabs from the Aden Police and a half-witted renegade Moslem mullah. Guled and "El Hammal", the two policemen, were to prove fervid partisans of Burton's; Abdy Abokr, the ex-mullah, was an ingenious scoundrel nicknamed the End of Time, he had so much the appearance which one of the Moslem priesthood would surely bear in that cosmic day of corruption that was foretold ere the end of the world. Burton himself was clad as a merchant: outside Aden, civilization being left behind, his companions and the crew of the boat proceeded to divest themselves of all the garments they had, and to indulge in a feast and the singing of improper songs. Burton joined in these refreshments, young still, dark, scoundrelly-looking, soft-hearted, muddle-headed, exhilarated at this his second venture out on the road to the Fortunate Land, to a second Forbidden City, Harar, there somewhere in the dim west behind the louring African shores, the home and fount of the slave trade, black and concealed and unfriendly, the Dragon awaiting the coming of its St. George.

§ 6

Zayla Creek was entered on the 31st of October; the governor of Zayla, a placid, benignant, and murderous individual who took an instant liking to Burton, was a pensioner of the Aden Government; he provided every facility for the march into the interior. Unfortunately, this provision was very small. His power extended but a short direction up into the bush. Burton spent an impatient three weeks gathering together his caravan and perfecting himself in the rumours and legends of the surrounding countryside. Particularly he studied all that could be read, seen, overheard or smelt about the Somali, that remarkable race among which he now found himself, the compeers, opponents and old-time friends of the vaguely Christianized Abyssinians of the North.

He considered them a vain and somewhat cowardly people, their civilization an odd hotch-potch of the unsavoury elements of most of the ancient and modern cultures; and recent research has done nothing to disprove that mid-Victorian estimate. But Burton, though he looked on those scrofulous, quarrelsome, under-fed souls with no great favour, was unique enough in the travellers of that era in his complete lack of disgust or contempt. He accepted them as human beings, rated them and their achievements, and passed on: he had none of the white man's belief in innate superiority, he had little care to either reform or suppress. He was, in fact, the typical earth conqueror unfolding in embryo.

Two routes connected Zayla with Harar: the direct one, taking between five and ten days; and a winding one, southwards along the coast and then branching tentatively in through the hills, west. The first route was closed by tribal feuds. The second Burton prepared for and on the 27th of September departed from Zayla with a small caravan, five camels and various mules, foot-followers and guards to some number, and the blessings of that polite scoundrel, the Hajj of Zayla.

It was a day of blistering heat. They travelled over a hard, stoneless, alluvial plain, across boggy creeks and along warty flats of black mould for hour on hour as the day-heat rose and intensified. The caravan would have liked to rest. The genial merchant-ruffian pressed them on. Night came at last, and camp was made, dates eaten, and Burton betook himself to his blanket, reflections on his Isabel, and a rapid and undisturbed slumber.

Next day they came in more populous parts, and halted for a day at an encampment of Bedouins who flocked to stare at Burton, to finger his raiment, to plan his end: imperturbably he pointed to a flight of vultures and lifting his gun killed one. Cries of amazement arose. The Somali were still in the spear-throwing, bow-and-arrow stage. It was evident that the merchant—no one believed him a merchant—was a notable and uncanny being. Burton was left in an awed peace for his sketching and note-taking.

On the 30th of November, still following the line of the sea-shore, they came on a tribe in trek, thousands of sheep and cows and camels driven forward by a couple of hundred spearmen, women and the sick loaded on to camels, dysentery very prevalent, dust rising like a thick and blinding fog, and all the landscape pervaded with a dreadful stench. Burton rode wide of them, coming to the village of Kuranyali. More egress of astounded natives, more begging, stealing, muttering of vague threats. Dark and scowling and imperturbable outwardly, inwardly still exhilarated at the feel and being of those days and journeyings, Burton took to his notes.

On the 2nd of December they left the sea and at last commenced the direct—more or less—trek upon Harar. Very soon it was evident that it was less than more. The way straggled and halted and debouched and paused and yawned. The Somali porters, feeble folk, sweated and panted under their loads ; even the mounted Somalis could hardly bear the weight of their spears "and preferred sitting upon them to spare their shoulders" ! Halting at night, it became intensely cold, and Burton's Aden companions shivered and complained very bitterly. They were passing up through country where it was considered dangerous to light a fire, what of prowling raiders. Burton disdained the tabu : they crouched and thawed themselves and slept, amidst the teeth-chattering of the guides, the sleep of the reckless.

Lions infested this new country into which they pushed—these and a miserable, warlike population which gazed with longing upon most of the accoutrements, arms and possessions of Ruffian Dick. These were the Eesa, degenerate Somali, or perhaps members of an autochthonous race. Republicans, they owed a nebulous loyalty to an equally nebulous potentate—one Prince Roblay the Rain-Maker. Drought of all things was feared in those parched hills.

The hills grew ever the more striking, day on day, piling up great granitic masses on the forward horizon. Rain and mists were encountered here. Halting in a lion-haunted village on the evening of the 6th of December, Burton cast eyes on the one prepossessing individual he had encountered in the course of the expedition—a charming girl. Undiplomatically, his poet's heart moved at the sight, he presented her with a few necklaces and toys in gratitude for her good looks. Her husband stood by: it was a tense moment. But the husband merely nodded a drowsy approval. That night the din of the lions round Burton's hut was exceedingly vexatious: he could find little sleep because of the continual commotion.

Now and again, in the hill-tracks, they passed great cairns erected against the sky—the tombs, these, of the men of old time, saints in Moslem or local theology, or perhaps antedating Mohammed. Sometimes entire and deserted villages littered the hillsides. Continually as evening fell a cold and piercing wind arose. Food and fodder were both scarce: presently the camels grew so weak they could hardly walk, and Burton's mule displayed a spine like a ridged hump borrowed from the neighbouring hills.

They were now at an altitude of 3350 feet. Halting beneath a sycamore of such great age that there were carved on its trunk words in the script of a pre-Arab race, Burton found buttercups growing in a hollow and heard a woodpecker tapping. These homely sounds moved him a little, but only for a moment. Harar was still far.

He had been attacked by dysentery, but rode on uncomplaining. On the 23rd of December, after various negotiations with minor chiefs who attempted to bar the way, to raise tribute from the caravan, to marry Burton off to their relatives and otherwise impede his progress, he rode his caravan forward across the fertile prairie of Marar and placed himself under the protection of the Gerad Adan, a powerful, unscrupulous and warlike chief who dominated the forward road to the forbidden city.

Harar itself, and at last, was undistant.

§ 7

Fresh difficulties arose here. The Gerad Adan was on bad terms with the Amir of Harar: no "Arab" friend of his would be allowed inside the Forbidden City. Neither, of course, would any infidel hitherto. But times, as Burton guessed

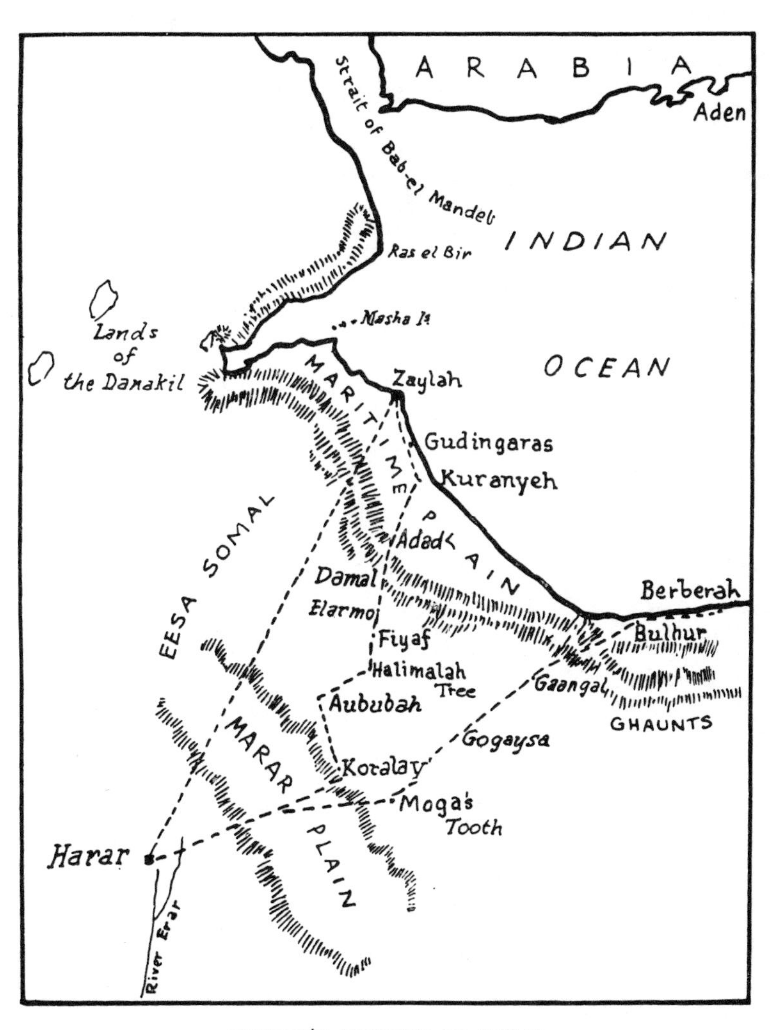

BURTON'S JOURNEY TO HARAR

shrewdly enough, were changing. The ruler of Harar might be as glad as other princelings to receive the friendship and the frequent subsidies of the Government at Aden. Accordingly, he sat down and wrote a letter ostensibly from the Political Agent at Aden, addressed to the Amir of Harar, and introducing himself as the accredited representative of the British Government ! With this precious and audacious forgery in his possession, he mounted his caravan next morning and took the road to Harar. His friends at the Gerad Adan's village assembled and bade him the farewell given to the dying.

Surmounting a hill-top shortly afterwards, they saw "thirty miles away, and separated by a series of blue valleys, lay a dark speck upon a tawny sheet of stubble—Harar".

It took two days to reach it, days of camping and debating with hesitant border guards, suspicious fellow-travellers and the like. But at length the walls of the famed Forbidden City rose in view—long and low, a dirty white, unimpressive they seemed to Burton's disappointed eye. At the main gate he sent a message to the Amir stating that he had come on a mission from Aden ; and sat and waited the reply, wondering if it would be in the shape of a knife in his neck.

Instead, he was presently led in in company with his companions. If Harar had looked disappointing from the outside, it looked worse from within. There were tortuous, narrow and stench-laden streets ; there were straying pariah dogs ; there were lacklustre children in great abundance. But of the gilded colleges of learning, the towers and temples, not a glimpse. Somali legend and Somali lies had decorated a miserable townlet in East Africa with the odours of a sanctity it never possessed, the luxury of a wealth it had never visioned !

A bored and chastened man, Ruffian Dick allowed himself to be led within the courtyard of the "palace"—it had acute resemblances to a great cluster of cowsheds—doffed his shoes, and came into the presence of the dreaded ruler of Harar. This was almost coping stone to the shocks of the day. The Amir was a small, scrofulous individual with yellow, claw-like hands, an appearance in general of a small Indian Rajah inadequately nourished and looking upon life with a myopic disfavour. He permitted Burton to kiss his not over-clean hand, listened to the ingenious lies which Burton had to tell of his reasons for visiting Harar, and then graciously gave him permission to retire.

I was under the roof of a bigoted prince whose least word was death; amongst a people who destest foreigners; the only European that had ever passed over their inhospitable threshold; and the fated instrument of their future downfall.

§ 8

He spent ten days in Harar, computing its position as 9° 20′ N, 42° 17′ E, wandering its decaying streets and studying its decaying population. Once it had been the capital of the great Moslem Empire of Hadiyah which through long centuries had waged unceasing war against Christian Abyssinia. But it had fallen from its ancient glories to a dun dullness, a population of a few thousands, an all-pervading stench of decay and no-life; it had still its own tongue, neither Arabic nor Amharic, incomprehensible to the stranger without its walls; it had three Moslem teachers of a crude and introverted theology. . . . And there was little or nothing else of interest in the place!

Burton created interests during his short stay. He collected —secretly, for he was closely watched and dare not write— materials for compiling a skeleton Harari grammar and vocabulary; inspected, surreptitiously, the Harari army—fifty ragged and depressed-looking souls armed with matchlocks; and assessed the unimportant ivory trade. But slaves, captured in the surrounding regions, were the principal export, though Burton saw little of them. A tall, dark-browed figure, he strode to and fro the streets, dined with the mullahs, listened with a contemptuous disregard of royalty to the complaining suspicions of the Amir, and resolved to depart from Harar seeking the coast by way of Berberah.

So this second venture passed, as did the first in which he had sought Mecca. On the 13th of January in the new year he looked from the mountain-top to see the last of Harar, nestling deceptive, mysterious again in distance, in the heat-hazed African valleys; and turned to the dust and din and the unceasing dangers of the coastward ride. On the 30th of January Berberah was sighted. Burton rode into it, and halted to rest after the excitements and peril of the passage from Harar. But rest was foreign to his nature. Hearing of numerous ruins in the neighbourhood, he rode out and spent several days in inspecting them, brooding upon their genesis and fate. Finally, however, he resolved to depart for Aden by sea.

Even yet he might not hold there by any straight route. There were islands on the way with further ruins, great wells long disused and guarded by a surly populace. Burton had the boat moored, leapt ashore, pacified the inhabitants, inspected the wells, and then allowed the boat to resume its slow passage up the coast.

So, with halting and delays and quarrels innumerable with the boatmen, they passed up the African coast, once encountering a terrible storm which Ruffian Dick alone enjoyed, until on the morning of Friday, the 9th of February, 1855,

we hove in sight of Jebel Shamsan, the loftiest peak of the Aden crater. And ere evening fell, I had the pleasure of seeing the faces of friends and comrades once more.

§ 9

He had accomplished much: indeed, as earth-conqueror, he had accomplished the most significant journey of his life. But that was inapparent to him. He thought of the conquest of Harar as a mere prelude to a still greater drive into the heart of unknown Africa. In Aden he set about raising and equipping a large expedition to penetrate directly inwards from Berberah. On the 7th of April the astounded inhabitants of Berberah looked out to see disembark on their shores the tall Infidel, come again, this time with a bodyguard of forty-two, impertinent intentions, and a disposition to resist both imposts and queries.

Berberah endured it for a little. But the local Fair was on, the town was filling up with wild Somalis who had as little respect for the white man as they had a keen desire to sample his goods. Burton had camped his host at a little distance from the town while he collected guides and information about the forward route. Between two and three o'clock on the morning of the nineteenth he was awakened by the sound of pistol-shots, and rushing out from his tent found a Bedouin raid in progress.

Over three hundred and fifty natives had attacked the encampment. A very confused and for a little while indeterminate fight raged amidst the tents. Burton and Speke and Stroyan defended the central tent until it was plain that that course was merely folly, and then attempted to cut their way through to the shore. So doing, Burton became separated from his companions. A Somali rushed up and thrust his javelin into Burton's mouth, lacerating his lips and cheek. He beat him off and staggered away into the darkness. A servant found him and guided him away from the fight, towards that sought-for shore. But again a stray eddy from the looting battle caught them and they became separated. Now and then Burton lay on the ground and rolled in agony, what of his lacerated face. But at last he managed to stagger to a boat and make the ship.

Meantime Stroyan had been clubbed to death, and Speke, attempting to break through, was captured and had his hands tied. Sitting so, he was several times assaulted and wounded. He managed to work his hands clear and run, dodging a hail of missiles. Some of them, nevertheless, found mark. Desperately wounded, he also succeeded in making the ship . . .

So ended the Third Attempt upon the Fortunate Land. Most unfortunate of all, in the opinion of Burton's admirers in later years, was the fact that Stroyan died, not Speke. But of the latter's salvation as disaster Ruffian Dick, tight-mouthed in pain, had no glimpse as he ordered the ship to put out for Aden. Soft-hearted, grief-stricken at memory of Stroyan's fate, he had still one resolve strong upon him.

He would return to Africa.

§ 10

There ensued a long hiatus before that Fourth Attempt could be put in operation. Speke, wounded, departed for England, and apparently out of Burton's life. Burton himself, having settled the last details of the Third ill-fated Expedition, followed. At home he wrote his *First Footsteps in East Africa*, and was greeted with a little fame in consequence. And he met again his Isabel, though in a stilted and somewhat unenthusiastic greeting. The Arundels were still obdurate against the consummation of the passion of their remarkable daughter and this remarkably suspicious-looking adventurer. They temporized. When he had made a name in his own profession——

Burton was more than willing. But he was a soldier of John Company, India was at peace, and he was too little liked for there ever to be much chance of peace-time promotion. At this hour of indecision the Crimean War broke out with an obliging readiness.

So, evidently, it appeared at first to Burton. He had little belief in the sanctity of human life, he was a child of his era in most matters military and imperial, he hungered for a command, the disposal of men, the sight and sound of great guns at dawn lifting blunt mouths against massed ranks of infantry. He saw these things as poetry.

He volunteered assiduously, continually, and for a while ineffectively. The War Office had other things on hand than to provide commands and pickings for tall and reputedly scoundrelly persons from India or Africa—unorthodox officers were anathema in that Army which went out to battle in bearskin helmets and dolmans, with few doctors and no sanitary equipment at all. Burton grew desperate. If the mountain would not come to Mohammed, he remembered, the Prophet had obligingly journeyed to the mountain. He resolved to sail for the Crimea on his own responsibility.

He did so and again appeared to arrive at a fortunate time. Beatson's Irregular Horse had just been raised for the benefit of such as himself. Burton enlisted, became adjutant, drew up elaborate plans for new modes of cavalry attack and general tactics, and impatiently awaited action.

He waited in vain. The Crimean War dragged on, by now a war of siege and sortie and repulse, having little or no need for gay irregulars in cavalry uniform. Burton sank to a quick despondency. The horrors and filth of the war appear to have affected him little—or at least he kept an air of ruffianly bravado in face of that which perhaps he found sickening enough. When the whole ill business was over he returned to England with his fortunes as regards Isabel no further advanced.

But another plan had risen up, slowly perhaps diminishing her image in his mind. When the war finished (he had planned in those Crimean nights) he would make Africa again, lead a stout expedition up from the East Coast—Zanzibar, perhaps—and seek out the sources of the Nile in that debatable land vaguely rumoured of as the Mountains of the Moon. . . .

Back to England and the arms of his Isabel. She consented to marry him when he returned from the new expedition. It would probably last several years, but those were unhasting days ; our wonder over that long and dragging courtship on the part of two such ardent souls as the combative Isabel and the reputedly Ruffian Richard are probably unwarranted. Neither was very deeply sexed, their interests were men and women and belief and thought and the magic of the geographically unknown and—disastrously, finally, for both of them—religions and the gropings of the human mind in those tenebrous regions of near-thought whence first arose in some antique Egyptian brain the dream of the Fortunate Isles.

Burton laid his plans before the Royal Geographical Society. The Society proved agreeable. It debated the matter, remembered Harar, and remembered also the news of Livingstone's discoveries in the Southern parts of Central Africa. Burton had proposed the ascertaining of the limits of the Sea of Ujiji—a great sheet of water of which the rumour had travelled down to the East Coast—as the primary object of the expedition. Financed, he would also make investigations on "the exportable produce of the interior and the ethnography of its tribes".

Agreeing, the Society raised a thousand pounds, appointed Burton to lead the expedition, and laid down his instructions in this his final assault upon *Terra Incognita*:

> The great object of the expedition is to penetrate inland from Kilwa or some other place on the east coast of Africa, and make the best of your way to the reputed lake Nyasa. . . . Having obtained all the information you require in this quarter, you are to proceed northward toward the range of mountains marked upon our maps as containing the probable source. . . . You will be at liberty to return to England by descending the Nile, or you may return by the route by which you advanced or otherwise, always having regard to the means at your disposal.

Burton had obtained a leave of a further two years from the Indian Army, and had also secured Speke as his lieutenant. He made a sentimentally tender farewell to his Isabel—she urged him "with flashing eyes" to go "and win greatness"—and set out, as he himself might have phrased it in one of those odd lapses to pedestrianism that occur in his writings, on the Fourth Lap to Fortune.

§ 11

It was a large and well-equipped expedition which disembarked at Zanzibar on the 19th of December, 1856. Burton had expended the thousand pounds of the Royal Geographical Society with his usual flamboyant efficiency, he had ample provisions and arms to arm the guard he proposed to raise; and he had as his chief assistant the quieter, dourer Speke. The two men seem always to have been strangers to each other, neither liking nor disliking. Their mental habits and conditions were poles dissimilar, Speke a commercial traveller of exploration, it might be said, but that would be in a measure an unfair assessment. He was something more. Almost he verged upon that scientific accuracy and fine judgment that were to follow him as the hallmark of the explorer in the next century. He had few of Burton's enthusiasms, none of his swashbuckling certainties.

Speke might have thought the immediate objectives the rumoured Sea of Ujiji and the sources of the Nile. But Burton, as ever ready to halt and inspect the milestones on the road to fortune, to brood above them and speculate on their shape and origin, insisted on exploring the island of Zanzibar with detail and attention, piling up in a great and stupefyingly impenetrable mound of erudition all he could learn of the geology, botany, metallurgy, zoology, ethnology, culture waves and racial migrations that bore even remotely upon the famed island. Month after month went by in these pursuits, and towards the end even Burton's interest may have begun to flag. He turned towards the West.

Meantime Speke and he had been gathering information enough on the Sea of Ujiji. There was a definite caravan-route thither, but in the way a multitude of tribes of varying degrees of culture but an unvarying degree of unpleasantness. So the rumours went, and judging from various brushes with the coastal tribes, Burton judged them unexaggerated. He felt no qualms. On the 27th of June he set his caravan in motion for the interior.

In eighteen days he covered a hundred and eighteen miles.

There had never, in his opinion, been such travelling in the world. He either knew little then of Mungo Park—whom later he was to rate so low—or honestly believed the privations of the march greater than those of the eighteenth century Scotsman's. Tribes haggled with him for passage: ferocious tribesmen clung on the skirts of the march of his fever-stricken caravan—it had been struck with marsh-fever very early. Horses died and porters deserted. Speke struggled on at the head of the caravan, as ill as the ferocious Ruffian Dick who brought up the van. Forward, slow plodding day on day, a jungly, river-sected land, sometimes dry and parched in long stretches, sometimes broken with the jagged shapes of hills. And at night the expedition lay down in this and that kraal, in verminous filthy huts, and haggled wearying hours with this and that potentate on the price of chickens, on the amount of backsheesh to be paid for the privilege of being allowed to exist. . . .

It grew warmer and warmer. A long halt was made and Burton retired into the delirium tremens of fever. Speke, in not much better case, prospected the country ahead through the agency of rumour and gossip. Ujiji was near. Burton roused himself to the dizzying tracks again.

The tracks were those of the Arab slave-traders who dominated all this countryside. Sometimes the blacks along the track had revolted, and naturally identified Burton and Speke with their oppressors. Sometimes the Arabs, trade-jealous, put all in their way possible to stop that slow ant-crawl, like a sick centipede, into the west. But at last, on the 9th of November, 1857, Kazeh on its high plantation was reached, the home of the Arab traders, the great trade-centre of that part of Africa.

Burton was very ill and the welcome—the somewhat surprising welcome—of the Arabs even could not arouse him. They were still afar from their objective. Again Burton dragged his way back to health, reorganized his disintegrating caravan, doctored Speke, bribed, bullied and coaxed the Arab overlords of Kazeh to his assistance. And again, through bush and forest and under the craggy overhang of the hills of the African winter, seeping in great rains, they took the road towards that lodestone of the Fourth Expedition, the Sea of Ujiji.

On the 13th of February, marching into Ujiji, Burton lifted swimming eyes and saw a great sheet of water spread before him in the evening light—the great lake of Tanganyika, himself the first white man to look upon it.

It was the greatest day and date of his life, but he was too sick and irritated to realize that. It was here that ended his greatest search into the mysteries of the geographically unknown, here that he was to touch most closely the fringes of that bright land that had fled the explorer's feet for nine long centuries. We see in the event a drama that even Burton, with all his powers of self-dramatization, could not envisage. From there, that point of Tanganyika's first glimpse, he might have called, with the Greeks of the Anabasis :

"Thalassa ! Thalassa !"

§ 12

He was then thirty-seven ; he had accomplished three conspicuous enterprises ; he was still free from the sense of public neglect ; and he was not yet married to the remarkable woman whose influence was, on the whole, unfortunate.

At this peak of his career, ill though he was, Burton set about plans for a thorough exploration of the lake region. He believed Tanganyika the source of the Nile, and despatched Speke, ill as himself, to explore the northern shores. He himself made a short voyage from Ujiji, following all the while his usual passions—topographical and ethnological predominated—to the utmost limit. Finally, as might have been said in the phrase of that day, outraged nature intervened. Both he and his lieutenant were worn out. He resolved to seek the coast.

This meant the abandonment of the attempt to reach the rumoured Lake Nyasa, and meant with it the abandonment of making certain (for Speke had been unable to fulfil the task) whether or not a river—the presumptive Nile—entered or left Tanganyika to the north. Another expedition, Burton resolved buoyantly even in his sickness, would see to that. That he himself would neither command it nor be on its staff never entered his head.

The homewards journey was as toilsome as most homeward trekkings of the great earth-conquerors. Speke recovered considerably ; Burton steadily grew worse. Rain pelted the retreating caravan, they were vexed with fever and famine. At Tabora Speke was summoned by Burton and a tentative plan laid before him. This was to strike northward and see what truth there was in the existence of a rumoured great lake in that direction. Speke agreed to accept a half of the command and set out on the mission.

The caravan straggled on towards the coast. When Speke —the uncommunicative Speke—rejoined the caravan, he had news of a sort to impart. Yes, he had discovered the Lake—he had named it the Victoria Nyanza in honour of the Queen. Yes, a greak lake . . . Burton irritably gave up questioning him, longing in a sick despair for the coast.

At last, early in March of 1859, Zanzibar again came in sight, shining across the sea. Burton had a ship chartered, and his men and surviving goods, his sick self and his lieutenant Speke, loaded into it. It made an easy voyage to Aden, that depot of dust and sunglare redeemed for Burton by the blessings of a hospital, attention, a clean bed and clean faces to look on again. He sank to sleep the first night with a thankfulness in his heart he had never known before, the returned earth-conqueror as weary as he was triumphant.

. . . . .

Speke hastened to England, leaving Burton in hospital, published an account of the expedition, stressed his own discovery of the Victoria Nyanza, made no mention of Burton, and affirmed his opinion that the Nile rose in the Victoria Nyanza. He was greeted with great acclaim, honoured everywhere, and funds raised to equip under his command a new expedition.

Burton arrived in England a man robbed of his fame as surely as though Speke had stolen his purse.

§ 13

So Ruffian Dick as the earth-conqueror passed from the scene. He lived many years thereafter ; he did many things, both of an ill repute and a good, but it would seem that something died in him when he found out the treachery of Speke. That something was certainly nothing in the nature of a "broken heart", he had never trusted Speke greatly, or cared for him greatly ; nor had he had any great affection for either the British public or its servant, the Royal Geographical Society. Neither they nor Speke killed any faith that he held in human-kind or in human decency. It was a subtler slaying. There died in him then, it would seem, that flaring conviction in himself as the geographically invincible, the predestined conqueror of the Fortunate Land.

He wrote bitter polemics against Speke ; and he looked

around for a fresh means of livelihood, that "life of an explorer" which he had envisaged being denied to him. He went off to America to inspect the Mormon territory and the Mormons at close hand; the reputedly scoundrelly Brigham Young he fled to for consolation from the decencies, the truly scoundrelly decencies, of a more normal theology and civilization. From that he returned to write the usual and—in his case—the unescapable book. Then he married his Isabel, at long last.

On his marriage day he "looked a wreck", though not with apprehension. He loved Isabel very completely and truly all the days of his life; he remained tall and dark and scowling of appearance, cherishing that pathetic desire to shock the world if he could not make it happy. He was appointed consul to Fernando Po, and explored vaguely and ineffectively in the Cameroons. He wrote seven books in those four years, with volcanic energy, but diminished vision. He was transferred (he and Isabel) to Brazil, to Damascus, to Trieste, and in each of these consulships played his reputedly scoundrelly part. Gradually his character because as undermined with the mystic Christianity of his wife as his body was undermined with the continual privations which, well over fifty, he loved to dare, riding out in search of the Gold Mines of Midian from Damascus, holidaying with vigour in Iceland, writing and writing and writing with a kind of unstayable passion, an unstayable escape.

Finally, between 1885 and 1888 he set to the translating, the literal and unbowdlerized translating of the complete *Arabian Nights*. Humanity had refused him his destined life of the earth-conqueror, earth-wanderer, and he had accepted instead the mission of shocking it. This work he intended as the final and complete shock.

Humanity was scandalized, horrified—and enthralled. It purchased Burton in great quantities, volume after volume of the sixteen volumes as they came from the press. It made of Burton a rich man. And finally it drew about him the luscious indecencies of the sheets of the *Arabian Nights* and smothered him in their folds.

X

FRIDTJOF NANSEN SEEKS THE POLE

§ 1

IN the quest of those Fortunate Isles that first awoke in men's imaginings with the burial of the dead on Nile Bank five thousand years before the birth of Christ we have seen profoundly affected the characters and actions of eight of the great explorers in the second Christian millennium. The ninth was born into a world that had narrowed considerably the geographical outlet to the quest: beyond Amazonia and Africa and thin little tracts of Arabia and Indo-China there remained only the great white stretches of *terra incognita* about the Poles when the last of the great earth conquerors touched with the wings of that ancient quest was born in Oslo in 1861.

Arctica had haunted the fringe of the Norse consciousness for many centuries. Arctic exploration ante-dated the Vikings. Pytheas, who came from the Mediterranean in the third century before Christ, circumnavigated Britain, and penetrated perhaps as far as Iceland, was the first of the Arctic explorers on record, followed in a long train by those wandering dispossessed farmers and fishers who quested with Eirik Raude for new homes out of Iceland. Whales laired in the northern waters and were hunted with harpoon and boat, and led the hunts up long craggy lanes overshadowed by fringing mountains of ice. Beyond those lay lands of snow as untrodden for the European as the moon: and quite as debatable.

Questing the North-East and the North-West passages in search of the Fortunate Isles of the East Indies had come the seventeenth and eighteenth century Dutch and English, naming the fringing territories, garnering in bitter experience some knowledge of the rigours and risks of the Arctic as a field of exploration. The eighteenth century looked elsewhere for trade-routes to the East than through those Northern passages. But with the coming of the nineteenth century the quest of the North-West sea passage (at least) awakened again into favour.

It was Ross's expedition in 1818 to Baffin Bay which opened the question of route anew, Parry's expedition of 1820 sailed its ships six hundred and thirty miles up Barrow Strait through what had previously appeared as land on the charts and maps. Thereafter expeditions were almost an annual affair to the bleak straits and islands that fringe northernmost Canada—leading to the tragic expedition of that unfortunate and unforgettable soul, the resolute Franklin, wrecked and lost and vanishing with his starving thirty into the wild lands on the fringes of the world, to be stared at by Eskimo, curiously, as a man at a starving spider; holding south, the sun in the memory of their faces, on a road to food and lights: and so vanishing and perishing between Adelaide Peninsula and the Great Fish River. Beyond the night of their attempt followed Rae and McLintock, equipped by Lady Franklin, searching out and charting eight hundred miles of sea and shore along that route that ultimately, long years after this subject was of fame, found its triumphant way across America by sea—the voyage of Amundsen's *Gjoa* in 1903–5 which crossed the roof of America from East to West for the first time and (it is likely) the last in history.

But still the true Arctic remained barely limned. From the searchings for the North-East passage came Novaya Zemlya, a long tale of journeyings carried out now from the east (utmost Siberia) now from Norway and European Russia. There both tale and occasion are simpler than in the lands beyond Greenland—unexplored Greenland. For in 1820 Wrangel heard rumours of high lands to the extreme north of the Kolyma river; and for another half century it was the search for that land that drew all the travellers up and around the lands north of the storm-driven Bering Straits. It was supposed to be a great Arctic Continental mass—Gama Land, the Fortunate Isles, reappearing undiscouraged. De Long in 1879 sailed north with the *Jeanette* in search of it. He found no land mass, his ship was crushed and sunk, he tramped back to the north coast of Asia with the news and died before help came to succour his exhaustion from those leagues of frost and desolation, silence and the cry of strange storm-birds. Thereon the Fortunate Land betook itself to the regions about the Pole.

In 1876 A. E. Nordenskiöld, leaving Novaya Zemlya, reached the mouth of the Yenisei, in the *Vega*, halted there a while, and in July of 1878 started on the second lap of the voyage through that North-East passage of myth and high hope that had beguiled so many of the heroic Dutch explorers of the sixteenth and seventeenth centuries. On 19th of July, 1879, he rounded the utmost peninsula of Asia and steered the *Vega* into the North Pacific.

But beyond still lay the true Arctic, barely touched. Franz Josef Land and Spitzbergen had been discovered, their coasts were known vaguely, vaguely mapped. Beyond the bulk of Northern Greenland lay great glacial tracts in which almost anything was possible, almost any country might exist. Remotely into this unknown (though known at its base since the days of the Iceland Vikings), stretched Greenland, shining high and resplendent its snow jokulls in summer as the whaler crews stood off and watched for the bubblings of the great mammals they came to hunt. It tailed off out of human recognition and mapping into a seeming jumble of ice-lands and passages that were suspected of being culs-de-sac, impassable and unpenetrable in their extremities.

Inglefield, Kane, Hall, and Nares worked up this coast in the early half of the nineteenth century: in 1853 Rink began his series of inland explorations in Greenland—South Greenland; in 1870 the redoubtable Nordenskiöld, that conqueror of the North-East Passage, attempted to cross Greenland from Disko Island. But he found it a tougher task than even the sailing of the bitter Siberian coasts, and turned back. Thirteen years later he made a second attempt, crossing all but a last seventy-five miles, and again being forced to retreat.

Beyond still lay the unknown Arctic.

In 1827 came the first direct attack upon it—an authenticated first attempt to reach the Pole. This was Parry's, turning back at 82° 45′ N. Nordenskiöld and Koldeway carried through major expeditions, neither of them reaching so far as Parry. The Polar regions remained thick-strewn with imaginary continents and catastrophic geographical phenomena—even, in the less responsible mind, with lost cities and tribes, those residua of the romantic imagination that is itself the religious imagination softened. It was a last refuge of the unknown. What lay there?

§ 2

Although it is unlikely he would have answered in so many words, the boy born to Baldur Nansen and his wife on the small estate of Store From near Oslo in 1861 was to grow and answer in very clear accents indeed: "The Fortunate Isles. A strange wealth of deep and irrelevant knowledge is there, experiences and curious sensations, cold winds to bring you to the edge of consciousness till the human reason stands aghast at its own existence, silences so deep you can hear the Galaxy turn, the edge of the Eternally Unknowable, North, the Fortunate Isles."

Baldur Fridtjof had been Reporter to the Supreme Court, a descendant of Danish merchants and seamen. In spite of that descent, heredity might have made him the last to father Fridtjof (Peace-Scarer), he was a cool and precise and methodical man, he had the world and fate and time docketed and put in place, one gathers the impression of a Victorian father very fully and completely realized indeed, repressed, grave, taciturn, tyrannical, uxorious and generous in a bourgeois tradition of gentlemanliness as Norwegian as it was American or English. His wife, Fridtjof's mother, was indeed of different quality, strong and self-reliant, a great ski-er for her time and sex, apt at churning and baking and choring as at correction of the misdemeanours of small and ebullient youth, efficient and strong. Fridtjof found her very lovely.

He learned from her, perhaps, to think of women as his equals as well as remote and delightful and mysterious persons. He found himself in a world of great if frugal fun, with a sister and a brother, hard and bright and boisterous children like himself. Behind Store From rose the forests and hills, rich with the green of the Norwegian woods: long summer nights the sun never went to bed, hardly Fridtjof or his brother. They swam and hunted and sometimes were let loose in the Forest for days on end in search of their own sustenance, building fires and shelters, sleeping under trees into the breathless hush of those summer mornings discovered in youth alone, Fridtjof a grave and wide-eyed lad staring at those fleckings of saffron on the wind-breaks at dawn. His feet very early were set on a path more Aryan than any other ever listed.

He was a great and terrible bore to the grown-ups, the stray elder encountered in forest and wood, cornered visitors in the rooms of Store From. For he wanted to know, in detail, exasperatingly, the why and becoming of all things under the sun. It was more than the normal aimless inquisitiveness of childhood as he grew on in years: it was a definite cast of mind moulded wonderfully and mysteriously by the play of the innumerable chances and encounters which mould us all so differently from the same human clay. Coupled with that unending curiosity, record the biographers (generally disapprovingly, for their ideal of Nansen remains that of a foolish adventurer, a hardy viking of romance, not reality) were occasional long moody fits, abstractions from which Store From would seek to shake him roughly enough. Whatever had come on the boy ? . . . One visions Fru Nansen, tall, efficient, a medicine bottle and spoon in hand, mounting resolutely the wooden stairs to young Fridtjof's bedroom.

But the occasions were not too frequent. Instead, he was normal in sport and fun and frolic throughout boyhood ; at seventeen, however, beyond normal. He won in that year the Norwegian distance skating championship, next year the world's skating record for the mile. He discovered abruptly the wonder of human nerve and muscle fine trained to hair-breadth accuracies, he discovered the wonder of his own body with a certain scientific eagerness, a commingling of coldness and excitement exceptional enough in such discoveries. He took to ski-ing the year following the second skating triumph, trained vigorously if slightly unlaboriously, and won the national cross-country race at the first attempt.

He paragoned at sport easily enough : but at Oslo University from 1880 onwards he was very bored. But Natural Science, a wide-reaching branch of study in those days, covering almost as many sins as subjects, gradually drew him out of a sportsman's yawn at the whole affair of education. Here were intriguing things, beasts and birds and the wherefore of the rocks. He began to specialize, earnestly, ski-champion-like, in "science". But which Science. Physics ? Chemistry ?

Every day as he walked home for dinner from lectures he would encounter a burly-looking being with heavy brows and eyes to match, an immense moustache and the touch of a roll in his gait. The student grew aware of this phenomenon passing so continuously across his vision. Idly, he asked who the man was, and learned he was Axel Krefting, a sealing skipper, a famous Arctic skipper.

And at that news it seems that Nansen's imagination suddenly turned north for the first time, the imagination from his studies, the imagination from his sports. Sealing ? The Arctic ? . . . Crouching behind hummocks watching the

FRIDTJOF NANSEN

beasts creep from the air-holes. Crouching on board a flying ship and seeing pile on the horizons the great ice mountains of the true roof of the world. . . . Abruptly, hearing that Krefting was sailing out a new sealer, the *Viking*, on her maiden voyage, Nansen introduced himself, had himself enrolled as student supercargo, told Store From and the university he was off to study the life of the Arctic animals, Zoology was his irrevocable choice: and on the 11th of March, 1882, looked back on Arendal fading hull-down on the horizon.

§ 3

He was over six feet in height, tall and burly, with a frank open look belied by a certain quality in his eyes, a brooding quality of a certain darkness and stillness. He found the life on the *Viking* shocking at first, perhaps, it was as crude and comradely and equalitarian as it well might be. But he entered it soon with the zest of youth, climbing the crow's nest during a storm, wrestling with the captain, beating him badly, staring at the lift and play of the sails at night on a lightless sea as they drove north in haste for the sealing grounds between Iceland and Spitzbergen; strangely moved at the drummle and hiss of the living ship in that wild waste of darkness and water at night, unstarred, with flying spray . . . Then he would turn back from those glimpses—those glimpses that were to haunt his soul—to the life and smoking lights and horseplay of the cabin.

He saw his first ice on the 18th of March, a tremulous white-blue line on the horizon, and stared at it with a mixture of exultation and sickness, as long afterwards he recorded. The sensations were surely premonitory. Then father Baldur's son recollected that he was a scientist. He made careful observations of the drift-ice, theorized on the currents, carried out tests on the sea-water, took readings of the ocean's temperature with a physician-like gravity. The crew laughed: young Nansen was a lanky favourite, somewhat puzzling.

Not till mid-June did they come on profitable sealing grounds. Nansen was a good sealer: he killed and skinned with an ease and celerity and a cold-blooded lack of imagination that astounded Krefting: he considered his pupil would become "a good vet". That imagination which could let itself loose on the pale tintings of the Borealis or the quest of Nothingness beyond the rim of the Ice Continent controlled itself readily enough in this matter of death and blood that was the sealing industry: he was as yet, indeed, no more than a half-awakened hobbledehoy, a hobbledehoy who could kill seals all day and then, while the rest of the crew dragged themselves to their bunks in sheer exhaustion, could sit up all night catching Greenland sharks. . . . Steadily he grew something of a legend; he has left, or others leave of him, innumerable tales and legends in the Norse tradition of those months—encounters with Polar bears, swimming feats in freezing waters, stuff of a like matter that gave little promise of his future except that they verified the magnificent physical stamina necessary to carry out the feats of the last seeker for the Earthly Paradise.

Early in July, from the crow's nest of the *Viking*, he caught his first glimpse of the Greenland coast, and was duly and reasonably thrilled. It would be more than fun, thought the hobbledehoy, to cross the interior of that unknown land, for what was there no one knew. Some day . . .

But the sealing season was ending. The *Viking* turned home. Nansen had been blooded with blood and hardship and imagination. Almost it seems he had received a surfeit. He secured appointment as Curator of the Zoological Museum at Bergen. For six years he was curator there. But for rare vacations when he crossed the Central mountains on ski and hunted and explored the wilder parts of Northern wild Norway he abandoned the enthusiasms of the *Viking* for the wonder kingdoms of scientific research. That other self whom in later years he was to refer to, with a kind of childish whimsicality, as "Master Irresponsible" was severely in leash.

I went in, body and soul, for Zoology, and especially for microscopical Anatomy. For six years I lived in a microscope. It was an entirely new world, and Master Irresponsible kept fairly quiet during those years, and we were well on the way to becoming a promising zoologist. . . . I wrote some works, especially on the microscopical anatomy of the nervous system. They contained some discoveries of value, I believe, but still more important were perhaps the new problems which they raised. We were full of ambitious plans for new investigations to solve these problems. Most of these investigations have later been made by others, but some of the problems are still waiting to be solved, I believe.

There is a naïve vanity in the last sentence, characteristic of the man, and plus it a kind of dullness that haunts all his writings and sayings, a kind of blindness to his own ephemeral quality (as all mankind are ephemeral), which go strangely with the broodings of the lonely figure in the remote Arctic that was not yet his. One may think of those lapses into the pedestrian as his refuge from both himself and the appalling visionings of time and space that were yet to hold strange hours.

§ 4

He had never forgotten that glimpse of the Greenland shore. Yawning over a newspaper at Bergen in 1883 he read of the failure of Nordenskiöld's attempt upon the Greenland interior—an attempt in which he had employed two Lapps, skilled skiers. The item stuck in his mind. Skilled ski-ing—might not that solve the entire problem ?

Meantime his scientific work went on. He published various papers on subjects such as the Myzostomida and the Central Nervous System and the like—papers over which father Baldur, with no training in anatomy or chemistry, confessed a puzzled pride. He had soothed out into a strange applauding shadow, the stout and grave bourgeois of Store From : he died in 1885, and Nansen was very deeply moved by the passing of that being so alien to himself in all but a few essentials. He took a holiday to Naples to escape Norway and that memory for a time. In the Marine Biological Museum there he found escape; a tall and burly and moody young man the Italians found him, apt at times to dance all night and sing the moon into morning, at others to retreat to the seashore and into the shell of himself for hours on end, staring across the warm Italian sea at the smoking summit of Vesuvius.

Because the thoughts of those days are for ever beyond the pryings of others they invite that interpretation that he himself might have encouraged. . . . He was looking out into that remoteness of the human spirit that is man's terrible heritage, seeing man himself a lonely figure in the wastes of a little planet wheeling about a little sun, without guide or light or surety or safety, uncompanioned by God or devil, hope and fear but the staves that he carves for himself. . . . So Baldur's death had left him, though presently—else he would not have survived it—that mist went and he went back to Norway with its passing.

But a new restlessness had made Bergen distasteful, even after he had met and fallen in love with the singer Eva Sars. (Their encounter was such as we should expect of Nansen. He was ski-ing in the woods near Oslo when he saw two feet sticking forth appealingly from the snow. On investigation, they proved to belong to his future wife—he seems to have decided almost at that moment that they belonged to his future wife.) The planning of an expedition to cross Greenland from east to west began to occupy all his spare hours. He published the plan in *Naturen* of January 1888.

The main reaction to the plan was horrified incredulity. Nansen proposed to attain as close to the eastern coastline as a ship could carry him, abandon ship, seek the ice floes with boats, attain the shore, climb the interior mountains, reach the presumed interior ice-cap, and from there slide carelessly down on skis to the western coast. It showed, said the critics—travellers, not writers—an insanity, a recklessness, a hobbledehoy presumption which placed it outside the sphere of criticism. They were very bitterly firm on its presumption to claim a critic's attention at all. He "betrayed absolute ignorance of the true conditions". A Bergen newspaper came humorously to his aid with an authentic advertisement:

> NOTICE: In the month of June next Curator Nansen will give a ski-ing display, with long jumps, on the Inland Ice of Greenland. Reserved seats in the crevssaes. Return ticket necessary.

All previous attempts at the crossing of the misnamed Greenland of Eric the Red's fancy had been made from the West, with bases and rest camps pushing up into the interior. Nansen's daring was in his resolve, Rubicon-like, to burn, or rather, abandon his boats when the east coast was attained, and then push through the unknown country till he reached the thinly inhabited western coast. There would be no going back, for return would mean certain starvation. The expedition's only salvation would be to hasten steadily west.

He went and consulted the aged hero Nordenskiöld, old and cynical and sceptical, but not refusing his aid and advice in pack and trek and sledge equipment. Finances were the next consideration. Nansen applied to the University of Norway, an enlightened institution, but itself unwealthy even to the extent of collecting the less than £300 which the reckless young man required. It recommended a grant to the Norwegian Parliament, the Storting. Sensible and bourgeois, the Storting refused. Then a Copenhagen philanthropist came to the rescue. Peace-Scarer's expedition was assured its finances.

There was no special technique of Arctic exploration in those times: Nansen perforce perfected his own in matters of sledges, cookers, sleeping-bags, and the like, the cookers odd and complicated instruments made to his own exclusive design and seldom copied by his successors. On the skis was his main reliance: they were specially made for the peculiar footings in Greenland snow.

Only Scandinavians in that era were ski-ers, so limiting the personnel of the expedition to the three North countries. From a host of applicants—that cheerful awaiting fringe on the verge of every new adventure—Nansen made his selection of three Norwegians and two Lapps, Sverdrup—the great and gallant Sverdrup with whom he was to be so long associated—Dietrichson, Trana, Balto, Ravna. Trana was twenty-four years old, which gave the leader of the expedition some doubts as to his suitability. He himself was an aged twenty-six.

§ 5

On the 4th of June, 1888, the *Jason*, Captain Jacobsen, a sealing steamer with a sealing crew, groped its way out of Isafjord in Iceland and turned west. On board were Nansen and his expedition, his famous cookers, his collapsible boat, his skis, and a pony he took as an experiment, a forlorn hope.

On the 11th of July, after much cruising, in fog, the Greenland coast was sighted and Nansen stared at the awakening of the first of the two great epochs of his life, in his eyes the same hope as had led Leif Ericsson long centuries before, Columbus to the Bahamas, Magellan round the Cape. Pack ice swirled dangerously down the rugged and forbidding coast; it was very evident the *Jason* would never draw inshore in safety. Fogs descended and rose with an exasperatingly regular irregularity, the *Jason* cruised offshore blindly, fodder grew scarce and the pony had to be shot: in all, unpropitious beginnings. The crew ailed from various diseases, mostly filth. Nansen, that sardonic doctor, suggested scrubbing as he turned to stare at the pack-ice's drift. This proved a surprising cure.

But on the 16th Cape Dan at the head of Sermilik Fjord was sighted, guarded by the broken ice-belt. Nansen determined to attempt the coast. He had his specially constructed boat lowered, borrowed from the captain a small sealing boat, packed in his expedition and its equipment, and set out for Greenland. Presently the *Jason* vanished from sight.

Ensued hours of toil, blisters, vain hopes and rising dismays. The boats had to be dragged over stretches of ice from one channel of clear water to another. The ice belt cruised steadily south, plain they would never make Cape Dan. A storm gathered, rain fell, darkness came and in the darkness the crash and grind of the bergs sounded all about them. Nansen had the tent pitched, they crept into it and slept with sheer exhaustion, soaked to the skin.

They were on a floe, grinding and drumming southwards along the Greenland coast. On the 18th and 19th they sought in vain to cross the intervening ice to the land. The floe turned about malignantly and sought the open sea. The Lapps took to reading the New Testament: Nansen, with Old Testament hardness, evicted them from this pursuit in the shelter of the tent and set them again to attempt dragging the boats to a less uncertain floe. Thereat the seawards making floe, with a bland surprise, turned about and made cautiously towards the land again.

For eight more days the floe kept them prisoners, about them the infernal roar and upheaval of the Arctic ice seas. Nansen filled in his diary and sketched and calmed his soul with staring moody exultation at the roll and pour, southwards, of the long billows of the Greenland coast. Then, on the morning of the 28th they saw the shore at length close at hand, launched the boats again and attained solid land, Kekertarsuak Island.

Nansen's original plan had been to cross from Sermilik Fjord, about 66° N. They had drifted south a long three hundred and fifty miles, and to cross from the spot where they landed would have been a comparatively short hundred miles or so, a poor and heartbreakingly easy substitute for the rigours and attractions of the original plan. Nansen decided to row up the coast as far as time would allow: the Greenland summer was passing.

They set out. Two toilsome days brought them to Cape Bille where they fell in with a tribe of Eskimos, simple and kindly and unwashed folk who stank very abominably, had stone weapons, and astounded Nansen. For in spite of their stenches they were unsavage, unspoilt, Christians it seemed to him without Christianity. They were, in fact, a last Northern reside of that primitive kindly stock of the Golden Age that had once endured all over the planet. Nansen researched in their huts and beliefs a long evening, then pushed north again.

Mount Katak came in sight on the 11th of August. They had come north a hundred and thirty-eight miles, and to attempt a further northing would be merely foolhardy. They camped under the towering cape, set to overhauling their gear, stacked the boats in a cleft to astound the straying Eskimo in after years, and on the evening of the 15th of August marched out across Greenland to Christianshaab.

§ 6

Days of arduous and painful travel followed, dragging the sledges over rough and crevassed ice. On the 20th a storm of such violence descended that they had to make camp and seek shelter in the tent. The storm raged for three days, great howling blasts sweeping across the deserted face of the unknown country, rising shrill and fierce in the hummock shapes while Nansen and his companions, stretched in their sleeping-bags, turned to light literature for amusement—the Nautical Almanac and the Logarithmic tables. The storm died in a whisper on a cold grey morning. They crept out and set out, still climbing into misty heights they might not discern far ahead.

Now they found themselves in a great waste of giant crevasses, cracks that yawned down into cavernous depths, blue and cold-green far down towards the earth foundations of this immense ice-house amid the roofs of which they stumbled and fell ever west and up. Ice and ice, no land to be seen, though far below them Nansen knew that land rested, once green and verdant in long past ages, now covered with the last residue of the shrinkage of the Fourth Glacial Age.

By the 21st of August they had climbed 3000 feet. Peaks rose above the surface of the snow, snow that curled in frozen billows up to those craggy peaks, under the low shimmering sun of the Greenland night—they travelled always by night, overhead the glory of the low Greenland stars when the sun went and the Northern Lights resumed their play. Nansen had never been so well. He dragged his sledge untiringly, staring at that splendour upon the sky, staring almost appalled at the great Arctic moons that came and seemed to refuse a setting; close to the earth they hung so that the conviction of the earth as a tiny globe in space amidst strange kin wanderers sunk into the naked consciousness like a frozen knife. Sometimes Nansen found himself humanizing that unearthly terror—or did so in his record long afterwards—into stillness and peace where indeed there was only negation.

They changed to day-trekking. The way remained toilsome, now amidst the great peaks of the Greenland mountains. Nothing moved or cried or had its being in that desolate land, except the unceasing wind driving frozen snow in their faces. Each morning they dug out the sledges and unroped the tent. They had food in plenty, though water had to be secured toilsomely from melted snow. Except for sprained knees and touches of snow-blindness, all kept their healths magnificently. Sails were erected on a smooth stretch of the ice and the sledges fled west with heartening rapidity and frequent capsizes till on the 29th the wind dropped and vanished.

It was late in the year. Even though they attained Christianshaab in safety the last ship for home would long have left. Nansen determined to shorten the journey and make for Godthaab, south-west, that settlement founded long before by Eirik Raude.

7930 feet up, a distance of 240 miles travel: and still they climbed, though the peaks had now vanished, the snow world remained unspecked by alien matter but themselves, that waste of snow a frozen and terrifying thing. The wind awoke afresh, a chilling and dreadful wind that speedily developed into the worst storm yet met. They took to the tent for two long days and nights, every moment expecting the canvas above their heads to levitate north into that inferno of storm and leave them unsheltered. But ropes and canvas held as they lay and listened and cooked with difficulty and much oil and soot, their faces and hands and bodies by this time deep-caked in a protective layer of filth.

The storm passed, they trekked forward and up again. But on the 11th of September it came on Nansen that they climbed no longer. Instead, the slope led imperceptibly downwards in front of their weary feet. Things grew more easy and their spirits rose, all except those of the old Lapp, Ravan, terrified and depressed in the lifeless deserts of no-colour. They hoisted sails on their sledges again and the going was good for some little while. On the 19th land, distant and smoky in the mist, was sighted ; then the easy going ceased. Crevasses appeared, cliff-edged and terrible, and after one of their most arduous days they crawled into the tent and into sleep like men revived from drowning.

But awakening in the morning Nansen looked out and saw a sight he was never to forget—the long, storm-beaten Western coast of Greenland about and below Godthaabsfjord, black cañons and high peaks glistening under new-fallen snow. It seemed near at that first glimpse, then he realized his height and his distance yet from that objective. He roused the others to an exceptional breakfast and exceptional marching endeavours.

It took them three days to attain the shore of that Earthly Paradise that had led them across the Inland Ice—the first crossing in the history of the white races, perhaps of any race. The ice was unsafe, great boulders barred their way, they came to cañons that might not be crossed but must be skirted in long and toilsome detours. By this time the Lapps were almost finished, though the three Norse plodded on grimly without complaint. They had come much further north than they had calculated: Godthaab, even when they should attain the shore, would be distant in the south. For only blessing, the weather kept unstormy.

And at length, on the 23rd of September, they descended the last steep, snow-sheathed shelves, and

like boys released, ran wildly about the shore. Words cannot describe what it was for us only to have the earth and stones again beneath our feet, or the thrill that went through us as we felt the elastic heather on which we trod, and smelt the fragrant scent of grass and moss. Behind us lay the Inland Ice, its cold grey slope sinking slowly towards the lake; before us lay the genial land. Away down the valley we could see headland beyond headland, covering and overlapping each other as far as the eye could reach.

He had crossed the Inland Ice of Greenland. A month later, voyaging and trekking down the coast, they came to Godthaab, and there made an encounter that cannot be better told than in Nansen's own words :

> "Presently a European appeared. He came up to us, we exchanged salutations. . . . 'May I ask your name ?' 'My name is Nansen, and we have just come fron the interior.' 'Oh, allow me to congratulate you on taking your doctor's degree.' This came like a thunderbolt from a blue sky, and it was all I could do to keep myself from laughing outright. To put it very mildly it struck me as comical that I should cross Greenland to receive congratulations upon my doctor's degree."

§ 7

Not until the 30th of May of the following year, 1889, did Nansen and the rest of the expedition return to Norway, so long they had to wait a ship at Godthaab of the Good Hope. They had spent the weary months of the winter unwearied enough, Nansen had betaken himself to the communities of the Eskimo, living the Eskimo life, sleeping in their snow huts, eating their food, staring in their faces, listening to their tales.

He came back with memory of them profoundly impressed in his mind, the Nansen discovery of the Eskimo was one of the great turning-points in anthropology, for his observations of that life of the remotest North brought additional facts to verify the beliefs of the school of historians that was soon to arise—that school which claimed man as a free and undiseased and happy animal in the day before civilization dawned on the world, that school that was to dispose once and for all of the theories of animism, totemism and the like muddled guessings on the origins of religion and social life called forth by misapprehension of the processes of biological evolution, mistakenly applied to human affairs. In that discovery, and fittingly as the last of the great earth-conquerors under the ancient spell, Nansen glimpsed that Earthly Paradise that had once been all mankind's.

But the world to which the tall and broad-cheeked youth returned at first knew little of this primary discovery of his, it was a world that had pored with some excitement over the map of Greenland, and now collected its honours to shower upon the first white man to traverse that unkindly Interior. Nansen was met by a fleet of steamers in Oslo Fjord, he was bemedalled and bedecorated by most of the learned societies of the world, in his account of the expedition, *The First Crossing of Greenland*, there creeps in a certain flattish note of complacency that is oddly displeasing. But *Eskimo Life*, the revolutionary account of his native hosts, had lost the naïvety of the adulation-surfeited. He had glimpsed a permanent and unsubduable surprise in the Eskimo: behind them loomed the greater wastes no feet had trod, the Arctic that now began, in the easy honours of his new position as Museum Curator of Oslo University, to haunt his leisure hours and his quiet nights.

He had married his singer, Eva Sars, and taken her to a home at Lysaker at the head of Oslo Fjord. He loved her with a deep and strange and lovely love that few of the earth conquerors, Mungo Park apart, had known or practised. Fru Nansen was a worthy mate for the tall, strange boy—he was little more—who could not forget the Arctic. He and Fru Nansen went winter expeditions into the mountains, ski-ing and mountain-climbing; they lost themselves in snowstorms and were romantically rescued and applauded and recognized; they lived very full and happy and complete lives, physically and mentally; and deeper and deeper Nansen immersed himself in the plans for an expedition to strike right at the heart of that mystery that surrounded the ultimate abiding-place of the Fortunate Isles, the Northern Pole itself.

Long before, as he tells, the root of the plan had formed in his mind: it formed when he read of the fate of the *Jeannette* expedition of De Long in 1879. Something of that expedition, in quest of a mythic Polar continent north of Siberia, has already been related. Now the sequel to the wreck of the *Jeannette* is pertinent. She was crushed in the ice off Bering Strait, in 77° 15′ N. 155° E. And three years afterwards, at the thither side of the Americas, relics, undisputable relics of the *Jeannette*, were discovered off Julianhaab on the West Coast of Greenland.

How had they drifted there?

A Professor Molm had investigated the relics, collated all the relevant data, and enunciated a startling theory that was long forgotten when Nansen broached his project to the world. The theory had been that the relics had been ice-drifted across the Polar area itself.

If relics, why not a ship, deliberately frozen into the ice, to be carried by the ice-drift over the Polar regions—perhaps the

Pole itself—from Siberia to Greenland? If a ship of sufficient strength could be made, if no land were encountered throughout the drift, it was—to Nansen—the sane and only way to attempt the reaching of the Pole.

He delayed, perfecting the defence of a scheme already determined in his mind. Then he went to England to address the Royal Geographical Society and lectured it on his plan, inviting criticism. He received it in bulk. . . . There was no Arctic current. His ship would be crushed to matchwood. He himself and his crew would perish. It was folly to fling away his life so in defiance of all the rules and conventions of Arctic exploration. The Royal Geographical Society admired and liked him and bade him good-bye regretfully. He went home, unperturbed, and published his plan.

There blew up such storm of opposition as he had expected. From America, from A. W. Greely, there came caustic and even spiteful comments on "Dr. Nansen's illogical scheme of self-destruction". But there was some admiration too, and no lack of volunteers for this expedition in quest of the Earthly Paradise in the mists and long fogs of the North. He found a great shipbuilder to construct for him the unique *Fram*, uniquely strong and felt-lined, baulked against the crushings of the ice; he found encouragement and help in Fru Nansen, though it wrung him a bitter moment, the thought of parting with her and his only child, Liv; he found the Norwegian Government subscribe £15,000 to the expedition—£25,000 in all was subscribed. He was young, strong, tall and immensely healthy and cool, with a fanatic look in his eyes, a Viking of romance if never such as reality had previously known. He sailed for the Siberian ice on the 24th of June, 1893.

Few of the orthodox shipbuilders, even when they heard of the *Fram's* unique specifications, believed she would survive her deliberate embedding in the Arctic ice. Her builder has left a note on the expedition's chances as generally viewed:

> Nor were the accounts of previous voyages in high latitudes encouraging. Many a fine ship had been tried and found wanting, thus adding strength to the general belief that the pressure of the ice is irresistible. When therefore the *Fram* was fitted out and ready for sea, it was undoubtedly still the prevailing opinion among those who had seen her while being built, that we *might* see Nansen and his men again; but the ship—never.

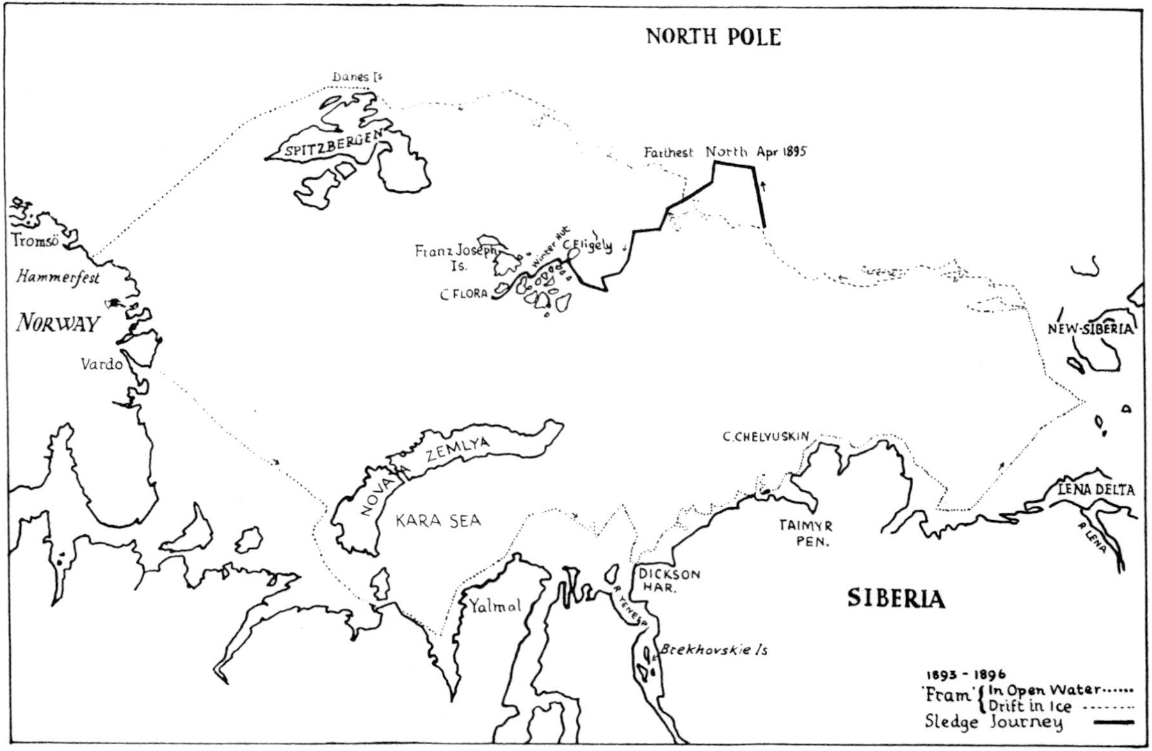

NORTH POLE

Danes Is

SPITZBERGEN

Farthest North Apr 1895

Tromsö

Hammerfest

NORWAY

Vardo

Franz Joseph Is.

Winter Hut

C. Eligely

C FLORA

NEW-SIBERIA

NOVAYA ZEMLYA

KARA SEA

C.CHELYUSKIN

TAIMYR PEN.

LENA DELTA

R LENA

DICKSON HAR.

R YENESP

Yalmal

SIBERIA

Brekhovskie Is

1893 - 1896
'Fram' { In Open Water ......
'Fram' { Drift in Ice - - - - - -
Sledge Journey ——

NANSEN'S VOYAGE IN THE "FRAM"

§ 8

The *Fram*, that famous Argo, is worthy a short description to herself. From stem to stern she measured only 128 feet, the extreme breadth was 36 feet, the sides were inclined, saucer-wise, in a fashion so that pressure would tend to elevate the ship. The outside timbers were paper smooth so that the crushing ice would find no grip in its task of elevation; and those sides, of Italian oak, were from 24 to 28 inches thick. The ship was rigged as a three-masted fore-and-aft schooner; under steam it was calculated her engines could attain for her a speed of six or seven knots; wells were provided for both screw and rudder so that they could be hoisted on deck in emergencies among the cruising ice. Between them, Nansen and Archer had evolved a vessel as unique in construction as she was to prove in performance.

Of the crew Sverdrup from the Greenland venture had inevitably been appointed commander, the others are a listing of very gallant names of whom only Hjalmar Johansen, the ship's stoker, need be mentioned here. Nansen had promulgated and was to enforce a strict enough discipline, but little on military or naval models, it was a discipline imposed by a directing equal upon fellow equals, eating, sleeping and working were much in common, there was little of ward-room and forecastle spirit in the ship that saw Vardo, the last of Norway sink behind on the 21st of July.

Through free running, foggy seas the *Fram*, built for endurance, not comfort, held a lurching way north eastwards. Presently ice was encountered and twisting amidst its channels the ship behaved to admiration. Nevertheless, Nansen became worried even thus early. Such ice argued ill for the condition of the Kara Sea.

But the icy waters slipped off and about the *Fram* with an admirable ease: on the 29th of July they put in at Tront-heim, collected the dog-teams of the expedition, great brutes on which Nansen looked with displeasure, for most of the males had been gelded and he had planned to breed litters of puppies during the polar drift. However, it was too late in the year to collect other beasts. They were tried out on the ice, to the hilarity and danger of the sledgers, Nansen, according to himself, "sitting dumb with fright" while the teams tangled and fought. They were disentangled, whipped to obedience, bidden recognize their masters and shipped aboard the *Fram*.

They sailed again on the 3rd of August, on the fourth crept into the dreaded Kara Sea, veiled in great fog banks. Here they anchored, and Nansen went ashore, staring anxiously at the twining mists that made further progress momentarily impossible. They must lift soon or the easterning he planned would be seriously curtailed.

They lifted on the 9th. All about the Kara drifted loose cakings of ice, a sea dangerous and inadequately charted over which the *Fram* began to creep. Islands rose black peaks out of the blue green of the sailing ice, day on day, as they made good speed, sunshine presently coming, the weather awaiting their passing.

On the 20th of August, still in that sunshine, they reached the Kjellman Islands, and anchored to refit the boiler and go ashore in search of fresh game. They had ample food and supplies, but Nansen's great legs longed for the land. He sighted a herd of reindeer and hunted it, he and Sverdrup, complicatedly. The deer ran : so did Nansen. The deer hid : so did Nansen. Finally, several reindeer were killed, then a polar bear encountered and also slaughtered. Rejoicing, the hunters returned to their boat and found it awash and most of the goods in it ruined. The tide was running against their return to the *Fram*, and they reached it exhausted. Arctic sport had its risks.

Winter was near. The ice closed in about them, seemingly in an impenetrable block as the *Fram* cruised to and fro in search of an eastward channel. They landed and hunted again and stared at the sky and the ice in a foreboding hopelessness, as Nansen was to tell. Should they be forced to winter here and explore this meagre neighbourhood instead of attempting the great venture of the drift ? But on the 5th of September a great storm arose, howling in the rigging of the *Fram*. Next day they looked out and saw a channel winding eastwards, ice-clear. It had opened for them, miraculously, and for five days they made good speed through it. Cape Cheluskin was made on the 10th, the northernmost point of land. Beyond that point they must seek the chances of the ice-drift.

Now, far south, in Central Asia, in the black tropic lands of Siberia, rises the Lena, flowing north into tundra and gold-field and emptying its yet warm waters by the New

Siberia Islands. Around that outlet the water is clear and unimpeded for many leagues. The *Fram* found itself again sailing an open sea. But on the 20th of September the ice-belt was again sighted, "long and compact, shining through the fog". They were in 77° 44′ N. latitude.

Here came the fogs again, curling carded from the grind and uproar of that strange mass of ice which swayed on the hinterlands of the warm Lena currents. Cruising its verge, it seemed to Nansen that verily it moved. But a doubt of himself and all his enterprise came upon him. Was that movement continuous, wide and deep over the shallow sea he had postulated as a necessity for the trans-Polar drift of the *Fram* ? Or merely a delusion ?

There was nothing to do but put it to the test, to attempt the strangest venture yet made in quest of the Fortunate Isles, those impossible Isles lying back and beyond that blanket of the dark to the North. September was nearing its end and there was no sign of a fresh channel through the ice to lead them further into the drift and make assurance doubly sure of the position of the *Fram* in that drift. They sailed up within reach of a great ice-block and made fast to it with anchors.

Monday, September 25th. Frozen in faster and faster. Beautiful still weather ; 13 degrees of frost last night. Winter is coming now.

§ 9

They made themselves fast for that winter to the berg, foreknowing the long while—perhaps a stretch of years—that the *Fram* must anchor there. Workshops were fitted up, a windmill erected to drive the dynamo for the electric plant, arrangements made for the taking of regular observations. It was a little community established in the ice, awaiting the northing of the drift.

And very speedily there came doubts of that northing. Between the 20th of September, when they moored themselves to the ice and the 7th of November, a month and a half later, the wind shifted them to and fro, and on the seventh they found themselves back in the original latitude of the ship. There was no sign of that continuous current, Pole-sweeping, that Nansen had calculated would drive the ice from the warm mouth of the Lena across the shallow Polar sea. Instead, month after month the soundings proved the sea the reverse of shallow: soundings of two thousand fathoms were recorded. To appearance the orthodox in their calculations had been right, Nansen himself deplorably wrong. There seemed no more than an outward drift (were the wind in good position) from the Siberian shore, and cessation of that drift, and then a slow and uncertain backwards wash towards the shore again.

To and fro, fast in the grip of the ice as the old year waned and the new came in went the *Fram*; Christmas Day and New Year's Day were celebrated with much feasting and genial clowning, but Nansen turned to stare again at the chart-markings with furrowed brows. About was the grind and clash of the ice under the unlifting Arctic night, sometimes broken by the crying of a far coyote, the howlings of the dogs on deck as they scented raiding bears, the sound of the wheeling arms of the windmill, now droning deeply, now laggard and hesitant as the wind currents ebbed and veered and died. Before the first of April 1894 they had crossed the 80th parallel three times.

> One degree in five months. If we go on at this rate we shall be at the Pole in forty-five, or say fifty, months, and in ninety or one hundred months at 80°N. lat. on the other side of it. . . . At best, if things go on as they are doing now, we shall be home in eight years.

The *Fram* was provisioned for five. But was his calculating backed by the evidence at all? . . . And then he would remember the relics of the *Jeannette*, and, undisputable, the only theory that could account for their drift from Bering to Greenland. A drift there must be.

Bears came killing the dogs in their kennels on deck and were hunted away and killed in their turn. Birds were seen now and again as the winter night lessened; Nansen ordered out all the crew for two hours ski-ing practice daily in case of a raid on the Pole or the chance of the *Fram* being crushed. But the ship was as steadfast as Nansen wished he himself could be, looking at that zigzagging of the chart around and over and over yet again the line of the 80th parallel.

With the spring the big floes about them took to titanic gambollings, breaking and smashing and rearing great masses one upon the other—masses that sometimes overtowered the *Fram* in threatening attitude. The din of the ice was continuous, the *Fram* quivered and groaned unceasingly; but the

Italian timber was seasoned and strong, the calculations and architecture of Colin Archer unimpeachable. Sometimes the violent quiverings of the ship, hours' long, was as agonizing as extreme toothache, and Nansen would escape in the sport and exercise on the ice.

Summer came and the ice cracked away into innumerable channels, too small to be worth the trouble of attempting to force the *Fram* through. The drift continued confusingly about the 80th parallel and Nansen was slowly tempered in that time of adversity to an austereness of outlook that had never been his before in all his sanguine life. He tasted of the bitter wine of unfulfilment that had wetted the lips of many another of the earth conquerors in their quests—the same quest as his. Then the summer, even the unending summer, waned at last. Birds left them. The ice-groaning ceased as the bergs froze up again. And with that happening came a strange and (by this time) unlooked-for miracle. The slow drifting and counter-drifting ceased. A consistent north-west drift set in. By the 1st of November the *Fram* had crossed the eighty-second parallel, and high hopes rose in Nansen's heart. Then the speed of the drift lessened. Still the northing held. At New Year's Day, 1895, they were beyond the 83rd.

But that winter was long and terrifying in moments when a man was alone as Nansen was often alone, with the full responsibility of the expedition on his shoulders. And sometimes that burden slipped aside and another took its place, till it seemed in the frozen silences of the Arctic night that all the burden of the strange adventure of humanity was borne by him under the white, cold, unfriendly stars. He would walk out on the ice alone and stand and look at that great arching of the Galaxy above him and realize again the loneliness of Man, what a little adventure in truth was his, how strange the puny aims and hopes and fears he had in this brief flicker of light betwixt darkness that he called life. And he filled the space of that flicker not with ease and peace and sustenance and friendship and lust, but with a wild debating and crying and adventuring in quest of—he knew not what! . . . Till at last, all over the world would descend again when the sun cooled great ice-sheets even as those that cased the *Fram*; and Man and his strange adventure cease for ever, that Earthly Paradise unattained.

Yet—it had been attempted. . . .

Such the mood in page on page of his journal, the modern Stoic's acceptance of the terror and beauty and ultimate tragedy of all life. It left an enduring mark in Nansen, even in that subsequent inconsequent career of his. That it was justified either by science or hope we may question: that it was the mood proper to the last earth conqueror the artist at least can appreciate. . . .

And down through the night the howl of a fox.

> Oh, at times this inactivity crushes one's very soul; one's life seems as dark as the winter night outside; there is sunlight upon no part of it except the past and the far, far distant future.

§ 10

Early in the dark winter-night of 1895 the *Fram* took a list to port under the enormous pressures of the ice. Nansen feared that it would be necessary to abandon the ship and gave orders for stores to be carried out on the ice, together with all the necessary gear and sledges for a retreat on foot. But even under the enormous pressures, and a ridge that rode over the rest of the ice-surface and capsized over and about the *Fram* till it half-buried the vessel, the ship held. Then the pressure stopped and slowly the ship began to right herself.

As the spring of the new year came Nansen perfected a plan that had been slowly shaping to being throughout the previous year. He now was certain of the Polar drift, but almost equally certain that that drift would never carry the ship across the Pole itself. And, though he had set out with the avowed intention of exploring the Polar area, not attempting theatrical risks to attain that "actual mere mathematical point" it was the mathematical point more than anything else that had really drawn him, though all his life he refused to confess it. . . . If the *Fram* might not make the voyage, men on foot could surely make the journey.

He decided to take two kayaks, three sledges, all the serviceable dogs, and only one human companion on this dash for the Earthly Paradise. The *Fram* he was to leave under the command of Sverdrup, with instructions to the latter to continue all observations and scientific work possible, to abandon the ship only at the direst necessity, and when at length it freed from the ice to take it back to Norway from whatever point in the Arctic Circle clear water was attained. He gave much careful thought to provisions and training for the attempt on the Pole, planning to march the 450 miles in fifty days and then turn back and attempt the Seven Isles, north of Spitzbergen, a distance of 720 miles.

It would be a trek of eleven hundred miles over unknown country, or rather ice.

He discussed the plan with Sverdrup and finally chose as his companion Hjalmar Johansen, a genial, strong and healthy man with whom he was to keep the best of relations throughout their long months together—a task not too easy for one of Nansen's sanguine and impatient temperament, which so easily took on the appearance if not the reality of domineering. The rest of the crew appear to have viewed the chances of this fresh expedition with a commendable warmth. It was planned to start in mid-February.

But various reasons delayed the plan. After a false start they returned for additional sledges, finally setting out with six in all; again they halted and returned to the ship to rearrange the loads. So it was as late as the 14th of March before the two men finally took last leave of the ship, with three sledges, looking back at the *Fram* ensconced amidst the towering hummocks. She was in latitude 84° 4′ N. 102° E. long.

They were three hundred and fifty miles south of the Pole. At the calculated rate of travelling they should reach it in fifty days, leaving four months for the retreat to Spitzbergen—a race with the closing in of the winter night.

The cold grew ever more intense as they marched northward throughout March, over ice level and pleasing. They hoped it would keep in like condition till they reached the Pole. But towards the end of March the ice grew hummocky, great pressure ridges serrated all the forward horizon and travel record dropped from fourteen miles a day to sometimes half that amount. It grew even colder. At night they slept frozen in their clothes, eating painfully and exhaustedly with frost-encrusted lips. Still the progress was slow.

The dogs tired, fought, bit through their traces; some escaped. A north-east wind added its quota of discomfort for both dogs and men; the former were bitterly over-driven, lashed to death, and then abandoned. Their fate—their unescapable fate—was to haunt Nansen with moments of bitter self-reproach in after years. But now, in quest of that ultimate hope, he was ruthless.

Pressure ridges, snowstorms, and intersecting lanes of open water met them in April with their barriers to quick advance. The two fought on through and over difficulties like men possessed till Nansen found they were making less than four miles a day. Suddenly the insanity of a further pressing forward into those desolate regions of ice came upon him. Unless conditions improved——

They did not improve. Instead, they grew worse. Lanes, ice-ridges, endless cakings of ice-blocks piled up in front of their stumbling feet; the dogs pattered with bruised and swollen pads. Continually they had to stop and drag the sledges up and down the hummocks; continually free the teams from this and that angle. Forward, in that unknown North, the vision of the Pole grew fainter and fainter in Nansen's eyes. Even were they to keep their health and attain it at last, sometime in June it might be, it would be impossible ever to return. And as the vision faded and common sense came in its place, commendable, the triumph of the scientist over the earth-adventurer, there closed down finally the second great phase in Nansen's life. He was never quite again to attain to those heights of sublime and hopeless hope he had known in the long winter nights of the *Fram*, never to such high vision as in the early days of the dash on the Pole. On the 7th of April he decided to turn about, if the next day's trek proved as difficult.

> The ice grew worse and worse and we got no way. Ridge after ridge, and nothing but rubble to travel over. . . . It was a veritable chaos of ice-blocks stretching as far as the horizon. There is not much sense in keeping on longer; we are sacrificing valuable time and doing little.

They halted at the furthest point attained, 86° 14′ N. lat. within 235 nautical miles of the North Pole, having covered a hundred and fifteen miles in twenty-three days' sledging.

Turning about with the last Fortunate Isle still unglimpsed and untrodden (as indeed, it still remains untrodden, for Admiral Peary's claim to have reached it is of as doubtful authenticity as Dr. Cook's) they set out on the long trek for Spitzbergen.

§ 10

On the 21st of April they came on a huge piece of timber, mysteriously erupting from the face of the ice. They carved their initials upon it and went on. Was land near at hand ?

But they never sighted that land (if such land there is) though the trails of foxes crossed theirs now and again. They were again in a region traversed and retraversed by open water lanes which made the dragging of the sledges a vexation and a weariness to the flesh and spirit. Week on week they fought their way southward, killing the dogs as they abandoned the sledges, feeding dead dog to live dog which on the morrow would itself be dead. The dog-killing Nansen found a grisly business—he had softened from the joyous young butcher who helped to man the sealer *Viking*. Mid-May brought them to even wider lanes, filled with narwhals, unchancy beasts which they hunted, slew and devoured. Then they held south again.

There came no sign of land and sudden and devastating hopelessness assailed Nansen as he stared south at those rifting lanes in the ice—"we do not know where we are and we do not know when this will end". Summer though it was, and Arctic birds now common, food had run perilously short till on the 22nd of June Johansen shot a seal. Kayaks were launched and they took to the opening lanes.

But they had opened insufficiently to allow for a hurrying progress. The two men camped and waited for a wider dispersal of the ice. June passed while they waited, the ice showing no sign of widening its rifts. Bear came and were shot and skinned and provided thick furs on which to squat inside the smoke-blackened tent. At length, in mid-July, in desperation they took to scrambling south again.

So doing, they came in sight of land. They had drifted little for the good reason that land blocked the drift. While they made the black peaks rising from the surface of the ice they encountered a bear which bit Johansen and was with difficulty killed by Nansen, an heroic encounter in true old style. Then they took to the kayaks and so reached the unknown islands which Nansen christened White Land, landing on the solid ground for the first time in a fantastic long two years.

Good hunting conditions kept them alive and they sought a way south with the kayaks. But again and again they were driven back, and finally, with the rising of the August storms, it became plain to Nansen that they could not attempt the journey that year. The prospect was appalling, but they must stay in those islands if they were to live.

They set about building a house with loose stones and earth, in sight of astounded Arctic foxes.

On the 15th of October they saw the last of the sun. Their third Polar night was upon them, to be spent in the darkness and stench and chilly unease of a badly made stone hut. Beasts came and dragged away and devoured the carcases which they had stored for food. The grease and sweat and soot hardened to thick layers on their faces, it was impossible, even on such occasions as they achieved boiling water, to wash the filth from their clothes. The boredom was maddening: they would leave the hut alone and stalk the ice and Nansen glower south with that almost facile despair that came to him now so comparatively readily. Would they ever escape this dreadful life, ever again see the lights and the kindly faces of Norway, ever meet his Eva and his Liv again? Memory of his child was alternate hope and torture. Magnificent as a specimen in so many ways, the last of the earth conquerors was no less magnificent as the typical and splendid monogamist, a great lover and writer though he had turned his back on the Fortunate Isles and was never now to attain them.

Johansen snored of nights, an exasperation which drove Peace-Scarer to kick him violently. Placidly, Johansen shook himself and snored on. Their hair and beards grew long and matted—they grew them for the sake of warmth. Unending night unending unease, with bodies never properly dry, never clean, never free. Would the winter ever pass?

Yet even it at last was over. In March, just as the daylight came and their provisions were exhausted, a considerate bear put in an appearance. He was instantly killed and feasted upon. With April, loading the kayaks with their gear, they prepared for the journey south. On the 19th of May they began the journey, but with sledges. A running wind led them to hoist sails, as once Nansen had done in Greenland, and they made good progress for a time. Then face-biting snowstorms awoke and plagued the dragging treks of a long June.

In mid-June they took to the kayaks, fighting off walruses, obstreperous beasts which feared man not at all, but were filled with immense desire to gaze on the two scarecrows with the paddles. Once the kayaks were upset and they spent a day drying their goods. In a kayak a hole six inches long had been ripped. That was on the 15th of June.

On the morning of the 17th, rising and emerging from the ragged tent to set about the preparation of a meagre breakfast, Nansen was startled to hear far in the south a noise which he took to be the barking of dogs. Johansen came out and listened beside him. Nansen set off to investigate, his hands trembling.

"Suddenly I thought I heard a shout from a human voice, a strange voice, the first for three years." His habitual control left him. He stumbled up a shelving mass of hummocks, crying aloud, crying he knew not what, seeing behind that voice salvation, Norway again, the lights of Oslo, security from that awful darkness in the North that shrouded the unattained Earthly Paradise, seeing his Eva Sars again. . . .

And amidst the ice-ridges, towards him, came hurrying a man, shaved and clean and welcoming. A white man.

It was Jackson of the Jackson-Harmsworth Expedition to Spitzbergen.

§ 12

So he was freed and the great adventure accomplished. The *Windward* of the English Expedition took him and Johansen home to Norway, to Hammerfest where an intelligent cow was the only being that appeared to recognize him as he walked up the public street—the cow stared a bovine astonishment—to the arms of his Eva again. And at Hammerfest came the news that the *Fram* itself had won safely clear from the ice, after being frozen in a long three years, and also was on the way home to Norway. It put in at Skjeervo on the 20th of August, and Nansen made for it, and kindliness pulls down a veil on the gladness of the meeting with Sverdrup and his gallant Argonauts.

So we passed from town to town, from fête to fête, along the coast of Norway. It was on the 9th of September that the *Fram* steamed up Oslo Fjord and met with a reception such as a prince might have envied. The stout old men-of-war, *Nordstjernen* and *Elida*, the new and elegant *Valkyrie* and the nimble little torpedo boats, led the way for us. Steamboats swarmed round all black with people. There were flags high and low, salutes, hurrahs, waving of handkerchiefs and hats, radiant faces everywhere, the whole fjord one multitudinous welcome. There lay home and the well-known strand before it, glittering and smiling in the sunshine. Then steamers on steamers again, shouts after shouts; and we all stood, hat in hand, bowing as they cheered.

The whole of Peppervik was one mass of boats and people and flags and waving pennants. Then the men-of-war saluted with thirteen guns apiece, and the old fort of Akershus followed with its thirteen peals of thunder, that echoed from the hills around.

In the evening I stood on the strand out by the fjord. The echoes had died away, and the pinewoods stood silent and dark around. On the headland the last embers of a bonfire of welcome still smouldered and smoked, and the sea rippling at my feet seemed to whisper : "Now you are at home." The deep peace of the autumn evening sank beneficently over the weary spirit.

I could not but recall that rainy morning in June when I last set foot on this strand. More than three years had passed ; we had toiled and we had sown, and now the harvest had come. In my heart I sobbed and wept for joy and thankfulness.

The ice and the long moonlit Polar nights, with all their yearning, seemed like a far-off dream from another world—a dream that had come and passed away. But what would life be worth without its dreams ?

So he passes from our vision, the last of the great earth-conquerors, to that life that surely sometimes was to seem dimly irrelevant to the great quest of the Pole that had once been his : to a mean squabbling on home politics, to helping Norway attain her nationhood and all the prides and prejudices that went with that attainment, to minute dredgings and weighings in Northern seas, to a long, puzzled neutrality during the War—for even the eagle grows old ; to that ten years' spurt of energy in Russia and at Geneva which awoke for the world again the magic of the earth-conqueror's name—this time the conquest of pity and compassion, perhaps the truest conquest of all, the strait and undeniable way to those Fortunate Isles that his countryman Leif Ericsson first set forth to seek nine hundred years before.

THE END

SELECT BIBLIOGRAPHY

I

Human History. G. ELLIOT SMITH. 1930.

Social Organization. W. H. R. RIVERS. 1924.

Ancient Hunters. W. J. SOLLAS. 1924.

The Origin of Magic and Religion. W. J. PERRY. 1923.

The Children of the Sun. W. J. PERRY. 1926.

First Player. IVOR BROWN. 1927.

The Golden Age. H. J. MASSINGHAM. 1927

II

Discovery of America by Northmen. E. N. HORSFORD. 1888.

The Landfall of Leif Eiriksen, A.D. 1002. E. N. HORSFORD. 1892

Leif's House in Vineland. E. N. HORSFORD. 1893.

Leif Erikson. M. A. BROWN. 1888.

The Northmen in America. G. M. GATHORNE HARDY. 1924.

In Northern Mists. FRIDTJOF NANSEN. 1911.

La Saga d'Eirik le Rouge, version du Flatey Bók. 1924.
(In *La Découverte de l'Amérique par les Normandes.* LANGLOIS.)

III

The Book of Marco Polo. Trans. and comment. H. YULE. Three vols. 1903.

IV

Columbus and His Discovery of America. H. B. Adams and H. Wood. 1892.

Ymago Mundi . . . Cardinal P. d'Ailly. 1930.

Cristóbal Colon y Cristóforo Columbo. R. Beltràn y Rozpide. 1921.

The Geographical Conceptions of Columbus. G. E. Nunn. 1924.

The Voyages of Christopher Columbus. Cecil Jane. 1930.

Historia della vita e dei fatti di Cristoforo Colombo. F. Colombo. 1930.

V

Relaciòn de los naufragios y comentarios de Alvar Nuñez Cabeça de Vaca. M. Serrano y Sanz. 1904.

The Narrative of Alvar Nuñez Cabeza de Vaca. Trans. T. Buckingham Smith. 1907.

The Commentaries of A. Nuñez Cabeza de Vaca. Trans. L. L. Dominguez. 1891.

VI

La Primera Vuelta al Mundo. Relaciòn documentada del viaje de Hernando de Magallanes, etc. V. Llorens Asensio. 1903.

The Life of Ferdinand Magellan. F. H. H. Guillemard. 1925.

VII

Bering's Voyages. F. A. Golder. Two vols. 1922-25.

VIII

The Travels of Mungo Park (Everyman Library).

Niger: The Life of Mungo Park. Lewis Grassic Gibbon. 1934.

IX

First Footsteps in East Africa. R. F. Burton. Two vols. 1893.

The Lake Regions of Central Africa. R. F. Burton. Two vols. 1860.

Life of Captain Sir R. F. Burton. Lady Burton. 1889.

The Real Sir Richard Burton. W. P. Dodge. 1907.

X

The First Crossing of Greenland. F. Nansen. 1892.

Eskimo Life. F. Nansen. 1893.

Farthest North. F. Nansen. Two vols. 1897.

The Saga of Fridtjof Nansen. J. Sörensen. 1932.

Titles available in the Polygon Lewis Grassic Gibbo

Gay Hunter

Nine Against the Unknown

The Speak of the Mearns

Stained Radiance

Three Go Back

Persian Dawns, Egyptian Nights

The Grassic Gibbon Centre in Arbuthnott contains important archival material relating to Lewis Grassic Gibbon and his work. A wide variety of L. G. Gibbon publications and biographical studies can be found in its bookshop. The 'Friends of the Grassic Gibbon Centre' produces a bi-annual newsletter for sharing news and views about the author. For further information contact The Grassic Gibbon Centre, Arbuthnott, Laurencekirk, AB30 1PB Tel: 01561-361668; Fax: 361742; E-mail: lgginfo@grassicgibbon.com

http:// www.grassicgibbon.com